OMNIBUS

OMNIBUS

STAR WARS®: A NEW HOPE

by George Lucas

THE EMPIRE STRIKES BACK™
by Donald F. Glut

RETURN OF THE JEDI™
by James Kahn

WARNER BOOKS

A *Warner* Book

This omnibus edition first published in 1995 by Warner Books

Star Wars Omnibus copyright ® & © 1995 The Star Wars Corporation
and Lucasfilm Ltd

Previously published in Great Britain separately:

Star Wars first published in 1977 by Sphere Books
Copyright © 1976 by The Star Wars Corporation
The Empire Strikes Back first published in 1980 by Sphere Books
Copyright © 1980 Lucasfilm Ltd
Return of the Jedi first published in 1983 by Futura Publications
Copyright © 1983 by Lucasfilm Ltd (LFL)

The moral right of the author has been asserted.

A CIP catalogue record for this book is available from the British Library.

ISBN 0 7515 1324 5

Typeset by Solidus (Bristol) Limited
Printed and bound in Great Britain by
Clays Ltd, St. Ives PLC

Warner Books
A Division of
Little, Brown and Company (UK)
Brettenham House
Lancaster Place
London WC2E 7EN

Contents

Star Wars: A New Hope   1

The Empire Strikes Back   193

Return of the Jedi   351

EPISODE

IV

STAR WARS®:
A New Hope

From the Adventures of Luke Skywalker

A Novel by **George Lucas**

Prologue

ANOTHER galaxy, another time.

The Old Republic was the Republic of legend, greater than distance or time. No need to note where it was or whence it came, only to know that . . . it was *the* Republic.

Once, under the wise rule of the Senate and the protection of the Jedi Knights, the Republic throve and grew. But as often happens when wealth and power pass beyond the admirable and attain the awesome, then appear those evil ones who have greed to match.

So it was with the Republic at its height. Like the greatest of trees, able to withstand any external attack, the Republic rotted from within though the danger was not visible from outside.

Aided and abetted by restless, power-hungry individuals within the government, and the massive organs of commerce, the ambitious Senator Palpatine caused himself to be elected President of the Republic. He promised to reunite the disaffected among the people and to restore the remembered glory of the Republic.

Once secure in office he declared himself Emperor, shutting himself away from the populace. Soon he was controlled by the very assistants and boot-lickers he had appointed to high office, and the cries of the people for justice did not reach his ears.

Having exterminated through treachery and deception the Jedi Knights, guardians of justice in the galaxy, the Imperial governors and bureaucrats prepared to institute a reign of terror among the disheartened worlds of the galaxy. Many used the imperial forces and the name of the increasingly isolated Emperor to further their own personal ambitions.

But a small number of systems rebelled at these new outrages. Declaring themselves opposed to the New Order they began the great battle to restore the Old Republic.

From the beginning they were vastly outnumbered by the systems held in thrall by the Emperor. In those first dark days it seemed certain the bright flame of resistance would be extinguished before it could cast the light of new truth across a galaxy of oppressed and beaten peoples . . .

From the First Saga
Journal of the Whills

'They were in the wrong place at the wrong time. Naturally they became heroes.'

Leia Organa of Alderaan, Senator

I

IT was a vast, shining globe and it cast a light of lambent topaz into space – but it was not a sun. Thus, the planet had fooled men for a long time. Not until entering close orbit around it did its discoverers realize that this was a world in a binary system and not a third sun itself.

At first it seemed certain nothing could exist on such a planet, least of all humans. Yet both massive G1 and G2 stars orbited a common center with peculiar regularity, and Tatooine circled them far enough out to permit the development of a rather stable, if exquisitely hot, climate. Mostly this was a dry desert of a world, whose unusual starlike yellow glow was the result of double sunlight striking sodium-rich sands and flats. That same sunlight suddenly shone on the thin skin of a metallic shape falling crazily toward the atmosphere.

The erratic course the galactic cruiser was traveling was intentional, not the product of injury but of a desperate desire to avoid it. Long streaks of intense energy slid close past its hull, a multihued storm of destruction like a school of rainbow remoras fighting to attach themselves to a larger, unwilling host.

One of those probing, questing beams succeeded in touching the fleeing ship, striking its principal solar fin. Gemlike fragments of metal and plastic erupted into space as the end of the fin disintegrated. The vessel seemed to shudder.

The source of those multiple energy beams suddenly hove into view – a lumbering Imperial cruiser, its massive outline bristling cactuslike with dozens of heavy weapons emplacements. Light ceased arching from those spines now as the cruiser moved in close. Intermittent explosions and flashes of light could be seen in those portions of the smaller ship which had taken hits. In the absolute cold of space, the cruiser snuggled up alongside its wounded prey.

Another distant explosion shook the ship – but it certainly didn't feel distant to Artoo Detoo or See Threepio. The concussion bounced them around the narrow corridor like bearings in an old motor.

To look at these two, one would have supposed that the tall, human-like machine, Threepio, was the master and the stubby, tripodal robot, Artoo Detoo, an inferior. But while Threepio might have sniffed disdainfully at the suggestion, they were in fact equal in everything save loquacity. Here Threepio was clearly – and necessarily – the superior.

Still another explosion rattled the corridor, throwing Threepio off balance. His shorter companion had the better of it during such moments with his squat, cylindrical body's low center of gravity well balanced on thick, clawed legs.

Artoo glanced up at Threepio, who was steadying himself against a corridor wall. Lights blinked enigmatically around a single mechanical eye as the smaller robot studied the battered casing of his friend. A patina of metal and fibrous dust coated the usually gleaming bronze finish, and there were some visible dents – all the result of the pounding the rebel ship they were on had been taking.

Accompanying the last attack was a persistent deep hum which even the loudest explosion had not been able to drown out. Then, for no apparent reason, the basso thrumming abruptly ceased, and the only sounds in the otherwise deserted corridor came from the eerie dry-twig crackle of shorting relays or the pops of dying circuitry. Explosions began to echo through the ship once more, but they were far away from the corridor.

Threepio turned his smooth, humanlike head to one side. Metallic ears listened intently. The imitation of a human pose was hardly necessary – Threepio's auditory sensors were fully omnidirectional – but the slim robot had been programmed to blend perfectly among human company. This programming extended even to mimicry of human gestures.

'Did you hear that?' he inquired rhetorically of his patient companion, referring to the throbbing sound. 'They've shut down the main reactor and the drive.' His voice was as full of disbelief and concern as that of any human. One metallic palm rubbed dolefully at a patch of dull gray on his side, where a broken hull brace had fallen and scored the bronze finish. Threepio was a fastidious machine, and such things troubled him.

'Madness, this is madness.' He shook his head slowly. 'This time we'll be destroyed for sure.'

Artoo did not comment immediately. Barrel torso tilted backward, powerful legs gripping the deck, the meter-high robot was engrossed in studying the roof overhead. Though he did not have a head to cock in a listening posture like his friend, Artoo still somehow managed to convey that impression. A series of short beeps and chirps issued from his speaker. To even a sensitive human ear they would have been just so much static, but to Threepio they formed words as clear and pure as direct current.

'Yes, I suppose they did have to shut the drive down,' Threepio admitted, 'but what are we going to do now? We can't enter atmosphere with our main stablizer fin destroyed. I can't believe we're simply going to surrender.'

A small band of armed humans suddenly appeared, rifles held at the ready. Their expressions were as worry-wrinkled as their uniforms, and they carried about them the aura of men prepared to die.

Threepio watched silently until they had vanished around a far bend in the passageway, then looked back at Artoo. The smaller robot hadn't shifted from his position of listening. Threepio's gaze turned upward also though he knew Artoo's senses were slightly sharper than his own.

'What is it, Artoo?' A short burst of beeping came in response. Another moment, and there was no need for highly attuned sensors. For a minute or two more, the corridor remained deathly silent. Then a faint *scrape, scrape* could be heard, like a cat at a door, from somewhere above. That strange noise was produced by heavy footsteps and the movement of bulky equipment somewhere on the ship's hull.

When several muffled explosions sounded, Threepio murmured, 'They've broken in somewhere above us. There's no escape for the Captain this time.' Turning, he peered down at Artoo. 'I think we'd better—'

The shriek of overstressed metal filled the air before he could finish, and the far end of the passageway was lit by a blinding actinic flash. Somewhere down there the little cluster of armed crew who had passed by minutes before had encountered the ship's attackers.

Threepio turned his face and delicate photoreceptors away – just in time to avoid the fragments of metal that flew down the corridor. At the far end a gaping hole appeared in the roof, and reflective forms like big metal beads began dropping to the corridor floor. Both robots knew that no machine could match the fluidity with which those shapes moved and instantly assumed fighting postures. The new arrivals were humans in armor, not mechanicals.

One of them looked straight at Threepio – no, not at him, the panicked robot thought frantically, but past him. The figure shifted its big rifle around in armored hands – too late. A beam of intense light struck the head, sending pieces of armor, bone, and flesh flying in all directions.

Half the invading Imperial troops turned and began returning fire up the corridor – aiming past the two robots.

'Quick – this way!' Threepio ordered, intending to retreat from the Imperials. Artoo turned with him. They had taken only a couple of steps when they saw the rebel crewmen in position ahead, firing *down* the corridor. In seconds the passageway was filled with smoke and crisscrossing beams of energy.

Red, green and blue bolts ricocheted off polished sections of wall and floor or ripped long gashes in metal surfaces. Screams of injured and dying humans – a peculiarly unrobotic sound, Threepio thought – echoed piercingly above the inorganic destruction.

One beam struck near the robot's feet at the same time as a second one burst the wall directly behind him, exposing sparking circuitry and rows of conduits. The force of the twin blast tumbled Threepio into the shredded cables, where a dozen different currents turned him into a jerking, twisting display.

Strange sensations coursed through his metal nerve-ends. They caused no pain, only confusion. Every time he moved and tried to free himself there was another violent crackling as a fresh cluster of componentry broke. The noise and man-made lightning remained constant around him as the battle continued to rage.

Smoke began to fill the corridor. Artoo Detoo bustled about trying to help free his friend. The little robot evidenced a phlegmatic indifference to the ravening energies filling the passageway. He was built so low that most of the beams passed over him anyhow.

'*Help!*' Threepio yelled, suddenly frightened at a new message from an internal sensor. 'I think something is melting. Free my left leg – the trouble's near the pelvic servomotor.' Typically, his tone turned abruptly from pleading to berating.

'This is all your fault!' he shouted angrily. 'I should have known better than to trust the logic of a half-sized thermocapsulary dehousing assister. I don't know why you insisted we leave our assigned stations to come down this stupid access corridor. Not that it matters now. The whole ship must be—' Artoo Detoo cut him off in midspeech with some angry beepings and hoots of his own, though he continued to cut and pull with precision at the tangled high-voltage cables.

'Is that so?' Threepio sneered in reply. 'The same to you, you little . . .!'

An exceptionally violent explosion shook the passage, drowning him out. A lung-searing miasma of carbonized component filled the air, obscuring everything.

Two meters tall. Bipedal. Flowing black robes trailing from the figure and a face forever masked by a functional if bizarre black metal breath screen – a Dark Lord of the Sith was an awesome, threatening shape as it strode through the corridors of the rebel ship.

Fear followed the footsteps of all the Dark Lords. The cloud of evil which clung tight about this particular one was intense enough to cause hardened Imperial troops to back away, menacing enough to set them muttering nervously among themselves. Once-resolute rebel crew members ceased resisting, broke and ran in panic at the sight of the black armor – armor which, though black as it was, was not nearly as dark as the thoughts drifting through the mind within.

One purpose, one thought, one obsession dominated that mind

now. It burned in the brain of Darth Vader as he turned down another passageway in the broken fighter. There smoke was beginning to clear, though the sounds of faraway fighting still resounded through the hull. The battle here had ended and moved on.

Only a robot was left to stir freely in the wake of the Dark Lord's passing. See Threepio finally stepped clear of the last restraining cable. Somewhere behind him human screams could be heard from where relentless Imperial troops were mopping up the last remnants of rebel resistance.

Threepio glanced down and saw only scarred deck. As he looked around, his voice was full of concern. 'Artoo Detoo – where are you?' The smoke seemed to part just a bit more. Threepio found himself staring up the passageway.

Artoo Detoo, it seemed, was there. But he wasn't looking in Threepio's direction. Instead, the little robot appeared frozen in an attitude of attention. Leaning over him was – it was difficult for even Threepio's electronic photoreceptors to penetrate the clinging, acidic smoke – a human figure. It was young, slim, and by abstruse human standards of aesthetics, Threepio mused, of a calm beauty. One small hand seemed to be moving over the front of Artoo's torso.

Threepio started toward them as the haze thickened once more. But when he reached the end of the corridor, only Artoo stood there, waiting. Threepio peered past him, uncertain. Robots were occasionally subject to electronic hallucinations – but why should he hallucinate a human?

He shrugged ... Then again, why not, especially when one considered the confusing circumstances of the past hour and the dose of raw current he had recently absorbed. He shouldn't be surprised at anything his concatenated internal circuits conjured up.

'Where have you been?' Threepio finally asked. 'Hiding, I suppose.' He decided not to mention the maybe-human. If it had been a hallucination, he wasn't going to give Artoo the satisfaction of knowing how badly recent events had unsettled his logic circuits.

'They'll be coming back this way,' he went on, nodding down the corridor and not giving the small automaton a chance to reply, 'looking for human survivors. What are we going to do now? They won't trust the word of rebel-owned machines that we don't know anything of value. We'll be sent to the spice mines of Kessel or taken apart for spare components for other, less deserving robots. That's if they don't consider us potential program traps and blow us apart on sight. If we don't ...' But Artoo had already turned and was ambling quickly back down the passageway.

'Wait, where are you going? Haven't you been listening to me?' Uttering curses in several languages, some purely mechanical, Threepio raced fluidly after his friend. The Artoo unit, he thought to himself, could be downright close-circuited when it wanted to.

Outside the galactic cruiser's control center the corridor was crowded with sullen prisoners gathered by Imperial troops. Some lay wounded, some dying. Several officers had been separated from the enlisted ranks and stood in a small group by themselves, bestowing belligerent looks and threats on the silent knot of troops holding them at bay.

As if on command, everyone – Imperial troops as well as rebels – became silent as a massive caped form came into view from behind a turn in the passage. Two of the heretofore resolute, obstinate rebel officers began to shake. Stopping before one of the men, the towering figure reached out wordlessly. A massive hand closed around the man's neck and lifted him off the deck. The rebel officer's eyes bulged, but he kept his silence.

An Imperial officer, his armored helmet shoved back to reveal a recent scar where an energy beam had penetrated his shielding, scrambled down out of the fighter's control room, shaking his head briskly. 'Nothing, sir. Information retrieval system's been wiped clean.'

Darth Vader acknowledged this news with a barely perceptible nod. The impenetrable mask turned to regard the officer he was torturing. Metal-clad fingers contracted. Reaching up, the prisoner desperately tried to pry them loose, but to no avail.

'Where is the data you intercepted?' Vader rumbled dangerously. 'What have you done with the information tapes?'

'We – intercepted – no information,' the dangling officer gurgled, barely able to breathe. From somewhere deep within, he dredged up a squeal of outrage. 'This is a ... councilor vessel ... Did you not see our ... exterior markings? We're on a ... diplomatic ... mission.'

'Chaos take your mission!' Vader growled. 'Where are those tapes?' He squeezed harder, the threat in his grip implicit.

When he finally replied, the officer's voice was a bare, choked whisper. 'Only . . . the Commander knows.'

'This ship carries the system crest of Alderaan,' Vader growled, the gargoylelike breath mask leaning close. 'Is any of the royal family on board? Who are you carrying?' Thick fingers tightened further, and the officer's struggles became more and more frantic. His last words were muffled and choked past intelligibility.

Vader was not pleased. Even though the figure went limp with an awful, unquestionable finality, that hand continued to tighten, producing a chilling snapping and popping of bone, like a dog padding on plastic. Then with a disgusted wheeze Vader finally threw the doll-form of the dead man against a far wall. Several Imperial troops ducked out of the way just in time to avoid the grisly missile.

The massive form whirled unexpectedly, and Imperial officers shrank under that baleful sculptured stare. 'Start tearing this ship apart piece by piece, component by component, until you find those tapes. As for the passengers, if any, I want them alive.' He paused a moment, then added, *'Quickly!'*

Officers and men nearly fell over themselves in their haste to leave – not necessarily to carry out Vader's orders, but simply to retreat from that malevolent presence.

Artoo Detoo finally came to a halt in an empty corridor devoid of smoke and the signs of battle. A worried, confused Threepio pulled up behind him.

'You've led us through half the ship, and to what . . .?' He broke off, staring in disbelief as the squat robot reached up with one clawed limb and snapped the seal on a lifeboat hatch. Immediately a red warning light came on and a low hooting sounded in the corridor.

Threepio looked wildly in all directions, but the passageway remained empty. When he looked back, Artoo was already working his way into the cramped boat pod. It was just large enough to hold several humans, and its design was not laid out to accommodate mechanicals. Artoo had some trouble negotiating the awkward little compartment.

'Hey,' a startled Threepio called, admonishing, 'you're not permitted in there! It's restricted to humans only. We just might be able to convince the Imperials that we're not rebel programmed and are too valuable to break up, but if someone sees you in there we haven't got a chance. Come on out.'

Somehow Artoo had succeeded in wedging his body into position in front of the miniature control board. He cocked his body slightly and threw a stream of loud beeps and whistles at his reluctant companion.

Threepio listened. He couldn't frown, but he managed to give a good impression of doing so. 'Mission ... what mission? What are you talking about? You sound like you haven't got an integrated logic terminal left in your brain. No ... no more adventures. I'll take my chances with the Imperials – and I'm *not* getting in there.'

An angry electronic twang came from the Artoo unit.

'Don't call *me* a mindless philosopher,' Threepio snapped back, 'you overweight, unstreamlined glob of grease!'

Threepio was concocting an additional rejoinder when an explosion blew out the back wall of the corridor. Dust and metal debris whooshed through the narrow subpassageway, followed instantly by a series of secondary explosions. Flames began jumping hungrily from the exposed interior wall, reflecting off Threepio's isolated patches of polished skin.

Muttering the electronic equivalent of consigning his soul to the unknown, the lanky robot jumped into the life pod. 'I'm going to regret this,' he muttered more audibly as Artoo activated the safety door behind him. The smaller robot flipped a series of switches, snapped back a cover, and pressed three buttons in a certain sequence. With the thunder of explosive latches the life pod ejected from the crippled fighter.

When word came over the communicators that the last pocket of resistance on the rebel ship had been cleaned out, the Captain of the Imperial cruiser relaxed considerably. He was listening with pleasure to the proceedings on the captured vessel when one of his chief gunnery officers called to him. Moving to the man's position, the Captain stared into the circular viewscreen and saw a tiny dot dropping away toward the fiery world below.

'There goes another pod, sir. Instructions?' The officer's hand hovered over a computerized energy battery.

Casually, confident in the firepower and total control under his command, the Captain studied the nearby readouts monitoring the pod. All of them read blank.

'Hold your fire, Lieutenant Hija. Instruments show no life forms aboard. The pod's release mechanism must have short-circuited or received a false instruction. Don't waste your power.' He turned away, to listen with satisfaction to the reports of captured men and material coming from the rebel ship.

Glare from exploding panels and erupting circuitry reflected crazily off the armor of the lead storm trooper as he surveyed the passageway ahead. He was about to turn and call for those behind to follow him forward when he noticed something moving off to one side. It appeared to be crouching back in a small, dark alcove. Holding his pistol ready, he moved cautiously forward and peered into the recess.

A small, shivering figure clad in flowing white hugged the back of the recess and stared up at the man. Now he could see that he faced a young woman, and her physical description fit that of the one individual the Dark Lord was most interested in. The trooper grinned behind his helmet. A lucky encounter for him. He would be commended.

Within the armor his head turned slightly, directing his voice to the tiny condenser microphone. 'Here she is,' he called to those behind him. 'Set for stun forc—'

He never finished the sentence, just as he would never receive the hoped-for commendation. Once his attention turned from the girl to his communicator her shivering vanished with startling speed. The energy pistol she had held out of sight behind her came up and around as she burst from her hiding place.

The trooper who had been unlucky enough to find her fell first, his head a mass of melted bone and metal. The same fate met the second armored form coming up fast behind him. Then a bright green energy pole touched the woman's side and she slumped instantly to the deck, the pistol still locked in her small palm.

Metal-encased shapes clustered around her. One whose arm bore the insignia of a lower officer knelt and turned her over. He studied the paralyzed form with a practiced eye.

'She'll be all right,' he finally declared, looking up at his subordinates. 'Report to Lord Vader.'

Threepio stared, mesmerized, out of the small viewport set in the front of the tiny escape pod as the hot yellow eye of Tatooine began to swallow them up. Somewhere behind them, he knew, the crippled fighter and the Imperial cruiser were receding to imperceptibility.

That was fine with him. If they landed near a civilized city, he would seek elegant employment in a halcyon atmosphere, something more befitting his status and training. These past months had gifted him with entirely too much excitement and unpredictability for a mere machine.

Artoo's seemingly random manipulation of the pod controls promised anything but a smooth landing, however. Threepio regarded his squat companion with concern.

'Are you sure you know how to pilot this thing?'

Artoo replied with a noncommittal whistle that did nothing to alter the taller robot's jangled state of mind.

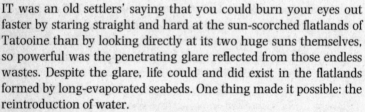

IT was an old settlers' saying that you could burn your eyes out faster by staring straight and hard at the sun-scorched flatlands of Tatooine than by looking directly at its two huge suns themselves, so powerful was the penetrating glare reflected from those endless wastes. Despite the glare, life could and did exist in the flatlands formed by long-evaporated seabeds. One thing made it possible: the reintroduction of water.

For human purposes, however, the water of Tatooine was only marginally accessible. The atmosphere yielded its moisture with reluctance. It had to be coaxed down out of the hard blue sky – coaxed, forced, yanked down to the parched surface.

Two figures whose concern was obtaining that moisture were standing on a slight rise of one of those inhospitable flats. One of the pair was stiff and metallic – a sand-pitted vaporator sunk securely through sand and into deeper rock. The figure next to it was a good deal more animated, though no less sunweathered.

Luke Skywalker was twice the age of the ten-year-old vaporator, but much less secure. At the moment he was swearing softly at a recalcitrant valve adjuster on the temperamental device. From time to time he resorted to some unsubtle pounding in place of using the appropriate tool. Neither method worked very well. Luke was sure that the lubricants used on the vaporators went out of their way to attract sand, beckoning seductively to small abrasive particles with an oily gleam. He wiped sweat from his forehead and leaned back for a moment. The most prepossessing thing about the young man was his name. A light breeze tugged at his shaggy hair and baggy work tunic as he regarded the device. No point in staying angry at it, he counseled himself. It's only an unintelligent machine.

As Luke considered his predicament, a third figure appeared, scooting out from behind the vaporator to fumble awkwardly at the damaged section. Only three of the Treadwell model robot's six arms were functioning, and these had seen more wear than the boots on Luke's feet. The machine moved with unsteady, stop-and-start motions.

Luke gazed at it sadly, then inclined his head to study the sky. Still no sign of a cloud, and he knew there never would be unless he got that vaporator working. He was about to try once again when a small, intense gleam of light caught his eye. Quickly he slipped the carefully cleaned set of macrobinoculars from his utility belt and focused the lenses skyward.

For long moments he stared, wishing all the while that he had a real telescope instead of the binocs. As he stared, vaporators, the heat, and the day's remaining chores were forgotten. Clipping the binoculars back onto his belt, Luke turned and dashed for the landspeeder. Halfway to the vehicle he thought to call behind him.

'Hurry up,' he shouted impatiently. 'What are you waiting for? Get it in gear.'

The Treadwell started toward him, hesitated, and then commenced spinning in a tight circle, smoke belching from every joint. Luke shouted further instructions, then finally gave up in disgust when he realized that it would take more than words to motivate the Treadwell again.

For a moment Luke hesitated at leaving the machine behind – but, he argued to himself, its vital components were obviously shot. So he jumped into the landspeeder, causing the recently repaired repulsion floater to list alarmingly to one side until he was able to equalize weight distribution by sliding behind the controls. Maintaining its altitude slightly above the sandy ground, the light-duty transport vehicle steadied itself like a boat in a heavy sea. Luke gunned the engine, which whined in protest, and sand erupted behind the floater as he aimed the craft toward the distant town of Anchorhead.

Behind him, a pitiful beacon of black smoke from the burning robot continued to rise into the clear desert air. It wouldn't be there when Luke returned. There were scavengers of metal as well as flesh in the wide wastes of Tatooine.

Metal and stone structures bleached white by the glaze of twin Tatoo I and II huddled together tightly, for company as much as for protection. They formed the nexus of the widespread farming community of Anchorhead.

Presently the dusty, unpaved streets were quiet, deserted. Sand-flies buzzed lazily in the cracked eaves of pourstone buildings. A dog barked in the distance, the sole sign of habitation until a lone old woman appeared and started across the street. Her metallic sun shawl was pulled tight around her.

Something made her look up, tired eyes squinting into the distance. The sound suddenly leaped in volume as a shining rectangular shape came roaring around a far corner. Her eyes popped as the vehicle bore down on her, showing no sign of altering its path. She had to scramble to get out of its way.

Panting and waving an angry fist after the landspeeder, she raised her voice over the sound of its passage. 'Won't you kids ever learn to slow down!'

Luke might have seen her, but he certainly didn't hear her. In both cases his attention was focused elsewhere as he pulled up behind a low, long concrete station. Various coils and rods jutted from its top and sides. Tatooine's relentless sand waves broke in frozen yellow spume against the station's walls. No one had bothered to clear them away. There was no point. They would only return again the following day.

Luke slammed the front door aside and shouted, 'Hey!'

A rugged young man in mechanic's dress sat sprawled in a chair behind the station's unkempt control desk. Sunscreen oil had kept his skin from burning. The skin of the girl on his lap had been equally protected, and there was a great deal more of the protected area in view. Somehow even dried sweat looked good on her.

'Hey, everybody!' Luke yelled again, having elicited something less than an overwhelming response with his first cry. He ran toward the instrument room at the rear of the station while the mechanic, half asleep, ran a hand across his face and mumbled, 'Did

I hear a young noise blast through here?'

The girl on his lap stretched sensuously, her well-worn clothing tugging in various intriguing directions. Her voice was casually throaty. 'Oh,' she yawned, 'that was just Wormie on one of his rampages.'

Deak and Windy looked up from the computer-assisted pool game as Luke burst into the room. They were dressed much like Luke, although their clothing was of better fit and somewhat less exercised.

All three youths contrasted strikingly with the burly, handsome player at the far side of the table. From neatly clipped hair to his precision-cut uniform he stood out in the room like an Oriental poppy in a sea of oats. Behind the three humans a soft hum came from where a repair robot was working patiently on a broken piece of station equipment.

'Shape it up, you guys,' Luke yelled excitedly. Then he noticed the older man in the uniform. The subject of his suddenly startled gaze recognized him simultaneously.

'Biggs!'

The man's face twisted in a half grin. 'Hello, Luke.' Then they were embracing each other warmly.

Luke finally stood away, openly admiring the other's uniform. 'I didn't know you were back. When did you get in?'

The confidence in the other's voice bordered the realm of smugness without quite entering it. 'Just a little while ago. I wanted to surprise you, hotshot.' He indicated the room. 'I thought you'd be here with these other two nightcrawlers.' Deak and Windy both smiled. 'I certainly didn't expect you to be out working.' He laughed easily, a laugh few people found resistible.

'The academy didn't change you much,' Luke commented. 'But you're back so soon.' His expression grew concerned. 'Hey, what happened – didn't you get your commission?'

There was something evasive about Biggs as he replied, looking slightly away, 'Of course I got it. Signed to serve aboard the freighter *Rand Ecliptic* just last week. First Mate Biggs Darklighter, at your service.' He performed a twisting salute, half serious and half humorous, then grinned that overbearing yet ingratiating grin again.

'I just came back to say good-bye to all you unfortunate

landlocked simpletons.' They all laughed, until Luke suddenly remembered what had brought him here in such a hurry.

'I almost forgot,' he told them, his initial excitement returning, 'there's a battle going on right here in our system. Come and look.'

Deak looked disappointed. 'Not another one of your epic battles, Luke. Haven't you dreamed up enough of them? Forget it.'

'Forget it, hell – I'm serious. It's a battle, all right.'

With words and shoves he managed to cajole the occupants of the station out into the strong sunlight. Camie in particular looked disgusted.

'This had better be worth it, Luke,' she warned him, shading her eyes against the glare.

Luke already had his macrobinoculars out and was searching the heavens. It took only a moment for him to fix on a particular spot. 'I told you,' he insisted. 'There they are.'

Biggs moved alongside him and reached for the binoculars as the others strained unaided eyes. A slight readjustment provided just enough magnification for Biggs to make out two silvery specks against the dark blue.

'That's no battle, hotshot,' he decided, lowering the binocs and regarding his friend gently. 'They're just sitting there. Two ships, all right – probably a barge loading a freighter, since Tatooine hasn't got an orbital station.'

'There was a lot of firing – earlier,' Luke added. His initial enthusiasm was beginning to falter under the withering assurance of his older friend.

Camie grabbed the binoculars away from Biggs, banging them slightly against a support pillar in the process. Luke took them away from her quickly, inspecting the casing for damage. 'Take it easy with those.'

'Don't worry so much, Wormie,' she sneered. Luke took a step toward her, then halted as the huskier mechanic easily interposed himself between them and favored Luke with a warning smile. Luke considered, shrugged the incident away.

'I keep telling you, Luke,' the mechanic said, with the air of a man tired of repeating the same story to no avail, 'the rebellion is a long way from here. I doubt if the Empire would fight to keep this system. Believe me, Tatooine is a big hunk of nothing.'

His audience began to fade back into the station before Luke could mutter a reply. Fixer had his arm around Camie, and the two of them were chuckling over Luke's ineptitude. Even Deak and Windy were murmuring among themselves – about him, Luke was certain.

He followed them, but not without a last glance back and up to the distant specks. One thing he was sure of were the flashes of light he had seen between the two ships. They hadn't been caused by the suns of Tatooine reflecting off metal.

The binding that locked the girl's hands behind her back was primitive and effective. The constant attention the squad of heavily armed troopers favored her with might have been out of place for one small female, except for the fact that their lives depended on her being delivered safely.

When she deliberately slowed her pace, however, it became apparent that her captors did not mind mistreating her a little. One of the armored figures shoved her brutally in the small of the back, and she nearly fell. Turning, she gave the offending soldier a vicious look. But she could not tell if it had any effect, since the man's face was completely hidden by his armored helmet.

The hallway they eventually emerged into was still smoking around the edges of the smoldering cavity blasted through the hull of the fighter. A portable accessway had been sealed to it and a circlet of light showed at the far end of the tunnel, bridging space between the rebel craft and the cruiser. A shadow moved over her as she turned from inspecting the accessway, startling her despite her usually unshakable self-control.

Above her towered the threatening bulk of Darth Vader, red eyes glaring behind the hideous breath mask. A muscle twitched in one smooth cheek, but other than that the girl didn't react. Nor was there the slightest shake in her voice.

'Darth Vader . . . I should have known. Only you would be so bold – and so stupid. Well, the Imperial Senate will not sit still for this. When they hear that you have attacked a diplomatic miss—'

'Senator Leia Organa,' Vader rumbled softly, though strongly enough to override her protests. His pleasure at finding her was evident in the way he savored every syllable.

'Don't play games with me, Your Highness,' he continued ominously. 'You aren't on any mercy mission this time. You passed directly through a restricted system, ignoring numerous warnings and completely disregarding orders to turn about – until it no longer mattered.'

The huge metal skull dipped close. 'I know that several transmissions were beamed to this vessel by spies within that system. When we traced those transmissions back to the individuals with whom they originated, they had the poor grace to kill themselves before they could be questioned. I want to know what happened to the data they sent you.'

Neither Vader's words nor his inimical presence appeared to have any effect on the girl. 'I don't know what you're blathering about,' she snapped, looking away from him. 'I'm a member of the Senate on a diplomatic mission to—'

'To your part of the rebel alliance,' Vader declared, cutting her off accusingly. 'You're also a traitor.' His gaze went to a nearby officer. 'Take her away.'

She succeeded in reaching him with her spit, which hissed against still-hot battle armor. He wiped the offensive matter away silently, watching her with interest as she was marched through the accessway into the cruiser.

A tall, slim soldier wearing the sign of an Imperial Commander attracted Vader's attention as he came up next to him. 'Holding her is dangerous,' he ventured, likewise looking after her as she was escorted toward the cruiser. 'If word of this does get out, there will be much unrest in the Senate. It will generate sympathy for the rebels.' The Commander looked up at the unreadable metal face, then added in an off-handed manner, 'She should be destroyed immediately.'

'No. My first duty is to locate that hidden fortress of theirs,' Vader replied easily. 'All the rebel spies have been eliminated – by our hand or by their own. Therefore she is now my only key to discovering its location. I intend to make full use of her. If necessary, I will use her up – but I *will* learn the location of the rebel base.'

The Commander pursed his lips, shook his head slightly, perhaps a bit sympathetically, as he considered the woman. 'She'll die before she gives you any information.'

Vader's reply was chilling in its indifference. 'Leave that to me.' He considered a moment, then went on. 'Send out a wide-band distress signal. Indicate that the Senator's ship encountered an unexpected meteorite cluster it could not avoid. Readings indicate that the shift shields were overridden and the ship was hulled to the point of vacating ninety-five percent of its atmosphere. Inform her father and the Senate that all aboard were killed.'

A cluster of tired-looking troops marched purposefully up to their Commander and the Dark Lord. Vader eyed them expectantly.

'The data tapes in question are not aboard the ship. There is no valuable information in the ship's storage banks and no evidence of bank erasure,' the officer in charge recited mechanically. 'Nor were any transmissions directed outward from the ship from the time we made contact. A malfunctioning lifeboat pod was ejected during the fighting, but it was confirmed at the time that no life forms were on board.'

Vader appeared thoughtful. 'It *could* have been a malfunctioning pod,' he mused, 'that might also have contained the tapes. Tapes are not life forms. In all probability any native finding them would be ignorant of their importance and would likely clear them for his own use. Still . . .

'Send down a detachment to retrieve them, or to make certain they are not in the pod,' he finally ordered the Commander and attentive officer. 'Be as subtle as possible; there is no need to attract attention, even on this miserable outpost world.'

As the officer and troops departed, Vader turned his gaze back to the Commander. 'Vaporize this fighter – we don't want to leave anything. As for the pod, I cannot take the chance it was a simple malfunction. The data it might contain could prove too damaging. See to this personally, Commander. If those data tapes exist, they must be retrieved or destroyed at all costs.' Then he added with satisfaction, 'With that accomplished and the Senator in our hands, we will see the end of this absurd rebellion.'

'It shall be as you direct, Lord Vader,' the Commander acknowledged. Both men entered the accessway to the cruiser.

'What a forsaken place this is!'

Threepio turned cautiously to look back at where the pod lay half buried in sand. His internal gyros were still unsteady from the rough landing. Landing! Mere application of the term unduly flattered his dull associate.

On the other hand, he supposed he ought to be grateful they had

come down in one piece. Although, he mused as he studied the
barren landscape, he still wasn't sure they were better off here than
they would have been had they remained on the captured cruiser.
High sandstone mesas dominated the skyline to one side. Every
other direction showed only endless series of marching dunes like
long yellow teeth stretching for kilometer on kilometer into the
distance. Sand ocean blended into sky-glare until it was impossible
to distinguish where one ended and the other began.

A faint cloud of minute dust particles rose in their wake as the
two robots marched away from the pod. That vehicle, its intended
function fully discharged, was now quite useless. Neither robot had
been designed for pedal locomotion on this kind of terrain, so they
had to fight their way across the unstable surface.

'We seem to have been made to suffer,' Threepio moaned in self-
pity. 'It's a rotten existence.' Something squeaked in his right leg
and he winced. 'I've got to rest before I fall apart. My internals still
haven't recovered from that headlong crash you called a landing.'

He paused, but Artoo Detoo did not. The little automaton had
performed a sharp turn and was now ambling slowly but steadily in
the direction of the nearest outjut of mesa.

'Hey,' Threepio yelled. Artoo ignored the call and continued
striding. 'Where do you think you're going?'

Now Artoo paused, emitting a stream of electronic explanation as
Threepio exhaustedly walked over to join him.

'Well, I'm not going that way,' Threepio declared when Artoo
had concluded his explanation. 'It's too rocky.' He gestured in the
direction they had been walking, at an angle away from the cliffs.
'This way is much easier.' A metal hand waved disparagingly at the
high mesas. 'What makes you think there are any settlements that
way, anyhow?'

A long whistle issued from the depths of Artoo.

'Don't get technical with me,' Threepio warned. 'I've had just
about enough of your decisions.'

Artoo beeped once.

'All right, go your way,' Threepio announced grandly. 'You'll be
sandlogged within a day, you nearsighted scrap pile.' He gave the
Artoo unit a contemptuous shove, sending the smaller robot
tumbling down a slight dune. As it struggled at the bottom to regain
its feet, Threepio started off toward the blurred, glaring horizon,

glancing back over his shoulder. 'Don't let me catch you following me, begging for help,' he warned, 'because you won't get it.'

Below the crest of the dune, the Artoo unit righted itself. It paused briefly to clean its single electronic eye with an auxiliary arm. Then it produced an electronic squeal which was almost, though not quite, a human expression of rage. Humming quietly to itself then, it turned and trudged off toward the sandstone ridges as if nothing had happened.

Several hours later a straining Threepio, his internal thermostat overloaded and edging dangerously toward overheat shutdown, struggled up the top of what he hoped was the last towering dune. Nearby, pillars and buttresses of bleached calcium, the bones of some enormous beast, formed an unpromising landmark. Reaching the crest of the dune, Threepio peered anxiously ahead. Instead of the hoped-for greenery of human civilization he saw only several dozen more dunes, identical in form and promise to the one he now stood upon. The farthest rose even higher than the one he presently surmounted.

Threepio turned and looked back toward the now far-off rocky plateau, which was beginning to grow indistinct with distance and heat distortion. 'You malfunctioning little twerp,' he muttered, unable even now to admit to himself that perhaps, just possibly, the Artoo unit might have been right. 'This is all your fault. You tricked me into going this way, but you'll do no better.'

Nor would he if he didn't continue on. So he took a step forward and heard something grind dully within a leg joint. Sitting down in an electronic funk, he began picking sand from his encrusted joints.

He could continue on his present course, he told himself. Or he could confess to an error in judgment and try to catch up again with Artoo Detoo. Neither prospect held much appeal for him.

But there was a third choice. He could sit here, shining in the sunlight, until his joints locked, his internals overheated, and the ultraviolet burned out his photoreceptors. He would become another monument to the destructive power of the binary, like the colossal organism whose picked corpse he had just encountered.

Already his receptors were beginning to go, he reflected. It seemed he saw something moving in the distance. Heat distortion, probably. No – no – it was definitely light on metal, and it was moving toward him. His hopes soared. Ignoring the warnings from his damaged leg, he rose and began waving frantically.

It was, he saw now, definitely a vehicle, though of a type unfamiliar to him. But a vehicle it was, and that implied intelligence and technology.

He neglected in his excitement to consider the possibility that it might not be of human origin.

'So I cut off my power, shut down the afterburners, and dropped in low on Deak's tail,' Luke finished, waving his arms wildly. He and Biggs were walking in the shade outside the power station. Sounds of metal being worked came from somewhere within, where Fixer had finally joined his robot assistant in performing repairs.

'I was so close to him,' Luke continued excitedly, 'I thought I was going to fry my instrumentation. As it was, I busted up the skyhopper pretty bad.' That recollection inspired a frown.

'Uncle Owen was pretty upset. He grounded me for the rest of the season.' Luke's depression was brief. Memory of his feat overrode its immorality.

'You should have been there, Biggs!'

'You ought to take it a little easier,' his friend cautioned. 'You may be the hottest bush pilot this side of Mos Eisley, Luke, but those little skyhoppers can be dangerous. They move awfully fast for tropospheric craft – faster than they need to. Keep playing engine jockey with one and someday, whammo!' He slammed one fist violently into his open palm. 'You're going to be nothing more than a dark spot on the damp side of a canyon wall.'

'Look who's talking,' Luke retorted. 'Now that you've been on a few big, automatic starships you're beginning to sound like my uncle. You've gotten soft in the cities.' He swung spiritedly at Biggs, who blocked the movement easily, making a halfhearted gesture of counterattack.

Biggs's easygoing smugness dissolved into something warmer. 'I've missed you, kid.'

Luke looked away, embarrassed. 'Things haven't exactly been the same since you left, either, Biggs. It's been so—' Luke hunted for the right word and finally finished helplessly, 'so *quiet*.' His gaze traveled across the sandy, deserted streets of Anchorhead. 'It's always been quiet, really.'

Biggs grew silent, thinking. He glanced around. They were alone out here. Everyone else was back inside the comparative coolness of the power station. As he leaned close Luke sensed an unaccustomed solemness in his friend's tone.

'Luke, I didn't come back just to say good-bye, or to crow over everyone because I got through the Academy.' Again he seemed to hesitate, unsure of himself. Then he blurted out rapidly, not giving himself a chance to back down, 'But I want somebody to know. I can't tell my parents.'

Gaping at Biggs, Luke could only gulp, 'Know what? What are you talking about?'

'I'm talking about the talking that's been going on at the Academy – and other places, Luke. Strong talking. I made some new friends, outsystem friends. We agreed about the way certain things are developing, and—' his voice dropped conspiratorially – 'when we reach one of the peripheral systems, we're going to jump ship and join the Alliance.'

Luke stared back at his friend, tried to picture Biggs – fun-loving, happy-go-lucky, live-for-today Biggs – as a patriot afire with rebellious fervor.

'You're going to join the rebellion?' he started. 'You've got to be kidding. How?'

'Damp down, will you?' the bigger man cautioned, glancing furtively back toward the power station. 'You've got a mouth like a crater.'

'I'm sorry,' Luke whispered rapidly. 'I'm quiet – listen how quiet I am. You can barely hear me—'

Biggs cut him off and continued. 'A friend of mine from the Academy has a friend on Bestine who might enable us to make contact with an armed rebel unit.'

'A friend of a— You're crazy,' Luke announced with conviction, certain his friend had gone mad. 'You could wander around forever trying to find a real rebel outpost. Most of them are only myths. This twice removed friend could be an imperial agent. You'd end up on Kessel, or worse. If rebel outposts were so easy to find, the Empire would have wiped them out years ago.'

'I know it's a long shot,' Biggs admitted reluctantly. 'If I don't contact them, then' – a peculiar light came into Biggs's eyes, a conglomeration of newfound maturity and . . . something else – 'I'll do what I can, on my own.'

He stared intensely at his friend. 'Luke, I'm not going to wait for the Empire to conscript me into its service. In spite of what you hear over the official information channels, the rebellion is growing, spreading. And I want to be on the right side – the side I believe in.' His voice altered unpleasantly, and Luke wondered what he saw in his mind's eye.

'You should have heard some of the stories I've heard, Luke, learned of some of the outrages I've learned about. The Empire may have been great and beautiful once, but the people in charge now—' He shook his head sharply. 'It's rotten, Luke, rotten.'

'And I can't do a damn thing,' Luke muttered morosely. 'I'm stuck here.' He kicked futilely at the ever-present sand of Anchorhead.

'I thought you were going to enter the Academy soon,' Biggs observed. 'If that's so, then you'll have your chance to get off this sandpile.'

Luke snorted derisively. 'Not likely. I had to withdraw my application.' He looked away, unable to meet his friend's disbelieving stare. 'I had to. There's been a lot of unrest among the sandpeople since you left, Biggs. They've even raided the outskirts of Anchorhead.'

Biggs shook his head, disregarding the excuse. 'Your uncle could hold off a whole colony of raiders with one blaster.'

'From the house, sure,' Luke agreed, 'but Uncle Owen's finally got enough vaporators installed and running to make the farm pay off big. But he can't guard all that land by himself, and he says he needs me for one more season. I can't run out on him now.'

Biggs sighed sadly. 'I feel for you, Luke. Someday you're going to have to learn to separate what seems to be important from what really is important.' He gestured around them.

'What good is all your uncle's work if it's taken over by the Empire? I've heard that they're starting to imperialize commerce in all the outlying systems. It won't be long before your uncle and everyone else on Tatooine are just tenants slaving for the greater glory of the Empire.'

'That couldn't happen here,' Luke objected with a confidence he didn't quite feel. 'You've said it yourself – the Empire won't bother with this rock.'

'Things change, Luke. Only the threat of rebellion keeps many in power from doing certain unmentionable things. If that threat is completely removed – well, there are two things men have never been able to satisfy: their curiosity and their greed. There isn't much the high Imperial bureaucrats are curious about.'

Both men stood silent. A sandwhirl traversed the street in silent majesty, collapsing against a wall to send newborn baby zephyrs in all directions.

'I wish I was going with you,' Luke finally murmured. He glanced up. 'Will you be around long?'

'No. As a matter of fact, I'm leaving in the morning to rendezvous with the *Ecliptic.*'

'Then I guess . . . I won't be seeing you again.'

'Maybe someday,' Biggs declared. He brightened, grinning that disarming grin. 'I'll keep a look out for you, hotshot. Try not to run into any canyon walls in the meantime.'

'I'll be at the Academy the season after,' Luke insisted, more to encourage himself than Biggs. 'After that, who knows where I'll end up?' He sounded determined. 'I won't be drafted into the starfleet, that's for sure. Take care of yourself. You'll . . . always be the best friend I've got.' There was no need for a handshake. These two had long since passed beyond that.

'So long, then, Luke,' Biggs said simply. He turned and re-entered the power station.

Luke watched him disappear through the door, his own thoughts as chaotic and frenetic as one of Tatooine's spontaneous dust storms.

There were any number of extraordinary features unique to Tatooine's surface. Outstanding among them were the mysterious mists which rose regularly from the ground at the points where desert sands washed up against unyielding cliffs and mesas.

Fog in a steaming desert seemed as out of place as cactus on a glacier, but it existed nonetheless. Meteorologists and geologists argued its origin among themselves, muttering hard-to-believe theories about water suspended in sandstone veins beneath the sand and incomprehensible chemical reactions which made water rise when the ground cooled, then fall underground again with the double sunrise. It was all very backward and very real.

Neither the mist nor the alien moans of nocturnal desert dwellers troubled Artoo Detoo, however, as he made his careful way up the rocky arroyo, hunting for the easiest pathway to the mesa top. His squarish, broad footpads made clicking sounds loud in the evening light as sand underfoot gave way gradually to gravel.

For a moment, he paused. He seemed to detect a noise – like metal on rock – ahead of him, instead of rock on rock. The sound wasn't repeated, though, and he quickly resumed his ambling ascent.

Up the arroyo, too far up to be seen from below, a pebble trickled loose from the stone wall. The tiny figure which had accidentally dislodged the pebble retreated mouselike into shadow. Two glowing points of light showed under overlapping folds of brown cape a meter from the narrowing canyon wall.

Only the reaction of the unsuspecting robot indicated the presence of the whining beam as it struck him. For a moment Artoo Detoo fluoresced eerily in the dimming light. There was a single short electronic squeak. Then the tripodal support unbalanced and the tiny automaton toppled over onto its back, the lights on its front blinking on and off erratically from the effects of the paralyzing beam.

Three travesties of men scurried out from behind concealing boulders. Their motions were more indicative of rodent than humankind, and they stood little taller than the Artoo unit. When they saw that the single burst of enervating energy had immobilized the robot, they holstered their peculiar weapons. Nevertheless, they approached the listless machine cautiously, with the trepidation of hereditary cowards.

Their cloaks were thickly coated with dust and sand. Unhealthy red-yellow pupils glowed catlike from the depths of their hoods as they studied their captive. The jawas conversed in low guttural croaks and scrambled analogs of human speech. If, as anthropologists hypothesized, they had ever been human, they had long since degenerated past anything resembling the human race.

Several more jawas appeared. Together they succeeded in alternately hoisting and dragging the robot back down the arroyo.

At the bottom of the canyon – like some monstrous prehistoric beast – was a sandcrawler as enormous as its owners and operators were tiny. Several dozen meters high, the vehicle towered above the ground on multiple treads that were taller than a tall man. Its metal epidermis was battered and pitted from withstanding untold sandstorms.

On reaching the crawler, the jawas resumed jabbering among themselves. Artoo Detoo could hear them but failed to comprehend anything. He need not have been embarrassed at his failure. If they so wished, only jawas could understand other jawas, for they employed a randomly variable language that drove linguists mad.

One of them removed a small disk from a belt pouch and sealed it to the Artoo unit's flank. A large tube protruded from one side of the gargantuan vehicle. They rolled him over to it and then moved clear. There was a brief moan, the *whoosh* of a powerful vacuum, and the small robot was sucked into the bowels of the sandcrawler as neatly as a pea up a straw. This part of the job completed, the jawas engaged in another bout of jabbering, following which they scurried into the crawler via tubes and ladders, for all the world like a nest of mice returning to their holes.

None too gently, the suction tube deposited Artoo in a small cubical. In addition to varied piles of broken instruments and outright scrap, a dozen or so robots of differing shapes and sizes populated the prison. A few were locked in electronic conversation. Others muddled aimlessly about. But when Artoo tumbled into the chamber, one voice burst out in surprise.

'Artoo Detoo – it's you, it's you!' called an excited Threepio from the near darkness. He made his way over to the still immobilized repair unit and embraced it most unmechanically. Spotting the small disk sealed onto Artoo's side, Threepio turned his gaze thoughtfully down to his own chest, where a similar device had likewise been attached.

Massive gears, poorly lubricated, started to move. With a groaning and grinding, the monster sandcrawler turned and lumbered with relentless patience into the desert night.

THE burnished conference table was as soulless and unyielding as the mood of the eight Imperial Senators and officers ranged around it. Imperial troopers stood guard at the entrance to the chamber, which was sparse and coldly lit from lights in the table and walls. One of the youngest of the eight was declaiming. He exhibited the attitude of one who had climbed far and fast by methods best not examined too closely. General Tagge did possess a certain twisted genius, but it was only partly that ability which had lifted him to his present exalted position. Other noisome talents had proven equally efficacious.

Though his uniform was as neatly molded and his body as clean as that of anyone else in the room, none of the remaining seven cared to touch him. A certain sliminess clung cloyingly to him, a sensation inferred rather than tactile. Despite this, many respected him. Or feared him.

'I tell you, he's gone too far this time,' the General was insisting vehemently. 'This Sith Lord inflicted on us at the urging of the Emperor will be our undoing. Until the battle station is fully operational, we remain vulnerable.

'Some of you still don't seem to realize how well equipped and organized the Rebel Alliance is. Their vessels are excellent, their pilots better. And they are propelled by something more powerful than mere engines: this perverse, reactionary fanaticism of theirs. They're more dangerous than most of you realize.'

An older officer, with facial scars so deeply engraved that even the best cosmetic surgery could not fully repair them, shifted nervously in his chair. 'Dangerous to your starfleet, General Tagge, but not to this battle station.' Wizened eyes hopped from man to man, traveling around the table. 'I happen to think Lord Vader knows what he's doing. The rebellion will continue only as long as those cowards have a sanctuary, a place where their pilots can relax and their machines can be repaired.'

Tagge objected. 'I beg to differ with you, Romodi. I think the construction of this station has more to do with Governor Tarkin's bid for personal power and recognition than with any justifiable military strategy. Within the Senate the rebels will continue to increase their support as long—'

The sound of the single doorway sliding aside and the guards snapping to attention cut him of. His head turned as did everyone else's.

Two individuals as different in appearance as they were united in objectives had entered the chamber. The nearest to Tagge was a thin, hatchet-faced man with hair and form borrowed from an old broom and the expression of a quiescent piranha. The Grand Moff Tarkin, Governor of numerous outlying Imperial territories, was dwarfed by the broad, armored bulk of Lord Darth Vader.

Tagge, unintimidated but subdued, slowly resumed his seat as Tarkin assumed his place at the end of the conference table. Vader stood next to him, a dominating presence behind the Governor's chair. For a minute Tarkin stared directly at Tagge, then glanced away as if he had seen nothing. Tagge fumed but remained silent.

As Tarkin's gaze roved around the table a razor-thin smile of satisfaction remained frozen in his features. 'The Imperial Senate will no longer be of any concern to us, gentlemen. I have just received word that the Emperor has permanently dissolved that misguided body.'

A ripple of astonishment ran through the assembly. 'The last remnants,' Tarkin continued, 'of the Old Republic have finally been swept away.'

'This is impossible,' Tagge interjected. 'How will the Emperor maintain control of the Imperial bureaucracy?'

'Senatorial representation has not been formally abolished, you must understand,' Tarkin explained. 'It has merely been superseded for the – ' he smiled a bit more – 'duration of the emergency. Regional Governors will now have direct control and a free hand in administering their territories. This means that the Imperial presence can at last be brought to bear properly on the vacillating worlds of the Empire. From now on, fear will keep potentially traitorous local governments in line. Fear of the Imperial fleet – and fear of this battle station.'

'And what of the existing rebellion?' Tagge wanted to know.

'If the rebels somehow managed to gain access to a complete technical schema of this battle station, it is remotely possible that they might be able to locate a weakness susceptible to minor exploitation.' Tarkin's smile shifted to a smirk. 'Of course, we all know how well guarded, how carefully protected, such vital data is. It could not possibly fall into rebel hands.'

'The technical data to which you are obliquely referring,' rumbled Darth Vader angrily, 'will soon be back in our hands. If—'

Tarkin shook the Dark Lord off, something no one else at the table would have dared to do. 'It is immaterial. Any attack made against this station by the rebels would be a suicidal gesture, suicidal and useless – regardless of any information they managed to obtain. After many long years of secretive construction,' he declared with evident pleasure, 'this station has become the decisive force in this part of the universe. Events in this region of the galaxy will no longer be determined by fate, by decree, or by any other agency. They will be decided by this station!'

A huge metal-clad hand gestured slightly, and one of the filled cups on the table drifted responsively into it. With a slightly admonishing tone the Dark Lord continued. 'Don't become too proud of this technological terror you've spawned, Tarkin. The ability to destroy a city, a world, a whole system is still insignificant when set against the Force.'

'The Force,' Tagge sneered. 'Don't try to frighten *us* with your sorcerer's ways, Lord Vader. Your sad devotion to that ancient mythology has not helped you to conjure up those stolen tapes, or gifted you with clairvoyance sufficient to locate the rebels' hidden fortress. Why, it's enough to make one laugh fit to—'

Tagge's eyes abruptly bulged and his hands went to his throat as he began to turn a disconcerting shade of blue.

'I find,' Vader ventured mildly, 'this lack of faith disturbing.'

'Enough of this,' Tarkin snapped, distressed. 'Vader, release him. This bickering among ourselves is pointless.'

Vader shrugged as if it were of no consequence. Tagge slumped in his seat, rubbing his throat, his wary gaze never leaving the dark giant.

'Lord Vader will provide us with the location of the rebel fortress by the time this station is certified operational,' Tarkin declared. 'That known, we will proceed to it and destroy it utterly, crushing this pathetic rebellion in one swift stroke.'

'As the Emperor wills it,' Vader added, not without sarcasm, 'so shall it be.'

If any of the powerful men seated around the table found this disrespectful tone objectionable, a glance at Tagge was sufficient to dissuade them from mentioning it.

The dim prison reeked of rancid oil and stale lubricants, a veritable metallic charnel house. Threepio endured the discomfiting atmosphere as best he could. It was a constant battle to avoid being thrown by every unexpected bounce into the walls or into a fellow machine.

To conserve power – and also to avoid the steady stream of complaints from his taller companion – Artoo Detoo had shut down all exterior functions. He lay inert among a pile of secondary parts, sublimely unconcerned at the moment as to their fate.

'Will this never end?' Threepio was moaning as another violent jolt roughly jostled the inhabitants of the prison. He had already formulated and discarded half a hundred horrible ends. He was certain only that their eventual disposition was sure to be worse than anything he could imagine.

Then, quite without warning, something more unsettling than even the most battering bump took place. The sandcrawler's whine died, and the vehicle came to a halt – almost as if in response to Threepio's query. A nervous buzz rose from those mechanicals who still retained a semblance of sentience as they speculated on their present location and probable fate.

At least Threepio was no longer ignorant of his captors or of their likely motives. Local captives had explained the nature of the quasi-human mechanic migrants, the jawas. Traveling in their enormous mobile fortress-homes, they scoured the most inhospitable regions of Tatooine in search of valuable minerals – and salvageable machinery. They had never been seen outside of their protective cloaks and sandmasks, so no one knew exactly what they looked like. But they were reputed to be extraordinarily ugly. Threepio did not have to be convinced.

Leaning over his still-motionless companion, he began a steady shaking of the barrel-like torso. Epidermal sensors were activated on the Artoo unit, and the lights on the front side of the little robot began a sequential awakening.

'Wake up, wake up,' Threepio urged. 'We've stopped someplace.' Like several of the other, more imaginative robots, his eyes were warily scanning metal walls, expecting a hidden panel to slide aside at any moment and a giant mechanical arm to come probing and fumbling for him.

'No doubt about it, we're doomed,' he recited mournfully as Artoo righted himself, returning to full activation. 'Do you think they'll melt us down?' He became silent for several minutes, then added, 'It's this waiting that gets to me.'

Abruptly the far wall of the chamber slid aside and the blinding white glare of a Tatooine morning rushed in on them. Threepio's sensitive photoreceptors were hard pressed to adjust in time to prevent serious damage.

Several of the repulsive-looking jawas scrambled agilely into the chamber, still dressed in the same swathings and filth Threepio had observed on them before. Using hand weapons of an unknown design, they prodded at the machines. Certain of them, Threepio noted with a mental swallow, did not stir.

Ignoring the immobile ones, the jawas herded those still capable of movement outside, Artoo and Threepio among them. Both robots found themselves part of an uneven mechanical line.

Shielding his eyes against the glare, Threepio saw that five of them were arranged alongside the huge sandcrawler. Thoughts of escape did not enter his mind. Such a concept was utterly alien to a mechanical. The more intelligent a robot was, the more abhorrent and unthinkable the concept. Besides, had he tried to escape, built-in sensors would have detected the critical logic malfunction and melted every circuit in his brain.

Instead, he studied the small domes and vaporators that indicated the presence of a larger underground human homestead. Though he was unfamiliar with this type of construction, all signs pointed to a modest, if isolated, habitation. Thoughts of being dismembered for parts or slaving in some high-temperature mine slowly faded. His spirits rose correspondingly.

'Maybe this won't be so bad after all,' he murmured hopefully. 'If we can convince these bipedal vermin to unload us here, we may enter into sensible human service again instead of being melted into slag.'

Artoo's sole reply was a noncommittal chirp. Both machines became silent as the jawas commenced scurrying around them, striving to straighten one poor machine with a badly bent spine, to disguise a dent or scrape with liquid and dust.

As two of them bustled about, working on his sandcoated skin, Threepio fought to stifle an expression of disgust. One of his many human-analog functions was the ability to react naturally to offensive odors. Apparently hygiene was unknown among the jawas. But he was certain no good would come of pointing this out to them.

Small insects drifted in clouds about the faces of the jawas, who ignored them. Apparently the tiny individualized plagues were regarded as just a different sort of appendage, like an extra arm or leg.

So intent was Threepio on his observation that he failed to notice the two figures moving toward them from the region of the largest dome. Artoo had to nudge him slightly before he looked up.

The first man wore an air of grim, semiperpetual exhaustion, sandblasted into his face by too many years of arguing with a hostile environment. His graying hair was frozen in tangled twists like gypsum helicites. Dust frosted his face, clothes, hands, and thoughts. But the body, if not the spirit, was still powerful.

Proportionately dwarfed by his uncle's wrestlerlike body, Luke strode slump-shouldered in his shadow, his present attitude one of dejection rather than exhaustion. He had a great deal on his mind, and it had very little to do with farming. Mostly it involved the rest of his life, and the commitment made by his best friend who had recently departed beyond the blue sky above to enter a harsher, yet more rewarding career.

The bigger man stopped before the assembly and entered into a peculiar squeaky dialogue with the jawa in charge. When they wished it, the jawas could be understood.

Luke stood nearby, listening indifferently. Then he shuffled along behind his uncle as the latter began inspecting the five machines, pausing only to mutter an occasional word or two to his nephew. It was hard to pay attention, even though he knew he ought to be learning.

'Luke – oh, Luke!' a voice called.

Turning away from the conversation, which consisted of the lead jawa extolling the unmatched virtues of all five machines and his uncle countering with derision, Luke walked over to the near edge of the subterranean courtyard and peered down.

A stout woman with the expression of a misplaced sparrow was busy working among decorative plants. She looked up at him. 'Be sure and tell Owen that if he buys a translator to make sure it speaks Bocce, Luke.'

Turning, Luke looked back over his shoulder and studied the motley collection of tired machines. 'It looks like we don't have much of a choice,' he called back down to her, 'but I'll remind him anyway.'

She nodded up at him and he turned to rejoin his uncle.

Apparently Owen Lars had already come to a decision, having settled on a small semi-agricultural robot. This one was similar in shape to Artoo Detoo, save that its multiple subsidiary arms were tipped with different functions. At an order it had stepped out of the line and was wobbling along behind Owen and the temporarily subdued jawa.

Proceeding to the end of the line, the farmer's eyes narrowed as he concentrated on the sand-scoured but still flashy bronze finish of the tall, humanoid Threepio.

'I presume you function,' he grumbled at the robot. 'Do you know customs and protocol?'

'Do I know protocol?' Threepio echoed as the farmer looked him up and down. Threepio was determined to embarrass the jawa when it came to selling his abilities. 'Do I know protocol! Why, it's my primary function. I am also well—'

'Don't need a protocol droid,' the farmer snapped dryly.

'I don't blame you, sir,' Threepio rapidly agreed. 'I couldn't be more in agreement. What could be more of a wasteful luxury in a climate like this? For someone of your interests, sir, a protocol droid would be a useless waste of money. No, sir – versatility is my middle name. See Vee Threepio – Vee for versatility – at your service. I've been programmed for over thirty secondary functions that require only . . .'

'I need,' the farmer broke in, demonstrating imperious disregard for Threepio's as yet unenumerated secondary functions, 'a droid that knows something about the binary language of independently programmable moisture vaporators.'

'Vaporators! We are both in luck,' Threepio countered. 'My first post-primary assignment was in programming binary load lifters. Very similar in construction and memory-function to your vaporators. You could almost say . . .'

Luke tapped his uncle on the shoulder and whispered something in his ear. His uncle nodded, then looked back at the attentive Threepio again.

'Do you speak Bocce?'

'Of course, sir,' Threepio replied, confident for a change with a wholly honest answer. 'It's like a second language to me. I'm as fluent in Bocce as—'

The farmer appeared determined never to allow him to conclude a sentence. 'Shut up.' Owen Lars looked down at the jawa. 'I'll take this one, too.'

'Shutting up, sir,' responded Threepio quickly, hard put to conceal his glee at being selected.

'Take them down to the garage, Luke,' his uncle instructed him. 'I want you to have both of them cleaned up by suppertime.'

Luke looked askance at his uncle. 'But I was going into Tosche station to pick up some new power converters and . . .'

'Don't lie to me, Luke,' his uncle warned him sternly. 'I don't mind you wasting time with your idle friends, but only after you've finished your chores. Now hop to it – and before supper, mind.'

Downcast, Luke directed his words irritably to Threepio and the small agricultural robot. He knew better than to argue with his uncle.

'Follow me, you two.' They started for the garage as Owen entered into price negotiations with the jawa.

Other jawas were leading the three remaining machines back

into the sandcrawler when something let out an almost pathetic beep. Luke turned to see an Artoo unit breaking formation and starting toward him. It was immediately restrained by a jawa wielding a control device that activated the disk sealed on the machine's front plate.

Luke studied the rebellious droid curiously. Threepio started to say something, considered the circumstances and thought better of it. Instead, he remained silent, staring straight ahead.

A minute later, something pinged sharply nearby. Glancing down, Luke saw that a head plate had popped off the top of the agricultural droid. A grinding noise was coming from within. A second later the machine was throwing internal components all over the sandy ground.

Leaning close, Luke peered inside the expectorating mechanical. He called out, 'Uncle Owen! The servomotor-central on this cultivator unit is shot. Look . . .' He reached in, tried to adjust the device, and pulled away hurriedly when it began a wild sparking. The odor of crisped insulation and corroded circuitry filled the clear desert air with a pungency redolent of mechanized death.

Owen Lars glared down at the nervous jawa. 'What kind of junk are you trying to push on us?'

The jawa responded loudly, indignantly, while simultaneously taking a couple of precautionary steps away from the big human. He was distressed that the man was between him and the soothing safety of the sandcrawler.

Meanwhile, Artoo Detoo had scuttled out of the group of machines being led back toward the mobile fortress. Doing so turned out to be simple enough, since all the jawas had their attention focused on the argument between their leader and Luke's uncle.

Lacking sufficient armature for wild gesticulation, the Artoo unit suddenly let out a high whistle, then broke it off when it was apparent he had gained Threepio's attention.

Tapping Luke gently on the shoulder, the tall droid whispered conspiratorially into his ear. 'If I might say so, young sir, that Artoo unit is a real bargain. In top condition. I don't believe these creatures have any idea what good shape he's really in. Don't let all the sand and dust deceive you.'

Luke was in the habit of making instant decisions – for good or bad – anyway. 'Uncle Owen!' he called.

Breaking off the argument without taking his attention from the jawa, his uncle glanced quickly at him. Luke gestured toward Artoo Detoo. 'We don't want any trouble. What about swapping this—' he indicated the burned-out agricultural droid – 'for that one?'

The older man studied the Artoo unit professionally, then considered the jawas. Though inherently cowards, the tiny desert scavengers *could* be pushed too far. The sandcrawler could flatten the homestead – at the risk of inciting the human community to lethal vengeance.

Faced with a no-win situation for either side if he pressed too hard, Owen resumed the argument for show's sake before gruffly assenting. The head jawa consented reluctantly to the trade, and both sides breathed a mental sigh of relief that hostilities had been avoided. While the jawa bowed and whined with impatient greed, Owen paid him off.

Meanwhile, Luke had led the two robots toward an opening in the dry ground. A few seconds later they were striding down a ramp kept clear of drifting sand by electrostatic repellers.

'Don't you ever forget this,' Threepio muttered to Artoo leaning over the smaller machine. 'Why I stick my neck out for you, when all you ever bring me is trouble, is beyond my capacity to comprehend.'

The passage widened into the garage proper, which was cluttered with tools and sections of farming machinery. Many looked heavily used, some to the point of collapse. But the lights were comforting to both droids, and there was a homeliness to the chamber which hinted at a tranquillity not experienced by either machine for a long time. Near the center of the garage was a large tub, and the aroma drifting from it made Threepio's principal olfactory sensors twitch.

Luke grinned, noting the robot's reaction. 'Yes, it's a lubrication bath.' He eyed the tall bronze robot appraisingly. 'And from the looks of it, you could use about a week's submergence. But we can't afford that so you'll have to settle for an afternoon.' Then Luke turned his attention to Artoo Detoo, walking up to him and flipping open a panel that shielded numerous gauges.

'As for you,' he continued, with a whistle of surprise, 'I don't know how you've kept running. Not surprising, knowing the jawas' reluctance to part with any erg-fraction they don't have to. It's recharge time for you.' He gestured toward a large power unit.

Artoo Detoo followed Luke's gesture, then beeped once and waddled over to the boxy construction. Finding the proper cord, he automatically flipped open a panel and plugged the triple prongs into his face.

Threepio had walked over to the large cistern, which was filled almost full with aromatic cleansing oil. With a remarkably human-like sigh he lowered himself slowly into the tank.

'You two behave yourselves,' Luke cautioned them as he moved to a small two-man skyhopper. A powerful little suborbital space-craft, it rested in the hangar section of the garage-workshop. 'I've got work of my own to do.'

Unfortunately, Luke's energies were still focused on his farewell encounter with Biggs, so that hours later he had finished few of his chores. Thinking about his friend's departure, Luke was running a caressing hand over the damaged port fin of the 'hopper – the fin he had damaged while running down an imaginary Tie fighter in the wrenching twists and turns of a narrow canyon. That was when the projecting ledge had clipped him as effectively as an energy beam.

Abruptly something came to a boil within him. With atypical violence he threw a power wrench across a worktable nearby. 'It just isn't fair!' he declared to no one in particular. His voice dropped disconsolately. 'Biggs is right. I'll never get out of here. He's planning rebellion against the Empire, and I'm trapped on a blight of a farm.'

'I beg your pardon, sir.'

Luke spun, startled, but it was only the tall droid, Threepio. The contrast in the robot was striking compared with Luke's initial sight of him. Bronze-colored alloy gleamed in the overhead lights of the garage, cleaned of pits and dust by the powerful oils.

'Is there anything I might do to help?' the robot asked solici-tously.

Luke studied the machine, and as he did so some of his anger drained away. There was no point in yelling cryptically at a robot.

'I doubt it,' he replied, 'unless you can alter time and speed up the harvest. Or else teleport me off this sandpile under Uncle Owen's nose.'

Sarcasm was difficult for even an extremely sophisticated robot to detect so Threepio considered the question objectively before finally replying, 'I don't think so, sir. I'm only a third-degree droid and not very knowledgeable about such things as transatomic physics.' Suddenly, the events of the past couple of days seemed to catch up with him all at once. 'As a matter of fact, young sir,' Threepio went on while looking around him with fresh vision, 'I'm not even sure which planet I'm on.'

Luke chuckled sardonically and assumed a mocking pose. 'If there's a bright center to this universe, you're on the world farthest from it.'

'Yes, Luke sir.'

The youth shook his head irritably. 'Never mind the "sir" – it's just Luke. And this world is called Tatooine.'

Threepio nodded slightly. 'Thank you, Luke s – Luke. I am See Threepio, human-droid relations specialist.' He jerked a casual metal thumb back toward the recharge unit. 'That is my companion, Artoo Detoo.'

'Pleased to meet you, Threepio,' Luke said easily. 'You too, Artoo.' Walking across the garage, he checked a gauge on the smaller machine's front panel, then gave a grunt of satisfaction. As he began unplugging the charge cord he saw something which made him frown and lean close.

'Something wrong, Luke?' Threepio inquired.

Luke went to a nearby tool wall and selected a small many-armed device. 'I don't know yet, Threepio.'

Returning to the recharger, Luke bent over Artoo and began scraping at several bumps in the small droid's top with a chromed pick. Occasionally he jerked back sharply as bits of corrosion were flicked into the air by the tiny tool.

Threepio watched, interested, as Luke worked. 'There's a lot of strange carbon scoring here of a type I'm not familiar with. Looks like you've both seen a lot of action out of the ordinary.'

'Indeed, sir,' Threepio admitted, forgetting to drop the honorific. This time Luke was too absorbed elsewhere to correct him. 'Sometimes I'm amazed we're in as good shape as we are.' He added as an afterthought, while still shying away from the thrust of Luke's question. 'What with the rebellion and all.'

Despite his caution, it seemed to Threepio that he must have given something away, for an almost jawa-like blaze appeared in

Luke's eyes. 'You know about the rebellion against the Empire?' he demanded.

'In a way,' Threepio confessed reluctantly. 'The rebellion was responsible for our coming into your service. We are refugees, you see.' He did not add from where.

Not that Luke appeared to care. 'Refugees! Then I did see a space battle!' He rambled on rapidly, excited. 'Tell me where you've been – in how many encounters. How is the rebellion going? Does the Empire take it seriously? Have you seen many ships destroyed?'

'A bit slower, please, sir,' Threepio pleaded. 'You misinterpret our status. We were innocent bystanders. Our involvement with the rebellion was of the most marginal nature.

'As to battles, we were in several, I think. It is difficult to tell when one is not directly in contact with the actual battle machinery.' He shrugged neatly. 'Beyond that, there is not much to say. Remember, sir, I am little more than a cosmeticized interpreter and not very good at telling stories or relating histories, and even less proficient at embellishing them. I am a very literal machine.'

Luke turned away, disappointed, and returned to his cleaning of Artoo Detoo. Additional scraping turned up something puzzling enough to demand his full attention. A small metal fragment was tightly lodged between two bar conduits that would normally form a linkage. Setting down the delicate pick, Luke switched to a larger instrument.

'Well, my little friend,' he murmured, 'you've ·got something jammed in here real good.' As he pushed and pried Luke directed half his attention to Threepio. 'Were you on a star freighter or was it—'

Metal gave way with a powerful *crack*, and the recoil sent Luke tumbling head over heels. Getting to his feet, he started to curse – then froze, motionless.

The front of the Artoo unit had begun to glow, exuding a three-dimensional image less than one-third of a meter square but precisely defined. The portrait formed within the box was so exquisite that in a couple of minutes Luke discovered he was out of breath – because he had forgotten to breathe.

Despite a superficial sharpness, the image flickered and jiggled unsteadily, as if the recording had been made and installed with haste. Luke stared at the atmosphere of the garage and started to form a question. But it was never finished. The lips on the figure moved, and the girl spoke – or rather, seemed to speak. Luke knew the aural accompaniment was generated somewhere within Artoo Detoo's squat torso.

'Obi-Wan Kenobi,' the voice implored huskily, 'help me! You're my only remaining hope.' A burst of static dissolved the face momentarily. Then it coalesced again, and once more the voice repeated, 'Obi-Wan Kenobi, you're my only remaining hope.'

With a raspy hum the hologram continued. Luke sat perfectly still for a long moment, considering what he was seeing, then he blinked and directed his words to the Artoo unit.

'What's this all about, Artoo Detoo?'

The stubby droid shifted slightly, the cubish portrait shifting with him, and beeped what sounded vaguely like a sheepish reply.

Threepio appeared as mystified as Luke. 'What is that?' he inquired sharply, gesturing at the speaking portrait and then at Luke. 'You were asked a question. What and who is that, and how are you originating it – and why?'

The Artoo unit generated a beep of surprise, for all the world as if just noticing the hologram. This was followed by a whistling stream of information.

Threepio digested the data, tried to frown, couldn't, and strove to convey his own confusion via the tone of his voice. 'He insists it's nothing, sir. Merely a malfunction – old data. A tape that should have been erased but was missed. He insists we pay it no mind.'

That was like telling Luke to ignore a cache of Durindfires he might stumble over in the desert. 'Who is she?' he demanded, staring enraptured at the hologram. 'She's beautiful.'

'I really don't know who she is,' Threepio confessed honestly. 'I think she might have been a passenger on our last voyage. From what I recall, she was a personage of some importance. This might have something to do with the fact that our Captain was attaché to—'

Luke cut him off, savoring the way sensuous lips formed and reformed the sentence fragment. 'Is there any more to this recording? It sounds like it's incomplete.' Getting to his feet, Luke reached out for the Artoo unit.

The robot moved backward and produced whistles of such frantic concern that Luke hesitated and held off reaching for the internal controls.

Threepio was shocked. 'Behave yourself, Artoo,' he finally chastised his companion. 'You're going to get us into trouble.' He had visions of the both of them being packed up as uncooperative and shipped back to the jawas, which was enough to make him imitate a shudder.

'It's all right – he's our master now.' Threepio indicated Luke. 'You can trust him. I feel that he has our best interests in mind.'

Detoo appeared to hesitate, uncertain. Then he whistled and beeped a long complexity at his friend.

'Well?' Luke prompted impatiently.

Threepio paused before replying. 'He says that he is the property of one Obi-Wan Kenobi, a resident of this world. Of this very region, in fact. The sentence fragment we are hearing is part of a private message intended for this person.'

Threepio shook his head slowly. 'Quite frankly, sir, I don't know what he's talking about. Our last master was Captain Colton. I never heard Artoo mention a prior master. I've certainly never heard of an Obi-Wan Kenobi. But with all we've been through,' he concluded apologetically, 'I'm afraid his logic circuits have gotten a bit scrambled. He's become decidedly eccentric at times.' And while Luke considered this turn of events, Threepio took the opportunity to throw Artoo a furious look of warning.

'Obi-Wan Kenobi,' Luke recited thoughtfully. His expression suddenly brightened. 'Say . . . I wonder if he could be referring to old Ben Kenobi.'

'Begging your pardon,' Threepio gulped, astonished beyond measure, 'but you actually know of such a person?'

'Not exactly,' he admitted in a more subdued voice. 'I don't know anyone named Obi-Wan – but old Ben lives somewhere out on the fringe of the Western Dune Sea. He's kind of a local character – a hermit. Uncle Owen and a few of the other farmers say he's a sorcerer.

'He comes around once in a while to trade things. I hardly ever talk to him, though. My uncle usually runs him off.' He paused and glanced across at the small robot again. 'But I never heard that old Ben owned a droid of any kind. At least, none that I ever heard tell of.'

Luke's gaze was drawn irresistibly back to the hologram. 'I wonder who she is. She must be important – especially if what you told me just now is true, Threepio. She sounds and looks as if she's in some kind of trouble. Maybe the message *is* important. We ought to hear the rest of it.'

He reached again for the Artoo's internal controls, and the robot scurried backward again, squeaking a blue streak.

'He says there's a restraining separator bolt that's circuiting out his self-motivation components.' Threepio translated. 'He suggests that if you move the bolt he might be able to repeat the entire message,' Threepio finished uncertainly. When Luke continued to stare at the portrait, Threepio added, more loudly, *'Sir!'*

Luke shook himself. 'What ... Oh, yes.' He considered the request. Then he moved and peered into the open panel. This time Artoo didn't retreat.

'I see it, I think. Well, I guess you're too small to run away from me if I take this off. I wonder what someone would be sending a message to old Ben for.'

Selecting the proper tool, Luke reached down into the exposed circuitry and popped the restraining bolt free. The first noticeable result of this action was that the portrait disappeared.

Luke stood back. 'There, now.' There was an uncomfortable pause during which the hologram showed no sign of returning. 'Where did she go?' Luke finally prompted. 'Make her come back. Play the entire message, Artoo Detoo.'

An innocent-sounding beep came from the robot. Threepio appeared embarrassed and nervous as he translated. 'He said, "What message?"'

Threepio's attention turned half angrily to his companion. 'What message? You know what message! The one you just played a fragment of for us. The one you're hauling around inside your recalcitrant, rust-ridden innards, you stubborn hunk of junk!'

Artoo sat and hummed softly to himself.

'I'm sorry, sir,' Threepio said slowly, 'but he shows signs of having developed an alarming flutter in his obedience-rational module. Perhaps if we—'

A voice from down a corridor interrupted him. 'Luke ... oh, Luke – come to dinner!'

Luke hesitated, then rose and turned away from the puzzling little droid. 'Okay,' he called, 'I'm coming, Aunt Beru!' He lowered his voice as he spoke to Threepio. 'See what you can do with him. I'll be back soon.' Tossing the just-removed restraining bolt on the workbench, he hurried from the chamber.

As soon as the human was gone, Threepio whirled on his shorter companion. 'You'd better consider playing that whole recording for him,' he growled, with a suggestive nod toward a workbench laden with dismembered machine parts. 'Otherwise he's liable to take up that cleaning pick again and go digging for it. He might not be too careful what he cuts through if he believes you're deliberately withholding something from him.'

A plaintive beep came from Artoo.

'No,' Threepio responded, 'I don't think he likes you at all.'

A second beep failed to alter the stern tone in the taller robot's voice. 'No, I don't like you, either.'

IV

LUKE'S Aunt Beru was filling a pitcher with blue liquid from a refrigerated container. Behind her, in the dining area, a steady buzz of conversation reached to the kitchen.

She sighed sadly. The mealtime discussions between her husband and Luke had grown steadily more acrimonious as the boy's restlessness pulled him in directions other than farming. Directions for which Owen, a stolid man of the soil if there ever was one, had absolutely no sympathy.

Returning the bulk container to the refrigerator unit, she placed the pitcher on a tray and hurried back to the dining room. Beru was not a brilliant woman, but she possessed an instinctive understanding of her important position in this household. She functioned like the damping rods in a nuclear reactor. As long as she was present, Owen and Luke would continue to generate a lot of heat, but if she was out of their presence for too long – *boom*!

Condenser units built into the bottom of each plate kept the food on the dining-room table hot as she hurried in. Immediately, both men lowered their voices to something civilized and shifted the subject. Beru pretended not to notice the change.

'I think that Artoo unit might have been stolen, Uncle Owen,' Luke was saying, as if that had been the topic of conversation all along.

His uncle helped himself to the milk pitcher, mumbling his reply around a mouthful of food. 'The jawas have a tendency to pick up anything that's not tied down, Luke, but remember, they're basically afraid of their own shadows. To resort to outright theft, they'd have to have considered the consequences of being pursued and punished. Theoretically, their minds shouldn't be capable of that. What makes you think the droid is stolen?'

'For one thing, it's in awfully good shape for a discard. It generated a hologram recording while I was cleaning—' Luke tried to conceal his horror at the slip. He added hastily, 'But that's not important. The reason I think it might be stolen is because it claims to be the property of someone it calls Obi-Wan Kenobi.'

Maybe something in the food, or perhaps the milk, caused Luke's uncle to gag. Then again, it might have been an expression of disgust, which was Owen's way of indicating his opinion of that peculiar personage. In any case, he continued eating without looking up at his nephew.

Luke pretended the display of graphic dislike had never happened. 'I thought,' he continued determinedly, 'it might have meant old Ben. The first name is different, but the last is identical.'

When his uncle steadfastly maintained his silence, Luke prompted him directly. 'Do *you* know who he's talking about, Uncle Owen?'

Surprisingly, his uncle looked uncomfortable instead of angry. 'It's nothing,' he mumbled, still not meeting Luke's gaze. 'A name from another time.' He squirmed nervously in his seat. 'A name that can only mean trouble.'

Luke refused to heed the implied warning and pressed on. 'Is it someone related to old Ben, then? I didn't know he had any relatives.'

'You stay away from that old wizard, you hear me!' his uncle exploded, awkwardly substituting threat for reason.

'Owen . . .' Aunt Beru started to interject gently, but the big farmer cut her off sternly.

'Now, this is important, Beru.' He turned his attention back to his nephew. 'I've told you about Kenobi before. He's a crazy old man; he's dangerous and full of mischief, and he's best left well alone.'

Beru's pleading gaze caused him to quiet somewhat. 'That droid has nothing to do with him. Couldn't have,' he grumbled half to himself. 'Recording – huh! Well, tomorrow I want you to take the unit into Anchorhead and have its memory flushed.'

Snorting, Owen bent to his half-eaten meal with determination. 'That will be the end of this foolishness. I don't care where that machine thinks it came from. I paid hard credit for it, and it belongs to us now.'

'But suppose it *does* belong to someone else,' Luke wondered. 'What if this Obi-Wan person comes looking for his droid?'

An expression between sorrow and a sneer crossed his uncle's seamed face at the remembrance. 'He won't. I don't think that man exists anymore. He died about the same time as your father.' A huge mouthful of hot food was shoveled inward. 'Now forget about it.'

'Then it *was* a real person,' Luke murmured, staring down at his plate. He added slowly, 'Did he know my father?'

'I said forget about it,' Owen snapped. 'Your only worry as far as those two droids are concerned is having them ready for work tomorrow. Remember, the last of our savings is tied up in those two. Wouldn't even have bought them if it wasn't so near harvest.' He shook a spoon at his nephew. 'In the morning I want you to have them working with the irrigation units up on the south ridge.

'You know,' Luke replied distantly, 'I think these droids are going to work out fine. In fact, I—' He hesitated, shooting his uncle a surreptitious glare. 'I was thinking about our agreement about me staying on for another season.'

His uncle failed to react, so Luke rushed on before his nerve failed. 'If these new droids do work out, I want to transmit my application to enter the Academy for next year.'

Owen scowled, trying to hide his displeasure with food. 'You mean, you want to transmit the *application* next year – after the harvest.'

'You have more than enough droids now, and they're in good condition. They'll last.'

'Droids, yes,' his uncle agreed, 'but droids can't replace a man, Luke. You know that. The harvest is when I need you the most. It's just for one more season after this one.' He looked away, bluster and anger gone now.

Luke toyed with his food, not eating, saying nothing.

'Listen,' his uncle told him, 'for the first time we've got a chance for a real fortune. We'll make enough to hire some extra hands for

next time. Not droids – people. Then you can go to the Academy.'
He fumbled over words, unaccustomed to pleading. 'I need you
here, Luke. You understand that, don't you?'

'It's another year,' his nephew objected sullenly. 'Another *year*.'

How many times had he heard that before? How many times had
they repeated this identical charade with the same result?

Convinced once more that Luke had come round to his way of
thinking, Owen shrugged the objection off. 'Time will pass before
you know it.'

Abruptly Luke rose, shoving his barely touched plate of food
aside. 'That's what you said last year when Biggs left.' He spun and
half ran from the room.

'Where are you going, Luke?' his aunt yelled worriedly after him.

Luke's reply was bleak, bitter. 'Looks like I'm going nowhere.'
Then he added, out of consideration for his aunt's sensibilities, 'I
have to finish cleaning those droids if they're going to be ready to
work tomorrow.'

Silence hung in the air of the dining room after Luke departed.
Husband and wife ate mechanically. Eventually Aunt Beru stopped
shoving her food around her plate, looked up, and pointed out
earnestly, 'Owen, you can't keep him here forever. Most of his
friends are gone, the people he grew up with. The Academy means
so much to him.'

Listlessly her husband replied, 'I'll make it up to him next year.
I promise. We'll have money – or maybe, the year after that.'

'Luke's just not a farmer, Owen,' she continued firmly. 'He never
will be, no matter how hard you try to make him one.' She shook
her head slowly. 'He's got too much of his father in him.'

For the first time all evening Owen Lars looked thoughtful as well
as concerned as he gazed down the passage Luke had taken. 'That's
what I'm afraid of,' he whispered.

Luke had gone topside. He stood on the sand watching the double
sunset as first one and then the other of Tatooine's twin suns sank
slowly behind the distant range of dunes. In the fading light the
sands turned gold, russet, and flaming red-orange before advancing
night put the bright colors to sleep for another day. Soon, for the
first time, those sands would blossom with food plants. This former
wasteland would see an eruption of green.

The thought ought to have sent a thrill of anticipation through Luke. He should have been as flushed with excitement as his uncle was whenever he described the coming harvest. Instead, Luke felt nothing but a vast indifferent emptiness. Not even the prospect of having a lot of money for the first time in his life excited him. What was there to do with money in Anchorhead – anywhere on Tatooine, for that matter?

Part of him, an increasingly large part, was growing more and more restless at remaining unfulfilled. This was not an uncommon feeling in youths his age, but for reasons Luke did not understand it was much stronger in him than in any of his friends.

As the night cold came creeping over the sand and up his legs, he brushed the grit from his trousers and descended into the garage. Maybe working on the droids would bury some of the remorse a little deeper in his mind. A quick survey of the chamber showed no movement. Neither of the new machines was in sight. Frowning slightly, Luke took a small control box from his belt and activated a couple of switches set into the plastic.

A low hum came from the box. The caller produced the taller of the two robots, Threepio. In fact, he gave a yell of surprise as he jumped up behind the skyhopper.

Luke started toward him, openly puzzled. 'What are you hiding back there for?'

The robot came stumbling around the prow of the craft, his attitude one of desperation. It occurred to Luke then that despite his activating the caller, the Artoo unit was still nowhere to be seen.

The reason for his absence – or something related to it – came pouring unbidden from Threepio. 'It wasn't my fault,' the robot begged frantically. 'Please don't deactivate me! I told him not to go, but he's faulty. He must be malfunctioning. Something has totally boiled his logic circuits. He kept babbling on about some sort of mission, sir. I never heard a robot with delusions of grandeur before. Such things shouldn't even be within the cogitative theory units of one that's as basic as an Artoo unit, and . . .'

'You mean . . .?' Luke started to gape.

'Yes, sir . . . he's gone.'

'And I removed his restraining coupling myself,' Luke muttered slowly. Already he could visualize his uncle's face. The last of their savings tied up in these droids, he had said.

Racing out of the garage, Luke hunted for non-existent reasons why the Artoo unit should go berserk. Threepio followed on his heels.

From a small ridge which formed the highest point close by the homestead, Luke had a panoramic view of the surrounding desert. Bringing out the precious macrobinoculars, he scanned the rapidly darkening horizons for something small, metallic, three-legged, and out of its mechanical mind.

Threepio fought his way up through the sand to stand beside Luke. 'That Artoo unit has always caused nothing but trouble,' he groaned. 'Astromech droids are becoming too iconoclastic even for me to understand, sometimes.'

The binoculars finally came down, and Luke commented matter-of-factly, 'Well, he's nowhere in sight.' He kicked furiously at the ground. 'Damn it – how could I have been so stupid, letting it trick me into removing that restrainer! Uncle Owen's going to kill me.'

'Begging your pardon, sir,' ventured a hopeful Threepio, visions of jawas dancing in his head, 'But can't we go after him?'

Luke turned. Studiously he examined the wall of black advancing toward them. 'Not at night. It's too dangerous with all the raiders around. I'm not too concerned about the jawas, but sandpeople . . . no, not in the dark. We'll have to wait until morning to try to track him.'

A shout rose from the homestead below. 'Luke – Luke, are you finished with those droids yet? I'm turning down the power for the night.'

'All right!' Luke responded, sidestepping the question. 'I'll be down in a few minutes, Uncle Owen!' Turning, he took one last look at the vanished horizon. 'Boy, am I in for it!' he muttered. 'That little droid's going to get me in a lot of trouble.'

'Oh, he excels at that, sir.' Threepio confirmed with mock cheerfulness. Luke threw him a sour look, and together they turned and descended into the garage.

'Luke . . . Luke!' Still rubbing the morning sleep from his eyes, Owen glanced from side to side, loosening his neck muscles. 'Where could that boy be loafing now?' he wondered aloud at the lack of response. There was no sign of movement in the homestead, and he had already checked above.

'Luke!' he yelled again. *Luke, Luke, Luke* ... the name echoed teasingly back at him from the homestead walls. Turning angrily, he stalked back into the kitchen, where Beru was preparing breakfast.

'Have you seen Luke this morning?' he asked as softly as he could manage.

She glanced briefly at him, then returned to her cooking. 'Yes. He said he had some things to do before he started out to the south ridge this morning, so he left early.'

'Before breakfast?' Owen frowned worriedly. 'That's not like him. Did he take the new droids with him?'

'I think so. I'm sure I saw at least one of them with him.'

'Well,' Owen mused, uncomfortable but with nothing to really hang imprecations on, 'he'd better have those ridge units repaired by midday or there'll be hell to pay.'

An unseen face shielded by smooth white metal emerged from the half-buried life pod that now formed the backbone of a dune slightly higher than its neighbors. The voice sounded efficient, but tired.

'Nothing,' the inspecting trooper muttered to his several companions. 'No tapes, and no sign of habitation.'

Powerful handguns lowered at the information that the pod was deserted. One of the armored men turned, calling out to an officer standing some distance away. 'This is definitely the pod that cleared the rebel ship, sir, but there's nothing on board.'

'Yet it set down intact,' the officer was murmuring to himself. 'It *could* have done so on automatics, but if it was a true malfunction, then they shouldn't have been engaged.' Something didn't make sense.

'Here's why there's nothing on board and no hint of life, sir,' a voice declared.

The officer turned and strode several paces to where another trooper was kneeling in the sand. He held up an object for the officer's inspection. It shone in the sun.

'Droid plating,' the officer observed after a quick glance at the metal fragment. Superior and underling exchanged a significant glance. Then their eyes turned simultaneously to the high mesas off to the north.

*

Gravel and fine sand formed a gritty fog beneath the landspeeder as it slid across the rippling wasteland of Tatooine on humming repulsors. Occasionally the craft would jog slightly as it encountered a dip or slight rise, to return to its smooth passage as its pilot compensated for the change in terrain.

Luke leaned back in the seat, luxuriating in unaccustomed relaxation as Threepio skillfully directed the powerful landcraft around dunes and rocky outcrops. 'You handle a landspeeder pretty well, for a machine,' he noted admiringly.

'Thank you, sir,' a gratified Threepio responded, his eyes never moving from the landscape ahead. 'I was not lying to your uncle when I claimed versatility as my middle name. In fact, on occasion I have been called upon to perform unexpected functions in circumstances which would have appalled my designers.'

Something pinged behind them, then pinged again.

Luke frowned and popped the speeder canopy. A few moments of digging in the motor casing eliminated the metallic bark.

'How's that?' he yelled forward.

Threepio signaled that the adjustment was satisfactory. Luke turned back into the cockpit and closed the canopy over them again. Silently he brushed his wind-whipped hair back out of his eyes as his attention returned to the dry desert ahead of them.

'Old Ben Kenobi is supposed to live out in this general direction. Even though nobody knows exactly where, I don't see how that Artoo unit could have come this far so quickly.' His expression was downcast. 'We must have missed him back in the dunes somewhere. He could be anywhere out here. And Uncle Owen must be wondering why I haven't called in from the south ridge by now.'

Threepio considered a moment, then ventured, 'Would it help, sir, if you told him that it was my fault?'

Luke appeared to brighten at the suggestion. 'Sure ... he needs you twice as much now. Probably he'll only deactivate you for a day or so, or give you a partial memory flush.'

Deactivate? Memory flush? Threepio added hastily, 'On second thoughts, sir, Artoo would still be around if you hadn't removed his restraining module.'

But something more important than fixing responsibility for the little robot's disappearance was on Luke's mind at the moment. 'Wait a minute,' he advised Threepio as he stared fixedly at the instrument panel. 'There's something dead ahead on the metal scanner. Can't distinguish outlines at this distance, but judging by size alone, it *could* be our wandering droid. Hit it.'

The landspeeder jumped forward as Threepio engaged the accelerator, but its occupants were totally unaware that other eyes were watching as the craft increased its speed.

Those eyes were not organic, but then, they weren't wholly mechanical, either. No one could say for certain, because no one had ever made that intimate a study of the Tusken Raiders – known less formally to the margin farmers of Tatooine simply as the sandpeople.

The Tuskens didn't permit close study of themselves, discouraging potential observers by methods as effective as they were uncivilized. A few xenologists thought they must be related to the jawas. Even fewer hypothesized that the jawas were actually the mature form of the sandpeople, but this theory was discounted by the majority of serious scientists.

Both races affected tight clothing to shield them from Tatooine's twin dose of solar radiation, but there most comparisons ended. Instead of heavy woven cloaks like the jawas wore, the sandpeople wrapped themselves mummylike in endless swathings and bandages and loose bits of cloth.

Where the jawas feared everything, a Tusken Raider feared little. The sandpeople were larger, stronger, and far more aggressive. Fortunately for the human colonists of Tatooine, they were not very numerous and elected to pursue their nomadic existence in some of Tatooine's most desolate regions. Contact between human and Tusken, therefore, was infrequent and uneasy, and they murdered no more than a handful of humans per year. Since the human population had claimed its share of Tuskens, not always with reason, a peace of a sort existed between the two – as long as neither side gained an advantage.

One of the pair felt that that unstable condition had temporarily shifted in his favor, and he was about to take full advantage of it as he raised his rifle toward the landspeeder. But his companion grabbed the weapon and shoved down on it before it could be fired. This set off a violent argument between the two. And, as they traded vociferous opinions in a language consisting mostly of consonants, the landspeeder sped on its way.

Either because the speeder had passed out of range or because the second Tusken had convinced the other, the two broke off the discussion and scrambled down the back side of the high ridge. Snuffling and a shifting of weight took place at the ridge bottom as the two Banthas stirred at the approach of their masters. Each was as large as a small dinosaur, with bright eyes and long, thick fur. They hissed anxiously as the two sandpeople approached, then mounted them from knee to saddle.

With a kick the Banthas rose. Moving slowly but with enormous strides, the two massive horned creatures swept down the back of the rugged bluff, urged on by their anxious, equally outrageous mahouts.

'It's him, all right,' Luke declared with mixed anger and satisfaction as the tiny tripodal form came into view. The speeder banked and swung down onto the floor of a huge sandstone canyon. Luke slipped his rifle out from behind the seat and swung it over his shoulder. 'Come round in front of him, Threepio,' he instructed.

'With pleasure, sir.'

The Artoo unit obviously noted their approach, but made no move to escape; it could hardly have outrun the landspeeder anyway. Artoo simply halted as soon as it detected them and waited until the craft swung around in a smooth arc. Threepio came to a sharp halt, sending up a low cloud of sand on the smaller robot's right. Then the whine from the landspeeder's engine dropped to a low idling hum as Threepio put it in parking mode. A last sigh and the craft stopped completely.

After finishing a cautious survey of the canyon, Luke led his companion out onto the gravelly surface and up to Artoo Detoo. 'Just where,' he inquired sharply, 'did you think you were going?'

A feeble whistle issued from the apologetic robot, but it was Threepio and not the recalcitrant rover who was abruptly doing most of the talking.

'Master Luke here is now your rightful owner, Artoo. How could you just amble away from him like this? Now that he's found you, let's have no more of this "Obi-Wan Kenobi" gibberish. I don't know where you picked that up – or that melodramatic hologram, either.'

Artoo started to beep in protest, but Threepio's indignation was too great to permit excuses. 'And don't talk to me about your mission. What rot! You're fortunate Master Luke doesn't blast you into a million pieces right here and now.'

'Not much chance of that,' admitted Luke, a bit overwhelmed by Threepio's casual vindictiveness. 'Come on – it's getting late.' He eyed the rapidly rising suns. 'I just hope we can get back before Uncle Owen really lets go.'

'If you don't mind my saying so,' Threepio suggested, apparently unwilling that the Artoo unit should get off so easily, 'I think you ought to deactivate the little fugitive until you've gotten him safely back in the garage.'

'No. He's not going to try anything.' Luke studied the softly beeping droid sternly. 'I hope he's learned his lesson. There's no need to—'

Without warning the Artoo unit suddenly leaped off the ground – no mean feat considering the weakness of the spring mechanisms in his three thick legs. His cylindrical body was twisting and spinning as he let out a frantic symphony of whistles, hoots, and electronic exclamations.

Luke was tired, not alarmed. 'What is it? What's wrong with him now?' He was beginning to see how Threepio's patience could be worn thin. He had had about enough of this addled instrument himself.

Undoubtedly the Artoo unit had acquired the holo of the girl by accident, then used it to entice Luke into removing his restraining module. Threepio probably had the right attitude. Still, once Luke got its circuits realigned and its logic couplings cleaned, it would make a perfectly serviceable farm unit. Only . . . if that was the case, then why was Threepio looking around so anxiously?

'Oh my, sir. Artoo claims there are several creatures of unknown type approaching from the southeast.'

That *could* be another attempt by Artoo to distract them, but Luke couldn't take the chance. Instantly he had his rifle off his shoulder and had activated the energy cell. He examined the horizon in the indicated direction and saw nothing. But then, sandpeople were experts at making themselves unseeable.

Luke suddenly realized exactly how far out they were, how much ground the landspeeder had covered that morning. 'I've never been

out in this direction this far from the farm before,' he informed
Threepio. 'There are some awfully strange things living out here.
Not all of them have been classified. It's better to treat anything as
dangerous until determined otherwise. Of course, if it's something
utterly new ...' His curiosity prodded him. In any case, this was
probably just another ruse of Artoo Detoo's. 'Let's take a look,' he
decided.

Moving cautiously forward and keeping his rifle ready, he led
Threepio toward the crest of a nearby high dune. At the same time
he took care not to let Artoo out of his sight.

Once at the top he lay flat and traded his rifle for the macrobinoculars. Below, another canyon spread out before them, rising
to a wind-weathered wall of rust and ocher. Advancing the binocs
slowly across the canyon floor, he settled unexpectedly on two
tethered shapes. Banthas – and riderless!

'Did you say something, sir?' wheezed Threepio, struggling up
behind Luke. His locomotors were not designed for such outer
climbing and scrambling.

'Banthas, all right,' Luke whispered over his shoulder, not
considering in the excitement of the moment that Threepio might
not know a Bantha from a panda.

He looked back into the eyepieces, refocusing slightly. 'Wait ...
it's sandpeople, sure. I see one of them.'

Something dark suddenly blocked his sight. For a moment he
thought that a rock might have moved in front of him. Irritably he
dropped the binoculars and reached out to move the blinding object
aside. His hand touched something like soft metal.

It was a bandaged leg about as big around as both of Luke's
together. Shocked, he looked up ... and up. The towering figure
glaring down at him was no jawa. It had seemingly erupted straight
from the sand.

Threepio took a startled step backward and found no footing. As
gyros whined in protest the tall robot tumbled backward down the
side of the dune. Frozen in place, Luke heard steadily fading bangs
and rattles as Threepio bounced down the steep slope behind him.

As the moment of confrontation passed, the Tusken let out a
terrifying grunt of fury and pleasure and brought down his heavy
gaderffii. The double-edged ax would have cleaved Luke's skull
neatly in two, except that he threw the rifle up in a gesture more

instinctive than calculated. His weapon deflected the blow, but would never do so again. Made from cannibalized freighter plating the huge ax shattered the barrel and made metallic confetti of the gun's delicate insides.

Luke scrambled backward and found himself against a steep drop. The Raider stalked him slowly, weapon held high over its rag-enclosed head. It uttered a gruesome, chuckling laugh, the sound made all the more inhuman by the distortion effect of its gridlike sandfilter.

Luke tried to view his situation objectively, as he had been instructed to do in survival school. Trouble was, his mouth was dry, his hands were shaking, and he was paralyzed with fear. With the Raider in front of him and a probably fatal drop behind, something else in his mind took over and opted for the least painful response. He fainted.

None of the Raiders noticed Artoo Detoo as the tiny robot forced himself into a small alcove in the rocks near the landspeeder. One of them was carrying the inert form of Luke. He dumped the unconscious youth in a heap next to the speeder, then joined his fellows as they began swarming over the open craft.

Supplies and spare parts were thrown in all directions. From time to time the plundering would be interrupted as several of them quibbled or fought over a particularly choice bit of booty.

Unexpectedly, distribution of the landspeeder's contents ceased, and with frightening speed the Raiders became part of the deserts-cape, looking in all directions.

A lost breeze idled absently down the canyon. Far off to the west, something howled. A rolling, booming drone ricocheted off canyon walls and crawled nervously up and down a gorgon scale.

The sandpeople remained poised a moment longer. Then they were uttering loud grunts and moans of fright as they rushed to get away from the highly visible landspeeder.

The shivering howl sounded again, nearer this time. By now the sandpeople were halfway to their waiting Banthas, that were likewise lowing tensely and tugging at their tethers.

Although the sound held no meaning for Artoo Detoo, the little droid tried to squeeze himself even deeper into the almost-cave. The booming howl came closer. Judging by the way the sandpeople had reacted, something monstrous beyond imagining had to be behind that rolling cry. Something monstrous and murder-bent which might not have the sense to distinguish between edible organics and inedible machines.

Not even the dust of their passing remained to mark where the Tusken Raiders had only minutes before been dismembering the interior of the landspeeder. Artoo Detoo shut down all but vital functions, trying to minimize noise and light as a swishing sound grew gradually audible. Moving toward the landspeeder, the creature appeared above the top of a nearby dune. . . .

IT was tall, but hardly monstrous. Artoo frowned inwardly as he checked ocular circuitry and reactivated his innards.

The monster looked very much like an old man. He was clad in a shabby cloak and loose robes hung with a few small straps, packs, and unrecognizable instruments. Artoo searched the human's wake but detected no evidence of a pursuing nightmare. Nor did the man appear threatened. Actually, Artoo thought, he looked kind of pleased.

It was impossible to tell where the odd arrival's overlapping attire ended and his skin began. That aged visage blended into the sand-stroked cloth, and his beard appeared but an extension of the loose threads covering his upper chest.

Hints of extreme climates other than desert, of ultimate cold and humidity, were etched into that seamed face. A questing beak of nose, like a high rock, protruded outward from a flashflood of wrinkles and scars. The eyes bordering it were a liquid crystal-azure. The man smiled through sand and dust and beard, squinting at the sight of the crumpled form lying quietly alongside the landspeeder.

Convinced that the sandpeople had been the victims of an auditory delusion of some kind – conveniently ignoring the fact that he had experienced it also – and likewise assured that this stranger meant Luke no harm, Artoo shifted his position slightly, trying to obtain a better view. The sound produced by a tiny pebble he dislodged was barely perceptible to his electronic sensors, but the man whirled as if shot. He stared straight at Artoo's alcove, still smiling gently.

'Hello there,' he called in a deep, surprisingly cheerful voice. 'Come here, my little friend. No need to be afraid.'

Something forthright and reassuring was in that voice. In any case, the association of an unknown human was preferable to remaining isolated in this wasteland. Waddling out into the sunlight, Artoo made his way over to where Luke lay sprawled. The robot's barrellike body inclined forward as he examined the limp form. Whistles and beeps of concern came from within.

Walking over, the old man bent beside Luke and reached out to touch his forehead, then his temple. Shortly, the unconscious youth was stirring and mumbling like a dreaming sleeper.

'Don't worry,' the human told Artoo, 'he'll be all right.'

As if to confirm this opinion, Luke blinked, stared upward uncomprehendingly, and muttered, 'What happened?'

'Rest easy, son,' the man instructed him as he sat back on his heels. 'You've had a busy day.' Again the boyish grin. 'You're mighty lucky your head's still attached to the rest of you.'

Luke looked around, his gaze coming to rest on the elderly face hovering above him. Recognition did wonders for his condition.

'Ben ... it's got to be!' A sudden remembrance made him look around fearfully. But there was no sign of sandpeople. Slowly he raised his body to a sitting position. 'Ben Kenobi ... am I glad to see you!'

Rising, the old man surveyed the canyon floor and rolling rimwall above. One foot played with the sand. 'The Jundland wastes are not to be traveled lightly. It's the misguided traveler who tempts the Tuskens' hospitality.' His gaze went back to his patient. 'Tell me, young man, what brings you out this far into nowhere?'

Luke indicated Artoo Detoo. 'This little droid. For a while I thought he'd gone crazy, claiming he was searching for a former master. Now I don't think so. I've never seen such devotion in a droid – misguided or otherwise. There seems to be no stopping him; he even resorted to tricking me.'

Luke's gaze shifted upward. 'He claims to be the property of someone called Obi-Wan Kenobi.' Luke watched closely, but the man showed no reaction. 'Is that a relative of yours? My uncle thinks he was a real person. Or is it just some unimportant bit of scrambled information that got shifted into his primary performance bank?'

An introspective frown did remarkable things to that sandblasted face. Kenobi appeared to ponder the question, scratching absently at his scruffy beard. 'Obi-Wan Kenobi!' he recited. 'Obi-Wan ... now, that's a name I haven't heard in a long time. A long time. Most curious.'

'My uncle said he was dead,' Luke supplied helpfully.

'Oh, he's not dead,' Kenobi corrected him easily. 'Not yet, not yet.'

Luke climbed excitedly to his feet, all thoughts of Tusken Raiders forgotten now. 'You know him, then?'

A smile of perverse youthfulness split that collage of wrinkled skin and beard. 'Of course I know him: he's me. Just as you probably suspected, Luke. I haven't gone by the name *Obi-Wan*, though, since before you were born.'

'Then,' Luke essayed, gesturing at Artoo Detoo, 'this droid does belong to you, as he claims.'

'Now, that's the peculiar part,' an openly puzzled Kenobi confessed, regarding the silent robot. 'I can't seem to remember owning a droid, least of all a modern Artoo unit. Most interesting, most interesting.'

Something drew the old man's gaze suddenly to the brow of nearby cliffs. 'I think it's best we make use of your landspeeder some. The sandpeople are easily startled, but they'll soon return in greater numbers. A landspeeder's not a prize readily conceded, and after all, jawas they're not.'

Placing both hands over his mouth in a peculiar fashion, Kenobi inhaled deeply and let out an unearthly howl that made Luke jump. 'That ought to keep any laggards running for a while yet,' the old man concluded with satisfaction.

'That's a krayt dragon call!' Luke gaped in astonishment. 'How did you do that?'

'I'll show you sometime, son. It's not too hard. Just takes the right attitude, a set of well-used vocal cords, and a lot of wind. Now, if you were an imperial bureaucrat, I could teach you right off, but you're not.' He scanned the cliff-spine again. 'And I don't think this is the time or place for it.'

'I won't argue that.' Luke was rubbing at the back of his head. 'Let's get started.'

That was when Artoo let out a pathetic beep and whirled. Luke couldn't interpret the electronic squeal, but he suddenly comprehended the reason behind it. 'Threepio.' Luke exclaimed, worriedly. Artoo was already moving as fast as possible away from the landspeeder. 'Come on, Ben.'

The little robot led them to the edge of a large sandpit. It stopped there, pointing downward and squeaking mournfully. Luke saw where Artoo was pointing, then started cautiously down the smooth, shifting slope while Kenobi followed effortlessly.

Threepio lay in the sand at the base of the slope down which he had rolled and tumbled. His casing was dented and badly mangled. One arm lay broken and bent a short distance away.

'*Threepio!*' Luke called. There was no response. Shaking the droid failed to activate anything. Opening a plate on the robot's back, Luke flipped a hidden switch on and off several times in succession. A low hum started, stopped, started again, and then dropped to a normal purr.

Using his remaining arm, Threepio rolled over and sat up. 'Where am I?' he murmured, as his photoreceptors continued to clear. Then he recognized Luke. 'Oh, I'm sorry, sir. I must have taken a bad step.'

'You're lucky any of your main circuits are still operational,' Luke informed him. He looked significantly toward the top of the hill. 'Can you stand? We've got to get out of here before the sandpeople return.'

Servomotors whined in protest until Threepio ceased struggling. 'I don't think I can make it. You go on, Master Luke. It doesn't make sense to risk yourself on my account. I'm finished.'

'No, you're not,' Luke shot back, unaccountably affected by this recently encountered machine. But then, Threepio was not the usual uncommunicative, agrifunctional device Luke was accustomed to dealing with. 'What kind of talk is that?'

'Logical,' Threepio informed him.

Luke shook his head angrily. 'Defeatist.'

With Luke and Ben Kenobi's aid, the battered droid somehow

managed to struggle erect. Little Artoo watched from the pit's rim.

Hesitating part way up the slope, Kenobi sniffed the air suspiciously. 'Quickly, son. They're on the move again.'

Trying to watch the surrounding rocks and his footsteps simultaneously, Luke fought to drag Threepio clear of the pit.

The decor of Ben Kenobi's well-concealed cave was Spartan without appearing uncomfortable. It would not have suited most people, reflecting as it did its owner's peculiarly eclectic tastes. The living area radiated an aura of lean comfort with more importance attached to mental comforts than those of the awkward human body.

They had succeeded in vacating the canyon before the Tusken Raiders could return in force. Under Kenobi's direction, Luke left a trail behind them so confusing that not even a hypernasal jawa could have followed it.

Luke spent several hours ignoring the temptations of Kenobi's cave. Instead he remained in the corner which was equipped as a compact yet complete repair shop, working to fix Threepio's severed arm.

Fortunately, the automatic overload disconnects had given way under the severe strain, sealing electronic nerves and ganglia without real damage. Repair was merely a matter of reattaching the limb to the shoulder, then activating the self-reseals. Had the arm been broken in mid-'bone' instead of at a joint, such repairs would have been impossible save at a factory shop.

While Luke was thus occupied, Kenobi's attention was concentrated on Artoo Detoo. The squat droid sat passively on the cool cavern floor while the old man fiddled with its metal insides. Finally the man sat back with a 'Humph!' of satisfaction and closed the open panels in the robot's rounded head. 'Now let's see if we can figure out what you are, my little friend, and where you came from.'

Luke was almost finished anyway, and Kenobi's words were sufficient to pull him away from the repair area. 'I saw part of the message,' he began, 'and I . . .'

Once more the striking portrait was being projected into empty space from the front of the little robot. Luke broke off, enraptured by its enigmatic beauty once again.

'Yes, I think that's got it,' Kenobi murmured contemplatively.

The image continued to flicker, indicating a tape hastily prepared. But it was much sharper, better defined now, Luke noted with admiration. One thing was apparent: Kenobi was skilled in subjects more specific than desert scavenging.

'General Obi-Wan Kenobi,' the mellifluous voice was saying, 'I present myself in the name of the world family of Alderaan and of the Alliance to Restore the Republic. I break your solitude at the bidding of my father, Bail Organa, Viceroy and First Chairman of the Alderaan system.'

Kenobi absorbed this extraordinary declamation while Luke's eyes bugged big enough to fall from his face.

'Years ago, General,' the voice continued, 'you served the Old Republic in the Clone Wars. Now my father begs you to aid us again in our most desperate hour. He would have you join him on Alderaan. You *must* go to him.

'I regret that I am unable to present my father's request to you in person. My mission to meet personally with you has failed. Hence I have been forced to resort to this secondary method of communication.

'Information vital to the survival of the Alliance has been secured in the mind of this Detoo droid. My father will know how to retrieve it. I plead with you to see this unit safely delivered to Alderaan.'

She paused, and when she continued, her words were hurried and less laced with formality. 'You *must* help me, Obi-Wan Kenobi. You are my last hope. I will be captured by agents of the Empire. They will learn nothing from me. Everything to be learned lies locked in the memory cells of this droid. Do not fail us, Obi-Wan Kenobi. Do not fail *me*.'

A small cloud of tridimensional static replaced the delicate portrait, then it vanished entirely. Artoo Detoo gazed up expectantly at Kenobi.

Luke's mind was as muddy as a pond laced with petroleum. Unanchored, his thoughts and eyes turned for stability to the quiet figure seated nearby.

The old man. The crazy wizard. The desert bum and all-around character whom his uncle and everyone else had known of for as long as Luke could recall.

If the breathless, anxiety-ridden message the unknown woman

had just spoken into the cool air of the cave had affected Kenobi in any way he gave no hint of it. Instead, he leaned back against the rock wall and tugged thoughtfully at his beard, puffing slowly on a water pipe of free-form tarnished chrome.

Luke visualized that simple yet lovely portrait. 'She's so – so—' His farming background didn't provide him with the requisite words. Suddenly something in the message caused him to stare disbelievingly at the oldster. 'General Kenobi, you fought in the Clone Wars? But . . . that was so long ago.'

'Um, yes,' Kenobi acknowledged, as casually as he might have discussed the recipe for shang stew. 'I guess it was a while back. I was a Jedi Knight once. Like,' he added, watching the youth appraisingly, 'your father.'

'A Jedi Knight,' Luke echoed. Then he looked confused. 'But my father didn't fight in the Clone Wars. He was no knight – just a navigator on a space freighter.'

Kenobi's smile enfolded the pipe's mouthpiece. 'Or so your uncle has told you.' His attention was suddenly focused elsewhere. 'Owen Lars didn't agree with your father's ideas, opinions, or with his philosophy of life. He believed that your father should have stayed here on Tatooine and not gotten involved in . . .' Again the seemingly indifferent shrug. 'Well, he thought he should have remained here and minded his farming.'

Luke said nothing, his body tense as the old man related bits and pieces of a personal history Luke had viewed only through his uncle's distortions.

'Owen was always afraid that your father's adventurous life might influence you, might pull you away from Anchorhead.' He shook his head slowly, regretfully at the remembrance. 'I'm afraid there wasn't much of the farmer in your father.'

Luke turned away. He returned to cleaning the last particles of sand from Threepio's healing armature. 'I wish I'd known him,' he finally whispered.

'He was the best pilot I ever knew,' Kenobi went on, 'and a smart fighter. The Force . . . the instinct was strong in him.' For a brief second Kenobi actually appeared old. 'He was also a good friend.'

Suddenly the boyish twinkle returned to those piercing eyes along with the old man's natural humor. 'I understand you're quite a pilot yourself. Piloting and navigation aren't hereditary, but a number of the things that can combine to make a good small-ship pilot are. Those you may have inherited. Still, even a duck has to be taught to swim.'

'What's a duck?' Luke asked curiously.

'Never mind. In many ways, you know, you are much like your father.' Kenobi's unabashed look of evaluation made Luke nervous. 'You've grown up quite a bit since the last time I saw you.'

Having no reply for that, Luke waited silently as Kenobi sank back into deep contemplation. After a while the old man stirred, evidently having reached an important decision.

'All this reminds me,' he declared with deceptive casualness, 'I have something here for you.' He rose and walked over to a bulky, old-fashioned chest and started rummaging through it. All sorts of intriguing items were removed and shoved around, only to be placed back in the bin. A few of them Luke recognized. As Kenobi was obviously intent on something important, he forbore inquiring about any of the other tantalizing flotsam.

'When you were old enough,' Kenobi was saying, 'your father wanted you to have this ... if I can ever find the blasted device. I tried to give it to you once before, but your uncle wouldn't allow it. He believed you might get some crazy ideas from it and end up following old Obi-Wan on some idealistic crusade.

'You see, Luke, that's where your father and your uncle Owen disagreed. Lars is not a man to let idealism interfere with business, whereas your father didn't think the question even worth discussing. His decision on such matters came like his piloting – instinctively.'

Luke nodded. He finished picking out the last of the grit and looked around for one remaining component to snap back into Threepio's open chest plate. Locating the restraining module, he opened the receiving latches in the machine and set about locking it back in place. Threepio watched the process and appeared to wince ever so perceptibly.

Luke stared into those metal and plastic photoreceptors for a long moment. Then he set the module pointedly on the workbench and closed the droid up. Threepio said nothing.

A grunt came from behind them, and Luke turned to see a pleased Kenobi walking over. He handed Luke a small, innocuous-looking device, which the youth studied with interest.

It consisted primarily of a short, thick handgrip with a couple of small switches set into the grip. Above this small post was a circular metal disk barely larger in diameter than his spread palm. A number of unfamiliar, jewellike components were built into both handle and disk, including what looked like the smallest power cell Luke had ever seen. The reverse side of the disk was polished to a mirror brightness. But it was the power cell that puzzled Luke the most. Whatever the thing was, it required a great deal of energy, according to the rating form of the cell.

Despite the claim that it had belonged to his father, the gizmo looked newly manufactured. Kenobi had obviously kept it carefully. Only a number of minute scratches on the handgrip hinted at previous usage.

'Sir?' came a familiar voice Luke hadn't heard in a while.

'What?' Luke was startled out of his examination.

'If you'll not be needing me,' Threepio declared, 'I think I'll shut down for a bit. It will help the armature nerves to knit, and I'm due for some internal self-cleansing anyhow.'

'Sure, go ahead,' Luke said absently, returning to his fascinated study of the whatever-it-was. Behind him, Threepio became silent, the glow fading temporarily from his eyes. Luke noticed that Kenobi was watching him with interest. 'What is it?' he finally asked, unable despite his best efforts to identify the device.

'Your father's lightsaber,' Kenobi told him. 'At one time they were widely used. Still are, in certain galactic quarters.'

Luke examined the controls on the handle, then tentatively touched a brightly colored button up near the mirrored pommel. Instantly the disk put forth a blue-white beam as thick around as his thumb. It was dense to the point of opacity and a little over a meter in length. It did not fade, but remained as brilliant and intense at its far end as it did next to the disk. Strangely, Luke felt no heat from it, though he was very careful not to touch it. He knew what a lightsaber could do, though he had never seen one before. It could drill a hole right through the rock wall of Kenobi's cave – or through a human being.

'This was the formal weapon of a Jedi Knight,' explained Kenobi. 'Not as clumsy or random as a blaster. More skill than simple sight was required for its use. An elegant weapon. It was a symbol as well. Anyone can use a blaster or fusioncutter – but to use a lightsaber *well* was a mark of someone a cut above the ordinary.' He was pacing the floor of the cave as he spoke.

'For over a thousand generations, Luke, the Jedi Knights were the most powerful, most respected force in the galaxy. They served as the guardians and guarantors of peace and justice in the Old Republic.'

When Luke failed to ask what had happened to them since, Kenobi looked up to see that the youth was staring vacantly into space, having absorbed little if any of the oldster's instruction. Some men would have chided Luke for not paying attention. Not Kenobi. More sensitive than most, he waited patiently until the silence weighed strong enough on Luke for him to resume speaking.

'How,' he asked slowly, 'did my father die?'

Kenobi hesitated, and Luke sensed that the old man had no wish to talk about this particular matter. Unlike Owen Lars, however, Kenobi was unable to take refuge in a comfortable lie.

'He was betrayed and murdered,' Kenobi declared solemnly, 'by a very young Jedi named Darth Vader.' He was not looking at Luke. 'A boy I was training. One of my brightest disciples . . . one of my greatest failures.'

Kenobi resumed his pacing. 'Vader used the training I gave him and the Force within him for evil, to help the later corrupt Emperors. With the Jedi knights disbanded, disorganized, or dead, there were few to oppose Vader. Today they are all but extinct.'

An indecipherable expression crossed Kenobi's face. 'In many ways they were too good, too trusting for their own health. They put too much trust in the stability of the Republic, failing to realize that while the body might be sound, the head was growing diseased and feeble, leaving it open to manipulation by such as the Emperor.

'I wish I knew what Vader was after. Sometimes I have the feeling he is marking time in preparation for some incomprehensible abomination. Such is the destiny of one who masters the force and is consumed by its dark side.'

Luke's face twisted in confusion. 'A force? That's the second time you've mentioned a "force."'

Kenobi nodded. 'I forget sometimes in whose presence I babble. Let us say simply that the force is something a Jedi must deal with. While it has never been properly explained, scientists have theorized it is an energy field generated by living things. Early man suspected its existence, yet remained in ignorance of its potential for millennia.

'Only certain individuals could recognize the force for what it was. They were mercilessly labeled: charlatans, fakers, mystics – and worse. Even fewer could make use of it. As it was usually beyond their primitive controls, it frequently was too powerful for them. They were misunderstood by their fellows – and worse.'

Kenobi made a wide, all-encompassing gesture with both arms. 'The force surrounds each and every one of us. Some men believe it directs our actions, and not the other way around. Knowledge of the force and how to manipulate it was what gave the Jedi his special power.'

The arms came down and Kenobi stared at Luke until the youth began to fidget uncomfortably. When he spoke again it was in a tone so crisp and unaged that Luke jumped in spite of himself. 'You must learn the ways of the force also, Luke – if you are to come with me to Alderaan.'

'Alderaan!' Luke hopped off the repair seat, looking dazed. 'I'm not going to Alderaan. I don't even know where Alderaan is.' Vaporators, droids, harvest – abruptly the surroundings seemed to close in on him, the formerly intriguing furnishings and alien artifacts now just a mite frightening. He looked around wildly, trying to avoid the piercing gaze of Ben Kenobi ... old Ben ... crazy Ben ... General Obi-Wan ...

'I've got to get back home,' he found himself muttering thickly. 'It's late. I'm in for it as it is.' Remembering something, he gestured toward the motionless bulk of Artoo Detoo. 'You can keep the droid. He seems to want you to. I'll think of something to tell my uncle – I hope,' he added forlornly.

'I need your help, Luke,' Kenobi explained, his manner a combination of sadness and steel. 'I'm getting too old for this kind of thing. Can't trust myself to finish it properly on my own. This mission is far too important.' He nodded toward Artoo Detoo. 'You heard and saw the message.'

'But ... I can't get involved with anything like that,' protested Luke. 'I've got work to do; we've got crops to bring in – even though Uncle Owen could always break down and hire a little extra help. I mean, one, I guess. But there's nothing I can do about it. Not now. Besides, that's all such a long way from here. The whole thing is really none of my business.'

'That sounds like your uncle talking,' Kenobi observed without rancor.

'Oh! My uncle Owen ... How am I going to explain all this to him?'

The old man suppressed a smile, aware that Luke's destiny had already been determined for him. It had been ordained five minutes before he had learned about the manner of his father's death. It had been ordered before that when he had heard the complete message. It had been fixed in the nature of things when he had first viewed the pleading portrait of the beautiful Senator Organa awkwardly projected by the little droid. Kenobi shrugged inwardly. Likely it had been finalized even before the boy was born. Not that Ben believed in predestination, but he did believe in heredity – and in the force.

'Remember, Luke, the suffering of one man is the suffering of all. Distances are irrelevant to injustice. If not stopped soon enough, evil eventually reaches out to engulf all men, whether they have opposed it or ignored it.'

'I suppose,' Luke confessed nervously, 'I *could* take you as far as Anchorhead. You can get transport from there to Mos Eisley, or wherever it is you want to go.'

'Very well,' agreed Kenobi. 'That will do for a beginning. Then you must do what you feel is *right*.'

Luke turned away, now thoroughly confused. 'Okay. Right now I don't feel too good ...'

The holding hole was deathly dim, with only the bare minimum of illumination provided. There was barely enough to see the black metal walls and the high ceiling overhead. The cell was designed to maximize a prisoner's feelings of helplessness, and this it achieved well. So much so that the single occupant started tensely as a hum came from one end of the chamber. The metal door which began moving aside was as thick as her body – as if, she mused bitterly, they were afraid she might break through anything less massive with her bare hands.

Straining to see outside, the girl saw several imperial guards assume positions just outside the doorway. Eyeing them defiantly, Leia Organa backed up against the far wall.

Her determined expression collapsed as soon as a monstrous black form entered the room, gliding smoothly as if on treads. Vader's presence crushed her spirit as thoroughly as an elephant would crush an eggshell. That villain was followed by an antiqued whip of a man who was only slightly less terrifying, despite his minuscule appearance alongside the Dark Lord.

Darth Vader made a gesture to someone outside. Something that hummed like a huge bee moved close and slipped inside the doorway. Leia choked on her own breath at the sight of the dark metal globe. It hung suspended on independent repulsors, a farrago of metal arms protruding from its sides. The arms were tipped with a multitude of delicate instruments.

Leia studied the contraption fearfully. She had heard rumors of such machines, but had never really believed that Imperial technicians would construct such a monstrosity. Incorporated into its soulless memory was every barbarity, every substantiated outrage known to mankind – and to several alien races as well.

Vader and Tarkin stood there quietly, giving her plenty of time to study the hovering nightmare. The Governor in particular did not delude himself into thinking that the mere presence of the device would shock her into giving up the information he needed. Not, he reflected, that the ensuing session would be especially unpleasant. There was always enlightenment and knowledge to be gained from such encounters, and the Senator promised to be a most interesting subject.

After a suitable interval had passed, he motioned to the machine. 'Now, Senator Organa, Princess Organa, we will discuss the location of the principal rebel base.'

The machine moved slowly toward her, traveling on a rising hum. Its indifferent spherical form blocked out Vader, the Governor, the rest of the cell . . . the light . . .

Muffled sounds penetrated the cell walls and thick door, drifting out into the hallway beyond. They barely intruded on the peace and quiet of the walkway running past the sealed chamber. Even so, the guards stationed immediately outside managed to find excuses to edge a sufficient distance away to where those oddly modulated sounds could no longer be heard at all.

VI

'LOOK over there, Luke,' Kenobi ordered, pointing to the southwest. The landspeeder continued to race over the gravelly desert floor beneath them. 'Smoke, I should think.'

Luke spared a glance at the indicated direction. 'I don't see anything, sir.'

'Let's angle over that way anyhow. Someone may be in trouble.'

Luke turned the speeder. Before long the rising wisps of smoke that Kenobi had somehow detected earlier became visible to him also.

Topping a slight rise, the speeder dropped down a gentle slope into a broad, shallow canyon that was filled with twisted, burned shapes, some of them inorganic, some not. Dead in the center of this carnage and looking like a beached metal whale lay the shattered hulk of a jawa sandcrawler.

Luke brought the speeder to a halt. Kenobi followed him onto the sand, and together they began to examine the detritus of destruction.

Several slight depressions in the sand caught Luke's attention. Walking a little faster, he came up next to them and studied them for a moment before calling back to Kenobi.

'Looks like the sandpeople did it, all right. Here's Bantha tracks...' Luke noticed a gleam of metal half buried in the sand.

'And there's a piece of one of those big double axes of theirs.' He shook his head in confusion. 'But I never heard of the Raiders hitting something this big.' He leaned back, staring up at the towering, burned-out bulk of the sandcrawler.

Kenobi had passed him. He was examining the broad, huge footprints in the sand. 'They didn't,' he declared casually, 'but they intended that we – and anyone else who might happen onto this – should think so.' Luke moved up alongside him.

'I don't understand, sir.'

'Look at these tracks carefully,' the older man directed him, pointing down at the nearest and then up at the others. 'Notice anything funny about them?' Luke shook his head. 'Whoever left here was riding Banthas side by side. Sandpeople always ride one Bantha behind another, single file, to hide their strength from any distant observers.'

Leaving Luke to gape at the parallel sets of tracks, Kenobi turned his attention to the sandcrawler. He pointed out where single weapons' bursts had blasted away portals, treads, and support beams. 'Look at the precision with which this firepower was applied. Sandpeople aren't this accurate. In fact, no one on Tatooine fires and destroys with this kind of efficiency.' Turning, he examined the horizon. One of those nearby bluffs concealed a secret – and a threat. 'Only Imperial troops would mount an attack on a sand-crawler with this kind of cold accuracy.'

Luke had walked over to one of the small, crumpled bodies and kicked it over onto its back. His face screwed up in distaste as he saw what remained of the pitiful creature.

'These are the same jawas who sold Uncle Owen and me Artoo and Threepio. I recognize this one's cloak design. Why would Imperial troops be slaughtering jawas and sandpeople? They must have killed some Raiders to get those Banthas.' His mind worked furiously, and he found himself growing unnaturally tense as he stared back at the landspeeder, past the rapidly deteriorating corpses of the jawas.

'But . . . if they tracked the droids to the jawas, then they had to learn first who they sold them to. That would lead them back to . . .' Luke was sprinting insanely for the landspeeder.

'Luke, wait . . . wait, Luke!' Kenobi called. 'It's too dangerous! You'd never . . .!'

Luke heard nothing except the roaring in his ears, felt nothing save the burning in his heart. He jumped into the speeder and was throwing the accelerator full over almost simultaneously. In an explosion of sand and gravel he left Kenobi and the two robots standing alone in the midst of smoldering bodies, framed by the still smoking wreck of the sandcrawler.

The smoke that Luke saw as he drew near the homestead was of a different consistency from that which had boiled out of the jawa machine. He barely remembered to shut down the landspeeder's engine as he popped the cockpit canopy and threw himself out. Dark smoke was drifting steadily from holes in the ground.

Those holes had been his home, the only one he had ever known. They might as well have been throats of small volcanoes now. Again and again he tried to penetrate the surface entrances to the below-ground complex. Again and again the still-intense heat drove him back, coughing and choking.

Weakly he found himself stumbling clear, his eyes watering not entirely from the smoke. Half blinded, he staggered over to the exterior entrance to the garage. It too was burning. But perhaps they managed to escape in the other landspeeder.

'Aunt Beru . . . Uncle Owen!' It was difficult to make out much of anything through the eye-stinging haze. Two smoking shapes showed down the tunnel barely visible through tears and haze. They almost looked like— He squinted harder, wiping angrily at his uncooperative eyes.

No.

Then he was spinning away, falling to his stomach and burying his face in the sand so he wouldn't have to look anymore.

The tridimensional solid screen filled one wall of the vast chamber from floor to ceiling. It showed a million star systems. A tiny portion of the galaxy, but an impressive display nonetheless when exhibited in such a fashion.

Below, far below, the huge shape of Darth Vader stood flanked on one side by Governor Tarkin and on the other by Admiral Motti and General Tagge, their private antagonisms forgotten in the awesomeness of this moment.

'The final checkout is complete,' Motti informed them. 'All

systems are operational.' He turned to the others. 'What shall be the first course we set?'

Vader appeared not to have heard as he mumbled softly, half to himself, 'She has a surprising amount of control. Her resistance to the interrogator is considerable.' He glanced down at Tarkin. 'It will be some time before we can extract any useful information from her.'

'I've always found the methods you recommend rather quaint, Vader.'

'They are efficient,' the Dark Lord argued softly. 'In the interests of accelerating the procedure, however, I am open to your suggestions.'

Tarkin looked thoughtful. 'Such stubbornness can often be detoured by applying threats to something other than the one involved.'

'What do you mean?'

'Only that I think it is time we demonstrated the full power of this station. We may do so in a fashion doubly useful.' He instructed the attentive Motti, 'Tell your programmers to set course for the Alderaan system.'

Kenobi's pride did not prevent him from wrapping an old scarf over nose and mouth to filter out a portion of the bonfire's drifting putrid odor. Though possessed of olfactory sensory apparatus, Artoo Detoo and Threepio had no need of such a screen. Even Threepio, who was equipped to discriminate among aromatic aesthetics, could be artifically selective when he so desired.

Working together, the two droids helped Kenobi throw the last of the bodies onto the blazing pyre, then stood back and watched the dead continue to burn. Not that the desert scavengers wouldn't have been equally efficient in picking the burned-out sandcrawler clean of flesh, but Kenobi retained values most modern men would have deemed archaic. He would consign no one to the bone-gnawers and gravel-maggots, not even a filthy jawa.

At a rising thrumming Kenobi turned from the residue of the noisome business to see the landspeeder approaching, now travel-ing at a sensible pace, far different from when it had left. It slowed and hovered nearby, but showed no signs of life.

Gesturing for the two robots to follow, Ben started toward the waiting craft. The canopy flipped open and up to reveal Luke sitting motionless in the pilot's seat. He didn't look up at Kenobi's inquiring glance. That in itself was enough to tell the old man what had happened.

'I share your sorrow, Luke,' he finally ventured softly. 'There was nothing you could have done. Had you been there, you'd be dead now, too, and the droid would be in the hands of the Imperials. Not even the Force—'

'Damn your Force!' Luke snarled with sudden violence. Now he turned and glared at Kenobi. There was a set to his jaw that belonged on a much older face.

'I'll take you to the spaceport at Mos Eisley, Ben. I want to go with you – to Alderaan. There's nothing left for me here now.' His eyes turned to look out across the desert, to focus on something beyond sand and rock and canyon walls. 'I want to learn to be a Jedi, like my father. I want . . .' He paused, the words backing up like a logjam in his throat.

Kenobi slid into the cockpit, put a hand gently on the youth's shoulder, then went forward to make room for the two robots. 'I'll do my best to see that you get what you want, Luke. For now, let's go to Mos Eisley.'

Luke nodded and closed the canopy. The landspeeder moved away to the southeast, leaving behind the still-smoldering sand-crawler, the jawa funeral pyre, and the only life Luke had ever known.

Leaving the speeder parked near the edge of the sandstone bluff, Luke and Ben walked over and peered down at the tiny regularized bumps erupting from the sun-baked plain below. The haphazard collage of low-grade concrete, stone, and plastoid structures spread outward from a central power-and-water-distribution plant like the spokes of a wheel.

Actually the town was considerably larger than it appeared, since a good portion of it lay underground. Looking like bomb craters from this distance, the smooth circular depressions of launch stations pockmarked the cityscape.

A brisk gale was scouring the tired ground. It whipped the sand about Luke's feet and legs as he adjusted his protective goggles.

'There it is,' Kenobi murmured, indicating the unimpressive

collection of buildings, 'Mos Eisley Spaceport – the ideal place for us to lose ourselves while we seek passage offplanet. Not a more wretched collection of villainy and disreputable types exists anywhere on Tatooine. The Empire has been alerted to us, so we must be very cautious, Luke. The population of Mos Eisley should disguise us well.'

Luke wore a determined look. 'I'm ready for anything, Obi-Wan.'

I wonder if you comprehend what that might entail, Luke, Kenobi thought. But he only nodded as he led the way back to the landspeeder.

Unlike Anchorhead, there were enough people in Mos Eisley to require movement in the heat of day. Built from the beginning with commerce in mind, even the oldest of the town's buildings had been designed to provide protection from the twin suns. They looked primitive from the outside, and many were. But oftentimes walls and arches of old stone masked durasteel double walls with circulating coolant flowing freely between.

Luke was maneuvering the landspeeder through the town's outskirts when several tall, gleaming forms appeared from nowhere and began to close a circle around him. For one panicked moment he considered gunning the engine and racing through the pedestrians and other vehicles. A startlingly firm grip on his arm both restrained and relaxed him. He glanced over to see Kenobi smiling, warning him.

So they continued at a normal town cruising speed, Luke hoping that the Imperial troops were bent on business elsewhere. No such luck. One of the troopers raised an armored hand. Luke had no choice but to respond. As he pulled the speeder over, he grew aware of the attention they were receiving from curious passersby. Worse yet, it seemed that the trooper's attention was in fact reserved not for Kenobi or himself, but for the two unmoving robots seated in the speeder behind them.

'How long have you had these droids?' the trooper who had raised his hand barked. Polite formalities were to be dispensed with, it appeared.

Looking blank for a second, Luke finally came up with 'Three or four seasons, I guess.'

'They're up for sale, if you want them – and the price is right,' Kenobi put in, giving a wonderful impression of a desert finagler out to cajole a few quick credits from ignorant Imperials.

The trooper in charge did not deign to reply. He was absorbed in a thorough examination of the landspeeder's underside.

'Did you come in from the south?' he asked.

'No ... no,' Luke answered quickly, 'we live in the west, near Bestine township.'

'Bestine?' the trooper murmured, walking around to study the speeder's front. Luke forced himself to stare straight ahead. Finally the armored figure concluded his examination. He moved to stand ominously close to Luke and snapped, 'Let me see your identification.'

Surely the man sensed his terror and nervousness by now, Luke thought wildly. His resolution of not long before to be ready to take on anything had already disintegrated under the unwinking stare of this professional soldier. He knew what would happen if they got a look at his formal ID, with the location of his homestead and the names of his nearest relatives on it. Something seemed to be buzzing inside his head; he felt faint.

Kenobi had leaned over and was talking easily to the trooper. 'You don't need to see his identification,' the old man informed the Imperial in an extremely peculiar voice.

Staring blankly back at him, the officer replied, as if it were self-evident, 'I don't need to see your identification.' His reaction was the opposite of Kenobi's: his voice was normal, but his expression peculiar.

'These aren't the droids you're looking for,' Kenobi told him pleasantly.

'These aren't the droids we're looking for.'

'He can go about his business.'

'You can go about your business,' the metal-masked officer informed Luke.

The expression of relief that spread across Luke's face ought to have been as revealing as his previous nervousness, but the Imperial ignored it.

'Move along,' Kenobi whispered.

'Move along,' the officer instructed Luke.

Unable to decide whether he should salute, nod, or give thanks to the man, Luke settled for nudging the accelerator. The landspeeder moved forward, drawing away from the circle of troops. As they prepared to round a corner, Luke risked a glance backward.

The officer who had inspected them appeared to be arguing with several comrades, though at this distance Luke couldn't be sure.

He peered up at his tall companion and started to say something. Kenobi only shook his head slowly and smiled. Swallowing his curiosity, Luke concentrated on guiding the speeder through steadily narrowing streets.

Kenobi seemed to have some idea where they were headed. Luke studied the run-down structures and equally unwholesome-looking individuals they were passing. They had entered the oldest section of Mos Eisley and consequently the one where the old vices flourished most strongly.

Kenobi pointed and Luke pulled the landspeeder up in front of what appeared to be one of the original spaceport's first block-houses. It had been converted into a cantina whose clientele was suggested by the diverse nature of transport parked outside. Some of them Luke recognized, others he had only heard rumors of. The cantina itself, he knew from the design of the building, must lie partially underground.

As the dusty but still sleek craft pulled into an open spot, a jawa materialized from nowhere and began running covetous hands over the metal sides. Luke leaned out and barked something harsh at the subhuman which caused it to scurry away.

'I can't abide those jawas,' murmured Threepio with lofty disdain. 'Disgusting creatures.'

Luke's mind was too full of their narrow escape for him to comment on Threepio's sentiments. 'I still can't understand how we got by those troops. I thought we were as good as dead.'

'The Force is in the mind, Luke, and can sometimes be used to influence others. It's a powerful ally. But as you come to know the Force, you will discover that it can also be a danger.'

Nodding without really understanding, Luke indicated the run-down though obviously popular cantina. 'Do you really think we can find a pilot here capable of taking us all the way to Alderaan?'

Kenobi was exiting from the speeder. 'Most of the good, independent freighter pilots frequent this place, though many can afford better. They can talk freely here. You should have learned by now, Luke, not to equate ability with appearance.' Luke saw the old man's shabby clothing anew and felt ashamed. 'Watch yourself, though. This place can be rough.'

Luke found himself squinting as they entered the cantina. It was darker inside than he would have liked. Perhaps the regular habitués of this place were unaccustomed to the light of day, or didn't wish to be seen clearly. It didn't occur to Luke that the dim interior in combination with the brilliantly lit entrance permitted everyone inside to see each newcomer before he could see them.

Moving inward, Luke was astonished at the variety of beings making use of the bar. There were one-eyed creatures and thousand-eyed, creatures with scales, creatures with fur, and some with skin that seemed to ripple and change consistency according to their feelings of the moment.

Hovering near the bar itself was a towering insectoid that Luke glimpsed only as a threatening shadow. It contrasted with two of the tallest women Luke had ever seen. They were among the most normal-looking of the outrageous assemblage of humans that mixed freely among alien counterparts. Tentacles, claws, and hands were wrapped around drinking utensils of various sizes and shapes. Conversation was a steady babble of human and alien tongues.

Leaning close, Kenobi gestured toward the far end of the bar. A small knot of rough-looking humans lounged there, drinking, laughing, and trading stories of dubious origin.

'Corellians – pirates, most likely.'

'I thought we were looking for an independent freighter captain with his own ship for hire,' Luke whispered back.

'So we are, young Luke, so we are,' agreed Kenobi. 'And there's bound to be one or two adequate for our needs among that group. It's just that in Corellian terminology the distinction between who owns what cargo tends to get a little muddled from time to time. Wait here.'

Luke nodded and watched as Kenobi worked his way through the crowd. The Correllians' suspicion at his approach vanished as soon as he engaged them in conversation.

Something grabbed Luke's shoulder and spun him around.

'Hey.' Looking around and struggling to regain his composure, he found himself staring up at an enormous, scruffy-looking human. Luke saw by the man's clothing that he must be the bartender, if not the owner of this cantina.

'We don't serve their kind in here,' the glaring form growled.

'What?' Luke replied dumbly. He still hadn't recovered from his sudden submergence into the cultures of several dozen races. It was rather different from the poolroom behind the Anchorhead power station. 'Your droids,' the bartender explained impatiently, gesturing with a thick thumb. Luke peered in the indicated direction, to see Artoo and Threepio standing quietly nearby. 'They'll have to wait outside. We don't serve them in here. I only carry stuff for organics, not,' he concluded with an expression of distaste, 'mechanicals.'

Luke didn't like the idea of kicking Threepio and Artoo out, but he didn't know how else to deal with the problem. The bartender didn't appear to be the sort who would readily respond to reason, and when he looked around for old Ben, Luke saw that he was locked in deep conversation with one of the Corellians.

Meanwhile, the discussion had attracted the attention of several especially gruesome-looking types who happened to be clustered within hearing range. All were regarding Luke and the two droids in a decidedly unfriendly fashion.

'Yes, of course,' Luke said, realizing this wasn't the time or place to force the issue of droid rights. 'I'm sorry.' He looked over at Threepio. 'You'd better stay outside with the speeder. We don't want any trouble in here.'

'I heartily agree with you, sir,' Threepio said, his gaze traveling past Luke and the bartender to take in the unfriendly stares at the bar. 'I don't feel the need for lubrication at the moment anyway.' With Artoo waddling in his wake, the tall robot hastily headed for the exit.

That finished things as far as the bartender was concerned, but Luke now found himself the subject of some unwanted attention. He abruptly became aware of his isolation and felt as if at one time or another every eye in the place rested a moment on him, that things human and otherwise were smirking and making comments about him behind his back.

Trying to maintain an air of quiet confidence, he returned his gaze to old Ben, and started when he saw what the oldster was talking to now. The Corellian was gone. In its place Kenobi was chatting with a towering anthropoid that showed a mouthful of teeth when it smiled.

Luke had heard about Wookiees, but he had never expected to see one, much less meet one. Despite an almost comical quasi-monkey face, the Wookiee was anything but gentle-looking. Only the large, glowing yellow eyes softened its otherwise awesome appearance. The massive torso was covered entirely with soft, thick russet fur. Less appealing cover consisted of a pair of chromed bandoliers which held lethal projectiles of a type unknown to Luke. Other than these, the Wookiees wore little.

Not, Luke knew, that anyone would laugh at the creature's mode of dress. He saw that other denizens of the bar eddied and swirled around the huge form without ever coming too close. All but old Ben – Ben who was talking to the Wookiee in its own language, quarreling and hooting softly like a native.

In the course of the conversation the old man had occasion to gesture in Luke's direction. Once the huge anthropoid stared directly at Luke and let out a horrifying howling laugh.

Disgruntled by the role he was evidently playing in the discussion, Luke turned away and pretended to ignore the whole conversation. He might be acting unfairly toward the creature, but he doubted that spine-quaking laugh was meant in gentle good-fellowship.

For the life of him he couldn't understand what Ben wanted with the monster, or why he was spending his time in guttural conversation with it instead of with the now-vanished Corellians. So he sat and sipped his drink in splendid silence, his eyes roving over the crowd in hopes of meeting a responsive gaze that held no belligerence.

Suddenly, something shoved him roughly from behind, so hard he almost fell. He turned angrily, but his fury spent itself in astonishment. He found himself confronted by a large squarish monstrosity of multiple eyes and indeterminate origin.

'*Negola dewaghi wooldugger?*' the apparition bubbled challengingly.

Luke had never seen its like before; he knew neither its species nor its language. The gabbling might have been an invitation to a fight, a request to share a drink, or a marriage proposal. Despite his ignorance, however, Luke could tell by the way the creature bobbed and wove unsteadily on its podal supports that it had imbibed too much of whatever it considered a pleasing intoxicant.

Not knowing what else to do, Luke tried turning back to his own drink while studiously ignoring the creature. As he did so, a thing

– a cross between a capybara and a small baboon – bounced over to stand (or squat) next to the quivering many-eye. A short, grubby-looking human also approached and put a companionable arm around the snuffling mass.

'He doesn't like you,' the stubby human informed Luke in a surprisingly deep voice.

'I'm sorry about that,' Luke admitted, wishing heartily he were somewhere else.

'I don't like you, either,' the smiling little man went on with brotherly negativity.

'I said I was sorry about it.'

Whether from the conversation it was having with the rodentlike creature or the overdose of booze, the apartment house for wayward eyeballs was obviously growing agitated. It leaned forward, almost toppling into Luke, and spewed a stream of unintelligible gibberish at him. Luke felt the eyes of a crowd on him as he grew increasingly more nervous.

'"Sorry,"' the human mimicked derisively, clearly deep into his own cups. 'Are you insulting us? You just better watch yourself. We're all wanted.' He indicated his drunken companions. 'I have the death sentence on me in twelve different systems.'

'I'll be careful, then,' Luke muttered.

The little man was smiling broadly. 'You'll be dead.'

At this the rodent let out a loud grunt. It was either a signal or a warning, because everything human or otherwise which had been leaning up at the bar immediately backed away, leaving a clear space around Luke and his antagonists.

Trying to salvage the situation, Luke essayed a wan smile. That faded rapidly when he saw that the three were readying hand weapons. Not only couldn't he have countered all three of them, he had no idea what a couple of the lethal-looking devices did.

'This little one isn't worth the trouble,' a calm voice said. Luke looked up, startled. He hadn't heard Kenobi come up alongside him. 'Come, let me buy you all something . . .'

By way of reply the bulky monster chittered hideously and swung out a massive limb. It caught an unprepared Luke across the temple and sent him spinning across the room, crashing through tables and shattering a large jug filled with a foul-smelling liquid.

The crowd edged back farther, a few grunts and warning snorts coming from some of them as the drunken monstrosity pulled a wicked-looking pistol from its service pouch. He started to wave it in Kenobi's direction.

That spurred the heretofore neutral bartender to life. He came charging clumsily around the end of the bar, waving his hands frantically but still taking care to stay out of range.

'No blasters, no blasters! Not in my place!'

The rodent thing chattered threateningly at him, while the weapon-wielding many-eye spared him a warning grunt.

In the split second when the gun and its owner's attention was off him, the old man's hand had moved to the disk slung at his side. The short human started to yell as a fiery blue-white light appeared in the dimness of the cantina.

He never finished the yell. It turned into a blink. When the blink was finished, the man found himself lying prone against the bar, moaning and whimpering as he stared at the stump of an arm.

In between the start of his yell and the conclusion of the blink, the rodent-thing had been cleft cleanly in half down the middle, its two halves falling in opposite directions. The giant multiocular creature still stood staring, dazed, at the old human who was poised motionless before it, the shining lightsaber held over his head in a peculiar fashion. The creature's chrome pistol fired once, blowing a hole in the door. Then the torso peeled away as neatly as had the body of the rodent, its two cauterized sections falling in opposite directions to lie motionless on the cool stone.

Only then did the suggestion of a sigh escape from Kenobi; only then did his body appear to relax. Bringing the lightsaber down, he flipped it carefully upward in a reflex saluting motion which ended with the deactivated weapon resting innocuously on his hip.

That final movement broke the total quiet which had enshrouded the room. Conversation resumed, as did the movement of bodies in chairs, the scraping of mugs and pitchers and other drinking devices on tabletops. The bartender and several assistants appeared to drag the unsightly corpses out of the room, while the mutilated human vanished wordlessly into the crowd, cradling the stump of his gun arm and counting himself fortunate.

To all appearances the cantina had returned to its former state, with one small exception. Ben Kenobi was given a respectful amount of space at the bar.

Luke barely heard the renewed conversation. He was still shaken by the speed of the fight and by the old man's unimagined abilities. As his mind cleared and he moved to rejoin Kenobi, he could overhear bits and snatches of the talk around him. Much of it centered on admiration for the cleanness and finality of the fight.

'You're hurt, Luke,' Kenobi observed solicitously.

Luke felt the bruise where the big creature had struck him. 'I . . .' he started to say, but old Ben cut him off. As if nothing had happened, he indicated the great hairy mass which was shoulder-ing its way through the crowd toward them.

'This is Chewbacca,' he explained when the anthropoid had joined them at the bar. 'He's first mate on a ship that might suit our needs. He'll take us to her captain-owner now.

'This way,' the Wookiee grunted – at least, it sounded something like that to Luke. In any case, the huge creature's follow-me gesture was unmistakable. They started to wend their way deeper into the bar, the Wookiee parting the crowd like a gravel storm cutting canyonettes.

Out in front of the cantina, Threepio paced nervously next to the landspeeder. Apparently unconcerned, Artoo Detoo was engaged in animated electronic conversation with a bright red R-2 unit belonging to another of the cantina's patrons.

'What could be taking them so long? They went to hire one ship – not a fleet.'

Abruptly Threepio paused, beckoning silently for Artoo to be quiet. Two Imperial troopers had appeared on the scene. They were met by an unkempt human who had emerged almost simultane-ously from the depths of the cantina.

'I do not like the looks of this,' the tall droid murmured.

Luke had appropriated someone else's drink from a waiter's tray as they made their way to the rear of the cantina. He gulped at it with the giddy air of one who feels himself under divine protection. That safe he was not, but in the company of Kenobi and the giant Wookiee he began to feel confident that no one in the bar would assault him with so much as a dirty look.

In a rear booth they encountered a sharp-featured young man per-haps five years older than Luke, perhaps a dozen – it was difficult to tell. He displayed the openness of the utterly confident – or the insanely reckless. At their approach the man sent the humanoid wench who had been wriggling on his lap on her way with a whispered something which left a wide, if inhuman, grin on her face.

The Wookiee Chewbacca rumbled something at the man, and he nodded in response, glancing up at the newcomers pleasantly.

'You're pretty handy with that saber, old man. Not often does one see that kind of swordplay in this part of the Empire anymore.' He downed a prodigious portion of whatever filled his mug. 'I'm Han Solo, captain of the *Millennium Falcon*.' Suddenly he became all business. 'Chewie tells me you're looking for passage to the Alderaan system?'

'That's right, son. If it's on a fast ship,' Kenobi told him. Solo didn't bridle at the 'son.'

'Fast ship? You mean you've never *heard* of the *Millennium Falcon*?'

Kenobi appeared amused. 'Should I?'

'It's the ship that made the Kessel run in less than twelve standard timeparts!' Solo told him indignantly. 'I've outrun Imperial starships and Corellian cruisers. I think she's fast enough for you, old man.' His outrage subsided rapidly. 'What's your cargo?'

'Only passengers. Myself, the boy, and two droids – no questions asked.'

'No questions.' Solo regarded his mug, finally looked up. 'Is it local trouble?'

'Let's just say we'd like to avoid any Imperial entanglements,' Kenobi replied easily.

'These days that can be a real trick. It'll cost you a little extra.' He did some mental figuring. 'All in all, about ten thousand. In advance.' He added with a smile, 'And no questions asked.'

Luke gaped at the pilot. 'Ten thousand! We could almost buy our own ship for that.'

Solo shrugged. 'Maybe you could and maybe you couldn't. In any case, could you fly it?'

'You bet I could,' Luke shot back, rising. 'I'm not such a bad pilot myself. I don't—'

Again the firm hand on his arm. 'We haven't that much with us,' Kenobi explained. 'But we could pay you two thousand now, plus another fifteen when we reach Alderaan.'

Solo leaned forward uncertainly. 'Fifteen ... You can really get your hands on that kind of money?'

'I promise it – from the government on Alderaan itself. At the worst, you'll have earned an honest fee: two thousand.'

But Solo seemed not to hear the last. 'Seventeen thousand ... All right, I'll chance it. You've got yourselves a ship. As for avoiding Imperial entanglements, you'd better twist out of here or even the *Millennium Falcon* won't be any help to you.' He nodded toward the cantina entrance, and added quickly, 'Docking bay ninety-four, first thing in the morning.'

Four Imperial troopers, their eyes darting rapidly from table to booth to bar, had entered the cantina. There was muttering from among the crowd, but whenever the eyes of one of the heavily armed troopers went hunting for the mutterers, the words died with sullen speed.

Moving to the bar, the officer in charge asked the bartender a couple of brief questions. The big man hesitated a moment, then pointed toward a place near the back of the room. As he did so, his eyes widened slightly. Those of the officer were unreadable.

The booth he was pointing to was empty.

VII

LUKE and Ben were securing Artoo Detoo in the back of the speeder while Threepio kept a lookout for any additional troops.

'If Solo's ship is as fast as his boasting, we should be all right,' the old man observed with satisfaction.

'But two thousand – and fifteen more when we reach Alderaan!'

'It's not the fifteen that worries me; it's the first two,' Kenobi explained. 'I'm afraid you'll have to sell your speeder.'

Luke let his gaze rove over the landspeeder, but the thrill it had once given him was gone – gone along with other things best not dwelt on.

'It's all right,' he assured Kenobi listlessly. 'I don't think I'll need it again.'

From their vantage point in another booth, Solo and Chewbacca watched as the Imperials strode through the bar. Two of them gave the Corellian a lingering glance. Chewbacca growled once and the two soldiers hurried their pace somewhat.

Solo grinned sardonically, turning to his partner. 'Chewie, this charter could save our necks. Seventeen thousand!' He shook his head in amazement. 'Those two must really be desperate. I wonder what they're wanted for. But I agreed, no questions. They're paying enough for it. Let's get going – the *Falcon* won't check itself out.'

'Going somewhere, Solo?'

The Corellian couldn't identify the voice, coming as it did through an electronic translator. But there was no problem recognizing the speaker or the gun it held stuck in Solo's side.

The creature was roughly man-sized and bipedal, but its head was something out of delirium by way of an upset stomach. It had huge, dull-faceted eyes, bulbous on a pea-green face. A ridge of short spines crested the high skull, while nostrils and mouth were contained in a tapirlike snout.

'As a matter of fact,' Solo replied slowly, 'I was just on my way to see your boss. You can tell Jabba I've got the money I owe him.'

'That's what you said yesterday – and last week – and the week prior to that. It's too late, Solo. I'm not going back to Jabba with another one of your stories.'

'But I've really got the money this time!' Solo protested.

'Fine. I'll take it now, please.'

Solo sat down slowly. Jabba's minions were apt to be cursed with nervous trigger fingers. The alien took the seat across from him, the muzzle of the ugly little pistol never straying from Solo's chest.

'I haven't got it here with me. Tell Jabba—'

'It's too late, I think. Jabba would rather have your ship.'

'Over my dead body,' Solo said unamiably.

The alien was not impressed. 'If you insist. Will you come outside with me, or must I finish it here?'

'I don't think they'd like another killing in here,' Solo pointed out.

Something which might have been a laugh came from the creature's translator. 'They'd hardly notice. Get up, Solo. I've been looking forward to this for a long time. You've embarrassed me in front of Jabba with your pious excuses for the last time.'

'I think you're right.'

Light and noise filled the little corner of the cantina, and when it had faded, all that remained of the unctuous alien was a smoking, slimy spot on the stone floor.

Solo brought his hand and the smoking weapon it held out from beneath the table, drawing bemused stares from several of the cantina's patrons and clucking sounds from its more knowledgeable ones. They had known the creature had committed its fatal mistake in allowing Solo the chance to get his hands under cover.

'It'll take a lot more than the likes of you to finish me off. Jabba the Hutt always did skimp when it came to hiring his hands.'

Leaving the booth, Solo flipped the bartender a handful of coins as he and Chewbacca moved off. 'Sorry for the mess. I always was a rotten host.'

Heavily armed troopers hurried down the narrow alleyway, glowering from time to time at the darkly clad beings who hawked exotic goods from dingy little stalls. Here in Mos Eisley's inner regions the walls were high and narrow, turning the passageway into a tunnel.

No one stared angrily back at them; no one shouted imprecations or mouthed obscenities. These armored figures moved with the authority of the Empire, their sidearms boldly displayed and activated. All around, men, not-men, and mechanicals were crouched in waste-littered doorways. Among accumulations of garbage and filth they exchanged information and concluded transactions of dubious legality.

A hot wind moaned down the alleyway and the troopers closed their formation. Their precision and order masked a fear of such claustrophobic quarters.

One paused to check a door, only to discover it tightly locked and bolted. A sand-encrusted human shambling nearby visited a half-mad harangue on the trooper. Shrugging inwardly, the soldier gave the crazy human a sour eye before moving on down the alley to join up again with his fellows.

As soon as they were well past, the door slid open a crack and a metallic face peered out. Below Threepio's leg, a squat barrel shape struggled for a view.

'I would rather have gone with Master Luke than stay here with you. Still, orders are orders. I don't quite know what all the trouble is about, but I'm sure it must be your fault.'

Artoo responded with a near impossibility: a sniggering beep.

'You watch your language,' the taller machine warned.

The number of old landspeeders and other powered transports in the dusty lot which were still capable of motion could be counted on the fingers of one hand. But that was not the concern of Luke and Ben as they stood bargaining with the tall, slightly insectoid owner. They were here not to buy, but to sell.

None of the passersby favored the hagglers with so much as a curious glance. Similar transactions which were the business of no one but the transactors took place half a thousand times daily in Mos Eisley.

Eventually there were no more pleas or threats to be exchanged. As though doling out vials of his own blood, the owner finalized the sale by passing a number of small metal shapes to Luke. Luke and the insectoid traded formal good-byes and then they parted, each convinced he had gotten the better of the deal.

'He says it's the best he can do. Since the XP-38 came out, they just aren't in demand anymore,' Luke sighed.

'Don't look so discouraged,' Kenobi chided him. 'What you've obtained will be sufficient. I've enough to cover the rest.'

Leaving the main street, they turned down an alleyway and walked past a small robot herding along a clutch of creatures resembling attenuated anteaters. As they rounded the corner Luke strained for a forlorn glimpse of the old landspeeder – his last link with his former life. Then there was no more time for looking back.

Something short and dark that might have been human underneath all its wrappings stepped out of the shadows as they moved away from the corner. It continued staring after them as they disappeared down a bend in the walkway.

The docking-bay entrance to the small saucer-shaped spacecraft was completely ringed by half a dozen men and aliens, of which the former were by half the most grotesque. A great mobile tub of muscle and suet topped by a shaggy scarred skull surveyed the semicircle of armed assassins with satisfaction. Moving forward from the center of the crescent, he shouted toward the ship.

'Come on out, Solo! We've got you surrounded.'

'If so, you're facing the wrong way,' came a calm voice.

Jabba the Hutt jumped – in itself a remarkable sight. His lackeys likewise whirled – to see Han Solo and Chewbacca standing behind them.

'You see, I've been waiting for you, Jabba.'

'I expected you would be,' the Hutt admitted, at once pleased and alarmed by the fact that neither Solo nor the big Wookiee appeared to be armed.

'I'm not the type to run,' Solo said.

'Run? Run from what!' Jabba countered. The absence of visible weapons bothered Jabba more than he cared to admit to himself. There was something peculiar here, and it would be better to make no hasty moves until he discovered what was amiss.

'Han, my boy, there are times when you disappoint me. I merely wish to know why you haven't paid me . . . as you should have long ago. And why did you have to fry poor Greedo like that? After all you and I have been through together.'

Solo grinned tightly. 'Shove it, Jabba. There isn't enough sentiment in your body to warm an orphaned bacterium. As for Greedo, you sent him to kill me.'

'Why, Han,' Jabba protested in surprise. 'Why would I do that? You're the best smuggler in the business. You're too valuable to fry. Greedo was only relaying my natural concern at your delays. He wasn't going to kill you.'

'I think he thought he was. Next time don't send one of those hired twerps. If you've got something to say, come see me yourself.'

Jabba shook his head and his jowls shook – lazy, fleshy echoes of his mock sorrow. 'Han, Han – if only you hadn't had to dump that shipment of spice! You understand . . . I just can't make an exception. Where would I be if every pilot who smuggled for me dumped his shipment at the first sign of an Imperial warship? And then simply showed empty pockets when I demanded recompense? It's not good business. I can be generous and forgiving – but not to the point of bankruptcy.'

'You know, even I get boarded sometimes, Jabba. Did you think I dumped that spice because I got tired of its smell? I wanted to deliver it as much as you wanted to receive it. I had no choice.' Again the sardonic smile. 'As you say, I'm too valuable to fry. But I've got a charter now and I can pay you back, plus a little extra. I just need some more time. I can give you a thousand on account, the rest in three weeks.'

The gross form seemed to consider, then directed his next words not to Solo but to his hirelings. 'Put your blasters away.' His gaze and a predatory smile turned to the wary Corellian.

'Han, my boy, I'm only doing this because you're the best and I'll need you again sometime. So, out of the greatness of my soul and a forgiving heart – and for an extra, say, twenty percent – I'll give you a little more time.' The voice nearly cracked with restraint. 'But this is the last time. If you disappoint me again, if you trample my

generosity in your mocking laughter, I'll put a price on your head
so large you won't be able to go near a civilized system for the rest
of your life, because on every one your name and face will be known
to men who'll gladly cut your guts out for one-tenth of what I'll
promise them.'

'I'm glad we both have my best interests at heart,' replied Solo
pleasantly as he and Chewbacca started past the staring eyes of the
Hutt's hired guns. 'Don't worry, Jabba, I'll pay you. But not because
you threaten me. I'll pay you because . . . it's my pleasure.'

'They're starting to search the spaceport central,' the Commander
declared, having to alternately run a couple of steps and then walk
to keep pace with the long strides of Darth Vader. The Dark Lord
was deep in thought as he strode down one of the battle station's
main corridors, trailed by several aides.

'The reports are just starting to come in,' the Commander went
on. 'It's only a matter of time before we have those droids.'

'Send in more men if you have to. Never mind the protests of the
planetary Governor – I must have those droids. It's her hope of that
data being used against us that is the pillar of her resistance to the
mind probes.'

'I understand, Lord Vader. Until then we must waste our time
with Governor Tarkin's foolish plan to break her.'

'There's docking bay ninety-four,' Luke told Kenobi and the robots
who had rejoined them, 'and there's Chewbacca. He seems excited
about something.'

Indeed, the big Wookiee was waving over the heads of the crowd
and jabbering loudly in their direction. Speeding their pace, none of
the foursome noticed the small, dark-clad thing that had followed
them from the transporter lot.

The creature moved into the doorway and pulled a tiny transmitter from a pouch concealed by its multifold robes. The transmitter looked far too new and modern to be in the grasp of so
decrepit a specimen, yet its manipulator was speaking into it with
steady assurance.

Docking bay ninety-four, Luke noted, was no different in appearance from a host of other grandiosely named docking bays scattered
throughout Mos Eisley. It consisted mostly of an entrance rampway

and an enormous pit gouged from the rocky soil. This served as clearance radii for the effects of the simple antigrav drive which boosted all spacecraft clear of the gravitational field of the planet.

The mathematics of spacedrive were simple enough even to Luke. Antigrav could operate only when there was a sufficient gravity well to push against – like that of a planet – whereas supralight travel could only take place when a ship was clear of that same gravity. Hence the necessity for the dual-drive system on any extrasystem craft.

The pit which formed docking bay ninety-four was as shabbily cut and run-down as the majority of Mos Eisley. Its sloping sides were crumbling in places instead of being smoothly fashioned as they were on more populous worlds. Luke felt it formed the perfect setting for the spacecraft Chewbacca was leading them toward.

That battered ellipsoid which could only loosely be labeled a ship appeared to have been pieced together out of old hull fragments and components discarded as unusable by other craft. The wonder of it, Luke mused, was that the thing actually held its shape. Trying to picture this vehicle as spaceworthy would have caused him to collapse in hysteria – were the situation not so serious. But to think of traveling to Alderaan in this pathetic . . .

'What a piece of junk,' he finally murmured, unable to hide his feelings any longer. They were walking up the rampway toward the open port. 'This thing couldn't possibly make it into hyperspace.'

Kenobi didn't comment, but merely gestured toward the port, where a figure was coming to meet them.

Either Solo had supernaturally acute hearing, or else he was used to the reaction the sight of the *Millennium Falcon* produced in prospective passengers. 'She may not look like much,' he confessed as he approached them, 'but she's all go. I've added a few unique modifications to her myself. In addition to piloting, I like to tinker. She'll make point five factors beyond lightspeed.'

Luke scratched his head as he tried to reassess the craft in view of its owner's claims. Either the Corellian was the biggest liar this side of the galactic center, or there was more to this vessel than met the eye. Luke thought back once more to old Ben's admonition never to trust surface impressions, and decided to reserve judgment on the ship and its pilot until after he had watched them in operation.

Chewbacca had lingered behind at the docking-bay entrance. Now he rushed up the ramp, a hairy whirlwind, and blabbered excitedly at Solo. The pilot regarded him coolly, nodding from time to time, then barked a brief reply. The Wookiee charged into the ship, pausing only to urge everyone to follow.

'We seem to be a bit rushed,' Solo explained cryptically, 'so if you'll hurry aboard, we'll be off.'

Luke was about to venture some questions, but Kenobi was already prodding him up the ramp. The droids followed.

Inside, Luke was slightly startled to see the bulky Chewbacca squirm and fight his way into a pilot's chair which, despite modifications, was still overwhelmed by his massive form. The Wookiee flipped several tiny switches with digits seemingly too big for the task. Those great paws drifted with surprising grace over the controls.

A deep throbbing started somewhere within the ship as the engines were activated. Luke and Ben began strapping themselves into the vacant seats in the main passageway.

Outside the docking-bay entrance a long, leathery snout protruded from dark folds of cloth, and somewhere in the depths to either side of that imposing proboscis, eyes stared intently. They turned, along with the rest of the head, as a squad of eight Imperial troops rushed up. Perhaps not surprisingly, they headed straight for the enigmatic figure who whispered something to the lead trooper and gestured to the docking bay.

The information must have been provocative. Activating their weapons and raising them to firing position, the troops charged en masse down the docking-bay entrance.

A glint of light on moving metal caught Solo's eyes as the unwelcome outlines of the first troops showed themselves. Solo thought it unlikely they would pause to engage in casual conversation. His suspicion was confirmed before he could open his mouth to protest their intrusion, as several dropped to their knees and opened fire on him. Solo ducked back inside, turning to yell forward.

'Chewie – deflector shields, quick! Get us out of here!'

A throaty roar of acknowledgment came back to him.

Drawing his own pistol, Solo managed to snap off a couple of bursts from the comparative safety of the hatchway. Seeing that their quarry was neither helpless nor comatose, the exposed troops dove for cover.

The low throbbing rose to a whine, then to a deafening howl as Solo's hand came down on the quick-release button. Immediately the overhead hatchcover slammed shut.

As the retreating troops raced out of the docking-bay entrance, the ground was trembling steadily. They ran smack into a second squad, which had just arrived in response to the rapidly spreading emergency call. One of the soldiers, gesticulating wildly, tried to explain to the newly arrived ranking officer what had happened back in the bay.

As soon as the panting trooper had finished, the officer whipped out a compact communicator and shouted into it, 'Flight deck ... they're trying to escape! Send everything you've got after this ship.'

All across Mos Eisley, alarms began to sound, spreading out from docking bay ninety-four in concentric circles of concern.

Several soldiers scouring one alleyway reacted to the citywide alarm at the same time as they saw the small freighter lift gracefully into the clear blue sky above Mos Eisley. It shrank to a pinpoint before any of them thought to bring a weapon to bear.

Luke and Ben were already undoing their acceleration straps as Solo walked past them, moving toward the cockpit with the easy, loose-limbed stride of the experienced spacer. Once forward, he fell rather than sat in the pilot's seat and immediately began checking readouts and gauges. In the seat next to him Chewbacca was growling and grunting like a poorly tuned speeder engine. He turned from studying his own instruments long enough to jab a massive finger at the tracking screen.

Solo gave it a quick glance, then turned irritably to his own panel. 'I know, I know ... looks like two, maybe three destroyers. Somebody certainly dislikes our passengers. Sure picked ourselves a hot one this time. Try to hold them off somehow until I can finish the programming for the supralight jump. Angle the deflectors for maximum shielding.'

With those instructions he ceased conversing with the huge Wookie as his hands flew over the computer input terminals. Solo did not even turn around when a small cylindrical shape appeared in the doorway behind him. Artoo Detoo beeped a few remarks, then scurried away.

Rear scanners showed the baleful lemon eye of Tatooine shrinking rapidly behind them. It wasn't rapid enough to eliminate the three points of light that indicated the presence of the pursuing Imperial warships.

Although Solo had ignored Artoo, he turned to acknowledge the entrance of his human passengers. 'We've got two more coming in from different angles,' he told them, scrutinizing the remorseless instrumentation. 'They're going to try to box up before we can jump. Five ships ... What did you two do to attract that kind of company?'

'Can't you outrun them?' Luke asked sarcastically, ignoring the pilot's question. 'I thought you said this thing was fast.'

'Watch your mouth, kid, or you'll find yourself floating home. There's too many of 'em, for one thing. But, we'll be safe enough once we've made the jump into hyperspace.' He grinned knowingly. 'Can't nobody track another ship accurately at supralight speeds. Plus, I know a few tricks that ought to lose any persistent stick-tights. I wish I'd known you boys were so popular.'

'Why?' Luke said challengingly. 'Would you have refused to take us?'

'Not necessarily,' the Corellian replied, refusing to be baited. 'But I sure's hell would've boosted your fare.'

Luke had a retort poised on his lips. It was wiped out as he threw up his arms to ward off a brilliant red flash which gave black space outside the viewport the temporary aspect of the surface of a sun. Kenobi, Solo, and even Chewbacca did likewise, since the proximity of the explosion nearly overrode the phototropic shielding.

'Here's where the situation gets interesting,' Solo muttered.

'How long before you can make the jump?' Kenobi inquired easily, apparently unconcerned that at any second they all might cease to exist.

'We're still within the gravitational influence of Tatooine,' came the cool response. 'It will be a few minutes yet before the navigation computer can compensate and effect an accurate jump. I could override its decision, but the hyperdrive would likely shred itself. That would give me a nice hold full of scrap metal in addition to you four.'

'A few minutes,' Luke blurted, staring at the screens. 'At the rate they're gaining . . .'

'Traveling through hyperspace isn't like dusting crops, boy. Ever tried calculating a hyperspace jump?' Luke had to shake his head. 'It's no mean trick. Be nice if we rushed it and passed right through a star or some other friendly spatial phenom like a black hole. That would end our trip real quick.'

Fresh explosions continued to flare close by despite Chewbacca's best efforts at evasion. On Solo's console a red warning light began to flash for attention.

'What's that?' Luke wondered nervously.

'We're losing a deflector shield,' Solo informed him with the air of a man about to have a tooth pulled. 'Better strap yourselves back in. We're almost ready to make the jump. It could get bad if we take a near-burst at the wrong moment.'

Back in the main hold area Threepio was already locked tightly into his seat by metal arms stronger then any acceleration straps. Artoo swayed back and forth under the concussion produced by increasingly powerful energy bursts against the ships deflectors.

'Was this trip really necessary?' the tall robot muttered in desperation. 'I'd forgotten how much I hate space travel.' He broke off as Luke and Ben appeared and began strapping themselves back into their chairs.

Oddly, Luke was thinking of a dog he had once owned when an immensely powerful something wrenched at the ship's hull with the strength of a fallen angel.

Admiral Motti entered the quiet conference room, his face streaked by the linear lights lining the walls. His gaze went to the spot where Governor Tarkin stood before the curved viewscreen, and he bowed slightly. Despite the evidence of the small green gem of a world entered in the screen, he formally announced, 'We have entered the Alderaan system. We await your order.'

The door signaled and Tarkin made a falsely gentle gesture to the admiral. 'Wait a moment yet, Motti.'

The door slid aside and Leia Organa entered, flanked by two armed guards, followed by Darth Vader.

'I am—' Tarkin began.

'I know who you are,' she spat, 'Governor Tarkin. I should have

expected to find you holding Vader's leash. I thought I recognized
your unique stench when I was first brought on board.'

'Charming to the last,' Tarkin declared in a fashion which
suggested he was anything but charmed. 'You don't know how
hard I found it to sign the order for your termination.' His
expression changed to one of mock sorrow. 'Of course, had you
cooperated in our investigation, things might be otherwise. Lord
Vader has informed me that your resistance to our traditional
methods of inquiry—'

'Torture, you mean,' she countered a trifle shakily.

'Let us not bandy semantics,' Tarkin smiled.

'I'm surprised you had the courage to take the responsibility for
issuing the order on yourself.'

Tarkin sighed reluctantly. 'I am a dedicated man, and the
pleasures I reserve for myself are few. One of them is that before
your execution I should like you to be my guest at a small
ceremony. It will certify this battle station's operational status while
at the same time ushering in a new era of Imperial technical
supremacy. This station is the final link in the new-forged Imperial
chain which will bind the million systems of the galactic Empire
together once and for all. Your petty Alliance will no longer be of
any concern to us. After today's demonstration no one will dare to
oppose Imperial decree, not even the Senate.'

Organa looked at him with contempt. 'Force will not keep the
Empire together. Force has never kept anything together for very
long. The more you tighten your grip, the more systems will slip
through your fingers. You're a foolish man, Governor. Foolish men
often choke to death on their own delusions.'

Tarkin smiled a death's-head smile, his face a parchment skull's.
'It will be interesting to see what manner of passing Lord Vader has
in mind for you. I am certain it will be worthy of you – and of him.

'But before you leave us, we must demonstrate the power of this
station once and for all, in a conclusive fashion. In a way, you have
determined the choice of subject for this demonstration. Since you
have proven reluctant to supply us with the location of the rebel
stronghold, I have deemed it appropriate to select as an alternate
subject your home planet of Alderaan.'

'No! You can't! Alderaan is a peaceful world, with no standing
armies. You can't . . .'

Tarkin's eyes gleamed. 'You would prefer another target? A military target, perhaps? We're agreeable ... name the system.' He shrugged elaborately. 'I grow tired of such games. For the last time, where is the main rebel base?'

A voice announced over a hidden speaker that they had approached within antigrav range of Alderaan – approximately six planetary diameters. That was enough to accomplish what all of Vader's infernal devices had failed to.

'Dantooine,' she whispered, staring at the deck, all pretense at defiance gone now. 'They're on Dantooine.'

Tarkin let out a slow sigh of satisfaction, then turned to the black figure nearby. 'There, you see, Lord Vader? She can be reasonable. One needs only frame the question properly to elicit the desired response.' He directed his attention to the other officers. 'After concluding our little test here we shall make haste to move on to Dantooine. You may proceed with the operation, gentlemen.'

It took several seconds for Tarkin's words, so casually uttered, to penetrate. '*What!*' Organa finally gasped.

'Dantooine,' Tarkin explained, examining his fingers, 'is too far from the centers of Imperial population to serve as the subject of an effective demonstration. You will understand that for reports of our power to spread rapidly through the Empire we require an obstreperous world more centrally located. Have no fear, though. We will deal with your rebel friends on Dantooine as soon as possible.'

'But you said ...' Organa started to protest.

'The only words which have meaning are the last ones spoken,' Tarkin declared cuttingly. 'We will proceed with the destruction of Alderaan as planned. Then you will enjoy watching with us as we obliterate the Dantooine center of this stupid and futile rebellion.'

He gestured to the two soldiers flanking her. 'Escort her to the principal observation level and,' he smiled, 'make certain she is provided with an unobstructed view.'

VIII

SOLO was busily checking readouts from gauges and dials in the hold area. Occasionally he would pass a small box across various sensors, study the result, and cluck with pleasure.

'You can stop worrying about your Imperial friends,' he told Luke and Ben. 'They'll never be able to track us now. Told you I'd lose them.'

Kenobi might have nodded briefly in response, but he was engaged in explaining something to Luke.

'Don't everybody thank me at once,' Solo grunted, slightly miffed. 'Anyway, navigation computer calculates our arrival in Alderaan orbit at oh-two-hundred. I'm afraid after this little adventure I'll have to forge a new registration.'

He returned to his checking, passing in front of a small circular table. The top was covered with small squares lit from beneath, while computer monitors were set into each side. Tiny three-dimensional figures were projected above the tabletop from various squares.

Chewbacca sat hunched over one side of the table, his chin resting in massive hands. His great eyes glowing and facial whiskers wrinkled upward, he gave every sign of being well pleased with himself.

At least, he did until Artoo Detoo reached up with a stubby clawed limb across from him and tapped his own computer monitor. One of the figures walked abruptly across the board to a new square and stopped there.

An expression of puzzlement, then anger crossed the Wookiee's face as he studied the new configuration. Glaring up and over the table, he vented a stream of abusive gibberish on the inoffensive machine. Artoo could only beep in reply, but Threepio soon interceded on behalf of his less eloquent companion and began arguing with the hulking anthropoid.

'He executed a fair move. Screaming about it won't help you.'

Attracted by the commotion, Solo looked back over his shoulder, frowning slightly. 'Let him have it. Your friend's way ahead anyhow. It's not wise to upset a Wookiee.'

'I can sympathize with that opinion, sir,' Threepio countered, 'but there is principle at stake here. There are certain standards any sentient creature must hold to. If one compromises them for any reason, including intimidation, then one is abrogating his right to be called intelligent.'

'I hope you'll both remember that,' Solo advised him, 'when Chewbacca is pulling the arms off you and your little friend.'

'Besides that, however,' Threepio continued without missing a beat, 'being greedy or taking advantage of someone in a weakened position is a clear sign of poor sportsmanship.'

That elicited a beep of outrage from Artoo, and the two robots were soon engaged in violent electronic argument while Chewbacca continued jabbering at each in turn, occasionally waving at them though the translucent pieces waiting patiently on the board.

Oblivious to the altercation, Luke stood frozen in the middle of the hold. He held an activated lightsaber in position over his head. A low hum came from the ancient instrument while Luke lunged and parried under Ben Kenobi's instructive gaze. As Solo glanced from time to time at Luke's awkward movements, his lean features were sprinkled with smugness.

'No, Luke, your cuts should flow, not be so choppy,' Kenobi instructed gently. 'Remember, the force is omnipresent. It envelops you as it radiates from you. A Jedi warrior can actually feel the force as a physical thing.'

'It is an energy field, then?' Luke inquired.

'It is an energy field and something more,' Kenobi went on, almost mystically. 'An aura that at once controls and obeys. It is a nothingness that can accomplish miracles.' He looked thoughtful for a moment.

'No one, not even the Jedi scientists, were able to truly define the Force. Possibly no one ever will. Sometimes there is as much magic as science in the explanations of the force. Yet what is a magician but a practicing theorist? Now, let's try again.'

The old man was hefting a silvery globe about the size of a man's fist. It was covered with fine antennae, some as delicate as those of a moth. He flipped it toward Luke and watched as it halted a couple of meters away from the boy's face.

Luke readied himself as the ball circled him slowly, turning to face it as it assumed a new position. Abruptly it executed a lightning-swift lunge, only to freeze about a meter away. Luke failed to succumb to the feint, and the ball soon backed off.

Moving slowly to one side in an effort to get around the ball's fore sensors, Luke drew the saber back preparatory to striking. As he did so the ball darted in behind *him*. A thin pencil of red light jumped from one of the antennae to the back of Luke's thigh, knocking him to the deck even as he was bringing his saber around – too late.

Rubbing at his tingling, sleeping leg, Luke tried to ignore the burst of accusing laughter from Solo. 'Hocus-pocus religions and archaic weapons are no substitute for a good blaster at your side,' the pilot sneered.

'You don't believe in the Force?' asked Luke, struggling back to his feet. The numbing effect of the beam wore off quickly.

'I've been from one end of this galaxy to the other,' the pilot boasted, 'and I've seen a lot of strange things. Too many to believe there couldn't be something like this "Force." Too many to think that there could be some such controlling one's actions. *I* determine my destiny – not some half-mystical energy field.' He gestured toward Kenobi. 'I wouldn't follow him so blindly, if I were you. He's a clever old man full of simple tricks and mischief. He might be using you for his own ends.'

Kenobi only smiled gently, then turned back to face Luke. 'I suggest you try it again, Luke,' he said soothingly. 'You must try to divorce your actions from conscious control. Try not to focus on anything concrete, visually or mentally. You must let your mind drift, drift; only then can you use the Force. You have to enter a state in which you act on what you sense, not on what you think beforehand. You must cease cogitation, relax, stop thinking ... let yourself drift ... free ... free ...'

The old man's voice had dropped to a mesmerizing buzz. As he finished, the chrome bulb darted at Luke. Dazed by Kenobi's hypnotic tone, Luke didn't see it charge. It's doubtful he saw much of anything with clarity. But as the ball neared, he whirled with amazing speed, the saber arcing up and out in a peculiar fashion. The red beam that the globe emitted was neatly deflected to one side. Its humming stopped and the ball bounced to the deck, all animation gone.

Blinking as if coming awake from a short nap, Luke stared in absolute astonishment at the inert remote.

'You see, you can do it,' Kenobi told him. 'One can teach only so much. Now you must learn to admit the Force when you want it, so that you can learn to control it consciously.'

Moving to one side, Kenobi took a large helmet from behind a locker and walked over to Luke. Placing the helmet over his head effectively eliminated the boy's vision.

'I can't see,' Luke muttered, turning around and forcing Kenobi to step back out of range of the dangerously wavering saber. 'How can I fight?'

'With the Force,' old Ben explained. 'You didn't really "see" the seeker when it went for your legs the last time, and yet you parried its beam. Try to let that sensation flow within you again.'

'I *can't* do it,' Luke moaned. 'I'll get hit again.'

'Not if you let yourself trust *you*,' Kenobi insisted, none too convincingly for Luke. 'This is the only way to be certain you're relying wholly on the Force.'

Noticing that the skeptical Corellian had turned to watch, Kenobi hesitated momentarily. It did Luke no good to have the self-assured pilot laugh every time a mistake was made. But coddling the boy would do him no good either, and there was no time for it anyway. Throw him in and hope he floats, Ben instructed himself firmly.

Bending over the chrome globe, he touched a control at its side. Then he tossed it straight up. It arched toward Luke. Braking in midfall, the ball plummeted stonelike toward the deck. Luke swung the saber at it. While it was a commendable try, it wasn't nearly fast enough. Once again the little antenna glowed. This time the crimson needle hit Luke square on the seat of his pants. Though it wasn't an incapacitating blow, it felt like one; and Luke let out a yelp of pain as he spun, trying to strike his invisible tormentor.

'Relax!' old Ben urged him. 'Be free. You're trying to use your eyes and ears. Stop predicting and use the rest of your mind.'

Suddenly the youth stopped, wavering slightly. The seeker was still behind him. Changing direction again, it made another dive and fired.

Simultaneously the lightsaber jerked around, as accurate as it was awkward in its motion, to deflect the bolt. This time the ball didn't fall motionless to the deck. Instead it backed up three meters and remained there, hovering.

Aware that the drone of the seeker remote no longer assaulted his ears, a cautious Luke peeked out from under the helmet. Sweat and exhaustion competed for space on his face.

'Did I—?'

'I told you you could,' Kenobi informed him with pleasure. 'Once you start to trust your inner self there'll be no stopping you. I told you there was much of your father in you.'

'I'd call it luck,' snorted Solo as he concluded his examination of the readouts.

'In my experience there is no such thing as luck, my young friend – only highly favorable adjustments of multiple factors to incline events in one's favor.'

'Call it what you like,' the Corellian sniffed indifferently, 'but good against a mechanical remote is one thing. Good against a living menace is another.'

As he was speaking a small telltale light on the far side of the hold had begun flashing. Chewbacca noticed it and called out to him.

Solo glanced at the board, then informed his passengers, 'We're coming up on Alderaan. We'll be slowing down shortly and going back under lightspeed. Come on, Chewie.'

Rising from the game table, the Wookiee followed his partner toward the cockpit. Luke watched them depart, but his mind wasn't on their imminent arrival at Alderaan. It was burning with something else, something that seemed to grow and mature at the back of his brain as he dwelt on it.

'You know,' he murmured, 'I did feel something. I could almost "see" the outlines of the remote.' He gestured at the hovering device behind him.

Kenobi's voice when he replied was solemn. 'Luke, you've taken the first step into a larger universe.'

Dozens of humming, buzzing instruments lent the freighter's cockpit the air of a busy hive. Solo and Chewbacca had their attention locked on the most vital of those instruments.

'Steady ... stand by, Chewie.' Solo adjusted several manual compensators. 'Ready to go sublight ... ready ... cut us in, Chewie.'

The Wookiee turned something on the console before him. At the same time Solo pulled back on a comparatively large lever. Abruptly the long streaks of Doppler-distorted starlight slowed to hyphen shapes, then finally to familiar bolts of fire. A gauge on the console registered zero.

Gigantic chunks of glowing stone appeared out of the nothingness, barely shunted aside by the ship's deflectors. The strain caused the *Millennium Falcon* to begin shuddering violently.

'What the—?' a thoroughly startled Solo muttered. Next to him, Chewbacca offered no comment of his own as he flipped off several controls and activated others. Only the fact that the cautious Solo always emerged from supralight travel with his deflectors up – just in case any of many unfriendly folks might be waiting for him – had saved the freighter from instant destruction.

Luke fought to keep his balance as he made his way into the cockpit. 'What's going on?'

'We're back in normal space,' Solo informed him, 'but we've come out in the middle of the worst asteriod storm I've ever seen. It's not on any of our charts.' He peered hard at several indicators. 'According to the galactic atlas, our position is correct. Only one thing is missing: Alderaan.'

'Missing? But – that's crazy!'

'I won't argue with you,' the Corellian replied grimly, 'but look for yourself.' He gestured out the port. 'I've triple-checked the coordinates, and there's nothing wrong with the nav 'puter. We ought to be standing out one planetary diameter from the surface. The planet's glow should be filling the cockpit, but – there's nothing out there. Nothing but debris.' He paused. 'Judging from the level of wild energy outside and the amount of solid waste, I'd guess that Alderaan's been ... blown away. Totally.'

'Destroyed,' Luke whispered, overwhelmed at the specter raised by such an unimaginable disaster. 'But – how?'

'The Empire,' a voice declared firmly. Ben Kenobi had come in behind Luke, and his attention was held by the emptiness ahead as well as the import behind it.

'No.' Solo was shaking his head slowly. In his own way even he was stunned by the enormity of what the old man was suggesting. That a human agency had been responsible for the annihilation of an entire population, of a planet itself . . .

'No . . . the entire Imperial fleet couldn't have done this. It would take a thousand ships massing a lot more firepower than has ever existed.'

'I wonder if we should get out of here,' Luke was murmuring, trying to see around the rims of the port. 'If by some chance it was the Empire . . .'

'I don't know what's happened here,' an angry Solo cursed, 'but I'll tell you one thing. The Empire isn't—'

Muffled alarms began humming loudly as a synchronous light flashed on the control console. Solo bent to the appropriate instrumentation.

'Another ship,' he announced. 'Can't judge the type yet.'

'A survivor, maybe – someone who might know what happened,' Luke ventured hopefully.

Ben Kenobi's next words shattered more than that hope. 'That's an Imperial fighter.'

Chewbacca suddenly gave an angry bark. A huge flower of destruction blossomed outside the port, battering the freighter violently. A tiny, double-winged ball raced past the cockpit port.

'It followed us!' Luke shouted.

'From Tatooine? It couldn't have,' objected a disbelieving Solo. 'Not in hyperspace.'

Kenobi was studying the configuration the tracking screen displayed. 'You're quite right, Han. It's the short-range TIE fighter.'

'But where did it come from?' the Corellian wanted to know. 'There are no Imperial bases near here. It couldn't have been a TIE job.'

'You saw it pass.'

'I know. It looked like a TIE fighter – but what about a base?'

'It's leaving in a big hurry,' Luke noted, studying the tracker. 'No matter where it's going, if it identifies us we're in big trouble.'

'Not if I can help it,' Solo declared. 'Chewie, jam its transmission. Lay in a pursuit course.'

'It would be best to let it go,' Kenobi ventured thoughtfully. 'It's already too far out of range.'

'Not for long.'

Several minutes followed, during which the cockpit was filled with a tense silence. All eyes were on the tracking screen and viewport.

At first the Imperial fighter tried a complex evasive course, to no avail. The surprisingly maneuverable freighter hung tight on its tail, continuing to make up the distance between them. Seeing that he couldn't shake his pursuers, the fighter pilot had obviously opened up his tiny engine all the way.

Ahead, one of the multitude of stars was becoming steadily brighter. Luke frowned. They were moving fast, but not nearly fast enough for any heavenly object to brighten so rapidly. Something here didn't make sense.

'Impossible for a fighter that small to be this deep in space on its own,' Solo observed.

'It must have gotten lost, been part of a convoy or something,' Luke hypothesized.

Solo's comment was gleeful. 'Well, he won't be around long enough to tell anyone about us. We'll be on top of him in a minute or two.'

The star ahead continued to brighten, its glow evidently coming from within. It assumed a circular outline.

'He's heading for that small moon,' Luke murmured.

'The Empire must have an outpost there,' Solo admitted. 'Although, according to the atlas, Alderaan had no moons.' He shrugged it off. 'Galactic topography was never one of my best subjects. I'm only interested in worlds and moons with customers on them. But I think I can get him before he gets there; he's almost in range.'

They drew steadily nearer. Gradually craters and mountains on the moon became visible. Yet there was something extremely odd about them. The craters were far too regular in outline, the mountains far too vertical, canyons and valleys impossibly straight and regularized. Nothing as capricious as volcanic action had formed those features.

'That's no moon,' Kenobi breathed softly. 'That's a space station.'

'But it's too big to be a space station,' Solo objected. 'The size of it! It can't be artificial – it can't!'

'I have a very strange feeling about this,' was Luke's comment.

Abruptly the usually calm Kenobi was shouting. 'Turn the ship around! Let's get out of here!'

'Yes, I think you're right, old man. Full reverse, Chewie.'

The Wookiee started adjusting controls, and the freighter seemed to slow, arcing around in a broad curve. The tiny fighter leaped instantly toward the monstrous station until it was swallowed up by its overpowering bulk.

Chewbacca chattered something at Solo as the ship shook and strained against unseen forces.

'Lock in auxiliary power!' Solo ordered.

Gauges began to whine in protest, and by ones and twos every instrument on the control console sequentially went berserk. Try as he might, Solo couldn't keep the surface of the gargantuan station from looming steadily larger, larger – until it became the heavens.

Luke stared wildly at secondary installations as big as mountains, dish antennae larger than all of Mos Eisley. 'Why are we still moving toward it?'

'Too late,' Kenobi whispered softly. A glance at Solo confirmed his concern.

'We're caught in a tractor beam – strongest one I ever saw. It's dragging us in,' the pilot muttered.

'You mean, there's nothing you can do?' Luke asked, feeling unbelievably helpless.

Solo studied the overloaded sensor readouts and shook his head. 'Not against this kind of power. I'm on full power myself, kid, and it's not shifting out of course a fraction of a degree. It's no use. I'm going to have to shut down or we'll melt our engines. But they're not going to suck me up like so much dust without a fight!'

He started to vacate the pilot's chair, but was restrained by an aged yet powerful hand on his shoulder. An expression of concern was on the old man's face – and yet, a suggestion of something somewhat less funereal.

'If it's a fight you cannot win – well, my boy, there are always alternatives to fighting . . .'

The true size of the battle station became apparent as the freighter was pulled closer and closer. Running around the station's equator was an artificial cluster of metal mountains, docking ports stretching beckoning fingers nearly two kilometers above the surface.

Now only a minuscule speck against the gray bulk of the station, the *Millennium Falcon* was sucked toward one of those steel pseudopods and finally swallowed by it. A lake of metal closed off the entryway, and the freighter vanished as if it had never existed.

Vader stared at the motley array of stars displayed on the conference-room map while Tarkin and Admiral Motti conferred nearby. Interestingly, the first use of the most powerful destructive machine ever constructed had seemingly had no influence at all on that map, which in itself represented only a tiny fraction of this section of one modest-sized galaxy.

It would take a microbreakdown of a portion of this map to reveal a slight reduction in spatial mass, caused by the disappearance of Alderaan. Alderaan, with its many cities, farms, factories, and towns – and traitors, Vader reminded himself.

Despite his advances and intricate technological methods of annihilation, the actions of mankind remained unnoticeable to an uncaring, unimaginably vast universe. If Vader's grandest plans ever came to pass, all that would change.

He was well aware that despite all their intelligence and drive, the vastness and wonder were lost on the two men who continued to chatter monkeylike behind him. Tarkin and Motti were talented and ambitious, but they saw things only on the scale of human pettiness. It was a pity, Vader thought, that they did not possess the scope to match their abilities.

Still, neither man was a Dark Lord. As such, little more could be expected of them. These two were useful now, and dangerous, but someday they, like Alderaan, would have to be swept aside. For now he could not afford to ignore them. And while he would have preferred the company of equals, he had to admit reluctantly that at this point, he *had* no equals.

Nonetheless, he turned to them and insinuated himself into their conversation. 'The defense systems on Alderaan, despite the Senator's protestations to the contrary, were as strong as any in the

Empire. I should conclude that our demonstration was as impressive as it was thorough.'

Tarkin turned to him, nodding. 'The Senate is being informed of our action at this very moment. Soon we will be able to announce the extermination of the Alliance itself, as soon as we have dealt with their main military base. Now that their main source of munitions, Alderaan, has been eliminated, the rest of those systems with secessionist inclinations will fall in line quickly enough, you'll see.'

Tarkin turned as an Imperial officer entered the chamber. 'Yes, what is it, Cass?'

The unlucky officer wore the expression of the mouse chosen to bell the cat. 'Governor, the advance scouts have reached and circumnavigated Dantooine. They have found the remains of a rebel base . . . which they estimate has been deserted for some time. Years, possibly. They are proceeding with an extensive survey of the remainder of the system.'

Tarkin turned apoplectic, his face darkening to a fine pomegranate fury. 'She lied! She lied to us!'

No one could see, but it seemed that Vader must have smiled behind his mask. 'Then we are even in the first exchange of "truths." I told you she would never betray the rebellion – unless she thought her confession could somehow destroy us in the process.'

'Terminate her immediately!' The Governor was barely able to form words.

'Calm yourself, Tarkin,' Vader advised him. 'You would throw away our only link to the real rebel base so casually? She can still be of value to us.'

'*Fagh!* You just said it yourself, Vader: we'll get nothing more out of her. I'll find that hidden fortress if I have to destroy every star system in this sector. I'll—'

A quiet yet demanding beep interrupted him.

'Yes, what is it?' he inquired irritably.

A voice reported over an unseen speaker. 'Sirs, we've captured a small freighter that was entering the remains of Alderaan. A standard check indicates that its markings apparently match that of the ship which blasted its way out of the quarantine at Mos Eisley, Tatooine system, and went hyper before the Imperial blockade craft there could close on it.'

Tarkin looked puzzled. 'Mos Eisley? Tatooine? What is this? What's this all about, Vader?'

'It means, Tarkin, that the last of our unresolved difficulties is about to be eliminated. Someone apparently received the missing data tapes, learned who transcribed them, and was trying to return them to her. We may be able to facilitate their meeting with the Senator.'

Tarkin started to say something, hesitated, then nodded in understanding. 'How convenient. I leave this matter in your hands, Vader.'

The Dark Lord bowed slightly, a gesture which Tarkin acknowledged with a perfunctory salute. Then he spun and strode from the room, leaving Motti looking from man to man in confusion.

The freighter sat listlessly in the docking hangar of the huge bay. Thirty armed Imperial troopers stood before the lowered main ramp leading into the ship. They snapped to attention when Vader and a Commander approached. Vader halted at the base of the ramp, studying the vessel as an officer and several soldiers came forward.

'There was no reply to our repeated signals, sir, so we activated the ramp from outside. We've made no contact with anyone aboard either by communicator or in person,' the officer reported.

'Send your men in,' Vader ordered.

Turning, the officer relayed the command to a noncom, who barked orders. A number of the heavily armored soldiers made their way up the ramp and entered the outer hold. They advanced with appreciable caution.

Inside, two men covered a third as he advanced. Moving in groups of three in this fashion, they rapidly spread through the ship. Corridors rang hollowly under metal-shod feet, and doors slid aside willingly as they were activated.

'Empty,' the Sergeant in charge finally declared in surprise. 'Check the cockpit.'

Several troopers made their way forward and slid the portal aside, only to discover the pilot's chairs as vacant as the rest of the freighter. The controls were deactivated and all systems shut down. Only a single light on the console winked on and off fitfully. The Sergeant moved forward, recognized the source of the light, and activated the appropriate controls. A printout appeared on a nearby screen. He studied it intently, then turned to convey the information to his superior, who was waiting by the main hatch.

That worthy listened carefully before he turned and called down to the Commander and Vader. 'There is no one aboard; the ship is completely deserted, sirs. According to the ship's log, her crew abandoned ship immediately after lift-off, then set her on automatics for Alderaan.'

'Possibly a decoy,' the Commander ventured aloud. 'Then they should still be on Tatooine!'

'Possibly,' Vader admitted reluctantly.

'Several of the escape pods have been jettisoned,' the officer went on.

'Did you find any droids on board?' Vader called.

'No, sir – nothing. If there were any, they must have abandoned the ship along with the organic crew.'

Vader hesitated before replying. When he did so, uncertainty was evident in his voice. 'This doesn't feel right. Send a fully equipped scanning team on board. I want every centimeter of that ship checked out. See to it as soon as possible.' With that, he whirled and stalked from the hangar, pursued by the infuriating feeling that he was overlooking something of vital importance.

The rest of the assembled soldiers were dismissed by the officer. On board the freighter, a last lone figure left off examining the space beneath the cockpit consoles and ran to join his comrades. He was anxious to be off this ghost ship and back in the comfortable surroundings of the barracks. His heavy footsteps echoed through the once more empty freighter.

Below, the muffled sounds of the officer giving final orders faded, leaving the interior in complete quiet. The quivering of a portion of the floor was the only movement on board.

Abruptly the quivering became a sharp upheaval. Two metal panels popped upward, followed by a pair of tousled heads. Han Solo and Luke looked around quickly, then managed to relax a little when it became clear that the ship was as empty as it sounded.

'Lucky you'd built these compartments,' Luke commented.

Solo was not as cheerily confident. 'Where did you think I kept smuggled goods – in the main hold? I admit I never expected to smuggle myself in them.' He started violently at a sudden sound, but it was only another of the panels shifting aside.

'This is ridiculous. It isn't going to work. Even if I could take off and get past the closed hatch' – he jabbed a thumb upward – 'we'd never get past that tractor beam.'

Another panel opened, revealing the face of an elderly imp. 'You leave that to me.'

'I was afraid you'd say something like that,' muttered Solo. 'You're a damn fool, old man.'

Kenobi grinned at him. 'What does that say of the man who allows himself to be hired by a fool?'

Solo muttered something under his breath as they pulled themselves clear of the compartments, Chewbacca doing so with a good deal of grunting and twisting.

Two technicians had arrived at the base of the ramp. They reported to the two bored soldiers guarding it.

'The ship's all yours,' one of the troopers told them. 'If the scanners pick up anything, report it immediately.'

The men nodded, then strained to lug their heavy equipment up the ramp. As soon as they disappeared inside, a loud crash was heard. Both guards whirled, then heard a voice call, 'Hey, down there, could you give us a hand with this?'

One trooper looked at his companion, who shrugged. They both started up the ramp, muttering at the inefficiency of mere technicians. A second crashing sound reverberated, but now there was no one left to hear it.

But the absence of the two troopers was noticed, soon thereafter. A gantry officer passing the window of a small command office near the freighter entrance glanced out, frowning when he saw no sign of the guards. Concerned but not alarmed, he moved to a comlink and spoke into it as he continued to stare at the ship.

'THX-1138, why aren't you at your post? THX-1138, do you copy?'

The speaker gave back only static.

'THX-1138, why don't you reply?' The officer was beginning to panic when an armored figure descended the ramp and waved toward him. Pointing to the portion of his helmet covering his right ear, the figured tapped it to indicate the comlink inside wasn't working.

Shaking his head in disgust, the gantry officer gave his busy aide an annoyed look as he made for the door. 'Take over here. We've got another bad transmitter. I'm going to see what I can do.' He activated the door, took a step forward as it slid aside – and stumbled backward in a state of shock.

Filling the door completely was a towering hairy form. Chewbacca leaned inward and with a bone splintering howl flattened the benumbed officer with one swipe of a pan-sized fist.

The aide was already on his feet and reaching for his sidearm when a narrow energy beam passed completely through him, piercing his heart. Solo flipped up the faceplate of his trooper helmet, then slid it back into place as he followed the Wookiee into the room. Kenobi and the droids squeezed in behind him, with Luke, also clad in the armor of a luckless Imperial soldier, bringing up the rear.

Luke was looking around nervously as he shut the door behind them. 'Between his howling and your blasting everything in sight, it's a wonder the entire station doesn't know we're here.'

'Bring 'em on,' Solo demanded, unreasonably enthused by their success so far. 'I prefer a straight fight to all this sneaking around.'

'Maybe you're in a hurry to die,' Luke snapped, 'but I'm not. All this sneaking around has kept us alive.'

The Corellian gave Luke a sour eye but said nothing.

They watched as Kenobi operated an incredibly complex computer console with the ease and confidence of one long accustomed to handling intricate machinery. A screen lit up promptly with a map of sections of the battle station. The old man leaned forward, scrutinizing the display carefully.

Meanwhile, Threepio and Artoo had been going over an equally complicated control panel nearby. Artoo suddenly froze and began whistling wildly at something he had found. Solo and Luke, their momentary disagreement over tactics forgotten, rushed over to where the robots were standing. Chewbacca busied himself hanging the gantry officer up by his toes.

'Plug him in,' Kenobi suggested, looking over from his place before the larger readout. 'He should be able to draw information from the entire station network. Let's see if he can find out where the tractor-beam power unit is located.'

'Why not just disconnect the beam from here, sir?' Luke wanted to know.

It was Solo who replied derisively, 'What, and have them lock it right back on us before we can get a ship's length outside the docking bay?'

Luke looked crestfallen. 'Oh. I hadn't thought of that.'

'We have to break the tractor at its power source in order to execute a clean escape, Luke,' old Ben chided gently as Artoo punched a claw arm into the open computer socket he had discovered. Immediately a galaxy of lights came to life on the panel in front of him and the room was filled with the hum of machinery working at high speed.

Several minutes passed while the little droid sucked up information like a metal sponge. Then the hum slowed and he turned to beep something back at them.

'He's found it, sir!' Threepio announced excitedly.

'The tractor beam is coupled to the main reactors at seven locations. Most of the pertinent data is restricted, but he'll try to pull the critical information through to the monitor.'

Kenobi turned his attention from the larger screen to a small readout near Artoo. Data began to race across it too fast for Luke to see, but apparently Kenobi somehow made something of the schematic blur. 'I don't think there's any way you boys can help with this,' he told them. 'I must go alone.'

'That suits me fine,' said Solo readily. 'I've already done more than I bargained for on this trip. But I think putting that tractor beam out of commission's going to take more than your magic, old man.'

Luke wasn't put off so easily. 'I want to go with you.'

'Don't be impatient, young Luke. This requires skills you haven't yet mastered. Stay and watch over the droids and wait for my signal. They must be delivered to the rebel forces or many more worlds will meet the same fate as Alderaan. Trust in the force, Luke – and wait.'

With a last look at the flow of information on the monitor, Kenobi adjusted the lightsaber at his waist. Stepping to the door, he slid it aside, looked once left, once right, and disappeared down a long, glowing hallway.

As soon as he was gone Chewbacca growled and Solo nodded agreement. 'You said it, Chewie!' He turned to Luke. 'Where'd you dig up that old fossil?'

'Ben Kenobi – *General* Kenobi – is a great man,' Luke protested loftily.

'Great at getting us into trouble,' Solo snorted. 'General, my afterburners! He's not going to get us out of here.'

'You got any better ideas?' Luke shot back challengingly.

'Anything would be better than just waiting here for them to come and pick us up. If we—'

A hysterical whistling and hooting came from the computer console. Luke hurried over to Artoo Detoo. The little droid was all but hopping about on stubby legs.

'What now?' Luke asked Threepio.

The taller robot looked puzzled himself. 'I'm afraid I don't understand either, sir. He says, "I found her," and keeps repeating, "She's here, she's here!"'

'Who? Who has he found?'

Artoo turned a flat blinking face toward Luke and whistled frantically.

'Princess Leia,' Threepio announced after listening carefully. 'Senator Organa – they seem to be one and the same. I believe she may be the person in the message he was carrying.'

That three-dimensional portrait of indescribable beauty coalesced in Luke's mind again. 'The Princess? She's here?'

Attracted by the commotion, Solo wandered over. 'Princess? What's going on?'

'Where? Where is she?' Luke demanded breathlessly, ignoring Solo completely.

Artoo whistled on while Threepio translated. 'Level five, detention block AA-23. According to the information, she is scheduled for slow termination.'

'No! We've got to do something.'

'What are you three blabbering about?' an exasperated Solo demanded.

'She's the one who programmed the message into Artoo Detoo,' Luke explained hurriedly, 'the one we were trying to deliver to Alderaan. We've got to help her.'

'Now, just a minute,' Solo cautioned him. 'This is going awful fast for me. Don't get any funny ideas. When I said I didn't have any "better ideas" I meant it. The old man said to wait here. I don't like it, but I'm not going off on some crazy maze through this place.'

'But Ben didn't know she was here,' Luke half pleaded, half argued. 'I'm sure that if he knew he would have changed his plans.'

Anxiety turned to thougtfulness. 'Now, if we could just figure a way to get into that detention block ...'

Solo shook his head and stepped back. 'Huh-uh – I'm not going into any Imperial detention blocks.'

'If we don't do something, they're going to execute her. A minute ago you said you didn't just want to sit here and wait to be captured. Now all you want to do is stay. Which is it, Han?'

The Corellian looked troubled – and confused. 'Marching into a detention area's not what I had in mind. We're likely to end up there anyway – why rush it?'

'But they're going to execute her!'

'Better her than me.'

'Where's your sense of chivalry, Han?'

Solo considered. 'Near as I can recall, I traded it for a ten-carat chrysopaz and three bottles of good brandy about five years ago on Commenor.'

'I've seen her,' Luke persisted desperately. 'She's beautiful.'

'So's life.'

'She's a rich and powerful Senator,' Luke pressed, hoping an appeal to Solo's baser instincts might be more effective. 'If we could save her, the reward could be substantial.'

'Uh ... rich?' Then Solo looked disdainful. 'Wait a minute ... Reward, from whom? From the government on Alderaan?' He made a sweeping gesture toward the hangar and by implication the space where Alderaan had once orbited.

Luke thought furiously. 'If she's being held here and is scheduled to be executed, that means she must be dangerous in some way to whoever destroyed Alderaan, to whoever had this station built. You can bet it had something to do with the Empire instituting a reign of full repression.

'I'll tell you who'll pay for her rescue, and for the information she holds. The Senate, the rebel Alliance, and every concern that did business with Alderaan. She could be the sole surviving heir of the off-world wealth of the entire system! The reward could be more wealth than you can imagine.'

'I don't know ... I can imagine quite a bit.' He glanced at Chewbacca, who grunted a terse reply. Solo shrugged back at the big Wookiee. 'All right, we'll give it a try. But you'd better be right about that reward. What's your plan, kid?'

Luke was momentarily taken aback. All his energies up till now had been concentrated on persuading Solo and Chewbacca to aid in a rescue attempt. That accomplished, Luke became aware he had no idea how to proceed. He had grown used to old Ben and Solo giving directions. Now the next move was up to him.

His eyes were caught by several metal circlets dangling from the belt of Solo's armor. 'Give me those binders and tell Chewbacca to come over here.'

Solo handed Luke the thin but quite unbreakable cuffs and relayed the request to Chewbacca. The Wookiee lumbered over and stood waiting next to Luke.

'Now, I'm going to put these on you,' Luke began, starting to move behind the Wookiee with the cuffs, 'and—'

Chewbacca made a sound low in his throat, and Luke jumped in spite of himself. 'Now,' he began again, 'Han is going to put these on you and ...' He sheepishly handed the binders to Solo, uncomfortably aware of the enormous anthropoid's glowing eyes on him.

Solo sounded amused as he moved forward. 'Don't worry, Chewie. I think I know what he has in mind.'

The cuffs barely fit around the thick wrists. Despite his partner's seeming confidence in the plan, the Wookiee wore a worried, frightened look as the restraints were activated.

'Luke, sir.' Luke looked over at Threepio. 'Pardon me for asking, but, ah – what should Artoo and I do if someone discovers us here in your absence?'

'Hope they don't have blasters,' Solo replied.

Threepio's tone indicated he didn't find the answer humorous. 'That isn't very reassuring.'

Solo and Luke were too engrossed in their coming expedition to pay much attention to the worried robot. They adjusted their helmets. Then, with Chewbacca wearing a half-real downcast expression, they started off along the corridor where Ben Kenobi had disappeared.

IX

AS they traveled farther and deeper into the bowels of the gigantic station, they found it increasingly difficult to maintain an air of casual indifference. Fortunately, those who might have sensed some nervousness on the part of the two armored troopers would regard it as only natural, considering their huge, dangerous Wookiee captive. Chewbacca also made it impossible for the two young men to be as inconspicuous as they would have liked.

The farther they traveled, the heavier the traffic became. Other soldiers, bureaucrats, technicians, and mechanicals bustled around them. Intent on their own assignments, they ignored the trio completely, only a few of the humans sparing the Wookiee a curious glance. Chewbacca's morose expression and the seeming confidence of his captors reassured the inquisitive.

Eventually they reached a wide bank of elevators. Luke breathed a sigh of relief. The computer-controlled transport ought to be capable of taking them just about anywhere on the station in response to a verbal command.

There was a nervous second when a minor official raced to get aboard. Solo gestured sharply, and the other, without voicing a protest, shifted to the next elevator tube in line.

Luke studied the operating panel, then tried to sound at once knowledgeable and important as he spoke into the pickup grid.

Instead, he sounded nervous and scared, but the elevator was a pure-response mechanism, not programmed to differentiate the appropriateness of emotions conveyed vocally. So the door slid shut and they were on their way. After what felt like hours but was in reality only minutes, the door opened and they stepped out into the security area.

It had been Luke's hope they would discover something like the old-fashioned barred cells of the kind used on Tatooine in towns like Mos Eisley. Instead, they saw only narrow ramps bordering a bottomless ventilation shaft. These walkways, several levels of them, ran parallel to smooth curving walls which held faceless detention cells. Alert-looking guards and energy gates seemed to be everywhere they looked.

Uncomfortably aware that the longer they stood frozen in place, the sooner someone was bound to come over and ask unanswerable questions, Luke searched frantically for a course of action.

'This isn't going to work,' Solo whispered, leaning toward him.

'Why didn't you say so before?' a frustrated, frightened Luke shot back.

'I think I did. I—'

'*Shssh!*'

Solo shut up as Luke's worst fears were realized. A tall, grim-looking officer approached them. He frowned as he examined the silent Chewbacca.

'Where are you two going with this – thing?'

Chewbacca snarled at the remark, and Solo quieted him with a hasty jab in the ribs. A panicky Luke found himself replying almost instinctively. 'Prisoner transfer from block TS-138.'

The officer looked puzzled. 'I wasn't notified. I'll have to clear it.'

Turning, the man walked to a small console nearby and began entering his request. Luke and Han hurriedly surveyed the situation, their gaze traveling from alarms, energy gates, and remote photosensors to the three other guards stationed in the area.

Solo nodded to Luke as he unfastened Chewbacca's cuffs. Then he whispered something to the Wookiee. An ear-splitting howl shook the corridor as Chewbacca threw up both hands, grabbing Solo's rifle from him.

'Look out!' a seemingly terrified Solo shouted. 'It's loose. It'll rip us all apart!'

Both he and Luke had darted clear of the rampaging Wookiee, pulled out their pistols, and were blasting away at him. Their reaction was excellent, their enthusiasm undeniable, and their aim execrable. Not a single shot came close to the dodging Wookiee. Instead, they blasted automatic cameras, energy-rate controls, and the three dumbfounded guards.

At this point it occurred to the officer in charge that the abominable aim of the two soldiers was a bit too selectively efficient. He was preparing to jab the general alarm when a burst from Luke's pistol caught him in the midsection and he fell without a word to the gray deck.

Solo rushed to the open comlink speaker, which was screeching anxious questions about what was going on. Apparently there were audio as well as visual links between this detention station and elsewhere.

Ignoring the barrage of alternate threats and queries, he checked the readout set in the panel nearby. 'We've got to find out which cell this Princess of yours is in. There must be a dozen levels and— Here it is. Cell 2187. Go on – Chewie and I'll hold them here.'

Luke nodded once and was racing down the narrow walkway.

After gesturing for the Wookiee to take up a position where he could cover the elevators, Solo took a deep breath and responded to the unceasing calls from the comlink.

'Everything's under control,' he said into the pickup, sounding reasonably official. 'Situation normal.'

'It didn't sound like that,' a voice snapped back in a no-nonsense tone. 'What happened?'

'Uh, well, one of the guards experienced a weapon malfunction,' Solo stammered, his temporary officialese lapsing into nervousness. 'No problem now – we're all fine, thanks. How about you?'

'We're sending a squad up,' the voice announced suddenly.

Han could almost smell the suspicion at the other end. What to say? He spoke more eloquently with the business end of a pistol.

'Negative – negative. We have an energy leak. Give us a few minutes to lock it down. Large leak – very dangerous.'

'Weapon malfunction, energy leak . . . Who is this? What's your operating— ?'

Pointing his pistol at the panels, Solo blew the instrumentation to silent scraps. 'It was a dumb conversation anyway,' he murmured. Turning, he shouted down the corridor, 'Hurry it up, Luke! We're going to have company.'

Luke heard, but he was absorbed in running from one cell to the next and studying the numbers glowing above each doorway. The cell 2187, it appeared, did not exist. But it did, and he found it just as he was about to give up and try the next level down.

For a long moment he examined the featureless convex metal wall. Turning his pistol to maximum and hoping it wouldn't melt in his hand before it broke through, he opened fire on the door. When the weapon became too hot to hold, he tossed it from hand to hand. As he did so the smoke had time to clear, and he saw with some surprise that the door had been blown away.

Peering through the smoke with an uncomprehending look on her face was the young woman whose portrait Artoo Detoo had projected in a garage on Tatooine several centuries ago, or so it seemed.

She was even more beautiful than her image, Luke decided, staring dazedly at her. 'You're even – more beautiful – than I—'

Her look of confusion and uncertainty was replaced by first puzzlement and then impatience. 'Aren't you a little short for a storm trooper?' she finally commented.

'What? Oh – the uniform.' He removed the helmet, regaining a little composure at the same time. 'I've come to rescue you. I'm Luke Skywalker.'

'I beg your pardon?' she said politely.

'I said, I've come to rescue you. Ben Kenobi is with me. We've got your two droids—'

The uncertainty was instantly replaced by hope at the mention of the oldster's name. 'Ben Kenobi!' She looked around Luke, ignoring him as she searched for the Jedi. 'Where is he? Obi-Wan!'

Governor Tarkin watched as Darth Vader paced rapidly back and forth in the otherwise empty conference room. Finally the Dark Lord paused, glancing around as though a great bell only he could hear had rung somewhere close by.

'He is here,' Vader stated unemotionally.

Tarkin looked startled. 'Obi-Wan Kenobi! That's impossible. What makes you think so?'

'A stirring in the Force, of a kind I've felt only in the presence of my old master. It is unmistakable.'

'Surely – surely he must be dead by now.'

Vader hesitated, his assurance suddenly gone. 'Perhaps ... It is gone now. It was only a brief sensation.'

'The Jedi are extinct,' declared Tarkin positively. 'Their fire was quenched decades ago. You, my friend, are all that's left of their ways.'

A comlink buzzed softly for attention. 'Yes?' Tarkin acknowledged.

'We have an emergency alert in detention block AA-23.'

'The Princess!' Tarkin yelped, jumping to his feet. Vader whirled, trying to stare through the walls.

'I knew it – Obi-Wan *is* here. I knew I could not mistake a stirring in the force of such power.'

'Put all sections on alert,' Tarkin ordered through the comlink. Then he turned to stare at Vader. 'If you're right, he must not be allowed to escape.'

'Escape may not be Obi-Wan Kenobi's intention,' Vader replied, struggling to control his emotions. 'He is the last of the Jedi – and the greatest. The danger he presents to us must not be under-estimated – yet only I can deal with him.' His head snapped around to stare fixedly at Tarkin. 'Alone.'

Luke and Leia had started back up the corridor when a series of blinding explosions ripped the walkway ahead of them. Several troopers had tried coming through the elevator, only to be crisped one after another by Chewbacca. Disdaining the elevators, they had blasted a gaping hole through a wall. The opening was too large for Solo and the Wookie to cover completely. In twos and threes, the Imperials were working their way into the detention block.

Retreating down the walkway, Han and Chewbacca encountered Luke and the Princess. 'We can't go back that way!' Solo told them, his face flushed with excitement and worry.

'No, it looks like you've managed to cut off our only escape route,' Leia agreed readily. 'This is a detention area, you know. They don't build them with multiple exits.'

Breathing heavily, Solo turned to look her up and down. 'Begging your forgiveness, Your Highness,' he said sarcastically, 'but maybe you'd prefer it back in your cell?' She looked away, her face impassive.

'There's got to be another way out,' Luke muttered, pulling a small transmitter unit from his belt and carefully adjusting the frequency: '*See Threepio . . . See Threepio!*'

A familiar voice responded with gratifying speed. 'Yes, sir?'

'We've been cut off here. Are there *any* other ways out of the detention area – anything at all?'

Static crackled over the tiny grid as Solo and Chewbacca kept the Imperial troops bottled up at the other end of the walkway.

'What was that . . .? I didn't copy.'

Back in the gantry office Artoo Detoo beeped and whistled frantically as Threepio adjusted controls, fighting to clear the awkward transmission. 'I said, all systems have been alerted to your presence, sir. The main entry seems to be the only way in or out of the cell block.' He pressed instruments, and the view on the nearby readouts changed steadily. 'All other information on your section is restricted.'

Someone began banging on the locked door to the office – evenly at first and then, when no response was forthcoming from within, more insistently.

'Oh, no!' Threepio groaned.

The smoke in the cell corridor was now so intense that it was difficult for Solo and Chewbacca to pick their targets. That was fortunate inasmuch as they were now badly outnumbered and the smoke confused the Imperials' fire with equal thoroughness.

Every so often one of the soldiers would attempt to move closer, only to stand exposed as he penetrated the smoke. Under the accurate fire of the two smugglers, he would rapidly join the accumulating mass of motionless figures on the rampway flooring.

Energy bolts continued to ricochet wildly through the block as Luke moved close to Solo.

'There isn't any other way out,' he yelled over the deafening roar of concentrated fire.

'Well, they're closing in on us. What do we do now?'

'This is some rescue,' an irritated voice complained from behind them. Both men turned to see a thoroughly disgusted Princess eyeing them with regal disapproval. 'When you came in here, didn't you have a plan for getting out?'

Solo nodded toward Luke. 'He's the brains, sweetheart.'

Luke managed an embarrassed grin and shrugged helplessly. He turned to help return fire, but before he could do so, the Princess had snatched the pistol from his hand.

'Hey!'

Luke stared as she moved along the wall, finally locating a small grate nearby. She pointed the pistol at it and fired.

Solo gazed at her in disbelief. 'What do you think you're doing?'

'It looks like it's up to me to save our skins. Get into that garbage chute, flyboy!'

While the others looked on in amazement, she jumped feet first into the opening and disappeared. Chewbacca rumbled threateningly, but Solo slowly shook his head.

'No, Chewie, I don't want you to rip her apart. I'm not sure about her yet. Either I'm beginning to like her, or I'm going to kill her myself.' The Wookiee snorted something else, and Solo yelled back at him, 'Go on in, you furry oaf! I don't care what you smell. This is no time to go dainty on me.'

Shoving the reluctant Wookiee toward the tiny opening, Solo helped jam the massive bulk through. As soon as he disappeared, the Corellian followed him in. Luke fired off a last series of blasts, more in the hope of creating a covering smoke than hitting anything, slid into the chute, and was gone.

Not wanting to incur further losses in such a confined space, the pursuing soldiers had momentarily halted to await the arrival of reinforcements and heavier weapons. Besides, they had their quarry trapped, and despite their dedication, none of them were anxious to die needlessly.

The chamber Luke tumbled into was dimly lit. Not that the light was needed to discern its contents. He smelled the decay long before he was dumped into it. Unadorned except for the concealed illuminants, the garbage room was at least a quarter full of slimy muck, much of which had already achieved a state of decomposition sufficient to wrinkle Luke's nose.

Solo was stumbling around the edge of the room, slipping and sinking up to his knees in the uncertain footing in an attempt to locate an exit. All he found was a small, thick hatchway which he grunted and heaved to pry open. The hatchcover refused to budge.

'The garbage chute was a wonderful idea,' he told the Princess sardonically, wiping the sweat from his forehead. 'What an incredible smell you've discovered. Unfortunately, we can't ride out of here on a drifting odor, and there doesn't seem to be any other exit. Unless I can get this hatch open.'

Stepping back, he pulled his pistol and fired at the cover. The bolt promptly went howling around the room as everyone sought cover in the garbage. A last glance and the bolt detonated almost on top of them.

Looking less dignified by the moment, Leia was the first to emerge from the pungent cover. 'Put that thing away,' she told Solo grimly, 'or you're going to get us all killed.'

'Yes, Your Worship,' Solo muttered in snide supplication. He made no move to reholster his weapon as he glanced back up toward the open chute above. 'It won't take long for them to figure out what happened to us. We had things well under control – until you led us down here.'

'Sure you did,' she shot back, brushing refuse from her hair and shoulders. 'Oh, well, it could be worse. . . .'

As if in reply, a piercing, horrible moaning filled the room. It seemed to come from somewhere beneath them. Chewbacca let out a terrified yowl of his own and tried to flatten himself against a wall. Luke drew his own pistol and peered hard at various clumps of debris, but saw nothing.

'What was that?' Solo asked.

'I'm not too sure.' Luke suddenly jumped, looking down and behind him. 'Something just moved past me, I think. Watch out—'

With shocking suddenness Luke disappeared straight down into the garbage.

'It's got Luke!' the Princess shouted. 'It took him under!' Solo looked around frantically for something to shoot at.

As abruptly as he had vanished, Luke reappeared – and so did part of something else. A thick whitish tentacle was wrapped tight around his throat.

'Shoot it, kill it!' Luke screamed.

'Shoot it! I can't even see it,' Solo protested.

Once again Luke was sucked under by whatever that gruesome appendage was attached to. Solo stared helplessly around the multicolored surface.

There was a distant rumble of heavy machinery, and two opposing walls of the chamber moved inward several centimeters. The rumble ceased and then it was quiet again. Luke appeared unexpectedly close to Solo, scrabbling his way clear of the suffocating mess and rubbing at the welt on his neck.

'What happened to it?' Leia wondered, eyeing the quiescent garbage warily.

Luke looked genuinely puzzled. 'I don't know. It had me – and then I was free. It just let me go and disappeared. Maybe I didn't smell bad enough for it.'

'I've got a very bad feeling about this,' Solo murmured.

Again the distant rumble filled the room; again the walls began their inward march. Only this time neither sound nor movement showed any sign of stopping.

'Don't just stand there gaping at each other!' the Princess urged them. 'Try to brace them with something.'

Even with the thick poles and old metal beams Chewbacca could handle, they were unable to find anything capable of slowing the walls' advance. It seemed as if the stronger the object was that they placed against the walls, the easier it was snapped.

Luke pulled out his comlink, simultaneously trying to talk and will the walls to retreat. 'Threepio . . . come in, Threepio!' A decent pause produced no response, causing Luke to look worriedly at his companions.

'I don't know why he doesn't answer.' He tried again. 'See Threepio, come in. Do you read?'

'See Threepio,' the muted voice continued to call, 'come in, See Threepio.' It was Luke's voice and it issued softly in between buzzings from the small hand comlink resting on the deserted computer console. Save for the intermittent pleading, the gantry office was silent.

A tremendous explosion drowned out the muffled pleadings. It blew the office door clean across the room, sending metal fragments flying in all directions. Several of them struck the comlink, sending it flying to the floor and cutting off Luke's voice in midtransmission.

In the wake of the minor cataclysm four armed and ready troopers entered through the blown portal. Initial study indicated the office was deserted – until a dim, frightened voice was heard coming from one of the tall supply cabinets near the back of the room.

'Help, help! Let us out!'

Several of the troopers bent to inspect the immobile bodies of the gantry officer and his aide while others opened the noisy cabinet. Two robots, one tall and humanoid, the other purely mechanical and three-legged, stepped out into the office. The taller one gave the impression of being half unbalanced with fear.

'They're madmen, I tell you, madmen!' He gestured urgently toward the doorway. 'I think they said something about heading for the prison level. They just left. If you hurry, you might catch them. That way, that way!'

Two of the troopers inside joined those waiting in the hallway in hustling off down the corridor. That left two guards to watch over the office. They totally ignored the robots as they discussed what might have taken place.

'All the excitement has overloaded the circuitry in my companion here,' Threepio explained carefully. 'If you don't mind, I'd like to take him down to Maintenance.'

'*Hmmm?*' One of the guards looked up indifferently and nodded to the robot. Threepio and Artoo hurried out the door without looking back. As they departed it occurred to the guard that the taller of the two droids was of a type he had never seen before. He shrugged. That was not surprising on a station of this size.

'That was too close,' Threepio muttered as they scurried down an empty corridor. 'Now we'll have to find another information-control console and plug you back in, or everything is lost.'

The garbage chamber grew remorselessly smaller, the smoothly fitting metal walls moving toward one another with stolid precision. Larger pieces of refuse performed a concerto of snapping and popping that was rising toward a final shuddering crescendo.

Chewbacca whined pitifully as he fought with all his incredible strength and weight to hold back one of the walls, looking like a hirsute Tantalus approaching his final summit.

'One thing's for sure,' Solo noted unhappily. 'We're all going to be much thinner. This could prove popular for slimming. The only trouble is its permanence.'

Luke paused for breath, shaking the innocent comlink angrily. 'What could have happened to Threepio?'

'Try the hatch again,' advised Leia. 'It's our only hope.'

Solo shielded his eyes and did so. The ineffectual blast echoed mockingly through the narrowing chamber.

The service bay was unoccupied, everyone apparently having been drawn away by the commotion elsewhere. After a cautious survey of the room Threepio beckoned for Artoo to follow. Together they commenced a hurried search of the many service panels. Artoo let out a beep, and Threepio rushed to him. He waited impatiently as the smaller unit plugged the receptive arm carefully into the open socket.

A superfast flurry of electronics spewed in undisciplined fashion from the grid of the little droid. Threepio made cautioning motions.

'Wait a minute, slow down!' The sounds dropped to a crawl. 'That's better. They're where? They what? Oh, no! They'll only come out of there as a liquid!'

Less than a meter of life was left to the trapped occupants of the garbage room. Leia and Solo had been forced to turn sideways, had ended up facing each other. For the first time the haughtiness was gone from the Princess's face. Reaching out, she took Solo's hand, clutching it convulsively as she felt the first touch of the closing walls.

Luke had fallen and was lying on his side, fighting to keep his head above the rising ooze. He nearly choked on a mouthful of compressed sludge when his comlink began buzzing for attention.

'Threepio!'

'Are you there, sir?' the droid replied. 'We've had some minor problems. You would not believe—'

'Shut up, Threepio!' Luke screamed into the unit. 'And shut down all the refuse units on the detention level or immediately below it. Do you copy? Shut down the refuse—'

Moments later Threepio grabbed at his head in pain as a terrific screeching and yelling sounded over the comlink.

'No, shut them *all* down!' he implored Artoo. 'Hurry! Oh, listen to them – they're dying, Artoo! I curse this metal body of mine. I was not fast enough. It was my fault. My poor master – all of them . . . no, no, *no!*'

The screaming and yelling, however, continued far beyond what seemed like a reasonable interval. In fact, they were shouts of relief.

The chamber walls had reversed direction automatically with Artoo's shutdown and were moving apart again.

'Artoo, Threepio,' Luke hollered into the comlink, 'it's all right, we're all right! Do you read me? We're okay – you did just fine.'

Brushing distastefully at the clinging slime, he made his way as rapidly as possible toward the hatchcover. Bending, he scraped accumulated detritus away, noting the number thus revealed.

'Open the pressure-maintenance hatch on unit 366-117891.'

'Yes, sir,' came Threepio's acknowledgment.

They may have been the happiest words Luke had ever heard.

LINED with power cables and circuitry conduits that rose from the depths and vanished into the heavens, the service trench appeared to be hundreds of kilometers deep. The narrow catwalk running around one side looked like a starched thread glued on a glowing ocean. It was barely wide enough for one man to traverse.

One man edged his way along that treacherous walkway now, his gaze intent on something ahead of him instead of the awesome metal abyss below. The clacking sounds of enormous switching devices resounded like captive leviathans in the vast open space, tireless and never sleeping.

Two thick cables joined beneath an overlay panel. It was locked, but after careful inspection of sides, top and bottom, Ben Kenobi pressed the panel cover in a particular fashion causing it to spring aside. A blinking computer terminal was revealed beneath.

With equal care he performed several adjustments to the terminal. His actions were rewarded when several indicator lights on the board changed from red to blue.

Without warning, a secondary door close behind him opened. Hurriedly reclosing the panel cover, the old man slipped deeper into the shadows. A detachment of troopers had appeared in the portal, and the officer in charge moved to within a couple of meters of the motionless, hidden figure.

'Secure this area until the alert has been cancelled.'

As they began to disperse, Kenobi became one with the dark.

Chewbacca grunted and wheezed, and barely succeeded in forcing his thick torso through the hatchway opening with Luke's and Solo's help. That accomplished, Luke turned to take stock of their surroundings.

The hallway they had emerged into showed dust on the floor. It gave the impression of not having been used since the station had been built. Probably it was only a repair access corridor. He had no idea where they were.

Something hit the wall behind them with a massive *thunk*, and Luke yelled for everyone to watch out as a long, gelatinous limb worked its way through the hatch and flailed hopefully about in the open corridor. Solo aimed his pistol at it as Leia tried to slip past the half-paralyzed Chewbacca.

'Somebody get this big hairy walking carpet out of my way.' Suddenly she noticed what Solo was preparing to do. 'No, wait! It'll be heard!'

Solo ignored her and fired at the hatchway. The burst of energy was rewarded with a distant roar as an avalanche of weakened wall and beaming all but buried the creature in the chamber beyond.

Magnified by the narrow corridor, the sounds continued to roll and echo for long minutes afterward. Luke shook his head in disgust, realizing that someone like Solo who spoke with the mouth of a gun might not always act sensibly. Until now he had sort of looked up to the Corellian. But the senseless gesture of firing at the hatchway brought them, for the first time in Luke's mind, to the same level.

The Princess's actions were more surprising than Solo's, however. 'Listen,' she began, staring up at him, 'I don't know where you came from, but I'm grateful.' Almost as an afterthought she glanced back at Luke, adding, 'To the both of you.' Her attention turned back to Solo. 'But from now on you do as I tell you.'

Solo gaped at her. This time the smug smile wouldn't come. 'Look, Your Holiness,' he was finally able to stammer, 'let's get something straight. I take orders only from one person – me.'

'It's a wonder you're still alive,' she shot back smoothly. A quick look down the corridor and she had started determinedly off in the other direction.

Solo looked at Luke, started to say something, then hesitated and simply shook his head slowly. 'No reward is worth this. I don't know if there's enough credit in the universe to pay for putting up with *her* . . . Hey, slow down!'

Leia had started around a bend in the corridor, and they ran swiftly to catch up with her.

The half dozen troops milling around the entrance to the power trench were more interested in discussing the peculiar disturbance in the detention block than in paying attention to their present boring duty. So engrossed were they in speculation as to the cause of the trouble that they failed to notice the fey wraith behind them. It moved from shadow to shadow like a night-stalking ferret, freezing when one of the troopers seemed to turn slightly in its direction, moving on again as if walking on air.

Several minutes later one of the troopers frowned inside his armor, turning to where he thought he had sensed a movement near the opening to the main passageway. There was nothing but an undefinable something which the ghost-like Kenobi had left behind. Acutely uncomfortable yet understandably unwilling to confess to hallucinations, the trooper turned back to the more prosaic conversation of his fellows.

Someone finally discovered the two unconscious guards tied in the service lockers on board the captured freighter. Both men remained comatose despite all efforts to revive them.

Under the direction of several bickering officers, troopers carried their two armorless comrades down the ramp and toward the nearest hospital bay. On the way they passed two forms hidden by a small open service panel. Threepio and Artoo went unnoticed, despite their proximity to the hangar.

As soon as the troops had passed, Artoo finished removing a socket cover and hurriedly shoved his sensor arm into the opening. Lights commenced a wild flashing on his face and smoke started issuing from several seams in the small droid before a frantic Threepio could pull the arm free.

Immediately the smoke vanished, the undisciplined blinking faded to normalcy. Artoo emitted a few wilted beeps, successfully giving the impression of a human who had expected a glass of mild wine and instead unwittingly downed several gulps of something 180 proof.

'Well, next time watch where you stick your sensors,' Threepio chastised his companion. 'You could have fried your insides.' He eyed the socket. 'That's a power outlet, stupid, not an information terminal.'

Artoo whistled a mournful apology. Together they hunted for the proper outlet.

Luke, Solo, Chewbacca, and the Princess reached the end of an empty hallway. It dead-ended before a large window which overlooked a hangar, giving them a sweeping, tantalizing view of the freighter just below.

Pulling out his comlink and looking around them with increasing nervousness, Luke spoke into the pickup. 'See Threepio ... do you copy?'

There was a threatening pause, then, 'I read you, sir. We had to abandon the region around the office.'

'Are you both safe?'

'For the moment, though I'm not sanguine about my old age. We're in the main hangar, across from the ship.'

Luke looked toward the bay window in surprise. 'I can't see you across the bay – we must be right above you. Stand by. We'll join you as soon as we can.' He clicked off, smiling suddenly at Threepio's reference to his 'old age.' Sometimes the tall droid was more human than people.

'Wonder if the old man was able to knock out the tractor,' Solo was muttering as he surveyed the scene below. A dozen or so troopers were moving in and out of the freighter.

'Getting back to the ship's going to be like flying through the five Fire Rings of Fornax.'

Leia Organa turned long enough to glance in surprise from the ship to Solo. 'You came here in that wreck? You're braver than I thought.'

At once praised and insulted, Solo wasn't sure how to react. He settled for giving her a dirty look as they started back down the hallway, Chewbacca bringing up the rear.

Rounding a corner, the three humans came to an abrupt halt. So did the twenty Imperial troopers marching toward them. Reacting naturally – which is to say, without thinking – Solo drew his pistol and charged the platoon, yelling and howling in several languages at the top of his lungs.

Startled by the totally unexpected assault and wrongly assuming their attacker knew what he was doing, the troopers started to back away. Several wild shots from the Corellian's pistol initiated complete panic. Ranks and composure shattered, the troopers broke and fled down the passage.

Drunk with his own prowess, Solo continued the chase, turning to shout back at Luke, 'Get to the ship. I'll take care of these!'

'Are you out of your mind?' Luke yelled at him. 'Where do you think you're going?'

But Solo had already rounded a far bend in the corridor and didn't hear. Not that it would have made any difference.

Upset at his partner's disappearance, Chewbacca let out a thunderous if unsettled howl and rushed down the hallway after him. That left Luke and Leia standing alone in the empty corridor.

'Maybe I was too hard on your friend,' she confessed reluctantly. 'He certainly is courageous.'

'He certainly is an idiot!' a furious Luke countered tightly. 'I don't know what good it'll do us if he gets himself killed.' Muted alarms suddenly sounded from the bay below and behind them.

'That's done it,' Luke growled disgustedly. 'Let's go.' Together they started off in search of a way down to a hangar-deck level.

Solo continued his rout of all opposition, running at top speed down the long hallway, yelling and brandishing his pistol. Occasionally he got off a shot whose effect was more valuable psychologically than tactically.

Half the troops had already scattered down various subpassages and corridors. The ten troopers he continued to harry still raced headlong away from him, returning his fire only indifferently. Then they came up against a dead end, which forced them to turn and confront their opponents.

Seeing that the ten had halted, Solo likewise slowed. Gradually he came to a complete stop. Corellian and Imperials regarded one another silently. Several of the troopers were staring, not at Han but past him.

It suddenly occurred to Solo that he was very much alone, and the same thought was beginning to seep into the minds of the guards he was confronting. Embarrassment gave way rapidly to anger. Rifles and pistols started to come up. Solo took a step backward, fired one shot, then turned and ran like hell.

Chewbacca heard the whistle and crump of energy weapons firing as he lumbered lightly down the corridor. There was something odd about them, though: they sounded as if they were coming closer instead of moving away.

He was debating what to do when Solo came tearing around a corner and nearly ran him down. Seeing ten troopers in pursuit, the Wookiee decided to reserve his questions for a less confused moment. He turned and followed Solo back up the hallway.

Luke grabbed the Princess and pulled her back into a recess. She was about to retort angrily at his brusqueness when the sound of marching feet caused her to shrink back into the darkness with him.

A squad of soldiers hurried past, responding to the alarms that continued to ring steadily. Luke looked out at the retreating backs and tried to catch his breath. 'Our only hope of reaching the ship is from the other side of the hangar. They already know someone's here.' He started back down the corridor, motioning for her to follow.

Two guards appeared at the far end of the passageway, paused, and pointed directly at them. Turning, Luke and Leia began running back the way they had come. A larger squad of troopers rounded the far bend and came racing toward them.

Blocked ahead and behind, they hunted frantically for another way out. Then Leia spotted the cramped subhallway and gestured to it.

Luke fired at the nearest of their pursuers and joined her in running down the narrow passage. It looked like a minor service corridor. Behind them, pursuit sounded deafeningly loud in the confining space. But at least it minimized the amount of fire the troops could concentrate on them.

A thick hatchway appeared ahead. The lighting beyond turned dimmer, raising Luke's hopes. If they could lock the hatch even for a few moments and lose themselves somewhere beyond, they might have a chance of shaking their immediate tormentors.

But the hatch stayed open, showing no inclination to close automatically. Luke was about to let out a shout of triumph when the ground suddenly vanished ahead of him. His toes hanging over nothingness, he flailed to regain his balance, succeeding just in time to nearly go over the edge of the retracted catwalk anyway as the Princess plowed into him from behind.

The catwalk had been reduced to a stub protruding into empty air. A cool draft caressed Luke's face as he studied walls that soared to unseen heights overhead and plunged to fathomless depths below. The service shaft was employed in circulating and recycling the atmosphere of the station.

At the moment Luke was too frightened and concerned to be angry with the Princess for nearly sending them over the edge. Besides, other dangers competed for his attention. A burst of energy exploded above their heads, sending metal slivers flying.

'I think we made a wrong turn,' he murmured, firing back at the advancing troops and illuminating the narrow corridor behind them with destruction.

An open hatchway showed on the other side of the chasm. It might as well have been a light-year away. Hunting along the rim of the doorway, Leia located a switch and hit it quickly. The hatch door behind them slid shut with a resounding boom. At least that cut off fire from the rapidly nearing soldiers. It also left the two fugitives balanced precariously on a small section of catwalk barely a meter square. If the remaining section were to unexpectedly withdraw into the wall, they would see more of the battle station's interior than either wished.

Gesturing for the Princess to move aside as much as possible, Luke shielded his eyes and aimed the pistol at the hatch controls. A brief burst of energy melted them flush with the wall, insuring that no one could open it easily from the other side. Then he turned his attention to the vast cavity blocking their path to the opposite portal. It beckoned invitingly – a small yellow rectangle of freedom.

Only the soft rush of air from below sounded until Luke commented, 'This is a shield-rated door, but it won't hold them back very long.'

'We've got to get across there somehow,' Leia agreed, once more examining the metal bordering the sealed doorway. 'Find the controls for extending the bridge.'

Some desperate searching produced nothing, while an ominous pounding and hissing sounded from behind the frozen door. A small spot of white appeared in the center of the metal, then began to spread and smoke.

'They're coming through!' Luke groaned.

The Princess turned carefully to stare across the gap. 'This must be a single-unit bridge, with the controls only on the other side.'

Reaching up to the point at the panel holding the unreachable controls, Luke's hand caught on something at his waist. A frustrated glance downward revealed the cause – and engendered a bit of practical insanity.

The cable coiled tightly in small loops was thin and fragile seeming, but it was general military-issue line and would have supported Chewbacca's weight easily. It certainly ought to hold Leia and himself. Pulling the cable free of the waist catch, he gauged its length, matching it against the width of the abyss. This should span the distance with plenty to spare.

'What now?' the Princess inquired curiously.

Luke didn't reply. Instead, he removed a small but heavy power unit from the utility belt of his armor and tied one end of the cable around it. Making sure the wrapping was secure, he stepped as close to the edge of their uncertain perch as he dared.

Whirling the weighted end of the cord in increasing circles, he let it arc across the gorge. It struck an outcropping of cylindrical conduits on the other side and fell downward. With forced patience he pulled the loose line back in, then recoiled it for another try.

Once again the weighted end orbited in ever greater circles, and again he flung it across the gap. He could feel the rising heat behind him as he let it go, heat from the melting metal doorway.

This time the heavy end looped around an outcropping of pipes above, wrapped itself several times around, and slipped, battery end down, into a crack between them. Leaning backward, he tugged and pulled on the cable, pulling on it at the same time as he tried to rest all his weight on it. The cable showed no sign of parting.

Wrapping the other end of the line several times around his waist and right arm, he reached out and pulled the Princess close to him with the other. The hatch door behind them was now a molten white, and liquid metal was running steadily from its borders.

Something warm and pleasant touched Luke's lips, alerting every nerve in his body. He looked down in shock at the Princess, his mouth still tingling from the kiss.

'Just for luck,' she murmured with a slight, almost embarrassed smile as she put her arms around him. 'We're going to need it.'

Gripping the thin cable as tightly as possible with his left hand,

Luke put his right over it, took a deep breath, and jumped out into air. If he had miscalculated the degree of arc in their swing, they would miss the open hatch and slam into the metal wall to either side or below it. If that happened he doubted he could maintain his grip on the rope.

The heart-halting transit was accomplished in less time than that thought. In a moment Luke was on the other side, scrambling on his knees to make sure they didn't fall back into the pit. Leia released her hold on him with admirable timing. She rolled forward and into the open hatchway, climbing gracefully to her feet as Luke fought to untangle himself from the cable.

A distant whine became a loud hiss, then a groan as the hatch door on the other side gave way. It collapsed inward and tumbled into the depths. If it touched bottom, Luke didn't hear it.

A few bolts struck the wall nearby. Luke turned his own weapon on the unsuccessful troopers and returned the fire even as Leia was pulling him into the passageway behind.

Once clear of the door he hit the activating switch. It shut tightly behind them. They would have several minutes, at least, without having to worry about being shot in the back. On the other hand, Luke didn't have the slightest idea where they were, and he found himself wondering what had happened to Han and Chewbacca.

Solo and his Wookiee partner had succeeded in shaking a portion of their pursuers. But it seemed that whenever they slipped free of several soldiers, more appeared to take their place. No question about it: the word was out on them.

Ahead, a series of shield doors was beginning to close.

'Hurry, Chewie!' Solo urged.

Chewbacca grunted once, breathing like an over-used engine. Despite his immense strength, the Wookiee was not built for long-distance sprinting. Only his enormous stride had enabled him to keep pace with the lithe Corellian. Chewbacca left a couple of hairs in one of the doors, but both slipped inside just before the five layers slammed shut.

'That ought to hold them for a while,' Solo crowed with delight. The Wookiee growled something at him, but his partner fairly fluoresced with confidence.

'Of course I can find the ship from here – Corellians can't get lost.' There came another growl, slightly accusing this time. Solo shrugged. 'Tocneppil doesn't count; he wasn't a Corellian. Besides, I was drunk.'

Ben Kenobi ducked into the shadows of a narrow passageway, seeming to become part of the metal itself as a large cluster of troopers hurried past him. Pausing to make certain they had all passed, he checked the corridor ahead before starting down it. But he failed to see the dark silhouette which eclipsed the light far behind him.

Kenobi had avoided one patrol after another, slowly working his way back toward the docking bay holding the freighter. Just another two turns and he should be at the hangar. What he would do then would be determined by how inconspicuous his charges had been.

That young Luke, the adventurous Corellian and his partner, and the two robots had been involved in something other than quiet napping he already suspected from the amount of activity he had observed while making his way back from the power trench. Surely all those troops hadn't been out hunting just for him!

But something else was troubling them, judging from the references he had overheard concerning a certain important prisoner, now escaped. That discovery had puzzled him, until he considered the restless natures of both Luke and Han Solo. Undoubtedly they were involved in some fashion.

Ben sensed something directly ahead and slowed cautiously. It had a most familiar feel to it, a half-remembered mental odor he could not quite place.

Then the figure stepped out in front of him, blocking his entry to the hangar not five meters away. The outline and size of the figure completed the momentary puzzle. It was the maturity of the mind he had sensed that had temporarily confused him. His hand moved naturally to the hilt of his deactivated saber.

'I have been waiting a long time, Obi-Wan Kenobi,' Darth Vader intoned solemnly. 'We meet again at last. The circle has been completed.' Kenobi sensed satisfaction beneath the hideous mask. 'The presence I sensed earlier could only have been you.'

Kenobi regarded the great form blocking his retreat and nodded slowly. He gave the impression of being more curious than impressed. 'You still have much to learn.'

'You were once my teacher,' Vader admitted, 'and I learned much from you. But the time of learning has long passed, and I am the master now.'

The logic that had constituted the missing link in his brilliant pupil remained as absent as before. There would be no reasoning here, Kenobi knew. Igniting his saber, he assumed the pose of warrior-ready, a movement accomplished with the ease and elegance of a dancer.

Rather roughly, Vader imitated the movement. Several minutes followed without motion as the two men remained staring at each other, as if waiting for some proper, as yet unspoken signal.

Kenobi blinked once, shook his head, and tried to clear his eyes, which had begun to water slightly. Sweat beaded up on his forehead, and his eyelids fluttered again.

'Your powers are weak,' Vader noted emotionlessly. 'Old man, you should never have come back. It will make your end less peaceful than you might have wished.'

'You sense only a part of the Force, Darth,' Kenobi murmured with the assurance of one to whom death is merely another sensation, like sleeping or making love or touching a candle. 'As always, you perceive its reality as little as a utensil perceives the taste of food.'

Executing a move of incredible swiftness for one so old, Kenobi lunged at the massive shape. Vader blocked the stab with equal speed, riposting with a counterslash that Kenobi barely parried. Another parry and Kenobi countered again, using this opportunity to move around the towering Dark Lord.

They continued to trade blows, with the old man now backing toward the hangar. Once, his saber and Vader's locked, the interaction of the two energy fields producing a violent sparking and flashing. A low buzzing sound rose from the straining power units as each saber sought to override the other.

Threepio peeked around the entrance to the docking bay, worriedly counting the number of troopers milling around the deserted freighter.

'Where could they be? Oh, oh.'

He ducked back out of sight just as one of the guards glanced in his direction. A second, more cautious appraisal was more rewarding. It revealed Han Solo and Chewbacca hugging the wall of another tunnel on the far side of the bay.

Solo also was nonplussed at the number of guards. He muttered, 'Didn't we just leave this party?'

Chewbacca grunted, and both turned, only to relax and lower their weapons at the sight of Luke and the Princess.

'What kept you?' Solo quipped mirthlessly.

'We ran into,' Leia explained, panting heavily, 'some old friends.'

Luke was staring at the freighter. 'Is the ship all right?'

'Seems okay,' was Solo's analysis. 'It doesn't look like they've removed anything or disturbed her engines. The problem's going to be getting to it.'

Leia suddenly pointed to one of the opposite tunnels. 'Look!'

Illuminated by the flare from contacting energy fields, Ben Kenobi and Darth Vader were backing toward the bay. The fight attracted the attention of others beside the Senator. Every one of the guards moved in for a better view of the Olympian conflict.

'Now's our chance,' Solo observed, starting forward.

All seven of the troopers guarding the ship broke and rushed toward the combatants, going to the Dark Lord's aid. Threepio barely ducked aside as they ran past him. Turning back into the alcove, he yelled to his companion.

'Unplug yourself, Artoo. We're leaving.' As soon as the Artoo unit slipped his sensor arm free of the socket, the two droids began to slowly edge out into the open bay.

Kenobi heard the approaching commotion and spared a glance back into the hangar. The squad of troopers bearing down on him was enough to show that he was trapped.

Vader took immediate advantage of the momentary distraction to bring his saber over and down. Kenobi somehow managed to deflect the sweeping blow, at once parrying and turning a complete circle.

'You still have your skill, but your power fades. Prepare to meet the Force, Obi-Wan.'

Kenobi gauged the shrinking distance between the oncoming troops and himself, then turned a pitying gaze on Vader. 'This is a fight you cannot win, Darth. Your power has matured since I taught you, but I too have grown much since our parting. If my blade finds its mark, you will cease to exist. But if you cut me down, I will only become more powerful. Heed my words.'

'Your philosophies no longer confuse me, old man,' Vader growled contemptuously. 'I am the master now.'

Once again he lunged forward, feinting, and then slashing in a deadly downward arc with the saber. It struck home, cutting the old man cleanly in half. There was a brief flash as Kenobi's cloak fluttered to the deck in two neat sections.

But Ben Kenobi was not in it. Wary of some trick, Vader poked at the empty cloak sections with the saber. There was no sign of the old man. He had vanished as though he had never existed.

The guards slowed their approach and joined Vader in examining the place where Kenobi had stood seconds before. Several of them muttered, and even the awesome presence of the Sith Lord couldn't keep a few of them from feeling a little afraid.

Once the guards had turned and dashed for the far tunnel, Solo and the others started for the starship – until Luke saw Kenobi cut in two. Instantly he shifted direction and was moving toward the guards.

'Ben!' he screamed, firing wildly toward the troops. Solo cursed, but turned to fire in support of Luke.

One of the energy bolts struck the safety release on the tunnel blast door. The emergency hold broken, the heavy door fairly exploded downward. Both the guards and Vader leaped clear – the guards into the bay and Vader backward, to the opposite side of the door.

Solo had turned and started for the entrance to the ship, but he paused as he saw Luke running toward the guards.

'It's too late!' Leia yelled at him. 'It's over.'

'No!' Luke half shouted, half sobbed.

A familiar, yet different voice rang in his ears – Ben's voice. 'Luke . . . listen!' was all it said.

Bewildered, Luke turned to hunt for the source of that admonition. He only saw Leia beckoning to him as she followed Artoo and Threepio up the ramp.

'Come on! There's no time.'

Hesitating, his mind still on that imagined voice (or was it imagined?), a confused Luke took aim and felled several soldiers before he, too, whirled and retreated into the freighter.

XI

DAZED, Luke staggered toward the front of the ship. He barely noticed the sound of energy bolts, too weak to penetrate the ship's deflectors, exploding harmlessly outside. His own safety was currently of little concern to him. With misty eyes he stared as Chewbacca and Solo adjusted controls.

'I hope that old man managed to knock out that tractor beam,' the Corellian was saying, 'or this is going to be a very short ride.'

Ignoring him, Luke returned to the hold area and slumped into a seat, his head falling into his hands. Leia Organa regarded him quietly for a while, then removed her cloak. Moving to him, she placed it gently around his shoulders.

'There wasn't anything you could have done,' she whispered comfortingly. 'It was all over in an instant.'

'I can't believe he's gone,' came Luke's reply, his voice a ghost of a whisper. 'I can't.'

Solo shifted a lever, staring nervously ahead. But the massive bay door was constructed to respond to the approach of any vessel. The safety feature now served to facilitate their escape as the freighter slipped quickly past the still-opening door and out into free space.

'Nothing,' Solo sighed, studying several readouts with profound satisfaction. 'Not so much as an erg of come-hither. He did it, all right.'

Chewbacca rumbled something, and the pilot's attention shifted to another series of gauges. 'Right, Chewie. I forget, for a moment, that there are other ways of persuading us to return.' His teeth flashed in a grin of determination. 'But the only way they'll get us back in that traveling tomb is in pieces. Take over.'

Whirling, he ran out of the cockpit. 'Come with me, kid,' he shouted at Luke as he entered the hold. 'We're not out of this yet.'

Luke didn't respond, didn't move, and Leia turned an angry face to Solo. 'Leave him alone. Can't you see what the old man meant to him?'

An explosion jarred the ship, nearly tumbling Solo to the deck.

'So what? The old man gave himself to give us a chance to get away. You want to waste that, Luke? You want Kenobi to have wasted himself?'

Luke's head came up and he stared with vacant eyes at the Corellian. No, not quite vacant . . . There was something too old and unpleasant shining blindly in the back of them. Without a word, he threw off the cloak and joined Solo.

Giving him a reassuring smile, Solo gestured down a narrow accessway. Luke looked in the indicated direction, smiled grimly, and rushed down it as Solo started down the opposing passage.

Luke found himself in a large rotating bubble protruding from the side of the ship. A long, wicked-looking tube whose purpose was instantly apparent projected from the apex of the transparent hemisphere. Luke settled himself into the seat and commenced a rapid study of the controls. Activator here, firing grip here . . . He had fired such weapons a thousand times before – in his dreams.

Forward, Chewbacca and Leia were searching the speckled pit outside for the attacking fighters represented by firepricks on several screens. Chewbacca suddenly growled throatily and pulled back on several controls as Leia let out a yelp.

'Here they come.'

The starfield wheeled around Luke as an Imperial TIE fighter raced toward him and then swung overhead to vanish into the distance. Within the tiny cockpit its pilot frowned as the supposedly battered freighter darted out of range. Adjusting his own controls, he swung up and over in a high arc intended to take him on a fresh intercept course with the escaping ship.

Solo fired at another fighter, and its pilot nearly slammed his engine through its mountings as he fought to avoid the powerful energy bolts. As he did so, his hurried maneuver brought him under and around to the other side of the freighter. Even as he was lowering the glare reflector over his eyes, Luke opened up on the racing fighter.

Chewbacca was alternating his attention between the instruments and the tracking screens, while Leia strained to separate distant stars from nearby assassins.

Two fighters dove simultaneously on the twisting, spiraling freighter, trying to line their weapons on the unexpectedly flexible craft. Solo fired at the descending globes, and Luke followed with his own weapon a second later. Both fired on the starship and then shot past.

'They're coming in too fast,' Luke yelled into his comlink.

Another enemy bolt struck the freighter forward and was barely shunted aside by its deflectors. The cockpit shuddered violently, and gauges whined in protest at the quantity of energy they were being asked to monitor and compensate for.

Chewbacca muttered something to Leia, and she murmured a soft reply as if she almost understood.

Another fighter unloosed a barrage on the freighter, only this time the bolt pierced an overloaded screen and actually struck the side of the ship. Though partially deflected, it still carried enough power to blow out a large control panel in the main passageway, sending a rain of sparks and smoke in all directions. Artoo Detoo started stolidly toward the miniature inferno as the ship lurched crazily, throwing the less stable Threepio into a cabinet full of component chips.

A warning light began to wink for attention in the cockpit. Chewbacca muttered to Leia, who stared at him worriedly and wished for the gift of Wookiee-gab.

Then a fighter floated down on the damaged freighter, right into Luke's sights. His mouth moving silently, Luke fired at it. The incredibly agile little vessel darted out of his range, but as it passed beneath them Solo picked it up instantly, and commenced a steady following fire. Without warning the fighter erupted in an incredible flash of multicolored light, throwing a billion bits of superheated metal to every section of the cosmos.

Solo whirled and gave Luke a victory wave, which the younger man gleefully returned. Then they turned back to their weapons as yet another fighter stormed over the freighter's hull, firing at its transmitter dish.

In the middle of the main passageway, angry flames raged around a stubby cylindrical shape. A fine white powdery spray issued from Artoo Detoo's head. Wherever it touched, the fire retreated sharply.

Luke tried to relax, to become a part of the weapon. Almost without being aware of it, he was firing at a retreating Imperial. When he blinked, it was to see the flaming fragments of the enemy craft forming a perfect ball of light outside the turret. It was his turn to spin and flash the Corellian a grin of triumph.

In the cockpit, Leia paid close attention to scattered readouts as well as searching the sky for additional ships. She directed her voice toward an open mike.

'There are still two more of them out there. Looks like we've lost the lateral monitors and the starboard deflector shield.'

'Don't worry,' Solo told her, with as much hope as confidence, 'she'll hold together.' He gave the walls a pleading stare. 'You hear me, ship? Hold together! Chewie, try to keep them on our port side. If we—'

He was forced to break off as a TIE fighter seemed to materialize out of nowhere, energy bolts reaching out from it toward him. Its companion craft came up on the freighter's other side and Luke found himself firing steadily at it, ignoring the immensely powerful energy it threw at him. At the last possible instant before it passed out of range, he swung the weapon's nozzle minutely, his finger tightening convulsively on the fire control. The Imperial fighter turned into a rapidly expanding cloud of phosphorescing dust. The other fighter apparently considered the shrunken odds, turned, and retreated at top speed.

'We've made it!' Leia shouted, turning to give the startled Wookiee an unexpected hug. He growled at her – very softly.

Darth Vader strode into the control room where Governor Tarkin stood staring at a huge, brilliantly lit screen. It displayed a sea of stars, but it was not the spectacular view which absorbed the Governor's thoughts at the moment. He barely glanced around as Vader entered.

'Are they away?' the Dark Lord demanded.

'They've just completed the jump to hyperspace. No doubt they are at this very moment congratulating themselves on their daring and success.' Now Tarkin turned to face Vader, a hint of warning in his tone.

'I'm taking an awful chance, on your insistence, Vader. This had better work. Are you certain the homing beacon is secure aboard their ship?'

Vader exuded confidence beneath the reflective black mask. 'There is nothing to fear. This will be a day long remembered. It already has been witness to the final extinction of the Jedi. Soon it will see the end of the Alliance and the rebellion.'

Solo switched places with Chewbacca, the Wookiee grateful for the opportunity to relinquish the controls. As the Corellian moved aft to check the extent of the damage, a determined-looking Leia passed him in the corridor.

'What do you think, sweetheart?' Solo inquired, well pleased with himself. 'Not a bad bit of rescuing. You know, sometimes I amaze even myself.'

'That doesn't sound too hard,' she admitted readily. 'The important thing is not my safety, but the fact that the information in the R-2 droid is still intact.'

'What's that droid carrying that's so important, anyway?'

Leia considered the blazing starfield forward. 'Complete technical schematics of the battle station. I only hope that when the data is analyzed, a weakness can be found. Until then, until the station itself is destroyed, we must go on. This war isn't over yet.'

'It is for me,' objected the pilot. 'I'm not on this mission for your revolution. Economics interest me, not politics. There's business to be done under any government. And I'm not doing it for you, Princess. I expect to be well paid for risking my ship and my hide.'

'You needn't worry about your reward,' she assured him sadly, turning to leave. 'If money is what you love . . . that's what you will receive.'

On leaving the cockpit she saw Luke coming forward, and she spoke softly to him in passing. 'Your friend is indeed a mercenary. I wonder if he really cares about anything – or anybody.'

Luke stared after her until she disappeared into the main hold area, then whispered, '*I* do ... *I* care.' Then he moved into the cockpit and sat in the seat Chewbacca had just vacated.

'What do you think of her, Han?'

Solo didn't hesitate. 'I try not to.'

Luke probably hadn't intended his response to be audible, but Solo overheard his murmur of 'Good' none the less.

'Still,' Solo ventured thoughtfully, 'she's got a lot of spirit to go with her sass. I don't know, do you think it's possible for a Princess and a guy like me ...?'

'No,' Luke cut him off sharply. He turned and looked away.

Solo smiled at the younger man's jealousy, uncertain in his own mind whether he had added the comment to bait his naive friend – or because it was the truth.

Yavin was not a habitable world. The huge gas giant was patterned with pastel high-altitude cloud formations. Here and there the softly lambent atmosphere was molded by cyclonic storms composed of six-hundred-kilometer-per-hour winds which boiled rolling gases up from the Yavinesque troposphere. It was a world of lingering beauty and quick death for any who might try to penetrate to its comparatively small core of frozen liquids.

Several of the giant planet's numerous moons, however, were planet-sized themselves, and of these, three could support humanoid life. Particularly inviting was the satellite designated by the system's discoverers as number four. It shone like an emerald in Yavin's necklace of moons, rich with plant and animal life. But it was not listed among those worlds supporting human settlement. Yavin was located too far from the settled regions of the galaxy.

Perhaps the latter reason, or both, or a combination of causes still unknown had been responsible for whatever race had once risen from satellite four's jungles, only to disappear quietly long before the first human explorer set foot on the tiny world. Little was known of them save that they left a number of impressive monuments, and that they were one of the many races which had aspired to the stars only to have their desperate reach fall short.

Now all that remained were the mounds and foliage-clad clumps formed by jungle-covered buildings. But though they had sunk back into the dust, their artifacts and their world continued to serve an important purpose.

Strange cries and barely perceptible moans sounded from every tree and copse; hoots and growls and strange mutterings issued from creatures content to remain concealed in the dense undergrowth. Whenever dawn broke over moon the fourth, heralding one of its long days, an especially feral chorus of shrieks and weirdly modulated screams would resound through the thick mist.

Even stranger sounds surged continually from one particular place. Here lay the most impressive of those edifices which a vanished race had raised toward the heavens. It was a temple, a roughly pyramidal structure so colossal that it seemed impossible it could have been built without the aid of modern gravitonic construction techniques. Yet all evidence pointed only to simple machines, hand technology – and, perhaps, devices alien and long lost.

While the science of this moon's inhabitants had led them to a dead end as far as offworld travel was concerned, they had produced several discoveries which in certain ways surpassed similar Imperial accomplishments – one of which involved a still unexplained method of cutting and transporting gargantuan blocks of stone from the crust of the moon.

From these monstrous blocks of solid rock, the massive temple had been constructed. The jungle had scaled even its soaring crest, clothing it in rich green and brown. Only near its base, in the temple front, did the jungle slide away completely, to reveal a long, dark entrance cut by its builders and enlarged to suit the needs of the structure's present occupants.

A tiny machine, its smooth metal sides and silvery hue incongruous amidst the all-pervasive green, appeared in the forest. It hummed like a fat, swollen beetle as it conveyed its cluster of passengers toward the open temple base. Crossing a considerable clearing, it was soon swallowed up by the dark maw in the front of the massive structure, leaving the jungle once more in the paws and claws of invisible squallers and screechers.

The original builders would never have recognized the interior of their temple. Seamed metal had replaced rock, and poured paneling did service for chamber division in place of wood. Nor would they have been able to see the buried layers excavated into the rock below, layers which contained hangar upon hangar linked by powerful elevators.

A landspeeder came to a gradual stop within the temple, whose first level was the uppermost of those ship-filled hangars. Its engine died obediently as the vehicle settled to the ground. A noisy cluster of humans waiting nearby ceased their conversation and rushed toward the craft.

Fortunately Leia Organa quickly emerged from the speeder, or the man who reached it first might have pulled her bodily from it, so great was his delight at the sight of her. He settled for giving her a smothering hug as his companion called their own greetings.

'You're safe! We'd feared you'd been killed.' Abruptly he composed himself, stepped away from her, and executed a formal bow. 'When we heard about Alderaan, we were afraid that you were ... lost along with the rest of the population.'

'All that is past history, Commander Willard,' she said. 'We have a future to live for. Alderaan and its people are gone.' Her voice turned bitter cold, frightening in so delicate-looking a person. 'We must see that such does not happen again.

'We don't have time for our sorrows, Commander,' she continued briskly. 'The battle station has surely tracked us here.'

Solo started to protest, but she shut him up with logic and a stern look.

'That's the only explanation for the ease of our escape. They sent only four TIE fighters after us. They could as easily have launched a hundred.'

Solo had no reply for that, but continued to fume silently. Then Leia gestured at Artoo Detoo.

'You must use the information locked in this R-2 droid to form a plan of attack. It's our only hope. The station itself is more powerful than anyone suspected.' Her voice dropped. 'If the data does not yield a weakness, there will be no stopping them.'

Luke was then treated to a sight unique in his experience, unique in most men's. Several rebel technicians walked up to Artoo Detoo, positioned themselves around him, and gently hoisted him in their arms. This was the first, and probably the last time he would ever see a robot being carried respectfully by men.

Theoretically, no weapon could penetrate the exceptionally dense stone of the ancient temple, but Luke had seen the shattered remains of Alderaan and knew that for those in the incredible battle station the entire moon would present simply another abstract problem in mass-energy conversion.

Little Artoo Detoo rested comfortably in a place of honor, his body radiating computer and data-bank hookups like a metal hairdo. On an array of screens and readouts nearby the technical information stored on the submicroscopic record tape within the robot's brain was being played out. Hours of it – diagrams, charts, statistics.

First the rush of material was slowed and digested by more sophisticated computer minds. Then the most critical information was turned over to human analysts for detailed evaluation.

All the while See Threepio stood close to Artoo, marveling at how so much complex data could be stored in the mind of so simple a droid.

The central briefing room was located deep within the bowels of the temple. The long, low-ceiling auditorium was dominated by a raised dais and huge electronic display screen at its far end. Pilots, navigators, and a sprinkling of Artoo units filled the seats. Impatient, and feeling very out of place, Han Solo and Chewbacca stood as far away from the stage, with its assemblage of officers and Senators, as possible. Solo scanned the crowd, searching for Luke. Despite some common sense entreaties, the crazy kid had gone and joined the regular pilots. He didn't see Luke, but he recognized the Princess as she talked somberly with some bemedaled oldster.

When a tall, dignified gentleman with too many deaths on his soul moved to stand by the far side of the screen, Solo turned his attention to him, as did everyone else in the room. As soon as an expectant silence had gripped the crowd, General Jan Dodonna adjusted the tiny mike on his chest and indicated the small group seated close to him.

'You all know these people,' he intoned with quiet power. 'They are the Senators and Generals whose worlds have given us support, whether open or covert. They have come to be with us in what may well prove to be the decisive moment.' He let his gaze touch many in the crowd, and none who were so favored remained unmoved.

'The Imperial battle station you now all have heard of is approaching from the far side of Yavin and its sun. That gives us a little extra time, but it must be stopped – once and for all – before it can reach this moon, before it can bring its weaponry to bear on

us as it did on Alderaan.' A murmur ran through the crowd at the
mention of that world, so callously obliterated.

'The station,' Dodonna went on, 'is heavily shielded and mounts
more firepower than half the Imperial fleet. But its defenses were
designed to fend off large-scale, capital ship assaults. A small, one-
or two-man fighter should be able to slip through its defensive
screens.'

A slim, supple man who resembled an older version of Han Solo
rose. Dodonna acknowledged his presence. 'What is it, Red Leader?'

The man gestured toward the display screen, which showed a
computer portrait of the battle station. 'Pardon me for asking, sir,
but what good are our *snub* fighters going to be against *that*?'

Dodonna considered. 'Well, the Empire doesn't think a one-man
fighter is any threat to anything except another small ship, like a
TIE fighter, or they would have provided tighter screens. Apparently
they're convinced that their defensive weaponry can fend off any
light attacks.

'But an analysis of the plans provided by Princess Leia has
revealed what we think is a weakness in the station's design. A big
ship couldn't get near it, but an X- or Y-wing fighter might.

'It's a small thermal exhaust port. Its size belies its importance, as
it appears to be an unshielded shaft that runs directly into the main
reactor system powering the station. Since this serves as an
emergency outlet for waste heat in the event of reactor over-
production, its usefulness would be eliminated by particle shielding.
A direct hit would initiate a chain reaction that would destroy the
station.'

Mutterings of disbelief ran through the room. The more experienced the pilot, the greater his expressed disbelief.

'I didn't say your approach would be easy,' Dodonna admonished
them. He gestured at the screen. 'You must maneuver straight in
down this shaft, level off in the trench, and skim the surface to – this
point. The target is only two meters across. It will take a precise hit
at exactly ninety degrees to reach the reactor systematization. And
only a direct hit will start the complete reaction.

'I said the port wasn't particle-shielded. However, it is completely
ray-shielded. That means no energy beams. You'll have to use
proton torpedoes.'

A few of the pilots laughed humorlessly. One of them was a

teenaged fighter jockey seated next to Luke who bore the unlikely name of Wedge Antilles. Artoo Detoo was there also, seated next to another Artoo unit who emitted a long whistle of hopelessness.

'A two-meter target at maximum speed – with a torpedo, yet,' Antilles snorted. 'That's impossible even for the computer.'

'But it's not impossible,' protested Luke. 'I used to bulls-eye womp-rats in my T-16 back home. They're not much bigger than two meters.'

'Is that so?' the rakishly uniformed youth noted derisively. 'Tell me, when you were going after your particular varmint, were there a thousand other, what did you call it, "womp-rats" armed with power rifles firing up at you?' He shook his head sadly.

'With all that firepower on the station directed at us, this will take a little more than barnyard marksmanship, believe me.'

As if to confirm Antilles' pessimism, Dodonna indicated a string of lights on the ever-changing schematic. 'Take special note of these emplacements. There's a heavy concentration of firepower on the latitudinal axes, as well as several dense circum-polar clusters.

'Also, their field generators will probably create a lot of distortion, especially in and around the trench. I figure that maneuverability in that sector will be less than point three.' This produced more murmurs and a few groans from the assembly.

'Remember,' the General went on, 'you must achieve a direct hit. Yellow squadron will cover for Red on the first run. Green will cover Blue on the second. Any questions?'

A muted buzz filled the room. One man stood, lean and handsome – too much so, it seemed, to be ready to throw away his life for something as abstract as freedom.

'What if both runs fail? What happens after that?'

Dodonna smiled tightly. 'There won't be any after that.' The man nodded slowly, understandingly, and sat down. 'Anyone else?' Silence now, pregnant with expectation.

'Then man your ships, and may the Force be with you.'

Like oil draining from a shallow pot, the seated ranks of men, women, and machines rose and flowed toward the exits.

Elevators hummed busily, lifting more and more deadly shapes from buried depths to the staging area in the primary temple hangar as Luke, Threepio, and Artoo Detoo walked toward the hangar entrance.

Neither the bustling flight crews, nor the pilots performing final checkouts, nor the massive sparks thrown off as power couplings were disconnected captured Luke's attention at the moment. Instead, it was held by the activity of two far more familiar figures.

Solo and Chewbacca were loading a pile of small strongboxes onto an armored landspeeder. They were completely absorbed with this activity, ignoring the preparations going on all around them.

Solo glanced up briefly as Luke and the robots approached, then returned to his loading. Luke simply watched sadly, conflicting emotions careening confusedly off one another inside him. Solo was cocky, reckless, intolerant, and smug. He was also brave to a fault, instructive, and unfailingly cheery. The combination made for a confusing friend – but a friend nonetheless.

'You got your reward,' Luke finally observed, indicating the boxes. Solo nodded once. 'And you're leaving, then?'

'That's right, kid. I've got some old debts to pay off, and even if I didn't, I don't think I'd be fool enough to stick around here.' He eyed Luke appraisingly. 'You're pretty good in a scrap, kid. Why don't you come with us? I could use you.'

The mercenary gleam in Solo's eyes only made Luke mad. 'Why don't you look around you and see something besides yourself for a change? You know what's going to happen here, what they're up against. They could use a good pilot. But you're turning your back on them.'

Solo didn't appear upset at Luke's tirade. 'What good's a reward if you're not around to spend it? Attacking that battle station isn't my idea of courage – more like suicide.'

'Yeah ... Take care of yourself, Han,' Luke said quietly, turning to leave. 'But I guess that's what you're best at, isn't it?' He started back into the hangar depths, flanked by the two droids.

Solo stared after him, hesitated, then called, 'Hey, Luke ... may the Force be with you.' Luke looked back to see Solo wink at him. He waved – sort of. Then he was swallowed up by moving mechanics and machinery.

Solo returned to his work, lifted a box – and stopped, to see Chewbacca gazing fixedly at him.

'What are you staring at, gruesome? I know what I'm doing. Get back to work!'

Slowly, still eyeing his partner, the Wookiee returned to the task of loading the heavy crates.

Sorrowful thoughts of Solo vanished when Luke saw the petite, slim figure standing by his ship – the ship he had been granted.

'Are you sure this is what you want?' Princess Leia asked him. 'It could be a deadly reward.'

Luke's eyes were filled with the sleek, venomous metal shape. 'More than anything.'

'Then what's wrong?'

Luke looked back at her and shrugged. 'It's Han. I thought he'd change his mind. I thought he'd join us.'

'A man must follow his own path,' she told him, sounding now like a Senator. 'No one can choose it for him. Han Solo's priorities differ from ours. I wish it were otherwise, but I can't find it in my heart to condemn him.' She stood on tiptoes, gave him a quick, almost embarrassed kiss, and turned to go. 'May the Force be with you.'

'I only wish,' Luke murmured to himself as he started back to his ship, 'Ben were here.'

So intent was he on thoughts of Kenobi, the Princess, and Han that he didn't notice the larger figure which tightly locked on to his arm. He turned, his initial anger gone instantly in astonishment as he recognized the figure.

'Luke!' the slightly older man exclaimed. 'I don't believe it! How'd you get here? Are you going out with us?'

'Biggs!' Luke embraced his friend warmly. 'Of course I'll be up there with you.' His smile faded slightly. 'I haven't got a choice, anymore.' Then he brightened again. 'Listen, have I got some stories to tell you . . .'

The steady whooping and laughing the two made was in marked contrast to the solemnity with which the other men and women in the hangar went about their business. The commotion attracted the attention of an older, war-worn man known to the younger pilots only as Blue Leader.

His face wrinkled with curiosity as he approached the two younger men. It was a face scorched by the same fire that flickered in his eyes, a blaze kindled not by revolutionary fervor but by years of living through and witnessing far too much injustice. Behind that fatherly visage a raging demon fought to escape. Soon, very soon, he would be free to let it loose.

Now he was interested in these two young men, who in a few hours were likely to be particles of frozen meat floating about Yavin. One of them he recognized.

'Aren't you Luke Skywalker? Have you been checked out on the Incom T-65?'

'Sir,' Biggs put in before his friend could reply, 'Luke's the best bush pilot in the outer-rim territories.'

The older man patted Luke reassuringly on the back as they studied his waiting ship. 'Something to be proud of. I've got over a thousand hours in an Incom skyhopper myself.' He paused a moment before going on.

'I met your father once when I was just a boy, Luke. He was a great pilot. You'll do all right out there. If you've got half your father's skill, you'll do a damn sight better than all right.'

'Thank you, sir. I'll try.'

'There's not much difference control-wise between an X-wing T-65,' Blue Leader went on, 'and a skyhopper.' His smile turned ferocious. 'Except the payload's of a somewhat different nature.'

He left them and hurried toward his own ship. Luke had a hundred questions to ask him, and no time for even one.

'I've got to get aboard my own boat, Luke. Listen, you'll tell me your stories when we come back. All right?'

'All right. I told you I'd make it here someday, Biggs.'

'You did.' His friend was moving toward a cluster of waiting fighters, adjusting his flight suit. 'It's going to be like old times, Luke. We're a couple of shooting stars that can't be stopped!'

Luke laughed. They used to reassure themselves with that cry when they piloted starships of sandhills and dead logs behind the flaking, pitted buildings of Anchorhead . . . years and years ago.

Once more Luke turned toward his ship, admiring its deadly lines. Despite Blue Leader's assurances, he had to admit that it didn't look much like an Incom skyhopper. Artoo Detoo was being snuggled into the R-2 socket behind the fighter cockpit. A forlorn metal figure stood below, watching the operation and shuffling nervously about.

'Hold on tight,' See Threepio was cautioning the smaller robot. 'You've got to come back. If you don't come back, who am I going to have to yell at?' For Threepio, that query amounted to an overwhelming outburst of emotion.

Artoo beeped confidently down at his friend, however, as Luke mounted the cockpit entry. Farther down the hangar he saw Blue Leader already set in his acceleration chair and signaling to his ground crew. Another roar was added to the monstrous din filling the hangar area as ship after ship activated its engines. In that enclosed rectangle of temple the steady thunder was overpowering.

Slipping into the cockpit seat, Luke studied the various controls as ground attendants began wiring him via cords and umbilicals into the ship. His confidence increased steadily. The instrumentation was necessarily simplified and, as Blue Leader had indicated, much like his old skyhopper.

Something patted his helmet, and he glanced left to see the crew chief leaning close. He had to shout to be heard above the deafening howl of multiple engines. 'That R-2 unit of yours seems a little beat up. Do you want a new one?'

Luke glanced briefly back at the secured droid before replying. Artoo Detoo looked like a permanent piece of the fighter.

'Not on your life. That droid and I have been through a lot together. All secure, Artoo?' The droid replied with a reassuring beep.

As the ground chief jumped clear, Luke commenced the final checkout of all instruments. It slowly occurred to him what he and the others were about to attempt. Not that his personal feelings could override his decision to join them. He was no longer an individual, functioning solely to satisfy his personal needs. Something now bound him to every other man and woman in this hangar.

All around him, scattered scenes of good-bye were taking place – some serious, some kidding, all with the true emotion of the moment masked by efficiency. Luke turned away from where one pilot left a mechanic, possibly a sister or wife, or just a friend, with a sharp, passionate kiss.

He wondered how many of them had their own little debts to settle with the Empire. Something crackled in his helmet. In response, he touched a small lever. The ship began to roll forward, slowly but with increasing speed, toward the gaping mouth of the temple.

XII

LEIA Organa sat silently before the huge display screen on which Yavin and its moons were displayed. A large red dot moved steadily toward the fourth of those satellites. Dodonna and several other field commanders of the Alliance stood behind her, their eyes also intent on the screen. Tiny green flecks began to appear around the fourth moon, to coalesce into small clouds like hovering emerald gnats.

Dodonna put a hand on her shoulder. It was comforting. 'The red represents the progress of the Imperial battle station as it moves deeper into Yavin's system.'

'Our ships are all away,' a Commander behind him declared.

A single man stood alone in the cylindrical hold, secured to the top of a rapier-thin tower. Staring through fixed-mount electro-binoculars, he was the sole visible representative of the vast technology buried in the green purgatory below.

Muted cries, moans, and primeval gurglings drifted up to him from the highest treetops. Some were frightening, some less so, but none were as indicative of power held in check as the four silvery starships which burst into view above the observer. Keeping a tight formation, they exploded through humid air to vanish in seconds into the morning cloud cover far above. Sound-shadows rattled the trees moments later, in a forlorn attempt to catch up to the engines which had produced them.

Slowly assuming attack formations combining X- and Y-wing ships, the various fighters began to move outward from the moon, out past the oceanic atmosphere of giant Yavin, out to meet the technologic executioner.

The man who had observed the byplay between Biggs and Luke now lowered his glare visor and adjusted his half-automatic, half-manual gunsights as he checked the ships to either side of him.

'Blue boys,' he addressed his intership pickup, 'this is Blue Leader. Adjust your selectors and check in. Approaching target at one point three ...'

Ahead, the bright sphere of what looked like one of Yavin's moons but wasn't began to glow with increasing brightness. It shone with an eerie metallic glow utterly unlike that of any natural satellite. As he watched the giant battle station make its way around the rim of Yavin, Blue Leader's thoughts traveled back over the years. Over the uncountable injustices, the innocents taken away for interrogation and never heard from again – the whole multitude of evils incurred by an increasingly corrupt and indifferent Imperial government. All those terrors and agonies were concentrated, magnified, represented by the single bloated feat of engineering they were approaching now.

'This is it, boys,' he said to the mike. 'Blue Two, you're too far out. Close it up, Wedge.'

The young pilot Luke had encountered in the temple briefing room glanced to starboard, then back to his instruments. He executed a slight adjustment, frowning. 'Sorry, boss. My ranger seems to be a few points off. I'll have to go on manual.'

'Check, Blue Two. Watch yourself. All ships, stand by to lock S-foils in attack mode.'

One after another, from Luke and Biggs, Wedge and the other members of Blue assault squadron, the replies came back. 'Standing by ...'

'Execute,' Blue Leader commanded, when John D. and Piggy had indicated they were in readiness.

The double wings on the X-wing fighters split apart, like narrow seeds. Each fighter now displayed four wings, its wing-mounted armament and quadruple engines now deployed for maximum firepower and maneuverability.

Ahead, the Imperial station continued to grow. Surface features became visible as each pilot recognized docking bays, broadcast antennae, and other man-made mountains and canyons.

As he neared that threatening black sphere for the second time, Luke's breathing grew faster. Automatic life-support machinery detected the respiratory shift and compensated properly.

Something began to buffet his ship, almost as if he were back in his skyhopper again, wrestling with the unpredictable winds of Tatooine. He experienced a bad moment of uncertainty until the calming voice of Blue Leader sounded in his ears.

'We're passing through their outer shields. Hold tight. Lock down freeze-floating controls and switch your own deflectors on, double front.'

The shaking and buffeting continued, worsened. Not knowing how to compensate, Luke did exactly what he should have: remained in control and followed orders. Then the turbulence was gone and the deathly cold peacefulness of space had returned.

'That's it, we're through,' Blue Leader told them quietly. 'Keep all channels silent until we're on top of them. It doesn't look like they're expecting much resistance.'

Though half the great station remained in shadow, they were now near enough for Luke to be able to discern individual lights on its surface. A ship that could show phases matching a moon ... once again he marveled at the misplaced ingenuity and effort which had gone into its construction. Thousands of lights scattered across its curving expanse gave it the appearance of a floating city.

Some of Luke's comrades, since this was their first sight of the station, were even more impressed. 'Look at the size of that thing!' Wedge Antilles gasped over his open pickup.

'Cut the chatter, Blue Two,' Blue Leader ordered. 'Accelerate to attack velocity.'

Grim determination showed in Luke's expression as he flipped several switches above his head and began adjusting his computer target readout. Artoo Detoo re-examined the nearing station and thought untranslatable electronic thoughts.

Blue Leader compared the station with the location of their proposed target area. 'Red Leader,' he called toward the pickup, 'this is Blue Leader. We're in position; you can go right in. The exhaust shaft is farther to the north. We'll keep 'em busy down here.'

Red Leader was the physical opposite of Luke's squadron commander. He resembled the popular notion of a credit accountant – short, slim, shy of face. His skills and dedication, however, easily matched those of his counterpart and old friend.

'We're starting for the target shaft now, Dutch. Stand by to take over if anything happens.'

'Check, Red Leader,' came the other's reply. 'We're going to cross their equatorial axis and try to draw their main fire. May the Force be with you.'

From the approaching swarm, two squads of fighters broke clear. The X-wing ships dove directly for the bulge of the station, far below, while the Y-ships curved down and northward over its surface.

Within the station, alarm sirens began a mournful, clangorous wail as slow-to-react personnel realized that the impregnable fortress was actually under organized attack. Admiral Motti and his tacticians had expected the Rebels' resistance to be centered around a massive defense of the moon itself. They were completely unprepared for an offensive response consisting of dozens of tiny snub ships.

Imperial efficiency was in the process of compensating for this strategic oversight. Soldiers scrambled to man enormous defensive-weapons emplacements. Servodrivers thrummed as powerful motors aligned the huge devices for firing. Soon a web of annihilation began to envelop the station as energy weapons, electrical bolts, and explosive solids ripped out at the oncoming rebel craft.

'This is Blue Five,' Luke announced to his mike as he nose dived his ship in a radical attempt to confuse any electronic predictors below. The gray surface of the battle station streaked past his ports. 'I'm going in.'

'I'm right behind you, Blue Five,' a voice recognizable as Biggs's sounded in his ears.

The target in Luke's sights was as stable as that of the Imperial defenders was evasive. Bolts flew from the tiny vessel's weapons. One started a huge fire on the dim surface below, which would burn until the crew of the station could shut off the flow of air to the damaged section.

Luke's glee turned to terror as he realized he couldn't swerve his craft in time to avoid passing through the fireball of unknown composition. 'Pull out, Luke, pull out!' Biggs was screaming at him.

But despite commands to shift course, the automatic pressors wouldn't allow the necessary centrifugal force. His fighter plunged into the expanding ball of superheated gases.

Then he was through and clear, on the other side. A rapid check of his controls enabled him to relax. Passage through the intense heat had been insufficient to damage anything vital – though all four wings bore streaks of black, carbonized testimony to the nearness of his escape.

Hell-flowers bloomed outside his ship as he swung it up and around in a sharp curve. 'You all right, Luke?' came Biggs's concerned query.

'I got a little toasted, but I'm okay.'

A different, stern voice sounded. 'Blue Five,' warned the squadron leader, 'you'd better give yourself more lead time or you're going to destroy yourself as well as the Imperial construction.'

'Yes, sir. I've got the hang of it now. Like you said, it's not *exactly* like flying a skyhopper.'

Energy bolts and sun-bright beams continued to create a chromatic maze in the space above the station as the rebel fighters crisscrossed back and forth over its surface, firing at whatever looked like a decent target. Two of the tiny craft concentrated on a power terminal. It blew up, throwing lightning-sized electric arcs from the station's innards.

Inside, troopers, mechanicals, and equipment were blown in all directions by subsidiary explosions as the effects of the blast traveled back down various conduits and cables. Where the explosion had hulled the station, escaping atmosphere sucked helpless soldiers and droids out into a bottomless black tomb.

Moving from position to position, a figure of dark calm amid the chaos, was Darth Vader. A harried Commander rushed up to him and reported breathlessly.

'Lord Vader, we count at least thirty of them, of two types. They are so small and quick the fixed guns cannot follow them accurately. They continuously evade the predictors.'

'Get all TIE crews to their fighters. We'll have to go out after them and destroy them ship by ship.'

Within numerous hangars red lights began flashing and an insistent alarm started to ring. Ground crews worked frantically to ready ships as flight-suited Imperial pilots grabbed for helmets and packs.

'Luke,' requested Blue Leader as he skimmed smoothly through a rain of fire, 'let me know when you're off the block.'

'I'm on my way now.'

'Watch yourself,' the voice urged over the cockpit speaker. 'There's a lot of fire coming from the starboard side of that deflection tower.'

'I'm on it, don't worry,' Luke responded confidently. Putting his fighter into a twisting dive, he sliced once more across metal horizons. Antennae and small protruding emplacements burst into transitory flame as bolts from his wing tips struck with deadly accuracy.

He grinned as he pulled up and away from the surface as intense lines of energy passed through space recently vacated. Darned if it *wasn't* like hunting womp-rats back home in the crumbling canyons of Tatooine's wastes.

Biggs followed Luke on a similar run, even as Imperial pilots prepared to lift clear of the station. Within the many docking bays technical crews rushed hurriedly to unlock power cables and conclude desperate final checks.

More care was taken in preparing a particular craft nearest one of the bay ports, the one into which Darth Vader barely succeeded in squeezing his huge frame. Once set in the seat he slid a second set of eye shields across his face.

The atmosphere of the war room back in the temple was one of nervous expectancy. Occasional blinks and buzzes from the main battle screen sounded louder than the soft sussuration of hopeful people trying to reassure one another. Near a far corner of the mass of flickering lights a technician leaned a little closer to his own readouts before speaking into the pickup suspended near his mouth.

'Squad leaders – attention; squad leaders – attention! We've picked up a new set of signals from the other side of the station. Enemy fighters coming your way.'

Luke received the report at the same time as everyone else. He began hunting the sky for the predicted Imperial craft, his gaze dropping to his instrumentation. 'My scope's negative. I don't see anything.'

'Maintain visual scanning,' Blue Leader directed. 'With all this energy flying, they'll be on top of you before your scope can pick them up. Remember, they can jam every instrument on your ship except your eyes.'

Luke turned again, and this time saw an Imperial already pursuing an X-wing – an X-wing with a number Luke quickly recognized.

'Biggs!' he shouted. 'You've picked one up. On your tail . . . watch it!'

'I can't see it,' came his friend's panicked response. 'Where is he? I can't see it.'

Luke watched helplessly as Biggs's ship shot away from the station surface and out into clear space, closely followed by the Imperial. The enemy vessel fired steadily at him, each successive bolt seeming to pass a little closer to Biggs's hull.

'He's on me tight,' the voice sounded in Luke's cockpit. 'I can't shake him.'

Twisting, spinning, Biggs looped back toward the battle station, but the pilot trailing him was persistent and showed no sign of relinquishing pursuit.

'Hang on, Biggs,' Luke called, wrenching his ship around so steeply that straining gyros whined. 'I'm coming in.'

So absorbed in his pursuit of Biggs was the Imperial pilot that he didn't see Luke, who rotated his own ship, flipped out of the concealing gray below and dropped in behind him.

Electronic crosshairs lined up according to the computer-readout instructions, and Luke fired repeatedly. There was a small explosion in space – tiny compared with the enormous energies being put out by the emplacements on the surface of the battle station. But the explosion was of particular significance to three people: Luke, Biggs, and, most particularly, to the pilot of the TIE fighter, who was vaporized with his ship.

'Got him!' Luke murmured.

'I've got one! I've got one!' came a less restrained cry of triumph over the open intercom. Luke identified the voice as belonging to a young pilot known as John D. Yes, that was Blue Six chasing another Imperial fighter across the metal landscape. Bolts jumped from the X-wing in steady succession until the TIE fighter blew in half, sending leaflike glittering metal fragments flying in all directions.

'Good shooting, Blue Six,' the squadron leader commented. Then he added quickly, 'Watch out, you've got one on your tail.'

Within the fighter's cockpit the gleeful smile on the young man's face vanished instantly as he looked around, unable to spot his pursuer. Something flared brightly nearby, so close that his starboard port burst. Then something hit even closer and the interior of the now open cockpit became a mass of flames.

'I'm hit, I'm hit!'

That was all he had time to scream before oblivion took him from behind. Far above and to one side Blue Leader saw John D.'s ship expand in a fiery ball. His lips may have whitened slightly. Otherwise he might as well never have seen the X-wing explode, for all the reaction he displayed. He had more important things to do.

On the fourth moon of Yavin a spacious screen chose that moment to flicker and die, much as John D. had. Worried technicians began rushing in all directions. One turned a drawn face to Leia, the expectant Commanders, and one tall, bronzed robot.

'The high-band receiver has failed. It will take some time to fix . . .'

'Do the best you can,' Leia snapped. 'Switch to audio only.'

Someone overheard, and in seconds the room was filled with the sounds of distant battle, interspersed with the voices of those involved.

'Tighten it up, Blue Two, tighten it up,' Blue Leader was saying. 'Watch those towers.'

'Heavy fire, Boss,' came the voice of Wedge Antilles, 'twenty-three degrees.'

'I see it. Pull in, pull in. We're picking up some interference.'

'I can't believe it,' Biggs was stammering. 'I've never seen such firepower!'

'Pull in, Blue Five. Pull in.' A pause, then, 'Luke, do you read me? Luke?'

'I'm all right, Chief,' came Luke's reply. 'I've got a target. I'm going to check it out.'

'There's too much action down there, Luke,' Biggs told him. 'Get out. Do you read me, Luke? Pull out.'

'Break off, Luke,' ordered the deeper tones of Blue Leader. 'We've hit too much interference here. Luke, I repeat, break off! I can't see him. Blue Two, can you see Blue Five?'

'Negative,' Wedge replied quickly. 'There's a fire zone here you wouldn't believe. My scanner's jammed. Blue Five, where are you? Luke, are you all right?'

'He's gone,' Biggs started to report solemnly. Then his voice rose. 'No, wait . . . there he is! Looks like a little fin damage, but the kid's fine.'

Relief swept the war room, and it was most noticeable in the face of the slightest, most beautiful Senator present.

On the battle station, troopers worn half to death or deafened by the concussion of the big guns were replaced by fresh crews. None of them had time to wonder how the battle was going, and at the moment none of them much cared, a malady shared by common soldiers since the dawn of history.

Luke skimmed daringly low over the station's surface, his attention riveted on a distant metal projection.

'Stick close, Blue Five,' the squadron commander directed him. 'Where are you going?'

'I've picked up what looks like a lateral stabilizer,' Luke replied. 'I'm going to try for it.'

'Watch yourself, Blue Five. Heavy fire in your area.'

Luke ignored the warning as he headed the fighter straight toward the oddly shaped protuberance. His determination was rewarded when, after saturating it with fire, he saw it erupt in a spectacular ball of superhot gas.

'Got it!' he exclaimed. 'Continuing south for another one.'

Within the rebel temple-fortress, Leia listened intently. She seemed simultaneously angry and frightened. Finally she turned to Threepio and muttered, 'Why is Luke taking so many chances?' The tall droid didn't reply.

'Watch your back, Luke,' Biggs's voice sounded over the speakers, 'watch your back! Fighters above you, coming in.'

Leia strained to see what she could only hear. She wasn't alone. 'Help him, Artoo,' Threepio was whispering to himself, 'and keep holding on.'

Luke continued his dive even as he looked back and spotted the object of Biggs's concern close on his tail. Reluctantly he pulled up and away from the station surface, abandoning his target. His tormentor was good, however, and continued closing on him.

'I can't shake him,' he reported.

Something cut across the sky toward both ships. 'I'm on him, Luke,' shouted Wedge Antilles. 'Hold on.'

Luke didn't have to for very long. Wedge's gunnery was precise, and the TIE fighter vanished brightly shortly thereafter.

'Thanks, Wedge,' Luke murmured, breathing a little more easily.

'Good shooting, Wedge.' That was Biggs again. 'Blue Four, I'm going in. Cover me, Porkins.'

'I'm right with you, Blue Three,' came the other pilot's assurance.

Biggs leveled them off, then let go with full weaponry. No one ever decided exactly what it was he hit, but the small tower that blew up under his energy bolts was obviously more important than it looked.

A series of sequential explosions hopscotched across a large section of the battle station's surface, leaping from one terminal to the next. Biggs had already shot past the area of disturbance, but his companion, following slightly behind, received a full dose of whatever energy was running wild down there.

'I've got a problem,' Porkins announced. 'My converter's running wild.' That was an understatement. Every instrument on his control panels had abruptly gone berserk.

'Eject – eject, Blue Four,' advised Biggs. 'Blue Four, do you read?'

'I'm okay,' Porkins replied. 'I can hold her. Give me a little room to run, Biggs.'

'You're too low,' his companion yelled. 'Pull up, pull up!'

With his instrumentation not providing proper information, and at the altitude he was traveling, Porkins's ship was simple for one of the big, clumsy gun emplacements to track. It did as its designers had intended it should. Porkins's demise was as glorious as it was abrupt.

It was comparatively quiet near the pole of the battle station. So intense and vicious had been Blue and Green squadron's assault on the equator that Imperial resistance had concentrated there. Red Leader surveyed the false peace with mournful satisfaction, knowing it wouldn't last for long.

'Blue Leader, this is Red Leader,' he announced into his mike. 'We're starting our attack run. The exhaust port is located and marked. No flak, no enemy fighters up here – yet. Looks like we'll get at least one smooth run at it.'

'I copy, Red Leader,' the voice of his counterpart responded. 'We'll try to keep them busy down here.'

Three Y-wing fighters dropped out of the stars, diving toward the battle-station surface. At the last possible minute they swerved to dip into a deep artificial canyon, one of many streaking the northern pole of the Death Star. Metal ramparts raced past on three sides of them.

Red Leader hunted around, noticed the temporary absence of Imperial fighters. He adjusted a control and addressed his squadron.

'This is it, boys. Remember, when you think you're close, go in closer before you drop that rock. Switch all power to front deflector screens – never mind what they throw at you from the side. We can't worry about that now.'

Imperial crews lining the trench rudely awoke to the fact that their heretofore ignored section of the station was coming under attack. They reacted speedily, and soon energy bolts were racing at the attacking ships in a steadily increasing volume. Occasionally one would explode near one of the onrushing Y-wings, jostling it without real damage.

'A little aggressive, aren't they,' Red Two reported over his mike.

Red Leader reacted quietly. 'How many guns do you think, Red Five?'

Red Five, known casually to most of the rebel pilots as Pops, somehow managed to make an estimate of the trench's defenses while simultaneously piloting his fighter through the growing hail of fire. His helmet was battered almost to the point of uselessness from the effects of more battles than anyone had a right to survive.

'I'd say about twenty emplacements,' he finally decided, 'some in the surface and some on the towers.'

Red Leader acknowledged the information with a grunt as he pulled his computer-targeting visor down in front of his face. Explosions continued to rock the fighter. 'Switch to targeting computers,' he declared.

'Red Two,' came one reply, 'computer locked in and I'm getting a signal.' The young pilot's rising excitement marked his reply.

But the senior pilot among all the rebels, Red Five, was expectantly cool and confident – though it didn't sound like it from what he murmured half to himself: 'No doubt about it, this is going to be some trick.'

Unexpectedly, all defensive fire from the surrounding emplacements ceased. An eerie quiet clung to the trench as the surface continued to blur past the skimming Y-wings.

'What's this?' Red Two blurted, looking around worriedly. 'They stopped. Why?'

'I don't like it,' growled Red Leader. But there was nothing to confuse their approach now, no energy bolts to avoid.

It was Pops who was first to properly evaluate this seeming aberration on the enemy's part. 'Stabilize your rear deflectors now. Watch for enemy fighters.'

'You pinned it, Pops,' Red Leader admitted, studying a readout. 'Here they come. Three marks at two-ten.'

A mechanical voice continued to recite the shrinking distance to their target, but it wasn't shrinking fast enough. 'We're sitting ducks down here,' he observed nervously.

'We'll just have to ride it out,' the old man told them all. 'We can't defend ourselves and go for the target at the same time.' He fought down old reflexes as his own screen revealed three TIE fighters in precision formation diving almost vertically down toward them.

'Three-eight-one-oh-four,' Darth Vader announced as he calmly adjusted his controls. The stars whipped past behind him. 'I'll take them myself. Cover me.'

Red Two was the first to die, the young pilot never knowing what hit him, never seeing his executioner. Despite his experience, Red Leader was on the verge of panic when he saw his wingman dissolve in flame.

'We're trapped down here. No way to maneuver – trench walls are too close. We've got to loosen it up somehow. Got—'

'Stay on target,' admonished an older voice. 'Stay on target.'

Red Leader took Pops's words like tonic, but it was all he could do to ignore the closing TIE fighters as the two remaining Y-wings continued to streak toward the target.

Above them, Vader permitted himself a moment of undisciplined pleasure as he readjusted his targeting 'puter. The rebel craft continued to travel a straight, unevasive course. Again Vader touched finger to fire control.

Something screeched in Red Leader's helmet, and fire started to consume his instrumentation. 'It's no good,' he yelled into his pickup, 'I'm hit. I'm hit . . .!'

A second Y-wing exploded in a ball of vaporized metal, scattering a few solid shards of debris across the trench. This second loss proved too much even for Red Five to take. He manipulated controls, and his ship commenced rising in a slow curve out of the trench. Behind him, the lead Imperial fighter moved to follow.

'Red Five to Blue Leader,' he reported. 'Aborting run under heavy fire. TIE fighters dropped on us out of nowhere. I can't – wait—'

Astern, a silent, remorseless enemy was touching a deadly button once more. The first bolts struck just as Pops had risen high enough to commence evasive action. But he had pulled clear a few seconds too late.

One energy beam seared his port engine, igniting gas within. The engine blew apart, taking controls and stabilizing elements with it. Unable to compensate, the out-of-control Y-wing began a long, graceful plunge toward the station surface.

'Are you all right, Red Five?' a troubled voice called over the intership system.

'Lost Tiree . . . lost Dutch,' Pops explained slowly, tiredly. 'They drop in behind you, and you can't maneuver in the trench. Sorry . . . it's your baby now. So long, Dave. . . .'

It was the last message of many from a veteran.

Blue Leader forced a crispness he didn't feel into his voice as he tried to shunt aside the death of his old friend. 'Blue boys, this is Blue Leader. Rendezvous at mark six point one. All wings report in.'

'Blue Leader, this is Blue Ten. I copy.'

'Blue Two here,' Wedge acknowledged. 'Coming toward you, Blue Leader.'

Luke was also waiting his turn to report when something beeped on his control board. A glance backward confirmed the electronic warning as he spotted an Imperial fighter slipping in behind him.

'This is Blue Five,' he declared, his ship wobbling as he tried to lose the TIE fighter. 'I have a problem here. Be right with you.'

He sent his ship into a steep dive toward the metal surface, then cut sharply up to avoid a burst of defensive fire from emplacements below. Neither maneuver shook his pursuit.

'I see you, Luke,' came a reassuring call from Biggs. 'Stay with it.'

Luke looked above, below, and to the sides, but there was no sign of his friend. Meanwhile, energy bolts from his trailing assailant were passing uncomfortably close.

'Blast it, Biggs, where are you?'

Something appeared, not to the sides or behind, but almost directly in front of him. It was bright and moving incredibly fast, and then it was firing just above him. Taken completely by surprise, the Imperial fighter came apart just as its pilot realized what had happened.

Luke turned for the rendezvous mark as Biggs shot past overhead. 'Good move, Biggs. Fooled me, too.'

'I'm just getting started,' his friend announced as he twisted his ship violently to avoid the fire from below. He hove into view over Luke's shoulder and executed a victory roll. 'Just point me at the target.'

Back alongside Yavin's indifferent bulk, Dodonna finished an intense discussion with several of his principal advisors, then moved to the long-range transmitter.

'Blue Leader, this is Base One. Double-check your own attack prior to commencement. Have your wingmen hold back and cover for you. Keep half your group out of range to make the next run.'

'Copy, Base One,' the response came. 'Blue Ten, Blue Twelve, join with me.'

Two ships leveled off to flank the squadron commander. Blue Leader checked them out. Satisfied that they were positioned properly for the attack run, he set the group to follow in case they should fail.

'Blue Five, this is Blue Leader, Luke, take Blue Two and Three with you. Hold up here out of their fire and wait for my signal to start your own run.'

'Copy, Blue Leader,' Luke acknowledged, trying to slow his heart slightly. 'May the force be with you. Biggs, Wedge, let's close it up.' Together, the three fighters assumed a tight formation high above the firefight still raging between other rebel craft of Green and Yellow squadrons and the imperial gunners below.

The horizon flip-flopped ahead of Blue Leader as he commenced his approach to the station surface. 'Blue Ten, Blue Twelve, stay back until we spot those fighters, then cover me.'

All three X-wings reached the surface, leveled off, then arced into the trench. His wingmen dropped farther and farther behind until Blue Leader was seemingly alone in the vast gray chasm.

No defensive fire greeted him as he raced toward the distant target. He found himself looking around nervously, checking and rechecking the same instruments.

'This doesn't look right,' he found himself muttering.

Blue Ten sounded equally concerned. 'You should be able to pick up the target by now.'

'I know. The disruption down here is unbelievable. I think my instruments are off. Is this the right trench?'

Suddenly, intense streaks of light began to shoot close by as the trench defenses opened up. Near misses shook the attackers. At the far end of the trench a huge tower dominated the metal ridge, vomiting enormous amounts of energy at the nearing ships.

'It's not going to be easy with that tower up there,' Blue Leader declared grimly. 'Stand by to close up a little when I tell you.'

Abruptly the energy bolts ceased and all was silent and dark in the trench once again. 'This is it,' Blue Leader announced, trying to locate the attack from above that had to be coming. 'Keep your eyes open for those fighters.'

'All short- and long-range scopes are blank,' Blue Ten reported tensely. 'Too much interference here. Blue Five, can you see them from where you are?'

Luke's attention was riveted to the surface of the station. 'No sign of— Wait!' Three rapidly moving points of light caught his eye. 'There they are. Coming in point three five.'

Blue Ten turned and looked in the indicated direction. Sun bounced off stabilizing fins as the TIE fighters looped downward. 'I see them.'

'It's the right trench, all right,' Blue Leader exclaimed as his tracking scope suddenly began a steady beeping. He adjusted his targeting instrumentation, pulling his visor down over his eyes. 'I'm almost in range. Targets ready ... coming up. Just hold them off me for a few seconds – keep 'em busy.'

But Darth Vader was already setting his own fire control as he dropped like a stone toward the trench. 'Close up the formation. I'll take them myself.'

Blue Twelve went first, both engines blown. A slight deviation in flight path and his ship slammed into the trench wall. Blue Ten slowed and accelerated, bobbed drunkenly, but could do little within the confines of those metal walls.

'I can't hold them long. You'd better fire while you can, Blue Leader – we're closing on you.'

The squadron commander was wholly absorbed in lining up two circles within his targeting visor. 'We're almost home. Steady, steady . . .'

Blue Ten glanced around frantically. 'They're right behind me!'

Blue Leader was amazed at how calm he was. The targeting device was partly responsible, enabling him to concentrate on tiny, abstract images to the exclusion of all else, helping him to shut out the rest of the inimical universe.

'Almost there, almost there . . .' he whispered. Then the two circles matched, turned red, and a steady buzzing sounded in his helmet. 'Torpedoes away, torpedoes away.'

Immediately after, Blue Ten let his own missiles loose. Both fighters pulled up sharply, just clearing the end of the trench as several explosions billowed in their wake.

'It's a hit! We've done it!' Blue Ten shouted hysterically.

Blue Leader's reply was thick with disappointment. 'No, we haven't. They didn't go in. They just exploded on the surface outside the shaft.'

Disappointment killed them, too, as they neglected to watch behind them. Three pursuing Imperial fighters continued up out of the fading light from the torpedo explosions. Blue Ten fell to Vader's precision fire, then the Dark Lord changed course slightly to fall in behind the squadron commander.

'I'll take the last one,' he announced coldly. 'You two go back.'

Luke was trying to pick the assault team out of the glowing gases below when Blue Leader's voice sounded over the communicator.

'Blue Five, this is Blue Leader. Move into position, Luke. Start your attack run – stay low and wait until you're right on top of it. It's not going to be easy.'

'Are you all right?'

'They're on top of me – but I'll shake them.'

'Blue Five to Blue pack,' Luke ordered, 'let's go!' The three ships peeled off and plunged toward the trench sector.

Meanwhile Vader finally succeeded in hitting his quarry, a glancing bolt that nonetheless started small, intense explosions in one engine. Its R-2 unit scrambled back toward the damaged wing and struggled to repair the crippled power plant.

'R-2, shut off the main feed to number-one starboard engine,' Blue Leader directed quietly, staring resignedly at instruments which were running impossibilities. 'Hang on tight, this could get rough.'

Luke saw that Blue Leader was in trouble. 'We're right above you, Blue Leader,' he declared. 'Turn to point oh five, and we'll cover for you.'

'I've lost my upper starboard engine,' came the reply.

'We'll come down for you.'

'Negative, negative. Stay there and get set up for your attack run.'

'You're sure you're all right?'

'I think so . . . Stand by for a minute.'

Actually, it was somewhat less than a minute before Blue Leader's gyrating X-wing plowed into the surface of the station.

Luke watched the huge explosion dissipate below him, knowing without question its cause, sensing fully for the first time the helplessness of his situation. 'We just lost Blue Leader,' he murmured absently, not particularly caring if his mike picked up the somber announcement.

On Yavin Four, Leia Organa rose from her chair and nervously began pacing the room. Normally perfect nails were now jagged and uneven from nervous chewing. It was the only indication of physical unease. The anxiety visible in her expression was far more revealing of her feelings, an anxiety and worry that filled the war room on the announcement of Blue Leader's death.

'Can they go on?' she finally asked Dodonna.

The general replied with gentle resolve. 'They must.'

'But we've lost so *many*. Without Blue or Red Leader, how will they regroup?'

Dodonna was about to reply, but held his words as more critical ones sounded over the speakers.

'Close it up, Wedge,' Luke was saying, thousands of kilometers away. 'Biggs, where are you?'

'Coming in right behind you.'

Wedge replied soon after. 'Okay, Boss, we're in position.'

Dodonna's gaze went to Leia. He looked concerned.

The three X-wings moved close together high above the battle station's surface. Luke studied his instruments and fought irritably with one control that appeared to be malfunctioning.

Someone's voice sounded in his ears. It was a young-old voice, a familiar voice: calm, content, confident, and reassuring – a voice he had listened to intently on the desert of Tatooine and in the guts of the station below, once upon a time.

'Trust your feelings, Luke,' was all the Kenobi-like voice said.

Luke tapped his helmet, unsure whether he had heard anything or not. This was no time for introspection. The steely horizon of the station tilted behind him.

'Wedge, Biggs, we're going in,' he told his wingmen. 'We'll go in full speed. Never mind finding the trench and then accelerating. Maybe that will keep those fighters far enough behind us.'

'We'll stay far enough back to cover you,' Biggs declared. 'At that speed will you be able to pull out in time?'

'Are you kidding?' Luke sneered playfully as they began their dive toward the surface. 'It'll be just like Beggars Canyon back home.'

'I'm right with you, *Boss*,' noted Wedge, emphasizing the title for the first time. 'Let's go . . .'

At high speed the three slim fighters charged the glowing surface, pulling out *after* the last moment. Luke skimmed so close over the station hull that the tip of one wing grazed a protruding antenna, sending metal splinters flying. Instantly they were enveloped in a meshwork of energy bolts and explosive projectiles. It intensified as they dropped down into the trench.

'We seem to have upset them,' Biggs chortled, treating the deadly display of energy as though it were all a show being put on for their amusement.

'This is fine,' Luke commented, surprised at the clear view ahead. 'I can see everything.'

Wedge wasn't quite as confident as he studied his own readouts. 'My scope shows the tower, but I can't make out the exhaust port. It must be awfully small. Are you sure the computer can target it?'

'It better,' Biggs muttered.

Luke didn't offer an evaluation – he was too busy holding a course through the turbulence produced by exploding bolts. Then, as if on command, the defensive fire ceased. He glanced around and up for signs of the expected TIE fighters, but saw nothing.

His hand went to drop the targeting visor into position, and for just a moment he hesitated. Then he swung it down in front of his eyes. 'Watch yourselves,' he ordered his companions.

'What about the tower?' Wedge asked worriedly.

'You worry about those fighters,' Luke snapped. 'I'll worry about the tower.'

They rushed on, closing on the target every second. Wedge stared upward, and his gaze suddenly froze. 'Here they come – oh point three.'

Vader was setting his controls when one of his wingmen broke attack silence. 'They're making their approach too fast – they'll never get out in time.'

'Stay with them,' Vader commanded.

'They're going too fast to get a fix,' his other pilot announced with certainty.

Vader studied several readouts and found that his sensors confirmed the other estimates. 'They'll still have to slow down before they reach that tower.'

Luke contemplated the view in his targeting visor. 'Almost home.' Seconds passed and the twin circlets achieved congruence. His finger convulsed on the firing control. 'Torpedoes away! Pull up, pull up.'

Two powerful explosions rocked the trench, striking harmlessly far to one side of the minute opening. Three TIE fighters shot out of the rapidly dissipating fireball, closing on the retreating rebels. 'Take them,' Vader ordered softly.

Luke detected the pursuit at the same time as his companions. 'Wedge, Biggs, split up – it's the only way we'll shake them.'

The three ships dropped toward the station, then abruptly raced off in three different directions. All three TIE fighters turned and followed Luke.

Vader fired on the crazily dodging ship, missed, and frowned to himself. 'The Force is strong with this one. Strange. I'll take him myself.'

Luke darted between defensive towers and wove a tight path around projecting docking bays, all to no avail. A single remaining TIE fighter stayed close behind. An energy bolt nicked one wing, close by an engine. It started to spark irregularly, threateningly. Luke fought to compensate and retain full control.

Still trying to shake his persistent assailant, he dropped back into a trench again. 'I'm hit,' he announced, 'but not bad. Artoo, see what you can do with it.'

The tiny droid unlocked himself and moved to work on the damaged engine as energy bolts flashed by dangerously close. 'Hang on back there,' Luke counseled the Artoo unit as he worked a path around projecting towers, the fighter spinning and twisting tightly through the topography of the station.

Fire remained intense as Luke randomly changed direction and speed. A series of indicators on the control panel slowly changed color; three vital gauges relaxed and returned to where they belonged.

'I think you've got it, Artoo,' Luke told him gratefully. 'I think – there, that's it. Just try to lock it down so it can't work loose again.'

Artoo beeped in reply while Luke studied the whirling panorama behind and above them. 'I think we've lost those fighters, too. Blue group, this is Blue Five. Are you clear?' He manipulated several controls and the X-wing shot out of the trench, still followed by emplacement fire.

'I'm up here waiting, Boss,' Wedge announced from his position high above the station. 'I can't see you.'

'I'm on my way. Blue Three, are you clear? Biggs?'

'I've had some trouble,' his friend explained, 'but I think I lost him.'

Something showed again, damnably, on Biggs's screen. A glance behind showed the TIE fighter that had been chasing him for the past several minutes dropping in once more behind him. He swung down toward the station again.

'Nope, not yet,' Biggs told the others. 'Hold on, Luke. I'll be right there.'

A thin, mechanical voice sounded over the speakers. 'Hang on, Artoo, hang on!' Back at the temple headquarters, Threepio turned away from the curious human faces which had turned to stare at him.

As Luke soared high above the station another X-wing swung in close to him. He recognized Wedge's ship and began hunting around anxiously for his friend.

'We're goin' in, Biggs – join up. Biggs, are you all right? Biggs!' There was no sign of the other fighter. 'Wedge, do you see him anywhere?'

Within the transparent canopy of the fighter bobbing close by, a helmeted head shook slowly. 'Nothing,' Wedge told him over the communicator. 'Wait a little longer. He'll show.'

Luke looked around, worried, studied several instruments, then came to a decision. 'We can't wait; we've got to go now. I don't think he made it.'

'Hey, you guys,' a cheerful voice demanded to know, 'what are you waiting for?'

Luke turned sharply to his right, in time to see another ship racing past and slowing slightly ahead of him. 'Don't ever give up on old Biggs,' the intercom directed as the figure in the X-wing ahead looked back at them.

Within the central control room of the battle station, a harried officer rushed up to a figure studying the great battle screen and waved a handful of printouts at him.

'Sir, we've completed an analysis of their attack plan. There is a danger. Should we break off the engagement or make plans to evacuate? Your ship is standing by.'

Governor Tarkin turned an incredulous gaze on the officer, who shrank back. 'Evacuate!' he roared. 'At our moment of triumph? We are about to destroy the last remnants of the Alliance, and you call for evacuation? You overestimate their chances badly . . . Now, get out!'

Overwhelmed by the Governor's fury, the subdued officer turned and retreated from the room.

'We're going in,' Luke declared as he commenced his dive toward the surface. Wedge and Biggs followed just aft.

'Let's go – Luke,' a voice he had heard before sounded inside his head. Again he tapped his helmet and looked around. It sounded as if the speaker were standing just behind him. But there was nothing, only silent metal and nonverbal instrumentation. Puzzled, Luke turned back to his controls.

Once more, energy bolts reached out for them, passing harmlessly on both sides as the surface of the battle station charged up into his face. But the defensive fire wasn't the cause of the renewed trembling Luke suddenly experienced. Several critical gauges were beginning their swing back into the danger zone again.

He leaned toward the pickup. 'Artoo, those stabilizing elements must have broken loose again. See if you can't lock it back down – I've got to have full control.'

Ignoring the bumpy ride, the energy beams and explosions lighting space around him, the little robot moved to repair the damage.

Additional, tireless explosions continued to buffet the three fighters as they dropped into the trench. Biggs and Wedge dropped behind to cover for Luke as he reached to pull down the targeting visor.

For the second time a peculiar hesitation swept through him. His hand was slower yet as he finally pulled the device down in front of his eyes, almost as if the nerves were in conflict with one another. As expected, the energy beams stopped as if on signal and he was barreling down the trench unchallenged.

'Here we go again,' Wedge declared as he spotted three Imperial fighters dropping down on them.

Biggs and Wedge began crossing behind Luke, trying to draw the coming fire away from him and confuse their pursuers. One TIE fighter ignored the maneuvers, continuing to gain inexorably on the rebel ships.

Luke stared into the targeting device – then reached up slowly to move it aside. For a long minute he pondered the deactivated instrument, staring at it as if hypnotized. Then he slid it sharply back in front of his face and studied the tiny screen as it displayed the shifting relationship of the X-wing to the nearing exhaust port.

'Hurry, Luke,' Biggs called out as he wrenched his ship in time to narrowly avoid a powerful beam. 'They're coming in faster this time. We can't hold them much longer.'

With inhuman precision, Darth Vader depressed the fire control of his fighter again. A loud, desperate shout sounded over the speakers, blending into a final agonized scream of flesh and metal as Biggs's fighter burst into a billion glowing splinters that rained down on the bottom of the trench.

Wedge heard the explosion over his speakers and hunted frantically behind him for the trailing enemy ships. 'We lost Biggs,' he yelled toward his own pickup.

Luke didn't reply immediately. His eyes were watering, and he angrily wiped them clear. They were blurring his view of the targeting readout.

'We're a couple of shooting stars, Biggs,' he whispered huskily, 'and we'll never be stopped.' His ship rocked slightly from a near miss and he directed his words to his remaining wingman, biting down hard on the end of each sentence.

'Close it up, Wedge. You can't do any more good back there. Artoo, try to give me a little more power on our rear reflectors.'

The Artoo unit hurried to comply as Wedge pulled up alongside Luke's ship. The trailing TIE fighters also increased their speed.

'I'm on the leader,' Vader informed his soldiers. 'Take the other one.'

Luke flew just in front of Wedge, slightly to port side. Energy bolts from the pursuing Imperials began to streak close about them. Both men crossed each other's path repeatedly, striving to present as confusing a target as possible.

Wedge was fighting with his controls when several small flashes and sparks lit his control board. One small panel exploded, leaving molten slag behind. Somehow he managed to retain control of the ship.

'I've got a bad malfunction, Luke. I can't stay with you.'

'Okay, Wedge, get clear.'

Wedge mumbled a heartfelt 'Sorry' and peeled up out of the trench.

Vader, concentrating his attention on the one ship remaining before him, fired.

Luke didn't see the near-lethal explosion which burst close behind him. Nor did he have time to examine the smoking shell of twisted metal which now rode alongside one engine. The arms went limp on the little droid.

All three TIE fighters continued to chase the remaining X-wing down the trench. It was only a matter of moments before one of them caught the bobbing fighter with a crippling burst. Except now there were only two Imperials pursuing. The third had become an expanding cylinder of decomposing debris, bits and pieces of which slammed into the walls of the canyon.

Vader's remaining wingman looked around in panic for the source of the attack. The same distortion fields that confused rebel instrumentation now did likewise to the two TIE fighters.

Only when the freighter fully eclipsed the sun forward did the new threat become visible. It was a Corellian transport, far larger than any fighter, and it was diving directly at the trench. But it didn't move precisely like a freighter, somehow.

Whoever was piloting that vehicle must have been unconscious or out of his mind, the wingman decided. Wildly he adjusted controls in an attempt to avoid the anticipated collision. The freighter swept by just overhead, but in missing it the wingman slid too far to one side.

A small explosion followed as two huge fins of the paralleling TIE fighters intersected. Screaming uselessly into his pickup, the wingman fluttered toward the near trench wall. He never touched it, his ship erupting in flame before contact.

To the other side, Darth Vader's fighter began spinning helplessly. Unimpressed by the Dark Lord's desperate glower, various controls and instruments gave back readings which were brutally truthful. Completely out of control, the tiny ship continued spinning in the opposite direction from the destroyed wingman – out into the endless reaches of deep space.

Whoever was at the controls of the supple freighter was neither unconscious nor insane – well, perhaps slightly touched, but fully in command nonetheless. It soared high above the trench, turning to run protectively above Luke.

'You're all clear now, kid,' a familiar voice informed him. 'Now blow this thing so we can all go home.'

This pep talk was followed by a reinforcing grunt which could only have been produced by a particularly large Wookiee.

Luke looked up through the canopy and smiled. But his smile faded as he turned back to the targeting visor. There was a tickling inside his head.

'Luke . . . trust me,' the tickle requested, forming words for the third time. He stared into the targeter. The emergency exhaust port was sliding toward the firing circle again, as it had once before – when he'd missed. He hesitated, but only briefly this time, then shoved the targeting screen aside. Closing his eyes, he appeared to mumble to himself, as if in internal conversation with something unseen. With the confidence of a blind man in familiar surroundings, Luke moved a thumb over several controls, then touched one. Soon after, a concerned voice filled the cockpit from the open speakers.

'Base One to Blue Five, your targeting device is switched off. What's wrong?'

'Nothing,' Luke murmured, barely audible. 'Nothing.'

He blinked and cleared his eyes. Had he been asleep? Looking around, he saw that he was out of the trench and shooting back into open space. A glance outside showed the familiar shape of Han Solo's ship shadowing him. Another, at the control board, indicated that he had released his remaining torpedoes, although he couldn't remember touching the firing stud. Still, he must have.

The cockpit speakers were alive with excitement. 'You did it! You did it!' Wedge was shouting over and over. 'I think they went right in.'

'Good shot kid.' Solo complimented him, having to raise his voice to be heard over Chewbacca's unrestrained howling.

Distant, muted rumblings shook Luke's ship, an omen of incipient success. He must have fired the torpedoes, mustn't he? Gradually he regained his composure.

'Glad ... you were here to see it. Now let's get some distance between us and that thing before it goes. I hope Wedge was right.'

Several X-wings, Y-wings, and one battered-looking freighter accelerated away from the battle station, racing toward the distant curve of Yavin.

Behind them small flashes of fading light marked the receding station. Without warning, something appeared in the sky in place of it which was brighter than the glowing gas giant, brighter than its far-off sun. For a few seconds the eternal night became day. No one dared look directly at it. Not even multiple shields set on high could dim that awesome flare.

Space filled temporarily with trillions of microscopic metal fragments, propelled past the retreating ships by the liberated energy of a small artificial sun. The collapsed residue of the battle station would continue to consume itself for several days, forming for that brief span of time the most impressive tombstone in this corner of the cosmos.

XIII

A CHEERING, gleeful throng of technicians, mechanics, and other inhabitants of the Alliance headquarters swarmed around each fighter as it touched down and taxied into the temple hangar. Several of the other surviving pilots had already vacated their ships and were waiting to greet Luke.

On the opposite side of the fighter, the crowd was far smaller and more restrained. It consisted of a couple of technicians and one tall, humanoid droid who watched worriedly as the humans mounted the scorched fighter and lifted a badly burned metal hulk from its back.

'Oh, my! Artoo?' Threepio pleaded, bending close to the carbonized robot. 'Can you hear me? Say something.' His unwinking gaze turned to one of the techs. 'You can repair him, can't you?'

'We'll do our best.' The man studied the vaporized metal, the dangling components. 'He's taken a terrible beating.'

'You must repair him! Sir, if any of my circuits or modules will help, I'll gladly donate them . . .'

They moved slowly away, oblivious to the noise and excitement around them. Between robots and the humans who repaired them there existed a very special relationship. Each partook a little of the other and sometimes the dividing line between man and machine was more blurred than many would admit.

The center of the carnival atmosphere was formed by three figures who battled to see who could compliment the others the most. When it came to congratulatory back-slapping, however, Chewbacca won by default. There was laughter as the Wookiee looked embarrassed at having nearly flattened Luke in his eagerness to greet him.

'I knew you'd come back,' Luke was shouting, 'I just knew it! I would've been nothing but dust if you hadn't sailed in like that, Han!'

Solo had lost none of his smug self-assurance. 'Well, I couldn't very well let a flying farm boy go up against that station all by himself. Besides, I was beginning to realize what could happen, and I felt terrible about it, Luke – leaving you to maybe take all the credit and get all the reward.'

As they laughed, a lithe figure, robes flowing, rushed up to Luke in a very unsenatorial fashion. 'You did it, Luke, you did it!' Leia was shouting.

She fell into his arms and hugged him as he spun her around. Then she moved to Solo and repeated the embrace. Expectantly, the Corellian was not quite as embarrassed.

Suddenly awed by the adulation of the crowd, Luke turned away. He gave the tired fighter a look of approval, then found his gaze traveling upward, up to the ceiling high overhead. For a second he thought he heard something faintly like a gratified sigh, a relaxing of muscles a crazy old man had once performed in moments of pleasure. Of course, it was probably the intruding hot wind of a steaming jungle world, but Luke smiled anyway at what he thought he saw up there.

There were many rooms in the vast expanse of the temple which had been converted for modern service by the technicians of the Alliance. Even in their desperate need, however, there was something too clean and classically beautiful about the ruins of the ancient throne room for the architects to modify. They had left it as it was, save for scouring it clear of creeping jungle growth and debris.

For the first time in thousands of years that spacious chamber was full. Hundreds of rebel troops and technicians stood assembled on the old stone floor, gathered together for one last time before dispersing to new posts and distant homes. For the first time ever the massed ranks of pressed uniforms and polished semi-armor stood arrayed together in a fitting show of Alliance might.

The banners of the many worlds which had lent support to the rebellion fluttered in the gentle breeze formed inside. At the far end of a long open aisle stood a vision gowned in formal white, barred with chalcedony waves – Leia Organa's signet of office.

Several figures appeared at the far end of the aisle. One, massive and hirsute, showed signs of running for cover, but was urged on down the open row by his companion. It took several minutes for Luke, Han, Chewie, and Threepio to cover the distance to the other end.

They stopped before Leia, and Luke recognized General Dodonna among the other dignitaries seated nearby. There was a pause and a gleaming, familiar Artoo unit joined the group, moving to stand next to a thoroughly awestruck Threepio.

Chewbacca shuffled nervously, giving every indication of wishing he were someplace else. Solo silenced him as Leia rose and came forward. At the same time banners tilted in unison and all those gathered in the great hall turned to face the dais.

She placed something heavy and golden around Solo's neck, then Chewbacca's – having to strain to do so – and finally around Luke's. Then she made a signal to the crowd, and the rigid discipline dissolved as every man, woman, and mechanical present was permitted to give full vent to their feelings.

As he stood awash in the cheers and shouts, Luke found that his mind was neither on his possible future with the Alliance nor on the chance of traveling adventurously with Han Solo and Chewbacca. Instead, unlikely as Solo had claimed it might be, he found his full attention occupied by the radiant Leia Organa.

She noticed his unabashed stare, but this time she only smiled.

EPISODE
V

STAR WARS®:

The Empire Strikes Back®

by **Donald F. Glut**

Based on a story by **George Lucas**

I

'NOW this is what I call cold!' Luke Skywalker's voice broke the silence he had observed since leaving the newly established Rebel base hours earlier. He was astride a Tauntaun, the only other living being as far as the eye could see. He felt tired and alone, and the sound of his own voice startled him.

Luke as well as his fellow members of the Rebel Alliance took turns exploring the white wastelands of Hoth, gathering information about their new home. They all returned to base with mixed feelings of comfort and loneliness. There was nothing to contradict their earliest findings that no intelligent lifeforms existed on this cold planet. All that Luke had seen on his solitary expeditions were barren white plains and ranges of blue-tinged mountains that seemed to vanish in the mists of the distant horizons.

Luke smiled behind the masklike gray bandana that protected him against Hoth's frigid winds. Peering out at the icy wastes through his goggles, he pulled his fur-lined cap down more snugly about his head.

One corner of his mouth curled upward as he tried to visualize the official researchers in the service of the Imperial government. 'The galaxy is peppered with settlements of colonizers who care little about the affairs of the Empire or its opposition, the Rebel Alliance,' he thought. 'But a settler would have to be crazy to stake his claims on Hoth. This planet doesn't have a thing to offer anyone – except *us*.'

The Rebel Alliance had established an outpost on the ice world little more than a month before. Luke was well-known on the base and, although barely twenty-three years old, he was addressed as *Commander* Skywalker by other Rebel warriors. The title made him feel a bit uncomfortable. Nonetheless, he was already in the position of giving orders to a band of seasoned soldiers. So much had happened to Luke and he had changed a great deal. Luke, himself, found it hard to believe that only three years ago he was a wide-eyed farm boy on his home world of Tatooine.

The youthful commander spurred his Tauntaun. 'Come on, girl,' he urged.

The snow-lizard's gray body was insulated from the cold by a covering of thick fur. It galloped on muscular hind legs, its tridactyl feet terminating in large hooked claws that dug up great plumes of snow. The Tauntaun's llamalike head thrust forward and its serpentine tail coiled out behind as the beast ran up the ice slope. The animal's horned head turned from side to side buffeting the winds that assaulted its shaggy muzzle.

Luke wished his mission were finished. His body felt nearly frozen in spite of his heavily padded Rebel-issue clothing. But he knew that it was his choice to be there; he had volunteered to ride across the ice fields looking for other lifeforms. He shivered as he looked at the long shadow he and the beast cast on the snow. 'The winds are picking up,' he thought. 'And these chilling winds bring unendur-able temperatures to the plains after nightfall.' He was tempted to return to the base a little early, but he knew the importance of establishing the certainty that the Rebels were alone on Hoth.

The Tauntaun quickly turned to the right, almost throwing Luke off-balance. He was still getting used to riding the unpredictable creatures. 'No offense,' he said to his mount, 'but I'd feel a lot more at ease in the cockpit of my old reliable landspeeder.' But for this mission, a Tauntaun – despite its disadvantages – was the most efficient and practical form of transportation available on Hoth.

When the beast reached the top of another ice slope, Luke brought the animal to halt. He pulled off his dark-lensed goggles and squinted for a few moments, just long enough for his eyes to adjust to the blinding glare of the snow.

Suddenly his attention was diverted by the appearance of an object streaking across the sky, leaving behind a lingering trail of smoke as it dipped toward the misty horizon. Luke flashed his gloved hand to his utility belt and clutched his pair of electrobinoculars. Apprehensive, he felt a chill that competed with the coldness of the Hoth atmosphere. What he had seen could have been man-made, perhaps even something launched by the Empire. The young commander, still focused on the object, followed its fiery course and watched intently as it crashed on the white ground and was consumed in its own explosive brilliance.

At the sound of the explosion, Luke's Tauntaun shuddered. A fearful growl escaped its muzzle and it began to claw nervously at the snow. Luke patted the animal's head, trying to reassure the beast. He found it difficult to hear himself over the blustering wind. 'Easy, girl, it's just another meteorite!' he shouted. The animal calmed and Luke brought the communicator to his mouth. 'Echo Three to Echo Seven. Han ol' buddy, do you read me?'

Static crackled from the receiver. Then a familiar voice cut through the interference. 'Is that you, kid? What's up?'

The voice sounded a little older and somewhat sharper than Luke's. For a moment Luke fondly recalled first meeting the Corellian space smuggler in that dark, alien-packed cantina at a spaceport on Tatooine. And now he was one of Luke's only friends who was not an official member of the Rebel Alliance.

'I've finished my circle and I haven't picked up any life readings,' Luke spoke into his comlink, pressing his mouth close to the transmitter.

'There isn't enough life on this ice cube to fill a space cruiser,' Han answered, fighting to make his voice heard above the whistling winds. 'My sentry markers are placed. I'm heading back to base.'

'See you shortly,' Luke replied. He still had his eye on the twisting column of dark smoke rising from a black spot in the distance. 'A meteorite just hit the ground near here and I want to check it out. I won't be long.'

Clicking off his comlink, Luke turned his attention to his Tauntaun. The reptilian creature was pacing, shifting its weight from one foot to the other. It gave out a deep-throated roar that seemed to signal fear.

'Whoa, girl!' he said, patting the Tauntaun's head. 'What's the matter . . . you smell something? There's nothing out there.'

But Luke, too, was beginning to feel uneasy, for the first time since he had set out from the hidden Rebel base. If he knew anything about these snowlizards, it was that their senses were keen. Without question the animal was trying to tell Luke that something, some danger, was near.

Not wasting a moment, Luke removed a small object from his utility belt and adjusted its miniature controls. The device was sensitive enough to zero in on even the most minute life readings by detecting body temperature and internal life systems. But as Luke began to scan the readings, he realized there was no need – or time – to continue.

A shadow crossed over him, towering above by a good meter and a half. Luke spun around and suddenly it seemed as if the terrain itself had come to life. A great white-furred bulk, perfectly camouflaged against the sprawling mounds of snow, rushed savagely at him.

'Son of a jumpin' . . .'

Luke's hand blaster never cleared its holster. The huge claw of the Wampa Ice Creature struck him hard and flat against his face, knocking him off the Tauntaun and into the freezing snow.

Unconsciousness came swiftly to Luke, so swiftly that he never even heard the pitiful screams of the Tauntaun nor the abrupt silence following the sound of a snapping neck. And he never felt his own ankle savagely gripped by his giant, hairy attacker, or felt his body dragged like a lifeless doll across the snow-covered plain.

Black smoke was still rising from the depression in the hillside where the air-borne thing had fallen. The smoky clouds had thinned considerably since the object had crashed to the ground and formed a smoldering crater, the dark fumes being dispersed over the plains by the icy Hoth winds.

Something stirred within the crater.

First there was only a sound, a droning mechanical sound swelling in intensity as if to compete with the howling wind. Then the thing moved – something that glinted in the bright afternoon light as it slowly began to rise from the crater.

The object appeared to be some form of alien organic life, its head a multiorbed, skull-like horror, its dark-lensed blister eyes training their cold gaze across the even colder reaches of wilderness. But as the thing rose higher from the crater, its form showed it clearly to be a machine of some sort, possessing a large cylindrical 'body' connected to a circular head, and equipped with cameras, sensors, and metal appendages, some of which terminated in crablike grasping pincers.

The machine hovered over the smoking crater and extended its appendages in various directions. Then a signal was set off within its internal mechanical systems, and the machine began to float across the icy plain.

The dark probe droid soon vanished over the distant horizon.

Another rider, bundled in winter clothing and mounted on a spotted gray Tauntaun, raced across the slopes of Hoth toward the Rebel base of operations.

The man's eyes, like points of cold metal, glanced without interest at the domes of dull gray, the myriad gun turrets and the colossal power generators that were the only indications of civilized life on this world. Han Solo gradually slowed his snow-lizard, guiding the reins so the creature trotted through the entrance of the enormous ice cave.

Han welcomed the relative warmth of the vast complex of caverns, warmed by Rebel heating units that obtained their power from the huge generators outside. This subterranean base was both a natural ice cave and a maze of angular tunnels blasted from a solid mountain of ice by Rebel lasers. The Corellian had been in more desolate hell-holes in the galaxy, but for the moment he couldn't remember the exact location of any one of them.

He dismounted his Tauntaun, then glanced around to watch the activity taking place inside the mammoth cave. Wherever he looked he saw things being carried, assembled, or repaired. Rebels in gray uniforms rushed to unload supplies and adjust equipment. And there were robots, mostly R2 units and power droids, that seemed to be everywhere, rolling or walking through the ice corridors, efficiently performing their innumerable tasks.

Han was beginning to wonder if he were mellowing with age. At first he had had no personal interest in or loyalty to this whole Rebel affair. His ultimate involvement in the conflict between Empire and Rebel Alliance began as a mere business transaction, selling his services and the use of his ship, the *Millennium Falcon*. The job had seemed simple enough: Just pilot Ben Kenobi, plus young Luke and two droids, to the Alderaan system. How could Han have known at the time that he would also be called on to rescue a princess from the Empire's most feared battle station, the Death Star?

Princess Leia Organa . . .

The more Solo thought about her, the more he realized how much trouble he eventually bought himself by accepting Ben Kenobi's money. All Han had wanted originally was to collect his fee and rocket off to pay back some bad debts that hung over his head like a meteor ready to fall. Never had he intended to become a hero.

And yet, something had kept him around to join Luke and his crazy Rebel friends as they launched the now-legendary space attack on the Death Star. Something. For the present, Han couldn't decide just what that something was.

Now, long after the Death Star's destruction, Han was still with the Rebel Alliance, lending his assistance to establish this base on Hoth, probably the bleakest of all planets in the galaxy. But all that was about to change, he told himself. As far as he was concerned, Han Solo and the Rebels were about to blast off on divergent courses.

He walked rapidly through the underground hangar deck where several Rebel fighter ships were docked and being serviced by men in gray assisted by droids of various designs. Of greatest concern to Han was the saucer-shaped freighter ship resting on its newly installed landing pods. This, the largest ship in the hangar, had garnered a few new dents in its metal hull since Han first hooked up with Skywalker and Kenobi. Yet the *Millennium Falcon* was famous not for its outward appearance but for its speed: This freighter was still the fastest ship ever to make the Kessel Run or to outrun an Imperial TIE fighter.

Much of the *Falcon*'s success could be attributed to its maintenance, now entrusted to the shaggy hands of a two-meter-tall mountain of brown hair, whose face was at the moment hidden behind a welder's mask.

Chewbacca, Han Solo's giant Wookiee copilot, was repairing the *Millennium Falcon*'s central lifter when he noticed Solo approaching. The Wookiee stopped his work and raised his face shield, exposing his furry countenance. A growl that few non-Wookiees in the universe could translate roared from his toothy mouth.

Han Solo was one of those few. '*Cold* isn't the word for it, Chewie,' the Corellian replied. 'I'll take a good fight any day over all this hiding and freezing!' He noticed the smoky wisps rising from the newly welded section of metal. 'How are you coming with those lifters?'

Chewbacca replied with a typical Wookiee grumble.

'All right,' Han said, fully agreeing with his friend's desire to return to space, to some other planet – anywhere but Hoth. 'I'll go report. Then I'll give you a hand. Soon as those lifters are fixed, we're out of here.'

The Wookiee barked, a joyful chuckle, and returned to his work as Han continued through the artificial ice cavern.

The command center was alive with electronic equipment and monitoring devices reaching toward the icy ceiling. As in the hangar, Rebel personnel filled the command center. The room was full of controllers, troopers, maintenance men – along with droids of varying models and sizes, all of whom were diligently involved in converting the chamber into a workable base to replace the one on Yavin.

The man Han Solo had come to see was busily engaged behind a great console, his attention riveted to a computer screen flashing brilliantly colored readouts. Rieekan, wearing the uniform of a Rebel general, straightened his tall frame to face Solo as he approached.

'General, there isn't a hint of life in the area,' Han reported. 'But all the perimeter markings are set, so you'll know if anyone comes calling.'

As usual, General Rieekan did not smile at Solo's flippancy. But he admired the young man's taking a kind of unofficial membership in the Rebellion. So impressed was Rieekan by Solo's qualities that he often considered giving him an honorary officer's commission.

'Has Commander Skywalker reported in yet?' the general inquired.

'He's checking out a meteorite that hit near him,' Han answered. 'He'll be in soon.'

Rieekan quickly glanced at a newly installed radar screen and studied the flashing images. 'With all the meteor activity in this system, it's going to be difficult to spot approaching ships.'

'General, I ...' Han hesitated. 'I think it's time for me to move on.'

Han's attention was drawn from General Rieekan to a steadily approaching figure. Her walk was both graceful and determined, and somehow the young woman's feminine features seemed incongruous with her white combat uniform. Even at this distance, Han could tell Princess Leia was upset.

'You're good in a fight,' the general remarked to Han, adding, 'I hate to lose you.'

'Thank you, General. But there's a price on my head. If I don't pay off Jabba the Hutt, I'm a walking dead man.'

'A death mark is not an easy thing to live with ... ' the officer began as Han turned to Princess Leia. Solo was not a sentimental sort, but he was aware that he was very emotional now. 'I guess this is it, Your Highness.' He paused, not knowing what response to expect from the princess.

'That's right,' Leia replied coldly. Her sudden aloofness was quickly evolving into genuine anger.

Han shook his head. Long ago he had told himself that females – mammalian, reptilian, or some biological class yet to be discovered – were beyond his meager powers of comprehension. Better leave them to mystery, he'd often advised himself.

But for a while, at least, Han had begun to believe that there was at least one female in all the cosmos that he was beginning to understand. And yet, he had been wrong before.

'Well,' Han said, 'don't go all mushy on me. So long, Princess.'

Abruptly turning his back to her, Han strode into the quiet corridor that connected with the command center. His destination was the hangar deck, where a giant Wookiee and a smuggler's freighter – two realities he did understand – were waiting for him. He was not about to stop walking.

'Han!' Leia was rushing after him, slightly out of breath.

Coolly, he stopped and turned toward her. 'Yes, Your Highness?'

'I thought you had decided to stay.'

There seemed to be real concern in Leia's voice, but Han could not be certain.

'That bounty hunter we ran into on Ord Mantell changed my mind.'

'Does Luke know?' she asked.

'He'll know when he gets back,' Han replied gruffly.

Princess Leia's eyes narrowed, her gaze judging him with a look he knew well. For a moment Han felt like one of the icicles on the surface of the planet.

'Don't give me that look,' he said sternly. 'Every day more bounty hunters are searching for me. I'm going to pay off Jabba before he sends any more of his remotes, Gank killers, and who knows what else. I've got to get this price off my head while I still *have* a head.'

Leia was obviously affected by his words, and Han could see that she was concerned for him as well as, perhaps, feeling something more.

'But we still need you,' she said.

'We?' he asked.

'Yes.'

'What about *you*?' Han was careful to emphasize the last word, but really wasn't certain why. Maybe it was something he had for some time wanted to say but had lacked the courage – no, he amended, the *stupidity* – to expose his feelings. At the moment there seemed to be little to lose, and he was ready for whatever she might say.

'Me?' she said bluntly. 'I don't know what you mean.'

Incredulous, Han Solo shook his head. 'No, you probably don't.'

'And what precisely *am* I supposed to know?' Anger was growing in her voice again, probably because, Han thought, she was finally beginning to understand.

He smiled. 'You want me to stay because of the way you feel about me.'

Again the princess mellowed. 'Well, yes, you've been a great help,' she said, pausing before going on, ' . . . to us. You're a natural leader—'

But Han refused to let her finish, cutting her off in midsentence. 'No, Your Worship. That's not it.'

Suddenly Leia was staring directly into Han's face, with eyes that were, at last, fully understanding. She started to laugh. 'You're imagining things.'

'Am I? I think you were afraid I was going to leave you without even a . . .' Han's eyes focused on her lips, ' . . . kiss.'

She began to laugh harder now. 'I'd just as soon kiss a Wookiee.'

'I can arrange that.' He moved closer to her, and she looked radiant even in the cold light of the ice chamber. 'Believe me, you could use a good kiss. You've been so busy giving orders, you've forgotten how to be a woman. If you'd have let go for a moment, I could have helped you. But it's too late now, sweetheart. Your big opportunity is flying out of here.'

'I think I can survive,' she said, obviously irked.

'Good luck!'

'You don't even care if the—'

He knew what she was going to say and didn't let her finish. 'Spare me, please!' he interrupted. 'Don't tell me about the Rebellion again. It's all you think about. You're as cold as this planet.'

'And you think you're the one to apply some heat?'

'Sure, if I were interested. But I don't think it'd be much fun.' With that, Han stepped back and looked at her again, appraising her coolly. 'We'll meet again,' he said. 'Maybe by then you'll have warmed up a little.' Her expression had changed again. Han had seen killers with kinder eyes.

'You have all the breeding of a Bantha,' she snarled, 'but not as much class. Enjoy your trip, hot shot!' Princess Leia quickly turned away from Han and hurried down the corridor.

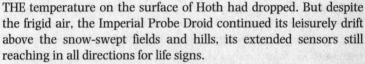

THE temperature on the surface of Hoth had dropped. But despite the frigid air, the Imperial Probe Droid continued its leisurely drift above the snow-swept fields and hills, its extended sensors still reaching in all directions for life signs.

The robot's heat sensors suddenly reacted. It had found a heat source in the vicinity, and warmth was a good indication of life. The head swiveled on its axis, the sensitive eyelike blisters noting the direction from which the heat source originated. Automatically the probe robot adjusted its speed and began to move at maximum velocity over the icy fields.

The insectlike machine slowed only when it neared a mound of snow bigger than the probe droid itself. The robot's scanners made note of the mound's size – nearly one-point-eight meters in height and an enormous six meters long. But the mound's size was of only secondary importance. What was truly astounding, if a surveillance machine could ever be astounded, was the amount of heat radiating from beneath the mound. The creature under that snowy hill must surely be well protected against the cold.

A thin blue-white beam of light shot from one of the probe robot's appendages, its intense heat boring into the white mound and scattering gleaming snow flecks in all directions.

The mound began to shiver, then to quake. Whatever existed beneath it was deeply irritated by the robot's probing laser beam.

Snow began to fall away from the mound in sizable clumps when, at one end, two eyes showed through the mass of white.

Huge yellow eyes peered like twin points of fire at the mechanical creature that continued to blast away with its painful beams. The eyes burned with primeval hatred for the thing that had interrupted its slumber.

The mound shook again, with a roar that nearly destroyed the probe droid's auditory sensors. It zoomed back several meters, widening the space between it and the creature. The droid had never before encountered a Wampa Ice Creature; its computers advised that the beast be dealt with expeditiously.

The droid made an internal adjustment to regulate the potency of its laser beam. Less than a moment later the beam was at maximum intensity. The machine aimed the laser at the creature, enveloping it in a great flaming and smoking cloud. Seconds later the few remaining particles of the Wampa were swept away by the icy winds.

The smoke disappeared, leaving behind no physical evidence – save for a large depression in the snow – that an Ice Creature had ever been there.

But its existence had been properly recorded in the memory of the probe droid, which was already continuing on its programmed mission.

The roars of another Wampa Ice Creature finally awakened the battered young Rebel commander.

Luke's head was spinning, aching, perhaps exploding for all he could tell. With painstaking effort he brought his vision into focus, discerning that he was in an ice gorge, its jagged walls reflecting the fading twilight.

He suddenly realized he was hanging upside down, arms dangling and fingertips some thirty centimeters from the snowy floor. His ankles were numb. He craned his neck and saw that his feet were frozen in ice hanging from the ceiling and that the ice was forming on his legs like stalactites. He could feel the frozen mask of his own blood caked on his face where the Wampa Ice Creature had viciously slashed him.

Again Luke heard the bestial moans, louder now as they resounded through the deep and narrow passageway of ice. The roars of the monster were deafening. He wondered which would kill him first, the cold or the fangs and claws of the thing that inhabited the gorge.

I've got to free myself, he thought, get free of this ice. His strength had not yet returned fully, but with a determined effort, he pulled himself up and reached for the confining bonds. Still too weak, Luke could not break the ice and fell back into his hanging position, the white floor rushing up at him.

'Relax,' he said to himself. 'Relax.'

The ice walls creaked with the ever-louder bellows of the approaching creature. Its feet crunched on the frigid ground, coming frighteningly nearer. It would not be long before the shaggy white horror would be back and possibly warming the cold young warrior in the darkness of its belly.

Luke's eyes darted about the gorge, finally spotting the pile of gear he had brought with him on his mission, now lying in a useless, crumpled heap on the floor. The equipment was nearly a full, unattainable meter beyond his grasp. And with that gear was a device that entirely captured his attention – a stout handgrip unit with a pair of small switches and a surmounting metal disk. The object had once belonged to his father, a former Jedi Knight who had been betrayed and murdered by the young Darth Vader. But now it was Luke's, given him by Ben Kenobi to be wielded with honor against Imperial tyranny.

In desperation Luke tried twisting his aching body, just enough to reach the discarded lightsaber. But the freezing cold coursing through his body slowed him down and weakened him. Luke was beginning to resign himself to his fate as he heard the snarling Wampa Ice Creature approaching. His last feelings of hope were nearly gone when he sensed the presence.

But it was not the presence of the white giant that dominated this gorge.

Rather, it was that soothing spiritual presence which occasionally visited Luke in moments of stress or danger. The presence that had first come to him only after old Ben, once again in his Jedi role of Obi-Wan Kenobi, vanished into a crumple of his own dark robes after being cut down by Darth Vader's lightsaber. The presence that was sometimes like a familiar voice, an almost silent whisper that spoke directly to Luke's mind.

'Luke.' The whisper was there again, hauntingly. 'Think of the lightsaber in your hand.'

The words made Luke's already aching head throb. Then he felt a sudden resurgence of strength, a feeling of confidence that urged him to continue fighting despite his apparently hopeless situation. His eyes fixed upon the lightsaber. His hand reached out painfully, the freezing in his limbs already taking its toll. He squeezed his eyes shut in concentration. But the weapon was still beyond his reach. He knew that the lightsaber would require more than just struggling to reach.

'Gotta relax,' Luke told himself, 'relax . . .'

Luke's mind whirled as he heard the words of his disembodied guardian. 'Let the Force flow, Luke.'

The Force!

Luke saw the inverted gorillalike image of the Wampa Ice Creature looming, its raised arms ending in enormous gleaming claws. He could see the apish face for the first time now, and shivered at the sight of the beast's ramlike horns, the quivering lower jaw with its protruding fangs.

But then the warrior divorced the creature from his thoughts. He stopped struggling for his weapon, his body relaxed and went limp, allowing his spirit to be receptive to his teacher's suggestion. Already he could feel coursing through him that energy field generated by all living beings, that bound the very universe together.

As Kenobi had taught him, the Force was within Luke to use as he saw fit.

The Wampa Ice Creature spread its black, hooked claws and lumbered toward the hanging youth. Suddenly the lightsaber, as if by magic, sprang to Luke's hand. Instantly, he depressed a colored button on the weapon, releasing a bladelike beam that quickly severed his icy bonds.

As Luke, weapon in hand, dropped to the floor, the monstrous figure towering over him took a cautious step backward. The beast's sulfurous eyes blinked incredulously at the humming lightshaft, a sight baffling to its primitive brain.

Though it was difficult to move, Luke jumped to his feet and waved his lightsaber at the snow-white mass of muscle and hair, forcing it back a step, another step. Bringing the weapon down,

Luke cut through the monster's hide with the blade of light. The Wampa Ice Creature shrieked, its hideous roar of agony shaking the gorge walls. It turned and hastily lumbered out of the gorge, its white bulk blending with the distant terrain.

The sky was already noticeably darker, and with the encroaching darkness came the colder winds. The Force was with Luke, but even that mysterious power could not warm him now. Every step he took as he stumbled out of the gorge was more difficult than the last. Finally, his vision dimming as rapidly as the daylight, Luke stumbled down an embankment of snow and was unconscious before he even reached the bottom.

In the subsurface main hangar dock, Chewie was getting the *Millennium Falcon* ready for takeoff. He looked up from his work to see a rather curious pair of figures that had just appeared from around a nearby corner to mingle with the usual Rebel activity in the hangar.

Neither of these figures was human, although one of them had a humanoid shape and gave the impression of a man in knightly golden armor. His movements were precise, almost too precise to be human, as he clanked stiffly through the corridor. His companion required no manlike legs for locomotion, for he was doing quite well rolling his shorter, barrel-like body along on miniature wheels.

The shorter of the two droids was beeping and whistling excitedly.

'It is *not* my fault, you malfunctioning tin can,' the tall, anthropomorphic droid stated, gesturing with a metallic hand. 'I did not ask you to turn on the thermal heater. I merely commented that it was freezing in her chamber. But it's *supposed* to be freezing. How are we going to get all her things dried out?... Ah! Here we are.'

See Threepio, the golden droid in human shape, paused to focus his optical sensors on the docked *Millennium Falcon*.

The other robot, Artoo Detoo, retracted his wheels and frontal leg, and rested his stout metal body on the ground. The smaller droid's sensors were reading the familiar figures of Han Solo and his Wookiee companion as those two continued the work of replacing the freighter's central lifters.

'Master Solo, sir,' Threepio called, the only one of the robotic twosome equipped with an imitation human voice. 'Might I have a word with you?'

Han was not particularly in a mood to be disturbed, especially by this fastidious droid. 'What is it?'

'Mistress Leia has been trying to reach you on the communicator,' Threepio informed him. 'It must be malfunctioning.'

But Han knew that it was not. 'I shut it off,' he said sharply as he continued to work on his ship. 'What does her royal holiness want?'

Threepio's auditory sensors identified the disdain in Han's voice but did not understand it. The robot mimicked a human gesture as he added, 'She is looking for Master Luke and assumed he would be here with you. No one seems to know—'

'Luke's not back yet?' Immediately Han became concerned. He could see that the sky beyond the ice cavern entrance had grown considerably darker since he and Chewbacca had begun to repair the *Millennium Falcon*. Han knew just how severely the temperatures dropped on the surface after nightfall and how deadly the winds could be.

In a flash he jumped off the *Falcon*'s lift, not even looking back toward the Wookiee. 'Bolt it down, Chewie. Officer of the Deck!' Han yelled, then brought his comlink to his mouth and asked, 'Security Control, has Commander Skywalker reported in yet?' A negative reply brought a scowl to Han's face.

The deck sergeant and his aide hurried up to Solo in response to his summons.

'Is Commander Skywalker back yet?' Han asked, tension in his voice.

'I haven't seen him,' the deck sergeant replied. 'It's possible he came in through the south entrance.'

'Check on it!' Solo snapped, though he was not in an official position to give commands. 'It's urgent.'

As the deck sergeant and his aide turned and rushed down the corridor, Artoo emitted a concerned whistle that rose inquiringly in pitch.

'I don't know, Artoo,' Threepio answered, stiffly turning his upper torso and head in Han's direction. 'Sir, might I inquire what's going on?'

Anger welled up inside Han as he grunted back at the robot, 'Go tell your precious princess that Luke is dead unless he shows up soon.'

Artoo began to whistle hysterically at Solo's grim prediction and his now-frightened golden partner exclaimed, 'Oh, no!'

The main tunnel was filled with activity when Han Solo rushed in. He saw a pair of Rebel troopers employing all their physical strength to restrain a nervous Tauntaun that was trying to break free.

From the opposite end, the deck officer rushed into the corridor, his eyes darting around the chamber until he had spotted Han. 'Sir,' he said frantically, 'Commander Skywalker hasn't come through the south entrance. He might have forgotten to check in.'

'Not likely,' Han snapped. 'Are the speeders ready?'

'Not yet,' the deck officer answered. 'Adapting them to the cold is proving difficult. Maybe by morning—'

Han cut him off. There wasn't any time to waste on machines that could and probably would break down. 'We'll have to go out on Tauntauns. I'll take sector four.'

'The temperature is falling too rapidly.'

'You bet it is,' Han growled, 'and Luke's out in it.'

The other officer volunteered, 'I'll cover sector twelve. Have control set screen alpha.'

But Han knew there was not time for control to get its surveillance cameras operating, not with Luke probably dying somewhere on the desolate plains above. He pushed his way through the assemblage of Rebel troops and took the reins of one of the trained Tauntauns, leaping onto the creature's back.

'The night storms will start before any of you can reach the first marker,' the deck officer warned.

'Then I'll see you in hell,' grunted Han, tugging the reins of his mount and maneuvering the animal out of the cave.

Snow was falling heavily as Han Solo raced his Tauntaun through the wilderness. Night was near and the winds were howling fiercely, piercing his heavy clothes. He knew that he would be as useless as an icicle to Luke unless he found the young warrior soon.

The Tauntaun was already feeling the effects of the temperature drop. Not even its layers of insulating fat or the matted gray fur could protect it from the elements after nightfall. Already the beast was wheezing, its breathing becoming increasingly labored.

Han prayed that the snow-lizard wouldn't drop, at least not until he had located Luke.

He drove his mount harder, forcing it on across the icy plains.

Another figure was moving across the snow, its metal body hovering above the frozen ground.

The Imperial Probe Droid paused briefly in midflight, its sensors twitching.

Then, satisfied with its findings, the robot gently lowered itself, coming to rest on the ground. Like spider legs, several probes separated from the metal hull, dislodging some of the snow that had settled there.

Something began to take shape around the robot, a pulsating glow that gradually covered the machine as if with a transparent dome. Quickly this force field solidified, repelling the blowing snow that brushed over the droid's hull.

After a moment the glow faded, and the blowing snow soon formed a perfect dome of white, completely concealing the droid and its protective force field.

The Tauntaun was racing at maximum speed, certainly too fast considering the distance it had traveled and the unbearable frigid air. No longer wheezing, it had begun moaning pitifully, and its legs were becoming more and more unsteady. Han felt sorry about the Tauntaun's pain, but at present the creature's life was only secondary to that of his friend Luke.

It was becoming difficult for Han to see through the thickening snowfall. Desperate, he searched for some interruption in the eternal plains, some distant spot that might actually be Luke. But there was nothing to see other than the darkening expanses of snow and ice.

Yet there was a sound.

Han drew the reins in, bringing the Tauntaun to an abrupt halt on the plain. Solo could not be certain, but there seemed to be some sound other than the howling of the winds that whipped past him. He strained to look in the direction of the sound.

Then he spurred his Tauntaun, forcing it to gallop across the snow-swept field.

*

Luke could have been a corpse, food for the scavengers, by the time the light of dawn returned. But somehow he was still alive, though barely, and struggling to stay that way even with the night storms violently assaulting him. Luke painfully pulled himself upright from the snow, only to be blasted back down by the freezing gale. As he fell he considered the irony of it all – a farm boy from Tatooine maturing to battle the Death Star, now perishing alone in a frozen alien wasteland.

It took all of Luke's remaining strength to drag himself a half meter before finally collapsing, sinking into the ever-deepening drifts. 'I can't . . .' he said, though no one could hear his words.

But someone, though still unseen, had heard.

'You must.' The words vibrated in Luke's mind. 'Luke, look at me!'

Luke could not ignore that command; the power of those softly spoken words was too great.

With a great effort, Luke lifted his head and saw what he thought was a hallucination. In front of him, apparently unaffected by the cold and still clad only in the shabby robes he had worn in the hot desert of Tatooine, stood Ben Kenobi.

Luke wanted to call out to him, but he was speechless.

The apparition spoke with the same gentle authority Ben had always used with the young man. 'You must survive, Luke.'

The young commander found the strength to move his lips again. 'I'm cold . . . so cold . . .'

'You must go to the Dagobah system,' the spectral figure of Ben Kenobi instructed. 'You will learn from Yoda, the Jedi Master, the one who taught me.'

Luke listened, then reached to touch the ghostly figure. 'Ben . . . Ben . . .' he groaned.

The figure remained unmoved by Luke's efforts to reach it. 'Luke,' it spoke again, 'you're our only hope.'

Our only hope.

Luke was confused. Yet before he could gather the strength to ask for an explanation, the figure began to fade. And when every trace of the apparition had passed from his sight, Luke thought he saw the approach of a Tauntaun with a human rider on its back. The snow-lizard was approaching, its gait unsteady. The rider was still too far away, too obscured by the storm for identification.

In desperation the young Rebel commander called out, 'Ben?!' before again dropping off into unconsciousness.

The snow-lizard was barely able to stand on its saurian hind legs when Han Solo reined it to a stop and dismounted.

Han looked with horror at the snow-covered, almost frozen form lying as if dead at his feet.

'Come on, buddy,' he appealed to Luke's inert figure, immediately forgetting his own nearly frozen body, 'you aren't dead yet. Give me a signal here.'

Han could detect no sign of life, and noticed that Luke's face, nearly covered with snow, was savagely torn. He rubbed at the youth's face, being careful not to touch the drying wounds. 'Don't do this, Luke. It's not your time.'

Finally a slight response. A low moan, barely audible over the winds, was strong enough to send a warm glow through Han's own shivering body. He grinned with relief. 'I knew you wouldn't leave me out here all alone! We've got to get you out of here.'

Knowing that Luke's salvation – and his own – lay in the speed of the Tauntaun, Han moved toward the beast, carrying the young warrior limply in his arms. But before he could drape the unconscious form over the animal's back, the snow-lizard gave an agonized roar, then fell into a shaggy gray heap on the snow. Laying his companion down, Han rushed to the side of the fallen creature. The Tauntaun made one final sound, not a roar or bellow but only a sickly rasp. Then the beast was silent.

Solo gripped the Tauntaun's hide, his numbed fingers searching for even the slightest indication of life. 'Deader than a Triton moon,' he said, knowing that Luke did not hear a word. 'We haven't got much time.'

Resting Luke's motionless form against the belly of the dead snow-lizard, Han proceeded to work. It might be something of a sacrilege, he mused, using a Jedi Knight's favorite weapon like this, but right now Luke's lightsaber was the most efficient and precise tool to cut through the thick skin of a Tauntaun.

At first the weapon felt strange in his hand, but momentarily he was cutting the animal's carcass from hairy head to scaly hind paws. Han winced at the foul odor that rose from the steaming incision. There were few things he could remember that stank like a snow-lizard's innards. Without deliberation he tossed the slippery entrails into the snow.

When the animal's corpse had been entirely eviscerated, Han shoved his friend inside the warm, hair-covered skin. 'I know this doesn't smell so good, Luke, but it'll keep you from freezing. I'm sure this Tauntaun wouldn't hesitate if it were the other way around.'

From the body of the snow-lizard, another blast of entrail-stench rose out of the disemboweled cavity. 'Whew!' Han almost gagged. 'It's just as well you're out cold, pal.'

There wasn't much time left to do what had to be done. Han's freezing hands went to the supply pack strapped to the Tauntaun's back and rummaged through the Rebel-issue items until he located the shelter container.

Before unpacking it, he spoke into his comlink. 'Echo Base, do you copy?'

No response.

'This comlink is useless!'

The sky had darkened ominously and the winds blew violently, making even breathing close to impossible. Han fought to open the shelter container and stiffly began to construct the one piece of Rebel equipment that might protect them both – if only for a short while longer.

'If I don't get this shelter up fast,' he grumbled to himself, 'Jabba won't need those bounty hunters.'

ARTOO DETOO stood just outside the entrance to the secret Rebel ice hangar, dusted with a layer of snow that had settled over his plug-shaped body. His inner timing mechanisms knew he had waited here a long time and his optical sensors told him that the sky was dark.

But the R2 unit was concerned only with his built-in probe-sensors that were still sending signals across the ice fields. His long and earnest sensorsearch for the missing Luke Skywalker and Han Solo had not turned up a thing.

The stout droid began beeping nervously when Threepio approached him, plodding stiffly through the snow.

'Artoo,' the gold-colored robot inclined the upper half of his form at the hip joints, 'there's nothing more you can do. You must come inside.' Threepio straightened to his full height again, simulating a human shiver as the night winds howled past his gleaming hull. 'Artoo, my joints are freezing up. Will you hurry . . . please? . . .' But before he could finish his own sentence, Threepio was hurrying back toward the hangar entrance.

Hoth's sky was then entirely black with night, and Princess Leia Organa stood inside the Rebel base entrance, maintaining a worried vigil. She shivered in the night wind as she tried to see into the Hoth darkness. Waiting near a deeply concerned Major Derlin, her mind was somewhere out on the ice fields.

The giant Wookiee sat nearby, his maned head lifting quickly from his hairy hands as the two droids Threepio and Artoo reentered the hangar.

Threepio was humanly distraught. 'Artoo has not been able to pick up any signals,' he reported, fretting, 'although he feels his range is probably too limited to cause us to give up hope.' Still, very little confidence could be detected in Threepio's artificial voice.

Leia gave the taller droid a nod of acknowledgment, but did not speak. Her thoughts were occupied with the pair of missing heroes. Most disturbing to her was that she found her mind focused on one of the two: a dark-haired Corellian whose words were not always to be taken literally.

As the princess kept watch, Major Derlin turned to acknowledge a Rebel lieutenant reporting in. 'All patrols are now in except Solo and Skywalker, sir.'

The major looked over at Princess Leia. 'Your Highness,' he said, his voice weighty with regret, 'nothing more can be done tonight. The temperature is dropping fast. The shield doors must be closed. I'm sorry.' Derlin waited a moment then addressed the lieutenant. 'Close the doors.'

The Rebel officer turned to carry out Derlin's order and immediately the chamber of ice seemed to drop even more in temperature as the mournful Wookiee howled his grief.

'The speeders should be ready in the morning,' the major said to Leia. 'They'll make the search easier.'

Not really expecting an affirmative reply, Leia asked, 'Is there any chance of their surviving until morning?'

'Slim,' Major Derlin answered with grim honesty. 'But yes, there's a chance.'

In response to the major's words, Artoo began to operate the miniature computers inside his barrellike metal body, taking only moments to juggle numerous sets of mathematical computations, and climaxing his figurings with a series of triumphant beeps.

'Ma'am,' Threepio interpreted, 'Artoo says the chances against survival are seven hundred twenty-five to one.' Then, tilting toward the shorter robot, the protocol droid grumbled, 'Actually, I don't think we needed to know that.'

No one responded to Threepio's translation. For several prolonged moments there was a solemn silence, broken only by the echoing clang of metal slamming against metal: the huge doors of the Rebel base were closed for the night. It was as if some heartless deity had officially severed the assembled group from the two men out on the ice plains and had, with a metallic bang, announced their deaths.

Chewbacca let out another suffering howl.

And a silent prayer, often spoken on an erstwhile world called Alderaan, crept into Leia's thoughts.

The sun that was creeping over Hoth's northern horizon was relatively dim, but its light was enough to shed some warmth on the planet's icy surface. The light crawled across the rolling hills of snow, fought to reach the darker recesses of the icy gorges, then finally came to rest on what must have been the only perfect white mound on the entire world.

So perfect was the snow-covered mound that it must have owed its existence to some power other than Nature. Then, as the sky grew steadily brighter, this mound began to hum. Anyone observing the mound now would have been startled as the snow dome seemed to erupt, sending its snowy outer covering skyward in a great burst of white particles. A droning machine began pulling back its retractable sensor arms, and its awesome bulk slowly rose from its frozen white bed.

The probe robot paused briefly in the windy air, then continued on its morning mission across the snow-covered plains.

Something else had invaded the morning air of the ice world – a relatively small, snub-nosed craft, with dark cockpit windows and laser guns mounted on each side. The Rebel snowspeeder was heavily armored and designed for warfare near the planet's surface. But this morning the small craft was on a reconnaissance mission, racing above the expansive white landscape and arcing over the contours of the snowdrifts.

Although the snowspeeder was designed for a two-man crew, Zev was the ship's only occupant. His eyes took in a panoramic scan of the desolate stretches below, and he prayed that he would find the objects of his search before he went snowblind.

Presently he heard a low beeping signal.

'Echo Base,' he shouted jubilantly into his cockpit comlink, 'I've got something! Not much, but it could be a sign of life. Sector four-six-one-four by eight-eight-two. I'm closing in.'

Frantically working the controls of his ship, Zev reduced its speed slightly and banked the craft over a snowdrift. He welcomed the sudden G-force pressing him against his seat and headed the snowspeeder in the direction of the faint signal.

As the white infinity of Hoth's terrain streaked under him, the Rebel pilot switched his comlink to a new frequency. 'Echo Three, this is Rogue Two. Do you copy? Commander Skywalker, this is Rogue Two.'

The only reply that came through his comlink receiver was static.

But then he heard a voice, a very distant-sounding voice, fighting its way through the crackling noise. 'Nice of you guys to drop by. Hope we didn't get you up too early.'

Zev welcomed the characteristic cynicism in Han Solo's voice. He switched his transmitter back to the hidden Rebel base. 'Echo Base, this is Rogue Two,' he reported, his voice suddenly rising in pitch. 'I found them. Repeat . . .'

As he spoke, the pilot pulled in a fine-tune fix on the signals winking on his cockpit monitor screens. Then he further reduced the speed of his craft, bringing it down close enough to the planet's surface so that he could better see a small object standing out against the fleecy plains.

The object, a portable Rebel-issue shelter, sat atop a snowdrift. On the shelter's windward side was a hard-packed layer of white. And resting gingerly against the upper part of the snowdrift was a makeshift radio antenna.

But a more welcome sight than any of this was the familiar human figure standing in front of the snow shelter, frantically waving his arms at the snowspeeder.

As Zev dipped his craft for a landing, he felt overwhelmingly grateful that at least one of the warriors he had been sent out to find was still alive.

Only a thick glass window separated the battered, near-frozen body of Luke Skywalker from five of his watchful friends.

Han Solo, who appreciated the relative warmth of the Rebel medical center, was standing beside Leia, his Wookiee copilot,

Artoo Detoo, and See Threepio. Han exhaled with relief. He knew that, despite the grim atmosphere of the chamber enclosing him, the young commander was finally out of danger and in the best of mechanical hands.

Clad only in white shorts, Luke hung in a vertical position inside a transparent cylinder with a combination breath mask and microphone covering his nose and mouth. The surgeon droid, Too-Onebee, was attending to the youth with the skill of the finest humanoid doctors. He was aided by his medical assistant droid, FX-7, which looked like nothing more than a metal-capped set of cylinders, wires, and appendages. Gracefully, the surgeon droid worked a switch that brought a gelatinous red fluid pouring down over his human patient. This bacta, Han knew, could work miracles, even with patients in such dire shape as Luke.

As the bubbling slime encapsulated his body, Luke began to thrash about and rave deliriously. 'Watch out,' he moaned. '... snow creatures. Dangerous ... Yoda ... go to Yoda ... only hope.'

Han had not the slightest idea what his friend was raving about. Chewbacca, also perplexed by the youth's babbling, expressed himself with an interrogative Wookiee bark.

'He doesn't make sense to me either, Chewie,' Han replied.

Threepio commented hopefully, 'I do hope he's all there, if you take my meaning. It would be most unfortunate if Master Luke were to develop a short circuit.'

'The kid ran into something,' Han observed matter-of-factly, 'and it wasn't just the cold.'

'It's those creatures he keeps talking about,' Leia said, looking at the grimly staring Solo. 'We've doubled the security, Han,' she began, tentatively trying to thank him, 'I don't know how—'

'Forget it,' he said brusquely. Right now he was concerned only with his friend in the red bacta fluid.

Luke's body sloshed through the brightly colored substance, the bacta's healing properties by now taking effect. For a while it appeared as if Luke were trying to resist the curative flow of the translucent muck. Then, at last, he gave up his mumbling and relaxed, succumbing to the bacta's powers.

Too-Onebee turned away from the human who had been entrusted to his care. He angled his skull-shaped head to gaze at Han and the others through the window. 'Commander Skywalker has been in dormo-shock but is responding well to the bacta,' the robot announced, his commanding, authoritative voice heard distinctly through the glass. 'He is now out of danger.'

The surgeon robot's words immediately wiped away the tension that had seized the group on the other side of the window. Leia sighed in relief, and Chewbacca grunted his approval of Too-Onebee's treatment.

Luke had no way of estimating how long he had been delirious. But now he was in full command of his mind and senses. He sat up on his bed in the Rebel medical center. What a relief, he thought, to be breathing real air again, however cold it might be.

A medical droid was removing the protective pad from his healing face. His eyes were uncovered and he was beginning to perceive the face of someone standing by his bed. Gradually the smiling image of Princess Leia came into focus. She gracefully moved toward him and gently brushed his hair out of his eyes.

'The bacta are growing well,' she said as she looked at his healing wounds. 'The scars should be gone in a day or so. Does it still hurt you?'

Across the room, the door banged open. Artoo beeped a cheerful greeting as he rolled toward Luke, and Threepio clanked noisily toward Luke's bed. 'Master Luke, it's good to see you functional again.'

'Thanks, Threepio.'

Artoo emitted a series of happy beeps and whistles.

'Artoo expresses his relief also,' Threepio translated helpfully.

Luke was certainly grateful for the robots' concern. But before he could reply to either of the droids, he met with yet another interruption.

'Hi, kid,' Han Solo greeted him boisterously as he and Chewbacca burst into the medical center.

The Wookiee growled a friendly greeting.

'You look strong enough to wrestle a Gundark,' Han observed.

Luke felt that strong, and felt grateful to his friend. 'Thanks to you.'

'That's two you owe me, junior.' Han gave the princess a wide, devilish grin. 'Well, Your Worship,' he said mockingly, 'it looks like you arranged to keep me close by for a while longer.'

'I had nothing to do with it,' Leia said hotly, annoyed at Han's vanity. 'General Rieekan thinks it's dangerous for any ships to leave the system until the generators are operational.'

'That makes a good story. But *I* think you just can't bear to let me out of your sight.'

'I don't know where you get your delusions, laser brains,' she retorted.

Chewbacca, amused by this verbal battle between two of the strongest human wills he had ever encountered, let out a roaring Wookiee laugh.

'Laugh it up, fuzz ball,' Han said goodnaturedly. 'You didn't see us alone in the south passage.'

Until now, Luke had scarcely listened to this lively exchange. Han and the princess had argued frequently enough in the past. But that reference to the south passage sparked his curiosity, and he looked at Leia for an explanation.

'She expressed her true feeling for me,' Han continued, delighting in the rosy flush that appeared on the princess's cheeks. 'Come on, Your Highness, you've already forgotten.'

'Why, you low-down, stuck-up, half-witted, scruffy-looking nerf-herder . . .' she sputtered in fury.

'Who's scruffy-looking?' he grinned. 'I tell ya, sweetheart, I must've hit pretty close to the mark to get you hoppin' like this. Doesn't it look that way to you, Luke?'

'Yeah,' he said, staring at the princess incredulously, 'it does . . . kind of.'

Leia looked over at Luke with a strange mixture of emotions showing on her flushed face. Something vulnerable, almost child-like, was reflected in her eyes for a moment. And then the tough mask fell again.

'Oh, it does, does it?' she said. 'Well, I guess you don't understand everything about women, do you?'

Luke agreed silently. He agreed even more when in the next moment Leia leaned over and kissed him firmly on the lips. Then she turned on her heel and marched across the room, slamming the door behind her. Everyone in the room – human, Wookiee, and droid – looked at one another, speechless.

In the distance, a warning alarm blared through the sub-terranean corridors.

*

General Rieekan and his head controller were conferring in the Rebel command center when Han Solo and Chewbacca burst into the room. Princess Leia and Threepio, who had been listening to the general and his officer, turned in anticipation at their approach.

A warning signal blared across the chamber from the huge console located behind Rieekan and monitored by Rebel control officers.

'General,' the sensor controller called.

Grimly attentive, General Rieekan watched the console screens. Suddenly he saw a flashing signal that had not been there a moment before. 'Princess,' he said, 'I think we have a visitor.'

Leia, Han, Chewbacca, and Threepio gathered around the general and watched the beeping monitor screens.

'We've picked up something outside the base in Zone Twelve. It's moving east,' said Rieekan.

'Whatever it is, it's metal,' the sensor controller observed.

Leia's eyes widened in surprise. 'Then it can't be one of those creatures that attacked Luke.'

'Could it be ours?' Han asked. 'A speeder?'

The sensor controller shook his head. 'No, there's no signal.' Then came a sound from another monitor. 'Wait, something very weak . . .'

Walking as rapidly as his stiff joints allowed, Threepio approached the console. His auditory sensors tuned in the strange signals. 'I must say, sir, I'm fluent in over sixty million forms of communication, but this is something new. Must be in a code or—'

Just then the voice of a Rebel trooper cut in through the console's comlink speaker. 'This is Echo Station Three-Eight. Unidentified object is in our scope. It's just over the ridge. We should have visual contact in about—' Without warning the voice filled with fear. 'What the—? Oh, no!'

A burst of radio static followed, then the transmission broke off completely.

Han frowned. 'Whatever it is,' he said, 'it isn't friendly. Let's have a look. Come on, Chewie.'

Even before Han and Chewbacca were out of the chamber, General Rieekan had dispatched Rogues Ten and Eleven to Station Three-Eight.

*

The mammoth Imperial Star Destroyer occupied a position of deadly prominence in the Emperor's fleet. The sleekly elongated ship was larger and even more ominous than the five wedge-shaped Imperial Star Destroyers guarding it. Together these six cruisers were the most dreaded and devastating warships in the galaxy, capable of reducing to cosmic scrap anything that strayed too close to their weapons.

Flanking the Star Destroyers were a number of smaller fighter ships and, darting about this great space armada, were the infamous TIE fighters.

Supreme confidence reigned in the heart of every crew member in this Imperial death squadron, especially among the personnel on the monstrous central Star Destroyer. But something also blazed within their souls. Fear – fear of merely the sound of the familiar heavy footsteps as they echoed through the enormous ship. Crew members dreaded these footfalls and shuddered whenever they were heard approaching, bringing their much feared, but much respected leader.

Towering above them in his black cloak and concealing black headgear, Darth Vader, Dark Lord of the Sith, entered the main control deck, and the men around him fell silent. In what seemed to be an endless moment, no sounds except those from the ship's control boards and the loud wheezes coming from the ebony figure's metal breath screen were to be heard.

As Darth Vader watched the endless array of stars, Captain Piett rushed across the wide bridge of the ship, carrying a message for the squat, evil-looking Admiral Ozzel, who was stationed on the bridge. 'I think we've found something, Admiral,' he announced nervously, looking from Ozzel to the Dark Lord.

'Yes, Captain?' The admiral was a supremely confident man who felt relaxed in the presence of his cloaked superior.

'The report we have is only a fragment, from a probe droid in the Hoth system. But it's the best lead we've had in—'

'We have had thousands of probe droids searching the galaxy,' Ozzel broke in angrily. 'I want proof, not leads. I don't intend to continue to chase around from one side of—'

Abruptly the figure in black approached the two and interrupted. 'You found something?' he asked, his voice somewhat distorted by the breath mask.

Captain Piett respectfully gazed at his master, who loomed above him like a black-robed, omnipotent god. 'Yes, sir,' Piett said slowly, choosing his words with caution. 'We have visuals. The system is supposed to be devoid of human forms . . .'

But Vader was no longer listening to the captain. His masked face turned toward an image beamed on one of the viewscreens – an image of a small squadron of Rebel snowspeeders streaking above the white fields.

'That's it,' Darth Vader boomed without further deliberation.

'My lord,' Admiral Ozzel protested, 'there are so many uncharted settlements. It could be smugglers—'

'That is the one!' the former Jedi Knight insisted, clenching a black-gloved fist. 'And Skywalker is with them. Bring in the patrol ships, Admiral, and set your course for the Hoth system.' Vader looked toward an officer wearing a green uniform with matching cap. 'General Veers,' the Dark Lord addressed him, 'prepare your men.'

As soon as Darth Vader had spoken, his men set about to launch his fearful plan.

The Imperial Probe Droid raised a large antenna from its buglike head and sent out a piercing, high-frequency signal. The robot's scanners had reacted to a lifeform hidden behind a great dune of snow and noted the appearance of a brown Wookiee head and the sound of a deep-throated growl. The blasters that had been built into the probe robot took aim at the furry giant. But before the robot had a chance to fire, a red beam from a hand blaster exploded from behind the Imperial Probe Droid and nicked its darkly finished hull.

As he ducked behind a large snow dune, Han Solo noticed Chewbacca still hidden, and then watched as the robot spun around in midair to face him. So far the ruse was working and now *he* was the target. Han had barely moved out of range as the floating machine fired, blasting chunks of snow from the edge of his dune. He fired again, hitting it square on with the beam of his weapon. Then he heard a high-pitched whine coming from the deadly machine, and in an instant the Imperial Probe Droid burst into a billion or more flaming pieces.

'. . . I'm afraid there's not much left,' Han said over the comlink as he concluded his report to the underground base.

Princess Leia and General Rieekan were still manning the console where they had maintained constant communication with Han. 'What is it?' Leia asked.

'Droid of some kind,' he answered. 'I didn't hit it that hard. It must have had a self-destruct.'

Leia paused as she considered this unwelcome piece of information. 'An Imperial droid,' she said, betraying some trepidation.

'If it was,' Han warned, 'the Empire surely knows we're here.'

General Rieekan shook his head slowly. 'We'd better start to evacuate the planet.'

IV

SIX ominous shapes appeared in the black space of the Hoth system and loomed like vast demons of destruction, ready to unleash the furies of their Imperial weapons. Inside the largest of the six Imperial Star Destroyers, Darth Vader sat alone in a small spherical room. A single shaft of light gleamed on his black helmet as he sat motionless in his raised meditation chamber.

As General Veers approached, the sphere opened slowly, the upper half lifting like a jagged-toothed mechanical jaw. To Veers, the dark figure seated inside the mouthlike cocoon hardly seemed alive, though a powerful aura of sheer evil emanated from him, sending a chilling fear through the officer.

Uncertain of his own courage, Veers took a step forward. He had a message to deliver but felt prepared to wait for hours if necessary rather than disturb Vader's meditation.

But Vader spoke immediately. 'What is it, Veers?'

'My lord,' the general replied, choosing each word with care, 'the fleet has moved out of light-speed. Com-Scan has detected an energy field protecting an area of the sixth planet in the Hoth system. The field is strong enough to deflect any bombardment.'

Vader stood, rising to his full two-meter height, his cloak swaying against the floor. 'So, the Rebel scum are alerted to our presence.' Furious, he clenched his black-gloved hands into fists. 'Admiral Ozzel came out of light-speed too close to the system.'

'He felt surprise was a wiser—'

'He's as clumsy as he is stupid,' Vader cut in, breathing heavily. 'A clean bombardment is impossible through their energy field. Prepare your troops for a surface attack.'

With military precision, General Veers turned and marched out of the meditation room, leaving behind an enraged Darth Vader. Alone in the chamber, Vader activated a large viewscreen that showed a brightly lit image of his Star Destroyer's vast bridge.

Admiral Ozzel, responding to Vader's summons, stepped forward, his face almost filling the Dark Lord's monitor screen. There was trepidation in Ozzel's voice when he announced, 'Lord Vader, the fleet has moved out of light-speed—'

But Vader's reply was addressed to the officer standing slightly behind Ozzel. 'Captain Piett.'

Knowing better than to delay, Captain Piett stepped forward instantly as the admiral staggered back a step, his hand automatically reaching for his throat.

'Yes, my lord,' Piett answered respectfully.

Ozzel began to gag now as his throat, as if in the grip of invisible talons, began to constrict.

'Make ready to land assault troops beyond the energy field,' Vader ordered. 'Then deploy the fleet so that nothing can get off that planet. You're in command now, Admiral Piett.'

Piett was simultaneously pleased and unsettled by this news. As he turned to carry out the orders, he saw a figure that might someday be himself. Ozzel's face was hideously contorted as he fought for one final breath of air; then he dropped into a dead heap on the floor.

The Empire had entered the system of Hoth.

Rebel troops rushed to their alert stations as the warning alarms wailed through the ice tunnels. Ground crews and droids of all sizes and makes hurried to perform their assigned duties, responding efficiently to the impending Imperial threat.

The armored snowspeeders were fueled as they waited in attack formation to blast out of the main cavern entranceway. Meanwhile, in the hangar, Princess Leia was addressing a small band of Rebel fighter pilots. 'The large transport ships will leave as soon as they're loaded. Only two fighter escorts per ship. The energy shield can only be opened for a split second, so you'll have to stay very close to the transports.'

Hobbie, a Rebel veteran of many battles, looked at the princess with concern. 'Two fighters against a Star Destroyer?'

'The ion cannon will fire several blasts which should destroy any ships in your flight path,' Leia explained. 'When you clear the energy shield, you will proceed to the rendezvous point. Good luck.'

Somewhat reassured, Hobbie and the other pilots raced toward their fighter cockpits.

Meanwhile, Han was working frantically to complete welding a lifter on the *Millennium Falcon*. Finishing quickly, he hopped to the hangar floor and switched on his comlink. 'All right, Chewie,' he said to the hairy figure seated at the *Falcon*'s controls, 'give it a try.'

Just then Leia walked past, throwing him an angry look. Han looked at her smugly while the freighter's lifters began to rise off the floor, whereupon the right lifter began to shake erratically, then broke partially loose to swing back down again with an embarrassing crash.

He turned away from Leia, catching only a glimpse of her face as she mockingly raised an eyebrow.

'Hold it, Chewie,' Han grunted into his small transmitter.

The *Avenger*, one of the Imperial armada's wedgelike Star Destroyers, hovered like a mechanized death angel in the sea of stars outside the Hoth system. As the colossal ship began to move closer to the ice world, the planet became clearly visible through the windows which stretched 100 meters or more across the huge bridge of the warship.

Captain Needa, commander of the *Avenger*'s crew, gazed out a main port, looking at the planet when a controller came up to him. 'Sir, Rebel ship coming into our sector.'

'Good,' Needa replied with a gleam in his eyes. 'Our first catch of the day.'

'Their first target will be the power generators,' General Rieekan told the princess.

'First transport Three Zone approaching shield,' one of the Rebel controllers said, tracking a bright image that could only be an Imperial Star Destroyer.

'Prepare to open shield,' a radarman ordered.

'Stand by, Ion Control,' another controller said.

A giant metal globe on Hoth's icy surface rotated into position and angled its great turret gun upward.

'Fire!' came the order from General Rieekan.

Suddenly two red beams of destructive energy were released into the cold skies. The beams almost immediately overtook the first of the racing Rebel transport craft, and sped on a direct course toward the huge Star Destroyer.

The twin red bolts struck the enormous ship and blasted its conning tower. Explosions set off by the blast began to rock the great flying fortress, spinning it out of control. The Star Destroyer plunged into deep space as the Rebel transport and its two fighter escorts streaked off to safety.

Luke Skywalker, preparing to depart, pulled on his heavy-weather gear and watched the pilots, gunners, and R2 units hurrying to complete their tasks. He started toward the row of snowspeeders that awaited him. On his way, the young commander paused at the tail section of the *Millennium Falcon*, where Han Solo and Chewbacca were working frenetically on the right lifter.

'Chewie,' Luke called, 'take care of yourself. And watch over this guy, will ya?'

The Wookiee barked a farewell, gave Luke a big hug, then turned back to his work on the lifters.

The two friends, Luke and Han, stood looking at each other, perhaps for the last time.

'I hope you make your peace with Jabba,' Luke said at last.

'Give 'em hell, kid,' the Corellian responded lightly.

The young commander began to walk away as memories of exploits shared with Han rushed to his mind. He stopped and looked back at the *Falcon*, and saw his friend still staring after him. As they gazed at each other for a brief moment, Chewbacca looked up and knew that each was wishing the other best, wherever their individual fates might take them.

The public address system broke in on their thoughts. 'First transport is clear,' a Rebel announcer proclaimed the good news.

At the announcement, a cheer burst from those gathered in the hangar. Luke turned and hurried over to his snowspeeder. When he reached it, Dack, his fresh-faced young gunner, was standing outside the ship waiting for him.

'How are you feeling, sir?' Dack asked enthusiastically.

'Like new, Dack. How about you?'

Dack beamed. 'Right now I feel like I could take on the whole Empire myself.'

'Yeah,' Luke said quietly, 'I know what you mean.' Though there were only a few years between them, at that moment Luke felt centuries older.

Princess Leia's voice came over the address system: 'Attention, speeder pilots . . . on the withdrawal signal assemble at South Slope. Your fighters are being prepared for takeoff. Code One Five will be transmitted when evacuation is complete.'

Threepio and Artoo stood amid the rapidly moving personnel as the pilots readied for departure. The golden droid tilted slightly as he turned his sensors on the little R2 robot. The shadows playing over Threepio's face gave the illusion that his faceplate had lengthened into a frown. 'Why is it,' he asked, 'when things seem to get settled, everything falls apart?' Leaning forward, he gently patted the other droid's hull. 'Take good care of Master Luke. And take good care of yourself.'

Artoo whistled and tooted a good-bye, then turned to roll down the ice corridor. Waving stiffly, Threepio watched as his stout and faithful friend moved away.

To an observer, it may have seemed that Threepio grew misty-eyed, but then it wasn't the first time he had gotten a drop of oil clogged before his optical sensors.

Finally turning, the human-shaped robot moved off in the opposite direction.

NO one on Hoth heard the sound. At first, it was simply too distant to carry above the whining winds. Besides, the Rebel troopers, fighting the cold as they prepared for battle, were too busy to really listen.

In the snow trenches, Rebel officers screamed out their orders to make themselves heard above the gale-force winds. Troopers hurried to carry out their commands, running through the snow with heavy bazookalike weapons on their shoulders, and lodging those death rays along the icy rims of the trenches.

The Rebel power generators near the gun towers began popping, buzzing, and crackling with deafening bursts of electrical power – enough to supply the vast underground complex. But above all this activity and noise a strange sound could be heard, an ominous thumping that was coming nearer and was beginning to shake the frozen ground. When it was close enough to attract the attention of an officer, he strained to see through the storm, looking for the source of the heavy, rhythmic pounding. Other men looked up from their work and saw what looked like a number of moving specks. Through the blizzard, the small dots seemed to be advancing at a slow yet steady pace, churning up clouds of snow as they moved toward the Rebel base.

The officer raised his electrobinoculars and focused on the

approaching objects. There must have been a dozen of them resolutely advancing through the snow, looking like creatures out of some uncharted past. But they were machines, each of them stalking like enormous ungulates on four jointed legs.

Walkers!

With a shock of recognition, the officer identified the Empire's All Terrain Armored Transports. Each machine was formidably armed with cannons placed on its foreside like the horns of some prehistoric beast. Moving like mechanized pachyderms, the walkers emitted deadly fire from their turnstile guns and cannons.

The officer grabbed his comlink. 'Rogue Leader ... Incoming! Point Zero Three.'

'Echo Station Five-Seven, we're on our way.'

Even as Luke Skywalker replied, an explosion sprayed ice and snow around the officer and his terror-struck men. The walkers already had them within range. The troopers knew their job was to divert attention while the transport ships were launched, but none of the Rebel soldiers was prepared to die under the feet or weapons of these horrible machines.

Brilliant billows of orange and yellow flames exploded from the walker guns. Nervously the Rebel troopers aimed their weapons at the walkers, each soldier feeling icy, unseen fingers pierce his body.

Of the twelve snowspeeders, four took the lead, soaring at full throttle as they moved toward the enemy. One All Terrain Armored Transport machine fired, barely missing the banking craft. A burst of gunfire blew another speeder into a ball of flaming oblivion that lit up the sky.

Luke saw the explosion of his squadron's first casualty as he looked from his cockpit window. Angrily, Luke fired his ship's guns at a walker, only to receive a hail of Imperial fire power that shook his speeder in a barrage of flak.

Regaining control of his ship, Luke was joined by another snowspeeder, Rogue Three. They swarmed like insects around the relentlessly stomping walkers, as other speeders continued to exchange fire with the Imperial assault machines. Rogue Leader and Rogue Three flitted alongside the lead walker, then moved away from each other, both banking to the right.

Luke saw the horizon tilt as he maneuvered his speeder between the walker's jointed legs and soared out from under the monster machine. Bringing his speeder back to horizontal flight, the young commander contacted his companion ship. 'Rogue Leader to Rogue Three.'

'Copy, Rogue Leader,' acknowledged Wedge, the pilot of Rogue Three.

'Wedge,' Luke called into his comlink, 'split your squad into pairs.' Luke's snowspeeder then banked and turned, while Wedge's ship moved off in the opposite direction with another Rebel craft.

The walkers, firing all cannons, continued their march across the snow. Inside one of the assault machines two Imperial pilots had spotted the Rebel guns, conspicuous against the white field. The pilots began to maneuver the walker toward the guns when they noticed a lone snowspeeder making a reckless charge directly toward their main viewport, guns blazing. A huge explosion flashed outside the impenetrable window and dissipated as the snowspeeder, roaring through the smoke, disappeared overhead.

As Luke soared up and away from the walker, he looked back. That armor is too strong for blasters, he thought. There *must* be some other way of attacking these horrors; something other than fire power. For a moment Luke thought of some of the simple tactics a farm boy might employ against a wild beast. Then, turning his snowspeeder for yet another run against the walkers, he made a decision.

'Rogue group,' he called into his comlink, 'use your harpoons and tow cables. Go for the legs. It's our only hope of stopping them. Hobbie, are you still with me?'

The reassuring voice immediately responded. 'Yes, sir.'

'Well, stick close now.'

As he leveled his ship, Luke was grimly determined to glide in tight formation with Hobbie. Together they veered, dropping nearer Hoth's surface.

In Luke's cockpit, his gunner, Dack, was jostled by the abrupt movement of the craft. Trying to keep his grip on the Rebel harpoon gun in his hand, he shouted, 'Whoea! Luke, I can't seem to find my restraints.'

Explosions rocked Luke's ship, tossing it about violently in the enveloping flak. Through the window he could see another walker that appeared to be unaffected by the full fire power of the Rebel attack speeders. This lumbering machine now became Luke's target as he flew, moving in a descending arc. The walker was firing directly at him, creating a wall of laser bolts and flak.

'Just hang on, Dack,' he yelled over the explosions, 'and get ready to fire that tow cable!'

Another great blast shook Luke's snowspeeder. He fought to regain control as the ship wobbled in its flight. Luke began to sweat profusely, despite the cold, as he desperately attempted to right his plunging ship. But the horizon still spun in front of him.

'Stand by, Dack. We're almost there. Are you okay?'

Dack didn't answer. Luke managed to turn and saw that Hobbie's speeder was maintaining its course next to him as they evaded the explosions bursting around them. He craned his head around and saw Dack, blood streaming from his forehead, slumped against the controls.

'Dack!'

On the ground, the gun towers near the Rebel power generators blasted away at the walking Imperial machines, but with no apparent effect. Imperial weapons bombarded the area all around them, blasting the snow skyward, almost blinding their human targets with the continuous onslaught. The officer who had first seen the incredible machines and fought alongside his men, was one of the first to be cut down by a walker's body-ripping rays. Troops rushed to his aid, but couldn't save him; too much of his blood had already spilled, making a scarlet stain against the snow.

More Rebel fire power blasted from one of the dishlike guns that had been erected near the power generators. Despite these tremendous explosions, the walkers continued to march. Another speeder made a heroic dive between a pair of the walkers, only to be caught by fire from one of the machines that exploded it into a great ball of rippling flames.

The surface explosions made the walls of the ice hangar tremble, causing deep cracks to spread.

Han Solo and Chewbacca were working frantically to complete their welding job. As they worked, it became obvious that the widening cracks would soon bring the entire ice ceiling smashing down upon them.

'First chance we get,' Han said, 'we're giving this crate a complete overhaul.' But he knew that first he would have to get the *Millennium Falcon* out of this white hell.

Even as he and the Wookiee labored on the ship, enormous pieces of ice, broken loose by the explosions, came tumbling down throughout the underground base. Princess Leia moved quickly, trying to avoid the falling frozen chunks, as she sought shelter in the Rebel command center.

'I'm not sure we can protect two transports at a time,' General Rieekan told her as she entered the chamber.

'It's risky,' she answered, 'but our holding action is faltering.' Leia realized that the transport launchings were taking too much time and that the procedure had to be hastened.

Rieekan issued a command through his comlink. 'Launch patrol, proceed with accelerated departures . . .'

As the general gave his order, Leia looked toward an aide and said, 'Begin clearing the remaining ground staff.' But she knew that their escape depended completely on Rebel success in the on-going battle above.

Inside the cold and cramped cockpit of the lead Imperial walker, General Veers moved between his snow-suited pilots. 'What is the distance to the power generators?'

Without looking away from the control panel, one of the pilots replied, 'Six-four-one.'

Satisfied, General Veers reached for an electrotelescope and peered through the viewfinder to focus on the bullet-shaped power generators and the Rebel soldiers fighting to save them. Suddenly the walker began to rock violently under a barrage of Rebel gunfire. As he was propelled backward, Veers saw his pilots scrambling over the controls to keep the machine from toppling over.

The Rogue Three snowspeeder had just attacked the lead walker. Its pilot, Wedge, hooted with a loud Rebel shout of victory as he saw the damage his guns had caused.

Other snowspeeders passed Wedge, racing in the opposite direction. He steered his craft on a direct course toward another walking death machine. As he approached the monster, Wedge shouted to his gunner, 'Activate harpoon!'

The gunner pressed the firing switch as his pilot daringly maneuvered their craft through the walker's legs. Immediately the harpoon whooshed from the rear of the speeder, a long length of cable unwinding behind it.

'Cable out!' the gunner yelled. 'Let her go!'

Wedge saw the harpoon plunge into one of the metal legs, the cable still connected to his snowspeeder. He checked his controls, then brought the speeder around in front of the Imperial machine. Making an abrupt turn, Wedge guided his ship around one of the hind legs, the cable banding around it like a metallic lariat.

So far, thought Wedge, Luke's plan was working. Now all he had to do was fly his speeder around to the tail end of the walker. Wedge caught a glimpse of Rogue Leader as he carried out the maneuver.

'Cable out!' shouted the speeder's gunner again as Wedge flew their craft alongside the cable-entangled walker, close to the metal hull. Wedge's gunner depressed another switch and released the cable from the rear of the snowspeeder.

The speeder zoomed away and Wedge laughed as he looked down at the results of their efforts. The walker was awkwardly struggling to continue on its way, but the Rebel cable had completely entangled its legs. Finally it leaned to one side and crashed against the ground, its impact stirring up a cloud of ice and snow.

'Rogue Leader ... One down, Luke,' Wedge announced to the pilot of his companion speeder.

'I see it, Wedge,' Commander Skywalker answered. 'Good work.'

In the trenches, Rebel troops cheered in triumph when they saw the assault machine topple. An officer leaped from his snow trench and signaled his men. Bolting out of the trench, he led his troopers in a boisterous charge against the fallen walker, reaching the great metallic hulk before a single Imperial soldier could pull himself free.

The Rebels were about to enter the walker when it suddenly exploded from within, hurtling great jagged chunks of torn metal at them, the impact of the blast flinging the stunned troops back against the snow.

Luke and Zev could see the destruction of the walker as they flew overhead, banking from right to left to avoid the flak bursting around them. When they finally leveled off, their craft were shaken by explosions from the walkers' cannons.

'Steady, Rogue Two,' Luke said, looking over at the snowspeeder flying parallel to his own ship. 'Set harpoon. I'll cover for you.'

But there was another explosion, this one damaging the front section of Zev's ship. The pilot could barely see through the engulfing cloud of smoke that fogged his windshield. He fought to keep his ship on a horizontal path, but more blasts by the enemy made it rock violently.

His view had become so obscured that it wasn't until Zev was directly in the line of fire that he saw the massive image of another Imperial walker. Rogue Two's pilot felt an instant of pain; then his snub-nosed craft, spewing smoke and hurtling on a collision course with the walker, suddenly erupted in flames amid a burst of cannon fire. Very little of Zev or his ship remained to hit the ground.

Luke saw the disintegration and was sickened by the loss of yet another friend. But he couldn't let himself dwell on his grief, especially now when so many other lives depended on his steady leadership.

He looked around desperately, then spoke into his comlink. 'Wedge . . . Wedge . . . Rogue Three. Set your harpoon and follow me on the next pass.'

As he spoke, Luke was hit hard by a terrific explosion that ripped through his speeder. He struggled with the controls in a futile attempt to keep the small craft under control. A chill of fear swept over him when he noticed the dense twisting funnel of black smoke pouring from his ship's aft section. He realized then that there was no way his damaged speeder could remain aloft. And, to make matters even worse, a walker loomed directly in his path.

Luke struggled with the controls as his ship plunged toward the ground, leaving a trail of smoke and flames behind. By then the heat in the cockpit was nearly unbearable. Flames were beginning to leap about inside the speeder and were coming uncomfortably close to Luke. He finally brought his ship down to skid and crash into the snow just a few meters away from one of the walking Imperial machines.

After impact, Luke struggled to pull himself from the cockpit and looked with horror at the looming figure of the approaching walker.

Gathering all his strength, Luke quickly squeezed himself from under the twisted metal of the control board and moved up against the top of his cockpit. Somehow he managed to open the hatch halfway and climbed out of the ship. With each elephantine step of the oncoming walker, the speeder shook violently. Luke had not realized just how enormous these four-legged horrors were until, unprotected by the shelter of his craft, he saw one up close.

Then he remembered Dack and returned to try and pull his friend's lifeless form from the wrecked speeder. But Luke had to give up. The body was too tightly wedged in the cockpit, and the walker was now almost upon him. Braving the flames, Luke reached into his speeder and grabbed the harpoon gun.

He gazed at the advancing mechanical behemoth and suddenly had an idea. He reached back inside the cockpit of the speeder and groped for a land mine attached to the ship's interior. With a great effort he stretched his fingers and firmly grasped the mine.

Luke leaped away from his vehicle just as the towering machine lifted a massive foot and planted it firmly on the snowspeeder, crushing it flat.

Luke crouched underneath the walker, moving with it to avoid its slow steps. Raising his head, he felt the cold wind slap against his face as he studied the monster's vast underbelly.

As he ran along under the machine, Luke aimed his harpoon gun and fired. A powerful magnet attached to a long thin cable was ejected from the gun and firmly attached itself to the machine's underbelly.

Still running, Luke yanked on the cable, testing to make sure its strength was sufficient to sustain his weight. Then he attached the cable drum to the buckle of his utility belt, allowing its mechanism to pull him up off the ground. Now, dangling from the monster's underbelly, Luke could see the remaining walkers and two Rebel snowspeeders continuing the battle as they soared through fiery explosions.

He climbed up to the machine's hull where he had observed a small hatch. Quickly cutting it open with his laser sword, Luke pulled open the hatch, threw in the land mine, and made a rapid descent along the cable. As he reached the end, Luke dropped hard onto the snow and became unconscious; his inert body was nearly brushed by one of the walker's hind feet.

As the walker passed over and away from him, a muffled explosion tore at its insides. Suddenly the tremendous bulk of the mechanical beast exploded at the seams, machinery and pieces of hull flying in every direction. The Imperial assault machine crumbled into a smoking, motionless heap coming to rest upon what remained of its four stiltlike legs.

VI

THE Rebel command center, its walls and ceiling still shaking and cracking under the force of the battle on the surface, was attempting to operate amid the destruction. Pipes, torn apart by the blasting, belched sprays of scalding steam. The white floors were littered with broken pieces of machinery and chunks of ice were scattered everywhere. Except for the distant rumblings of laser fire, the command center was forebodingly quiet.

There were still Rebel personnel on duty, including Princess Leia, who watched the images on the few still-functioning console screens. She wanted to be certain that the last of the transport ships had slipped past the Imperial armada and were approaching their rendezvous point in space.

Han Solo rushed into the command center, dodging great sections of the ice ceiling that came plunging down at him. One great chunk was followed by an avalanche of ice that poured onto the floor near the entrance to the chamber. Undaunted, Han hurried to the control board where Leia stood beside See Threepio.

'I heard the command center was hit.' Han appeared concerned. 'Are you all right?'

The princess nodded. She was surprised to see him there where the danger was severest.

'Come on,' he urged before she could reply. 'You've got to get to your ship.'

Leia looked exhausted. She had been standing at the console viewscreens for hours and had participated in dispatching Rebel personnel to their posts. Taking her hand, Han led her from the chamber, with the protocol droid clacking after them.

As they left, Leia gave one final order to the controller. 'Give the evacuation code signal . . . and get to the transport.'

Then, as Leia, Han, and Threepio made their hasty exit from the command center, a voice blared from the public address speakers, echoing in the nearby deserted ice corridors. 'Disengage, disengage! Begin retreat action!'

'Come on,' Han urged, grimacing. 'If you don't get there fast, your ship won't be able to take off.'

The walls quaked even more violently than before. Ice chunks continued to fall throughout the underground base as the three hurried toward the transport ships. They had nearly reached the hangar where Leia's transport ship was waiting, ready for departure. But as they neared the corner they found the entrance to the hangar completely blocked by ice and snow.

Han knew they would have to find some other route to Leia's escape ship – and quickly. He began to lead them back down the corridor, careful to avoid falling ice, and snapped on his comlink as they hurried toward the ship. 'Transport C One Seven!' he yelled into the small microphone. 'We're coming! Hold on!'

They were close enough to the hangar to hear Leia's escape vessel preparing for lift-off from the Rebel ice base. If he could lead them just a few meters more, the princess would be safe and—

The chamber suddenly quaked with a terrible noise that thundered through the underground base. In an instant the entire ceiling had crashed down in front of them, creating a solid barrier of ice between them and the hangar docks. They stared in shock at the dense white mass.

'We're cut off,' Han yelled into his comlink, knowing that if the transport were to make good its escape there could be no time wasted in melting down or blasting through the barricade. 'You'll have to take off without Princess Organa.' He turned to her. 'If we're lucky we can still make it to the *Falcon*.'

The princess and See Threepio followed as Han dashed toward

another chamber, hoping that the *Millennium Falcon* and his Wookiee copilot had not already been buried under an avalanche of ice.

Looking out across the white battlefield, the Rebel officer watched the remaining snowspeeders whisking through the air and the last of the Imperial vehicles as they passed the wreckage of the exploded walker. He flipped on his comlink and heard the order to retreat: 'Disengage, disengage. Begin retreat action.' As he signaled his men to move back inside the ice cavern, he noticed that the lead walker was still treading heavily in the direction of the power generators.

In the cockpit of that assault machine, General Veers stepped close to the port. From this position he could clearly see the target below. He studied the crackling power generators and observed the Rebel troops defending them.

'Point-three-point-three-point-five ... coming within range, sir,' reported his pilot.

The general turned to his assault officer. 'All troops will debark for ground assault,' Veers said. 'Prepare to target the main generator.'

The lead walker, flanked by two of the hulking machines, lurched forward, its guns blazing to scatter the retreating Rebel troops.

As more laser fire came from the oncoming walkers, Rebel bodies and parts of Rebel bodies were flung through the air. Many of the soldiers who had managed to avoid the obliterating laser beams were crushed into unrecognizable pulp beneath the walkers' stomping feet. The air was charged with the stink of blood and burning flesh, and thundering with the explosive noises of battle.

As they fled, the few surviving Rebel soldiers glimpsed a lone snowspeeder as it retreated in the distance, a black trail of smoke escaping its burning hull.

Although the smoke rising from his crippled speeder obstructed his view, Hobbie could still see some of the carnage that raged on the ground. His wounds from a walker's laser fire made it torture even to move, let alone operate the controls of his craft. But if he could manage to work them just long enough to return to the base, he might be able to find a medical robot and ...

No, he doubted he would survive even that long. He was dying – of that he was now certain – and the men in the trench would soon be dead, too, unless something were done to save them.

General Veers, proudly transmitting his report to Imperial head-quarters, was totally unaware of Rogue Four's approach. 'Yes, Lord Vader, I've reached the main power generators. The shield will be down in moments. You may commence your landing.'

As he ended his transmission, General Veers reached for the electrorangefinder and looked through the eyepiece to line up the main power generators. Electronic crosshairs aligned according to the information from the walker's computers. Then suddenly the readouts on the small monitor screens mysteriously vanished.

Confounded, General Veers moved away from the eyepiece of the electrorangefinder and turned instinctively toward a cockpit window. He flinched in terror at seeing a smoking projectile heading on a direct course toward his walker's cockpit.

The other pilots also saw the hurtling speeder, and knew that there was no time to turn the massive assault machine. 'He's going to—' one of the pilots began.

At that instant, Hobbie's burning ship crashed through the walker cockpit like a manned bomb, its fuel igniting into a cascade of flame and debris. For a second there were human screams, then fragments, and the entire machine crashed to the ground.

Perhaps it was the sound of this nearby blast that jarred Luke Skywalker back to consciousness. Dazed, he slowly lifted his head from the snow. He felt very weak and was achingly stiff with cold. The thought crossed his mind that frostbite might already have damaged his tissues. He hoped not; he had no desire to spend any more time in that sticky bacta fluid.

He tried to stand, but fell back against the snow, hoping he would not be spotted by any of the walker pilots. His comlink whistled, and somehow he found the strength to flick on its receiver.

'Forward units' withdrawal complete,' the broadcast voice reported.

Withdrawal? Luke thought a moment. Then Leia and the others must have escaped! Luke suddenly felt that all the fighting and the deaths of loyal Rebel personnel had not been for nothing. A warmth rushed through his body, and he gathered his strength to rise and begin making the long trek back toward a distant formation of ice.

*

Another explosion rocked the Rebel hangar deck, cracking the ceiling and almost burying the docked *Millennium Falcon* in a mound of ice. At any moment the entire ceiling might cave in. The only safe place in the hangar seemed to be underneath the ship itself where Chewbacca was impatiently awaiting the return of his captain. The Wookiee had begun to worry. If Han did not return soon, the *Falcon* would surely be buried in a tomb of ice. But loyalty to his partner kept Chewie from taking off in the freighter alone.

As the hangar started to tremble more violently, Chewbacca detected movement in the adjoining chamber. Throwing back his head, the shaggy giant filled the hangar with his loudest roar as he saw Han Solo climb over hills of ice and snow and enter the chamber, followed closely by Princess Leia and an obviously nervous See Threepio.

Not far from the hangar, Imperial stormtroopers, their faces shielded by white helmets and white snowscreens, had begun moving down deserted corridors. With them strode their leader, the dark-robed figure who surveyed the shambles that had been the Rebel base at Hoth. Darth Vader's black image stood out starkly against the white walls, ceiling, and floor. As he moved through the white catacombs, he regally stepped aside to avoid a falling section of the ice ceiling. Then he continued on his way with such quick strides that his troops had to hurry to keep up.

A low whine, rising in pitch, began to issue from the saucer-shaped freighter. Han Solo stood at the controls in the *Millennium Falcon*'s cockpit, at last feeling at home. He quickly flipped one switch after another, expecting to see the board flash its familiar mosaic of light; but only some of the lights were working.

Chewbacca had also noticed something amiss and barked with concern as Leia examined a gauge that seemed to be malfunctioning.

'How's that, Chewie?' asked Han anxiously.

The Wookiee's bark was distinctly negative.

'Would it help if I got out and pushed?' snapped Princess Leia, who was beginning to wonder if it were the Corellian's spit that held the ship together.

'Don't worry, Your Holiness. I'll get it started.'

See Threepio clanked into the hold and, gesturing, tried to get Han's attention. 'Sir,' the robot volunteered, 'I was wondering if I might—' But his scanners read the scowl on the face staring at him. 'It can wait,' he concluded.

Imperial stormtroopers, accompanied by the rapidly moving Darth Vader, thundered through the ice corridors of the Rebel base. Their pace quickened as they rushed in the direction of the low whine coming from the ion engines. Vader's body tensed slightly as, entering the hangar, he perceived the familiar saucer-shaped form of the *Millennium Falcon*.

Within the battered freighter ship, Han Solo and Chewbacca were trying desperately to get the craft moving.

'This bucket of bolts is never going to get us past that blockade,' Princess Leia complained.

Han pretended that he didn't hear her. Instead, he checked the *Falcon*'s controls and struggled to keep his patience even though his companion had so obviously lost hers. He flipped switches on the control console, ignoring the princess's look of disdain. Clearly, she doubted that this assemblage of spare parts and welded hunks of scrap metal would hold together even if they *did* manage to get beyond the blockade.

Han pushed a button on the intercom. 'Chewie ... come on!' Then, winking at Leia, he said, 'This baby's still got a few surprises left in her.'

'I'll be surprised if we start moving.'

Before Han could make a carefully honed retort, the *Falcon* was jolted by a blast of Imperial laser fire that flashed outside the cockpit window. They could all see the squad of Imperial stormtroopers rushing with drawn weapons into the far end of the ice hangar. Han knew that the *Falcon*'s dented hull might resist the force of those hand weapons, but would be destroyed by the more powerful bazooka-shaped weapon that two of the Imperial troopers were hurriedly setting up.

'Chewie!' Han yelled as he quickly strapped himself into his pilot's chair. Meanwhile, a somewhat subdued young woman seated herself in the navigator's chair.

Outside the *Millennium Falcon*, stormtroopers worked with military efficiency to set up their enormous gun. Behind them the hangar doors began to open. One of the *Falcon*'s powerful laser weapons appeared from the hull and swung about, aiming directly at the stormtroopers.

Han moved urgently to block the Imperial soldiers' efforts. Without hesitation he released a deadly blast from the powerful laser weapon he had aimed at the stormtroopers. The explosion scattered their armored bodies all over the hangar.

Chewbacca dashed into the cockpit.

'We'll just have to switch over,' Han announced, 'and hope for the best.'

The Wookiee hurled his hairy bulk into the copilot's seat as yet another laser blast erupted outside the window next to him. He yelled indignantly, then yanked back on the controls to bring the welcome roar of engine fire from deep inside the *Falcon*.

The Corellian grinned at the princess, a gleeful I-told-you-so gleam in his eyes.

'Someday,' she said with mild disgust, 'you're going to be wrong, and I just hope I'm there to see it.'

Han just smiled then turned to his copilot. 'Punch it!' he shouted.

The huge freighter's engines roared. And everything behind the craft instantly melted in the fiery exhaust billowing from its tailpiece. Chewbacca furiously worked the controls, watching out of the corner of his eyes the ice walls rushing past as the freighter blasted away.

At the last moment, just before takeoff, Han caught a glimpse of additional stormtroopers running into the hangar. In their wake strode a foreboding giant clad entirely in black. Then there was only the blue and the beckoning of billions of stars.

As the *Millennium Falcon* soared from the hangar, its flight was detected by Commander Luke Skywalker, who turned to smile at Wedge and his gunner. 'At least Han got away.' The three then trudged along to their waiting X-wing fighter ships. When they finally reached them, they shook hands and moved off toward their separate vehicles.

'Good luck, Luke,' Wedge said as they parted. 'See you at the rendezvous.'

Luke waved and began to walk toward his X-wing. Standing

there amid the mountains of ice and snow, he was overcome by a surge of loneliness. He felt desperately alone now that even Han was gone. Worse than that, Princess Leia was also somewhere else; she might just as well be an entire universe away . . .

Then out of nowhere a familiar whistle greeted Luke.

'Artoo!' he exclaimed. 'Is that you?'

Sitting snugly in the socket that had been installed for these helpful R2 units was the little barrel-shaped droid, his head peeking from the top of the ship. Artoo had scanned the approaching figure and had whistled with relief when his computers informed him it was Luke. The young commander was equally relieved to re-encounter the robot that had accompanied him on so many of his previous adventures.

As he climbed into the cockpit and seated himself behind the controls, Luke could hear the sound of Wedge's fighter roaring into the sky toward the Rebel rendezvous point. 'Activate the power and stop worrying. We'll soon be airborne,' Luke said in response to Artoo's nervous beeping.

His was the last Rebel ship to abandon what had, for a very brief time, been a secret outpost in the revolution against the tyranny of the Empire.

Darth Vader, a raven specter, quickly strode through the ruins of the Rebel ice fortress, forcing his accompanying men into a brisk jog to keep up. As they moved through the corridors, Admiral Piett rushed up to overtake his master.

'Seventeen ships destroyed,' he reported to the Dark Lord. 'We don't know how many got away.'

Without turning his head, Vader snarled through his mask, 'The *Millennium Falcon?*'

Piett paused a moment before replying. He would have preferred to avoid *that* issue. 'Our tracking scanners are on it now,' he responded a bit fearfully.

Vader turned to face the admiral, his towering figure looming over the frightened officer. Piett felt a chill course through his veins, and when the Dark Lord spoke again his voice conveyed an image of the dreadful fate that would be inflicted if his commands were not executed.

'I want that ship,' he hissed.

*

The ice planet was rapidly shrinking to a point of dim light as the *Millennium Falcon* sped into space. Soon that planet seemed nothing more than one of the billions of light specks scattered throughout the black void.

But the *Falcon* was not alone in its escape into deep space. Rather, it was followed by an Imperial fleet that included the *Avenger* Star Destroyer and a half-dozen TIE fighters. The fighters moved ahead of the huge, slower-moving Destroyer, and closed in on the fleeing *Millennium Falcon*.

Chewbacca howled over the roar of the *Falcon*'s engines. The ship was beginning to lurch with the buffeting flak blasted at it by the fighters.

'I know, I know, I see them,' Han shouted. It was taking everything he had to maintain control of the ship.

'See what?' Leia asked.

Han pointed out the window at two very bright objects.

'Two more Star Destroyers, and they're heading right at us.'

'I'm glad you said there was going to be no problem,' she commented with more than a touch of sarcasm, 'or I'd be worried.'

The ship rocked under the steady fire from the TIE fighters, making it difficult for Threepio to maintain his balance as he returned to the cockpit. His metal skin bumped and banged against the walls as he approached Han. 'Sir,' he began tentatively, 'I was wondering . . .'

Han Solo shot him a threatening glance. 'Either shut up or shut down,' Han warned the robot, who immediately did the former.

Still struggling with the controls to keep the *Millennium Falcon* on course, the pilot turned to the Wookiee. 'Chewie, how's the deflector shield holding up?'

The copilot adjusted an overhead switch and barked a reply that Solo interpreted as positive.

'Good,' said Han. 'At sublight, they may be faster, but we can still out-maneuver them. Hold on!' Suddenly the Corellian shifted his ship's course.

The two Imperial Star Destroyers had come almost within firing range of the *Falcon* as they loomed ahead; the pursuing TIE fighters and the *Avenger* were also dangerously close. Han felt he had no choice but to take the *Falcon* into a ninety-degree dive.

Leia and Chewbacca felt their stomachs leap into their throats as the *Falcon* executed its steep dive. Poor Threepio quickly had to alter his inner mechanisms if he wanted to remain on his metallic feet.

Han realized that his crew might think he was some kind of lunatic star jockey, pushing his ship on this madman's course. But he had a strategy in mind. With the *Falcon* no longer between them, the two Star Destroyers were now on a direct collision course with the *Avenger*. All he had to do was sit back and watch.

Alarms blared through the interiors of all three Star Destroyers. These ponderously massive ships could not respond quickly enough to such emergencies. Sluggishly one of the Destroyers began to move to the left in its effort to avoid collision with the *Avenger*. Unfortunately, as it veered, it brushed its companion ship, violently shaking up both spaceborne fortresses. The damaged Destroyers began to drift through space, while the *Avenger* continued in pursuit of the *Millennium Falcon* and its obviously insane pilot.

Two down, Han thought. There was still a quartet of TIE fighters tailing the *Falcon*, blasting at its stern with full laser fire, but Han thought he could outstrip them. The ship was buffeted violently by the fighters' laser blasts, forcing Leia to hold on in a desperate attempt to keep her seat.

'That slowed them down a bit!' Han exulted. 'Chewie, stand by to make the jump to lightspeed.' There was not a moment to waste – the laser attack was intense now, and the TIE fighters were almost on top of them.

'They're very close,' Leia warned, finally able to speak.

Han looked at her with a wicked glint in his eyes. 'Oh, yeah? Watch this.'

He threw the hyperspace throttle forward, desperate to escape, but also eager to impress the princess with both his own cleverness and his ship's fantastic power. Nothing happened! The stars that should by then have been mere blurs of light were still. Something was definitely wrong.

'Watch what?' Leia asked impatiently.

Instead of responding, Han worked the lightspeed controls a second time. Again, nothing. 'I think we're in trouble,' he muttered. His throat tightened. He knew 'trouble' was a gross under-statement.

'If I may say so, sir,' Threepio volunteered, 'I noticed earlier that the entire main para-light system seemed to have been damaged.'

Chewbacca threw back his head and let out a loud and miserable wail.

'We're in trouble!' Han repeated.

All around them, the laser attack had increased violently. The *Millennium Falcon* could only continue at its maximum sublight velocity as it moved deeper into space, closely followed by a swarm of TIE fighters and one gigantic Imperial Star Destroyer.

VII

THE double sets of wings on Luke Skywalker's X-wing fighter were pulled together to form one wing as the small, sleek craft streaked away from the planet of snow and ice.

During his flight, the young commander had time to reflect on the events of the past few days. He now had time to ponder the enigmatic words of the ghostly Ben Kenobi and think about his friendship with Han Solo, and also consider his tenuous relationship with Leia Organa. As he thought of the people he cared most about, he arrived at a sudden decision. Gazing back one last time at the small icy planet, he told himself there was no longer any turning back.

Luke flipped a number of switches on his control board and took the X-wing into a steep turn. He watched the heavens shift as he rocketed off in a new direction, flying at top velocity. He was bringing his craft back onto an even course when Artoo, still snug in his specially designed socket, began to whistle and beep.

The miniature computer installed in Luke's ship for translating the droid's language flashed the small droid's message onto a control panel viewscreen.

'There's nothing wrong, Artoo,' Luke replied after reading the translation. 'I'm just setting a new course.'

The small droid beeped excitedly, and Luke turned to read the updated printout on the viewscreen.

'No,' Luke replied, 'we're not going to regroup with the others.'

This news startled Artoo, who immediately emitted a series of galvanic noises.

'We're going to the Dagobah system,' answered Luke.

Again the robot beeped, calculating the amount of fuel carried by the X-wing.

'We have enough power.'

Artoo gave vent to a longer, singsong series of toots and whistles.

'They don't need us there,' said Luke to the droid's question about the planned Rebel rendezvous.

Artoo then gently beeped a reminder about Princess Leia's order. Exasperated, the young pilot exclaimed, 'I'm countermanding that order! Now, be still.'

The little droid fell silent. Luke was, after all, a commander in the Rebel Alliance and, as such, could countermand orders. He was making a few minor adjustments on the controls when Artoo chirped up again.

'Yes, Artoo,' sighed Luke.

This time the droid made a series of soft noises, selecting each beep and whistle carefully. He did not want to annoy Luke, but the findings on his computer were important enough to report.

'Yes, Artoo, I know the Dagobah system doesn't appear on any of our navigational charts. But don't worry. It's there.'

Another worried beep from the R2 unit.

'I'm very sure,' the youth said, trying to reassure his mechanical companion. 'Trust me.'

Whether or not Artoo did trust the human being at the X-wing's controls, he only vented a meek little sigh. For a moment he was completely silent, as if thinking. Then he beeped again.

'Yes, Artoo?'

This communication from the robot was even more carefully put forth than before – one might even call the whistle-sentences tactful. It seemed Artoo had no intention of offending the human to whom he had entrusted himself. But wasn't it possible, the robot calculated, that the human's brain was slightly malfunctioning? After all, he had lain a long time in the snowdrifts of Hoth. Or, another possibility computed by Artoo, perhaps the Wampa Ice Creature had struck him more seriously than Too-Onebee had diagnosed?...

'No,' Luke answered, 'no headache. I feel fine. Why?'

Artoo's chirp was coyly innocent.

'No dizziness, no drowsiness. Even the scars are gone.'

The next whistle rose questioningly in pitch.

'No, that's all right, Artoo. I'd rather keep it on manual control for a while.'

Then the stout robot delivered a final whimper that sounded to Luke like a noise of defeat. Luke was amused by the droid's concern for his health. 'Trust me, Artoo,' Luke said with a gentle smile. 'I know where I'm going and I'll get us there safely. It's not far.'

Han Solo was desperate now. The *Falcon* had still not been able to shrug off the four TIE fighters or the enormous Star Destroyer that pursued it.

Solo raced down to the ship's hold and began to work frantically on repairing the malfunctioning hyperdrive unit. It was all but impossible to carry out the delicate repair work necessary while the *Falcon* shook with each blast of flak from the fighters.

Han snapped orders at his copilot, who checked the mechanisms as he was commanded. 'Horizontal booster.'

The Wookiee barked. It looked fine to him.

'Alluvial damper.'

Another bark. That part was also in place.

'Chewie, get me the hydrospanners.'

Chewbacca rushed over to the pit with the tools. Han grabbed the spanners, then paused and looked at his faithful Wookiee friend.

'I don't know how we're going to get out of this one,' he confided.

Just then a resounding *thump* hit the *Falcon*'s side, making the ship pitch and turn radically.

Chewbacca barked anxiously.

Han braced himself at the impact, the hydrospanners flew from his hand. When he managed to regain his balance, he shouted at Chewbacca over the noise, 'That was no laser blast! Something hit us!'

'Han ... Han ...' Princess Leia called to him from the cockpit. She was frantic. 'Get up here!'

Like a shot, he lurched out of the hold and raced back to the cockpit with Chewbacca. They were stunned by what they saw through the windows.

'Asteroids!'

Enormous chunks of flying rock hurtled through space as far as they could see. As if those damn Imperial pursuit ships weren't trouble enough!

Han instantly returned to his pilot's seat, once more taking over the *Falcon*'s controls. His copilot settled himself back into his own seat just as a particularly large asteroid sped by the prow of the ship.

Han felt he had to stay as calm as possible; otherwise they might not last more than a few moments. 'Chewie,' he ordered, 'set two-seven-one.'

Leia gasped. She knew what Han's order meant and was stunned by so reckless a plan. 'You're not thinking of heading into the asteroid field?' she asked, hoping she had misunderstood his command.

'Don't worry, they won't follow us through this!' he shouted with glee.

'If I might remind you, sir,' Threepio offered, trying to be a rational influence, 'the possibility of successfully navigating through an asteroid field is approximately two thousand four hundred and sixty-seven to one.'

No one seemed to hear him.

Princess Leia scowled. 'You don't have to do this to impress me,' she said, as the *Falcon* was pummeled hard by another asteroid.

Han was enjoying himself enormously and chose to ignore her insinuations. 'Hang on, sweetheart,' he laughed, grasping the controls more tightly. 'We're gonna do some *flyin*'.'

Leia winced and, resigned, buckled herself firmly into her seat.

See Threepio, still muttering calculations, shut down his synthesized human voice when the Wookiee turned and growled at him.

But Han concentrated only on carrying out his plan. He knew it would work; it had to – there was no other choice. Flying more on instinct than on instruments, he steered his ship through the relentless rain of stone. Glancing quickly at his scanner screens, he saw that the TIE fighters and the *Avenger* had not yet abandoned the chase. It would be an Imperial funeral, he thought, as he maneuvered the *Falcon* through the asteroid hail.

He looked at another viewscreen and smiled as it showed a collision between an asteroid and a TIE fighter. The explosion registered on the screen with a burst of light. No survivors in *that* one, Han thought.

The TIE fighter pilots chasing the *Falcon* were among the best in the Empire. But they couldn't compete with Han Solo. Either they weren't good enough, or they weren't crazy enough. Only a lunatic would have plunged his ship into a suicidal journey through these asteroids. Crazy or not, these pilots had no choice but to follow in hot pursuit. They undoubtedly would be better off perishing in this bombardment of rocks than reporting failure to their dark master.

The greatest of all the Imperial Star Destroyers regally moved out of Hoth's orbit. It was flanked by two other Star Destroyers and the entire group was accompanied by a protective squadron of smaller warships. In the central Destroyer, Admiral Piett stood outside Darth Vader's private meditation chamber. The upper jaw slowly opened until Piett was able to glimpse his robed master standing in the shadows. 'My lord,' Piett said with reverence.

'Come in, Admiral.'

Admiral Piett felt great awe as he stepped into the dimly lit room and approached the Dark Lord of the Sith. His master stood silhouetted so that Piett could just barely make out the lines of a set of mechanical appendages as they retracted a respirator tube from Vader's head. He shuddered when he realized that he might be the first ever to have seen his master unmasked.

The sight was horrifying. Vader, his back turned to Piett, was entirely clothed in black; but above his studded black neck band gleamed his naked head. Though the admiral tried to avert his eyes, morbid fascination forced him to look at that hairless, skull-like head. It was covered with a maze of thick scar tissue that twisted around against Vader's corpse-pale skin. The thought crossed Piett's mind that there might be a heavy price for viewing what no one else had seen. Just then, the robot hands grasped the black helmet and gently lowered it over the Dark Lord's head.

His helmet back in place, Darth Vader turned to hear his admiral's report.

'Our pursuit ships have sighted the *Millennium Falcon*, my lord. It has entered an asteroid field.'

'Asteroids don't concern me, Admiral,' Vader said as he slowly clenched his fist. 'I want that ship, not excuses. How long until you will have Skywalker and the others in the *Millennium Falcon*?'

'Soon, Lord Vader,' the admiral answered, trembling in fear.

'Yes, Admiral . . .' Darth Vader said slowly, '. . . soon.'

*

Two gigantic asteroids hurtled toward the *Millennium Falcon*. Its pilot quickly made a daring banking maneuver that brought it skirring out of the path of those two asteroids, nearly to collide with a third.

As the *Falcon* darted in and out of the asteroid field, it was followed closely by three Imperial TIE fighters that veered through the rocks in hot pursuit. Suddenly one of the three was fatally scraped by a shapeless chunk of rock and spun off in another direction, hopelessly out of control. The other two TIE fighters continued their chase, accompanied by the Star Destroyer *Avenger*, which was blasting speeding asteroids in its path.

Han Solo glimpsed the pursuing ships through the windows of his cockpit as he spun his craft around, speeding under yet another oncoming asteroid, then bringing the freighter back to its right-side-up position. But the *Millennium Falcon* was not yet out of danger. Asteroids were still streaking past the freighter. A small one bounced off the ship with a loud, reverberating clang, terrifying Chewbacca and causing See Threepio to cover his eye lenses with a bronzed hand.

Han glanced at Leia and saw that she was sitting stone-faced as she stared at the swarm of asteroids. It looked to him as if she wished she were thousands of miles away.

'Well,' he remarked, 'you said you wanted to be around when I was wrong.'

She didn't look at him. 'I take it back.'

'That Star Destroyer is slowing down,' Han announced, checking his computer readings.

'Good,' she replied shortly.

The view outside the cockpit was still thick with racing asteroids. 'We're going to get pulverized if we stay out here much longer,' he observed.

'I'm against that,' Leia remarked dryly.

'We've got to get out of this shower.'

'That makes sense.'

'I'm going to get in closer to one of the big ones,' Han added.

That did *not* make sense.

'Closer!' Threepio exclaimed, throwing up his metal arms. His artificial brain could scarcely register what his auditory sensors had just perceived.

'Closer!' Leia repeated in disbelief.

Chewbacca stared at his pilot in amazement and barked.

None of the three could understand why their captain, who had risked his life to save them all, would now try to get them killed! Making a few simple adjustments on the cockpit controls, Han swerved the *Millennium Falcon* between a few larger asteroids, then aimed the craft directly at one the size of a moon.

A flashing shower of smaller rocks exploded against the enormous asteroid's craggy surface as the *Millennium Falcon*, with the Emperior's TIE fighters still in pursuit, flew directly above the asteroid. It was like skimming over the surface of a small planet, barren and devoid of all life.

With expert precision, Han Solo steered his ship toward still another giant asteroid, the largest one they had yet encountered. Summoning all the skill that had made his reputation known throughout the galaxy, he maneuvered the *Falcon* so that the only object between it and the TIE fighters was the deadly floating rock.

There was only a brief, brilliant flare of light, then nothing. The shattered remains of the two TIE fighters drifted away into the darkness and the tremendous asteroid – undeflected in its course – continued on its way.

Han felt an inner glow as bright as the spectacle that had just lighted up the view. He smiled to himself in quiet triumph.

Then he noticed an image on the main scope of his control console and nudged his hairy copilot. 'There.' Han pointed to the image. 'Chewie, get a reading on that. Looks pretty good.'

'What is it?' Leia asked.

The *Falcon*'s pilot ignored her question. 'That should do nicely,' he said.

As they flew near the asteroid's surface, Han looked down at the craggy terrain, his eye caught by a shadowy area that looked like a crater of mammoth proportions. He lowered the *Falcon* to surface level and flew it directly into the crater, its bowl-like walls suddenly rising up around his ship.

And still two TIE fighters chased after him, firing their laser cannons and attempting to mimic his every maneuver.

Han Solo knew he had to be trickier and more daring if he was to lose the deadly pursuit ships. Spotting a narrow chasm through his windscreen, he banked the *Millennium Falcon* to one side. The ship soared sideways through the high-walled rocky trench.

Unexpectedly the two TIE fighters followed. One of them even sparked as it grazed the walls with its metal hull.

Twisting, banking, and turning his ship, Han pressed through the narrow gorge. From behind, the black sky flared as the two TIE fighters crashed against one another, then exploded against the rocky ground.

Han reduced his speed. He still wasn't safe from the Imperial hunters. Searching about the canyon, he spotted something dark, a gaping cave mouth at the very bottom of the crater, large enough to hold the *Millennium Falcon* – perhaps. If not, he and his crew would know soon enough.

Slowing his ship, Han coursed into the cave entrance and through a large tunnel, which he hoped would make the ideal hiding place. He took a deep breath as his ship was promptly devoured by the cave's shadows.

A tiny X-wing was approaching the atmosphere of the Dagobah planet.

As he neared the planet, Luke Skywalker was able to glimpse a portion of its curved surface through a heavy cover of thick clouds. The planet was uncharted and virtually unknown. Somehow Luke had made his way there, though he wasn't certain whether it was his hand alone that had guided his ship into this unexplored sector of space.

Artoo Detoo, riding in the back of Luke's X-wing, scanned the passing stars, then addressed his remarks to Luke via the computer scope.

Luke read the viewscreen interpreter. 'Yes, that's Dagobah, Artoo,' he answered the little robot, then glanced out the cockpit window as the fighter ship began to descend toward the planet's surface. 'Looks a little grim, doesn't it?'

Artoo beeped, attempting for one last time to get his master back on a more sensible course.

'No,' Luke replied, 'I don't want to change my mind about this.' He checked the ship's monitors and began to feel a bit nervous. 'I'm not picking up any cities or technology. Massive life-form readings, though. There's something alive down there.'

Artoo was worried, too, and that was translated as an apprehensive inquiry.

'Yes, I'm sure it's perfectly safe for droids. Will you take it easy?'
Luke was beginning to get annoyed. 'We'll just have to see what
happens.'

He heard a pathetic electronic whimper from the rear of the
cockpit.

'*Don't worry!*'

The X-wing sailed through the twilight halo separating pitch
black space from the planet's surface. Luke took a deep breath, then
plunged his craft into the white blanket of mists.

He couldn't see a thing. His vision was entirely obstructed by the
dense whiteness pressing against the canopy windows of his ship.
His only choice was to control his X-wing solely by instruments. But
the scopes weren't registering anything, even as Luke flew ever
nearer to the planet. Desperately he worked his controls, no longer
able to discern even so much as his altitude.

When an alarm began to buzz, Artoo joined its clarion call with
his own frantic series of whistles and beeps.

'I know, I know!' Luke shouted, still fighting the controls of his
ship. 'All the scopes are dead! I can't see a thing. Hang on, I'm going
to start the landing cycle. Let's just hope there's something
underneath us.'

Artoo squealed again, but his sounds were effectively drowned by
the ear-splitting blast of the X-wing's retrorockets. Luke felt his
stomach plunge as the ship began to drop rapidly. He braced against
his pilot's seat, steeling himself for any possible impact. Then the
ship lunged and Luke heard an awful sound as if the limbs of trees
were being snapped off by his speeding craft.

When the X-wing finally screeched to a halt, it was with a
tremendous jolt that nearly flung its pilot through the cockpit
window. Certain, at last, that he was on the ground, Luke slumped
back in his chair and sighed with relief. He then pulled a switch that
lifted his ship's canopy. When he raised his head outside the ship to
get his first look at the alien world, Luke Skywalker gasped.

The X-wing was completely surrounded by mists, its bright
landing lights not illuminating more than a few feet in front of it.
Luke's eyes gradually began to grow accustomed to the gloom all
around him so that he could just barely see the twisted trunks and
roots of grotesque-looking trees. He pulled himself out of the cockpit
as Artoo detached his stout body from its cubbyhole plug.

'Artoo,' Luke said, 'you stay put while I look around.'

The enormous gray trees had gnarled and intertwining roots that rose far above Luke before they joined to form trunks. He tilted back his head and could see the branches, high above, that seemed to form a canopy with the low-hanging clouds. Luke cautiously climbed out onto the long nose of his ship and saw that he had crash-landed in a small, fog-shrouded body of water.

Artoo emitted a short beep – then there was a loud splash, followed by silence. Luke turned just in time to glimpse the droid's domed topside as it disappeared beneath the water's foggy surface.

'Artoo! Artoo!' Luke called. He kneeled down on the smooth hull of the ship and leaned forward, anxiously searching for his mechanical friend.

But the black waters were serene, revealing not a sign of the little R2 unit. Luke could not tell how deep this still, murky pond might be; but it looked *extremely* deep. He was suddenly gripped by the realization that he might never see his droid friend again. Just then, a tiny periscope broke through the surface of the water and Luke could hear a faint gurgling beep.

What a relief! Luke thought, as he watched the periscope make its way toward shore. He ran along the nose of his X-wing fighter, and when the shore line was less than three meters away, the young commander jumped into the water and scrambled up the shore. He looked back and saw that Artoo was still making his way toward the beach.

'Hurry, Artoo!' Luke shouted.

Whatever it was that suddenly moved through the water behind Artoo moved too quickly and was too obscured by the mist for Luke to clearly identify it. All he could see was a massive dark form. This creature rose up for a moment, then dove beneath the surface, making a loud bang against the little droid's metal hull. Luke heard the robot's pathetic electronic scream for help. Then, nothing ...

Luke stood there, horror-struck, as he continued to stare at the black waters, still as death itself. As he watched, a few tell-tale bubbles began to erupt at the surface. Luke's heart began to pound in fear as he realized he was standing too near the pool. But before he could move, the runt-size robot was spat out by the thing lurking beneath the black surface. Artoo made a graceful arc through the air and came crashing down onto a soft patch of gray moss.

'Artoo,' Luke yelled, running to him, 'are you okay?' Luke was grateful that the shadowy swamp lurker apparently found metal droids neither palatable nor digestible.

Feebly the robot replied with a series of faint whistles and beeps.

'If you're saying coming here was a bad idea, I'm beginning to agree with you,' Luke admitted, looking around at their dismal surroundings. At least, he thought, there was human companionship on the ice world. Here, except for Artoo, there seemed to be nothing but this murky bog – and creatures, as yet unseen, that might lurk in the falling darkness.

Dusk was quickly approaching. Luke shivered in the thickening fog that closed in on him like something alive. He helped Artoo-Detoo back onto his feet, then wiped away the swamp muck that covered the droid's cylindrical body. As he worked, Luke heard eerie and inhuman cries that emanated from the distant jungle and shuddered as he imagined the beasts that might be making them.

By the time he finished cleaning off Artoo, Luke observed that the sky had grown noticeably darker. Shadows loomed ominously all around him and the distant cries didn't seem quite so far away anymore. He and Artoo glanced around at the spooky swamp-jungle surrounding them, then huddled a bit closer. Suddenly, Luke noticed a pair of tiny but vicious eyes winking at them through the shadowy underbrush, then vanishing with a scutter of diminutive feet.

He hesitated to doubt the advice of Ben Kenobi, but now he was beginning to wonder if that robed specter had somehow made a mistake leading him to this planet with its mysterious Jedi teacher.

He looked over at his X-wing and groaned when he saw that the entire bottom section was completely submerged in the dark waters. 'How are we going to get that thing flying again?' The whole set of circumstances seemed hopeless and somewhat ridiculous. 'What are we doing here?' he moaned.

It was beyond the computerized abilities of Artoo to provide an answer for either of those questions, but he made a little comforting beep anyway.

'It's like part of a dream,' Luke said. He shook his head, feeling cold and frightened. 'Or maybe I'm going crazy.'

At least, he knew for certain, he couldn't have gotten himself into a crazier situation.

VIII

DARTH Vader looked like a great silent god as he stood on the main control deck of his mammoth Star Destroyer.

He was staring through the large rectangular window above the deck at the raging field of asteroids that was pelting his ship as it glided through space. Hundreds of rocks streaked past the windows. Some collided with one another and exploded in brilliant displays of vivid light.

As Vader watched, one of his smaller ships disintegrated under the impact of an enormous asteroid. Seemingly unmoved, he turned to look at a series of twenty holographic images. These twenty holograms re-created in three dimensions the features of twenty Imperial battleship commanders. The image of the commander whose ship had just been obliterated was fading rapidly, almost as quickly as the glowing particles of his exploded ship were being flung to oblivion.

Admiral Piett and an aide quietly moved to stand behind their black-garbed master as he turned to an image in the center of the twenty holograms which was continually interrupted by static and faded in and out as Captain Needa of the Star Destroyer *Avenger* made his report. His first words had already been drowned by static.

'... which was the last time they appeared in any of our scopes,'

Captain Needa continued. 'Considering the amount of damage we've sustained, they also must have been destroyed.'

Vader disagreed. He knew of the *Millennium Falcon*'s power and was quite familiar with the skills of her cocky pilot. 'No, Captain,' he snarled angrily, 'they're alive. I want every ship available to sweep the asteroid field until they're found.'

As soon as Vader had given his command, Captain Needa's image and those of the other nineteen captains faded completely. When the last hologram vanished, the Dark Lord, having sensed the two men standing behind him, turned. 'Now what is so important it couldn't wait, Admiral?' he asked imperiously. 'Speak up!'

The admiral's face turned pale with fear, his trembling voice shaking almost as much as his body. 'It was . . . the Emperor.'

'The Emperor?' the voice behind the black breath mask repeated.

'Yes,' the admiral replied. 'He commands you make contact with him.'

'Move this ship out of the asteroid field,' Vader ordered, 'into a position where we can send a clear transmission.'

'Yes, my lord.'

'And code the signal to my private chamber.'

The *Millennium Falcon* had come to rest hidden in the small cave which was pitch black and dripping with moisture. The *Falcon*'s crew turned down its engines until no sound at all was emitted from the small craft.

Inside the cockpit, Han Solo and his shaggy copilot were just completing shutting down the ship's electronic systems. As they did so, all the service lights dimmed and the interior of the ship became nearly as dark as its sheltering cave.

Han glanced over at Leia and flashed her a quick grin. 'Getting kind of romantic in here.'

Chewbacca growled. There was work to be done in here and the Wookiee needed Han's undivided attention if they were going to repair the malfunctioning hyperdrive.

Irritated, Han returned to his work. 'What are you so grouchy about?' he snapped.

Before the Wookiee could respond, the protocol droid timidly approached Han and posed a question of burning importance. 'Sir, I'm almost afraid to ask, but does shutting down all except emergency power systems include me?'

Chewbacca expressed his opinion with a resounding bark of affirmation, but Han disagreed. 'No,' he said, 'we're going to need you to talk to the old *Falcon* here and find out what happened to our hyperdrive.' He looked over at the princess and added, 'How are you with a macrofuser, Your Holiness?'

Before Leia could get off a suitable retort, the *Millennium Falcon* lurched forward as a sudden impact struck its hull. Everything that was not bolted down flew through the cockpit; even the giant Wookiee, howling boisterously, had to struggle to stay in his chair.

'Hang on!' Han yelled. 'Watch out!'

See Threepio clattered against a wall, then collected himself. 'Sir, it's very possible this asteroid is not stable.'

Han glared at him. 'I'm glad you're here to tell us these things.'

The ship rocked once more, even more violently than before.

The Wookiee howled again; Threepio stumbled backward, and Leia was hurled across the cabin directly into the waiting arms of Captain Solo.

The ship's rocking stopped as suddenly as it had started. But Leia still stood in Han's embrace. For once she did not draw away, and he could almost swear she was willingly embracing him. 'Why, Princess,' he said, pleasantly surprised, 'this is so sudden.'

At that, she began to pull back. 'Let go,' she insisted, trying to move out of his arms. 'I'm getting angry.'

Han saw the old familiar expression of arrogance beginning to return to her face. 'You don't look angry,' he lied.

'How do I look?'

'Beautiful,' he answered truthfully, with an emotion that surprised him.

Leia felt suddenly, unexpectedly shy. Her cheeks flushed pink and, when she realized she was blushing, she averted her eyes. But she still did not really try to get free.

Han somehow couldn't let the tender moment last. 'And excited,' he had to add.

Leia became infuriated. Once again the angry princess and haughty senator, she quickly moved away from him and drew herself up to her most regal bearing. 'Sorry, Captain,' she said, her cheeks now reddened in anger, 'being held by you isn't enough to get me excited.'

'Well, I hope you don't expect more,' he grunted, angrier at himself than at her stinging words.

'I don't expect anything,' Leia said indignantly, 'except to be left alone.'

'If you'll just get out of my way, I'll leave you alone.'

Embarrassed to realize that she was, indeed, still standing rather close, Leia stepped aside and made an effort to change the subject. 'Don't you think it's time we got to work on your ship?'

Han frowned. 'Fine with me,' he said coldly, not looking at her.

Leia quickly turned on her heel and left the cockpit.

For a moment Han stood there quietly, just gathering his composure. Sheepishly he looked at the now quiet Wookiee and droid, both of whom had witnessed the entire incident.

'Come on, Chewie, let's tear into this flying short circuit,' he said quickly to end the awkward moment.

The copilot barked in agreement, then joined his captain as they began to leave the cockpit. As they walked out, Han looked back at Threepio, who was still standing in the dim chamber looking dumbfounded. 'You too, goldenrod!'

'I must admit,' the robot muttered to himself as he began to shuffle out of the cockpit, 'there are times I don't understand human behavior.'

The lights of Luke Skywalker's X-wing fighter pierced the darkness of the bog planet. The ship had sunk deeper into the scummy waters, but there was still enough of it above the surface to let Luke carry needed supplies from the storage compartments. He knew it could not be much longer before his ship sank deeper – possibly all the way – beneath the water. He thought that his chance of survival might be increased if he gathered as many supplies as he could.

It was now so dark that Luke could scarcely see in front of him. Out in the dense jungle he heard a sharp snapping noise and felt a chill run through him. Grabbing his pistol, he prepared to blast anything that leaped from the jungle to attack him. But nothing did, and he clipped his weapon back onto its holster and continued to unpack his gear.

'You ready for some power?' Luke asked Artoo, who was patiently waiting for his own form of nourishment. Luke took a small fusion furnace from an equipment box and ignited it, welcoming even the tiny glow thrown off by the small heating device, then took a power cable and attached it to Artoo through a protuberance that roughly resembled a nose. As power radiated through Artoo's electronic innards, the stout robot whistled his appreciation.

Luke sat down and opened a container of processed food. As he began to eat, he talked to the robot. 'Now all I have to do is find this Yoda, if he even exists.'

He looked around nervously at the shadows in the jungle and felt frightened, miserable, and increasingly in doubt about his quest. 'This certainly seems like a strange place to find a Jedi Master,' he said to the little robot. 'Gives me the creeps.'

From the sound of his beep, it was clear Artoo shared Luke's opinion of the swamp world.

'Although,' Luke continued as he reluctantly tasted more of the food, 'there's something familiar about this place. I feel like—'

'You feel like what?'

That wasn't Artoo's voice! Luke leaped up, grabbed his pistol, then spun around, peering into the gloom to try to find the source of those words.

As he turned he saw a tiny creature standing directly in front of him. Luke immediately stepped back in surprise; this little being seemed to have materialized out of nowhere! It stood no more than half a meter in height, fearlessly holding its ground in front of the towering youth who wielded an awesome laser pistol.

The little wizened thing could have been any age. Its face was deeply lined, but was framed with elfin, pointed ears that gave it a look of eternal youth. Long white hair was parted down the middle and hung down on either side of the blue-skinned head. The being was bipedal, and stood on short legs that terminated in tridactyl, almost reptilian feet. It wore rags as gray as the mists of the swamp, and in such tatters that they must have approximated the creature's very age.

For the moment, Luke could not decide whether to be frightened or to laugh. But when he gazed into those bulbous eyes and sensed the being's kindly nature, he relaxed. At last the creature motioned toward the pistol in Luke's hand.

'Away put your weapon. I mean you no harm,' it said.

After some hesitation, Luke quietly put his pistol back into his belt. As he did so, he wondered why he felt impelled to obey this little creature.

'I am wondering,' the creature spoke again, 'why are you here?'

'I'm looking for someone,' Luke answered.

'Looking? Looking?' the creature repeated curiously with a wide smile beginning to crease his already-lined face. 'You've found someone I'd say. Heh? Yes!'

Luke had to force himself not to smile. 'Yeah.'

'Help you I can ... yes ... yes.'

Inexplicably Luke found himself trusting the odd creature, but wasn't at all sure that such a tiny individual could be of help on his important quest. 'I don't think so,' he replied gently. 'You see, I'm looking for a great warrior.'

'A *great* warrior?' The creature shook his head, the whitish hair flopping about his pointed ears. 'Wars don't make one great.'

A strange phrase, Luke thought. But before he could answer, Luke saw the tiny hominid hobble over to the top of the salvaged supply cases. Shocked, he watched as the creature began to rummage through the articles Luke had brought with him from Hoth.

'Get away from there,' he said, surprised at this sudden strange behavior.

Moving across the ground, Artoo waddled toward the pile of cases, standing just about at optical sensor level with the creature. The droid squealed his disapproval as he scanned the creature that was carelessly digging through the supplies.

The strange being grabbed the container holding the remains of Luke's food and took a bite.

'Hey, that's my dinner!' Luke exclaimed.

But no sooner had the creature taken his first bite than he spat out what he had tasted, his deeply lined face wrinkling like a prune. '*Peewh!*' he said, spitting. 'Thank you, no. How get you so big eating food of this kind?' He looked Luke up and down.

Before the astounded youth could reply, the creature flipped the food container in Luke's direction, then dipped one of his small and delicate hands into another supply case.

'Listen, friend,' Luke said, watching this bizarre scavenger, 'we didn't mean to land here. And if I could get my fighter out of this puddle I would, but I can't. So—'

'Can't get your ship out? Have you tried? Have you tried?' the creature goaded.

Luke had to admit to himself that he had not, but then the whole idea was patently ludicrous. He didn't have the proper equipment to—

Something in Luke's case had attracted the creature's interest. Luke finally reached the end of his patience when he saw the crazy little being snatch something out of the supply case. Knowing that survival depended on those supplies, he grabbed for the case. But the creature held on to his prize – a miniature power lamp that he gripped tightly in his blue-skinned hand. The little light came alive in the creature's hand, throwing its radiance up into his delighted face, and he immediately began to examine his treasure.

'Give me that!' Luke cried.

The creature retreated from the approaching youth like a petulant child. 'Mine! Mine! Or I'll help you not.'

Still clutching the lamp to his breast, the creature stepped backward, inadvertently bumping into Artoo-Detoo. Not remembering that the robot was at all animate, the being stood next to it as Luke approached.

'I don't want your help,' Luke said indignantly. 'I want my lamp back. I'll need it in this slimy mudhole.'

Luke instantly realized he had issued an insult.

'Mudhole? Slimy? My home this is!'

As they argued, Artoo slowly reached out a mechanical arm. Suddenly his appendage grabbed the pilfered lamp and immediately the two little figures were engaged in a tug-of-war over the stolen prize. As they spun about in battle, Artoo beeped a few electronic, 'give me that's.

'Mine, mine. Give it back,' the creature cried. Abruptly, though, he seemed to give up the bizarre struggle and lightly poked the droid with one bluish finger.

Artoo emitted a loud, startled squeal and immediately released the power lamp.

The victor grinned at the glowing object in his tiny hands, gleefully repeating, 'Mine, mine.'

Luke was about fed up with these antics and advised the robot that the battle was over. 'Okay, Artoo,' he said with a sigh, 'let him have it. Now get out of here, little fellow. We've got things to do.'

'No, no!' the creature pleaded excitedly. 'I'll stay and help you find your friend.'

'I'm not looking for a friend,' Luke said. 'I'm looking for a Jedi Master.'

'Oh,' the creature's eyes widened as he spoke, 'a Jedi Master. Different altogether. *Yoda*, you seek, Yoda.'

Mention of that name surprised Luke, but he felt skeptical. How could an elf like this know anything about a great teacher of the Jedi Knights? 'You know him?'

'Of course, yes,' the creature said proudly. 'I'll take you to him. But first we must eat. Good food. Come, come.'

With that, the creature scurried out of Luke's camp and into the shadows of the swamp. The tiny power lamp he carried was gradually dimming in the distance as Luke stood feeling baffled. At first he had no intention of pursuing the creature, but all at once he found himself diving into the fog after him.

As Luke started off into the jungle, he heard Artoo whistling and beeping as if he would blow his circuits. Luke turned around to see the little droid standing forlornly next to the miniature fission furnace.

'You'd better stay here and watch over the camp,' Luke instructed the robot.

But Artoo only intensified his noisy output, running through the entire gamut of his electronic articulations.

'Artoo, now settle down,' Luke called as he ran into the jungle. 'I can take care of myself. I'll be safe, okay?'

Artoo's electronic grumblings grew fainter as Luke hurried to catch up with the little guide. I must really be out of my mind, Luke thought, following this weird being into who-knows-what. But the creature *had* mentioned Yoda's name, and Luke felt compelled to accept any help he could get to find the Jedi Master. He stumbled in the dark over thick weeds and twisting roots as he pursued the flickering light ahead.

The creature was chattering gaily as he led the way through the swamp. 'Heh ... safe ... heh ... quite safe ... yes, of course.' Then, in his odd little way, this mysterious being started to laugh.

Two Imperial cruisers slowly moved across the surface of the great asteroid. The *Millennium Falcon* had to be hidden somewhere within – but where?

As the ships skimmed the surface of the asteroid, they dropped bombs on its pock-marked terrain, trying to scare out the freighter. The shock waves from the explosives violently shook the spheroid, but still there was no sign of the *Falcon*. As it drifted above the asteroid, one of the Imperial Star Destroyers cast an eclipsing shadow across the tunnel entrance. Yet the ship's scanners failed to note the curious hole in the bowl-like wall. Within that hole, in a winding tunnel not detected by the minions of the powerful Empire, sat the freighter. It rattled and vibrated with every explosion that pounded the surface above.

Inside, Chewbacca worked feverishly to repair the complex powertrain. He had scrambled into an overhead compartment to get at the wires that operated the hyperdrive system. But when he felt the first of the explosions, he popped his head out through the mass of wires and gave out a worried yelp.

Princess Leia, who was welding a damaged valve, stopped her work and looked up. The bombs sounded very close.

See Threepio glanced up at Leia and nervously tilted his head. 'Oh, my,' he said, 'they've found us.'

Everyone became quiet, as if fearing that the sound of their voices might somehow carry and betray their exact position. Again the ship was shaken by a blast, less intense than the last.

'They're moving away,' Leia said.

Han saw through their tactic. 'They're just trying to see if they can stir up something,' he told her. 'We're safe if we stay put.'

'Where have I heard that line before?' Leia said with an innocent air.

Ignoring her sarcasm, Han moved past her as he went back to work. The passageway in the hold was so narrow that he couldn't avoid brushing against her as he passed by – or could he?

With mixed emotions the princess watched him for a moment as he continued to work on his ship. And then she turned back to her welding.

See Threepio ignored all this odd human behavior. He was too busy trying to communicate with the *Falcon*, trying to find out what was wrong with its hyperdrive. Standing at the central control panel, Threepio was making uncharacteristic whistle and beep sounds. A moment later, the control panel whistled back.

'Where is Artoo when I need him?' sighed the golden robot. The control panel's response had been difficult for him to interpret. 'I don't know where your ship learned to communicate,' Threepio announced to Han, 'but its dialect leaves something to be desired. I believe, sir, it says the power coupling on the negative axis has been polarized. I'm afraid you'll have to replace it.'

'Of course I'll have to replace it,' Han snapped, then called up to Chewbacca, who was peering from the ceiling compartment. 'Replace it!' he whispered.

He noticed that Leia had finished her welding but was having trouble reengaging the valve, struggling with a lever that simply would not budge. He moved toward her and began offering to help, but she coldly turned her back to him and continued her battle with the valve.

'Easy, Your Worship,' he said. 'Only trying to help.'

Still struggling with the lever, Leia asked quietly, 'Would you please stop calling me that?'

Han was surprised at the princess's simple tone. He had expected a stinging retort or, at best, a cold silence. But her words were missing the mocking tone that he was accustomed to hearing. Was she finally bringing their relentless battle of wills to an end? 'Sure,' he said gently.

'You make things difficult sometimes,' Leia said as she shyly glanced at him.

He had to agree. 'I do, I really do.' But he added, 'You could be a little nicer, too. Come on, admit it, sometimes you think I'm all right.'

She let go of the lever and rubbed her sore hand. 'Sometimes,' she said with a little smile, 'maybe ... occasionally, when you aren't acting the scoundrel.'

'Scoundrel?' he laughed, finding her choice of words endearing. 'I like the sound of that.'

Without another word, he reached for Leia's hand and began to massage it.

'Stop it,' Leia protested.

Han continued to hold her hand. 'Stop what?' he asked softly.

Leia felt flustered, confused, embarrassed – a hundred things in that moment. But her sense of dignity prevailed. 'Stop that!' she said regally. 'My hands are dirty.'

Han smiled at her feeble excuse, but held on to her hand and looked right into her eyes. 'My hands are dirty, too. What are you afraid of?'

'Afraid?' She returned his direct gaze. 'Of getting my hands dirty.'

'That's why you're trembling?' he asked. He could see that she was affected by his closeness and by his touch, and her expression softened. Whereupon he reached out and took her other hand.

'I think you like me *because* I'm a scoundrel,' he said. 'I think you haven't had *enough* scoundrels in your life.' As he spoke he slowly drew her near.

Leia didn't resist his gentle pull. Now, as she looked at him, she thought he had never seemed more handsome, but she was still the princess. 'I happen to *like* nice men,' she chided in a whisper.

'And I'm not nice?' Han asked, teasing.

Chewbacca stuck his head out from the overhead compartment and watched the proceedings unnoticed.

'Yes,' she whispered, 'but you . . .'

Before she could finish, Han Solo drew her to him and felt her body tremble as he pressed his lips to hers. It seemed forever, it seemed an eternity to share between them, as he gently bent her body back. This time she didn't resist at all.

When they parted, Leia needed a moment to catch her breath. She tried to regain her composure and work up a measure of indignation, but she found it difficult to talk.

'Okay, hot shot,' she began. 'I—'

But then she stopped, and suddenly found herself kissing him, pulling him even closer than before.

When their lips finally parted, Han held Leia in his arms as they looked at each other. For a long moment there was a peaceful kind of emotion between them. Then Leia began to draw away, her thoughts and feelings a turmoil. She averted her eyes and began to disengage herself from Han's embrace. In the next second she turned and rushed from the cabin.

Han silently looked after her as she left the room. He then became acutely aware of the very curious Wookiee whose head was poking from the ceiling.

'Okay, Chewie!' he bellowed. 'Give me a hand with this valve.'

The fog, dispersed by a torrent of rain, snaked around the swamp in diaphanous swirls. Scooting along amid the pounding rain was a single R2 droid looking for his master.

Artoo Detoo's sensing devices were busily sending impulses to his electronic nerve ends. At the slightest sound, his auditory systems reacted – perhaps overreacted – and sent information to the robot's nervous computer brain.

It was too wet for Artoo in this murky jungle. He aimed his optical sensors in the direction of a strange little mud house on the edge of a dark lake. The robot, overtaken by an almost-human perception of loneliness, moved closer to the window of the tiny abode. Artoo extended his utility feet toward the window and peeked inside. He hoped no one inside noticed the slight shiver of his barrel-shaped form or heard his nervous little electronic whimper.

Somehow Luke Skywalker managed to squeeze inside the miniature house, where everything within was perfectly scaled to its tiny resident. Luke sat cross-legged on the dried mud floor in the living room, careful not to bang his skull against the low ceiling. There was a table in front of him and he could see a few containers holding what appeared to be hand-written scrolls.

The wrinkle-faced creature was in his kitchen, next to the living room, busily concocting an incredible meal. From where Luke sat he could see the little cook stirring steaming pots, chopping this, shredding that, scattering herbs over all, and scurrying back and forth to put platters on the table in front of the youth.

Fascinated as he was by this bustling activity, Luke was growing very impatient. As the creature made one of his frantic runs into the living room area, Luke reminded his host, 'I told you, I'm not hungry.'

'Patience,' the creature said, as he scuttled back into the steamy kitchen. 'It's time to eat.'

Luke tried to be polite. 'Look,' he said, 'it smells good. I'm sure it's delicious. But I don't know why we can't see Yoda now.'

'It's the Jedi's time to eat, too,' the creature answered.

But Luke was eager to be on his way. 'Will it take long to get there? How far is he?'

'Not far, not far. Be patient. Soon you will see him. Why wish you become a Jedi?'

'Because of my father, I guess,' Luke answered, as he reflected that he never really knew his father that well. In truth his deepest kinship with his father was through the lightsaber Ben had entrusted to him.

Luke noticed the curious look in the creature's eyes as he mentioned his father. 'Oh, your father,' the being said, sitting down to begin his vast meal. 'A powerful Jedi was he. Powerful Jedi.'

The youth wondered if the creature were mocking him. 'How could you know my father?' he asked a little angrily. 'You don't even know who I am.' He glanced around at the bizarre room and shook his head. 'I don't know what I'm doing here . . .'

Then he noticed that the creature had turned away from him and was talking to a corner of the room. This really is the final straw, Luke thought. Now this impossible creature is talking to thin air!

'No good is this,' the creature was saying irritably. 'This will not do. I cannot teach him. The boy has no patience!'

Luke's head spun in the direction the creature was facing. *Cannot teach. No patience.* Bewildered, he still saw no one there. Then the truth of the situation gradually became as plain to him as the deep lines on the little creature's face. Already he was being tested – and by none other than Yoda himself!

From the empty corner of the room, Luke heard the gentle, wise voice of Ben Kenobi responding to Yoda. 'He will learn patience,' Ben said.

'Much anger in him,' the dwarfish Jedi teacher persisted. 'Like in his father.'

'We've discussed this before,' Kenobi said.

Luke could no longer wait. 'I *can* be a Jedi,' he interrupted. It meant more than anything else to him to become a part of the noble band that had championed the causes of justice and peace. 'I'm ready, Ben . . . Ben . . .' The youth called to his invisible mentor, looking about the room in the hope of finding him. But all he saw was Yoda sitting across from him at the table.

'Ready are you?' the skeptical Yoda asked. 'What know you of ready? I have trained Jedi for eight hundred years. My own counsel I'll keep on who is to be trained.'

'Why not me?' Luke asked, insulted by Yoda's insinuation.

'To become a Jedi,' Yoda said gravely, 'takes the deepest commitment, the most serious mind.'

'He can do it,' Ben's voice said in defense of the youth.

Looking toward the invisible Kenobi, Yoda pointed at Luke. 'This

one I have watched a long time. All his life has he looked away ...
to the horizon, to the sky, to the future. Never his mind on where
he was, on what he was doing. Adventure, excitement.' Yoda shot
a glaring look at Luke. 'A Jedi craves not these things!'

Luke tried to defend his past. 'I have followed my feelings.'

'You are reckless!' the Jedi Master shouted.

'He will learn,' came the soothing voice of Kenobi.

'He's too old,' Yoda argued. 'Yes. Too old, too set in his ways to
start the training.'

Luke thought he heard a subtle softening in Yoda's voice.
Perhaps there was still a chance to sway him. 'I've learned much,'
Luke said. He couldn't give up now. He had come too far, endured
too much, *lost* too much for that.

Yoda seemed to look right through Luke as he spoke those words,
as if trying to determine how much he *had* learned. He turned to the
invisible Kenobi again. 'Will he finish what he begins?' Yoda asked.

'We've come this far,' was the answer. 'He is our only hope.'

'I will not fail you,' Luke said to both Yoda and Ben. 'I'm not
afraid.' And, indeed, at that moment, the young Skywalker felt he
could face anyone without fear.

But Yoda was not so optimistic. 'You will be, my young one,' he
warned. The Jedi Master turned slowly to face Luke as a strange
little smile appeared on his blue face. 'Heh. You will be.'

IX

ONLY one being in the entire universe could instill fear in the dark spirit of Darth Vader. As he stood, silent and alone in his dim chamber, the Dark Lord of the Sith waited for a visit from his own dreaded master.

As he waited, his Imperial Star Destroyer floated through a vast ocean of stars. No one on his ship would have dared disturb Darth Vader in his private cubicle. But if they had, they might have detected a slight trembling in that black-cloaked frame. And there might even have been a hint of terror to be seen upon his visage, had anyone been able to see through his concealing black breath mask.

But no one approached, and Vader remained motionless as he kept his lonely, patient vigil. Soon a strange electronic whine broke the dead silence of the room and a flickering light began to glimmer on the Dark Lord's cloak. Vader immediately bowed deeply in homage to his royal master.

The visitor arrived in the form of a hologram that materialized before Vader and towered above him. The three-dimensional figure was clad in simple robes and its face was concealed behind an enormous hood.

When the hologram of the Galactic Emperor finally spoke, it did so with a voice even deeper than Vader's. The Emperor's presence was awesome enough, but the sound of his voice sent a thrill of terror coursing through Vader's powerful frame. 'You may rise, my servant,' the Emperor commanded.

Immediately Vader straightened up. But he did not dare gaze into his master's face, and instead cast his eyes down at his own black boots.

'What is thy bidding, my master?' Vader asked with all the solemnity of a priest attending his god.

'There is a grave disturbance in the Force,' the Emperor said.

'I have felt it,' the Dark Lord replied solemnly.

The Emperor emphasized the danger as he continued. 'Our situation is most precarious. We have a new enemy who could bring about our destruction.'

'Our destruction? Who?'

'The son of Skywalker. You must destroy him, or he will be our undoing.'

Skywalker!

The thought was impossible. How could the Emperor be concerned with this insignificant youth?

'He's not a Jedi,' Vader reasoned. 'He's just a boy. Obi-Wan could not have taught him so much that—'

The Emperor broke in. 'The Force is strong in him,' he insisted. 'He must be destroyed.'

The Dark Lord reflected a moment. Perhaps there was another way to deal with the boy, a way that might benefit the Imperial cause. 'If he could be turned, he would be a powerful ally,' Vader suggested.

Silently the Emperor considered the possibility.

After a moment, he spoke again. 'Yes ... yes,' he said thoughtfully. 'He would be a great asset. Can it be done?'

For the first time in their meeting, Vader lifted his head to face his master directly. 'He will join us,' he answered firmly, 'or die, my master.'

With that, the encounter had come to an end. Vader kneeled before the Galactic Emperor, who passed his hand over his obedient servant. In the next moment, the holographic image had completely disappeared, leaving Darth Vader alone to formulate what would be, perhaps, his most subtle plan of attack.

The indicator lights on the control panel cast an eerie glow through the quiet cockpit of the *Millennium Falcon*. They softly lit Princess Leia's face as she sat in the pilot's chair, thinking about Han. Deep in thought, she ran her hand along the control panel in front of her. She knew something was churned up within her, but wasn't certain that she was willing to acknowledge it. And yet, could she deny it?

Suddenly her attention was attracted by a flurry of movement outside the cockpit window. A dark shape, at first too swift and too shadowy to identify, streaked toward the *Millennium Falcon*. In an instant it had attached itself to the ship's front window with something that looked like a soft suction cup. Cautiously Leia moved forward for a closer look at the black smudgelike shape. As she peered out the window, a set of large yellow eyes suddenly popped open and stared right at her.

Leia started in shock and stumbled backward into the pilot's seat. As she tried to compose herself, she heard the scurry of feet and an inhuman screech. Suddenly the black shape and its yellow eyes disappeared into the darkness of the asteroid cave.

She caught her breath, leaped up out of the chair, and raced to the ship's hold.

The *Falcon*'s crew was finishing its work on the ship's power system. As they worked, the lights flickered weakly, then came on and stayed on brightly. Han finished reconnecting the wires, and began setting a floor panel back in place while the Wookiee watched See Threepio complete his work at the control panel.

'Everything checks out here,' Threepio reported. 'If I might say so, I believe that should do it.'

Just then, the princess rushed breathlessly into the hold.

'There's something out there!' Leia cried.

Han looked up from his work. 'Where?'

'Outside,' she said, 'in the cave.'

As she spoke, they heard a sharp banging against the ship's hull. Chewbacca looked up and let out a loud bark of concern.

'Whatever it is sounds like it's trying to get in,' Threepio observed worriedly.

The captain began to move out of the hold. 'I'm going to see what it is,' he announced.

'Are you crazy?' Leia looked at him in astonishment.

The banging was getting louder.

'Look, we just got this bucket going again,' Han explained. 'I'm not about to let some varmint tear it apart.'

Before Leia could protest, he had grabbed a breath mask off a supply rack and pulled it down over his head. As Han walked out, the Wookiee hurried up behind him and grabbed his own face mask. Leia realized that, as part of the crew, she was duty-bound to join them.

'If there's more than one,' she told the captain, 'you're going to need help.'

Han looked at her affectionately as she removed a third breath mask and placed it over her lovely, but determined, face.

Then the three of them rushed out, leaving the protocol droid to complain pitifully to the empty hold: 'But that leaves me here all alone!'

The darkness outside the *Millennium Falcon* was thick and dank. It surrounded the three figures as they carefully moved around their ship. With each step they heard unsettling noises, *squishing* sounds, that echoed through the dripping cavern.

It was too dark to tell where the creature might be hiding. They moved cautiously, peering as well as they could into the deep gloom. Suddenly Chewbacca, who could see better in the dark than either his captain or the princess, emitted a muffled bark and pointed toward the thing that moved along the *Falcon*'s hull.

A shapeless leathery mass scurried over the top of the ship, apparently startled by the Wookiee's yelp. Han leveled his blaster at the creature and blasted the thing with a laser bolt. The black shape screeched, stumbled, then fell off the spaceship, landing with a *thud* at the princess's feet.

She leaned over to get a better look at the black mass. 'Looks like some kind of Mynock,' she told Han and Chewbacca.

Han glanced quickly around the dark tunnel. 'There will be more of them,' he predicted. 'They always travel in groups. And there's nothing they like better than to attach themselves to ships. Just what we need right now!'

But Leia was more distracted by the consistency of the tunnel floor. The tunnel itself struck her as peculiar; the smell of the place was unlike that of any cave she had ever known. The floor was especially cold and seemed to cling to her feet.

As she stamped her foot against the floor, she felt the ground give a bit beneath her heel. 'This asteroid has the strangest consistency,' she said. 'Look at the ground. It's not like rock at all.'

Han knelt to inspect the floor more closely and noted how pliable it was. As he studied the floor, he tried to make out how far it reached and to see the contours of the cave.

'There's an awful lot of moisture in here,' he said. He looked up and aimed his hand blaster at the far side of the cave, then fired toward the sound of a screeching Mynock in the distance; as soon as he shot the bolt, the entire cavern began to shake and the ground to buckle. 'I was afraid of that,' he shouted. 'Let's get out of here!'

Chewbacca barked in agreement, and bolted toward the *Millennium Falcon*. Close behind him, Leia and Han rushed toward the ship, covering their faces as a swarm of Mynocks flew past them. They reached the *Falcon* and ran up the platform into the ship. As soon as they were on board, Chewbacca closed the hatch after them, careful that none of the Mynocks could slip inside.

'Chewie, fire her up!' Han yelled as he and Leia darted through the ship's hold. 'We're getting out of here!'

Chewbacca hurriedly lumbered to his seat in the cockpit, while Han rushed to check the scopes on the hold control panel.

Leia, running to keep up, warned, 'They would spot us long before we could get up to speed.'

Han didn't seem to hear her. He checked the controls, then turned to rush back to the cockpit. But as he passed her, his comment made it clear he had heard every word. 'There's no time to discuss this in committee.'

And with that he was gone, racing to his pilot's chair, where he began working the engine throttles. The next minute the whine of the main engines resounded through the ship.

But Leia hurried after him. 'I am not a committee,' she shouted indignantly.

It didn't appear that he heard her. The sudden cave-quake was beginning to subside, but Han was determined to get his ship out – and out fast.

'You can't make the jump to light-speed in this asteroid field,' she called over the engine roar.

Solo grinned at her over his shoulder. 'Strap yourself in, sweetheart,' he said, 'we're taking off!'

'But the tremors have stopped!'

Han was not about to stop his ship now. Already the craft moved forward, quickly passing the craggy walls of the tunnel. Suddenly Chewbacca barked in horror as he stared out the front windscreen.

Directly in front of them stood a jagged white row of stalactites and stalagmites completely surrounding the cave's entrance.

'I see it, Chewie,' Han shouted. He pulled hard on the throttle, and the *Millennium Falcon* surged forward. 'Hang on!'

'The cave is collapsing,' Leia screamed as she saw the entrance ahead grow smaller.

'This is no cave.'

'What?!'

Threepio began jabbering in terror. 'Oh, my, no! We're doomed. Good-bye, Mistress Leia. Good-bye, Captain.'

Leia's mouth dropped open as she stared at the rapidly approaching tunnel opening.

Han was right; they were not in a cave. As they came nearer the opening, it was apparent that the white mineral formations were giant teeth. And it was very apparent that, as they soared out of this giant mouth, those teeth were beginning to close!

Chewbacca roared.

'Bank, Chewie!'

It was an impossible maneuver, but Chewbacca responded immediately and once again accomplished the impossible. He rolled the *Millennium Falcon* steeply on its side, tilting the ship as he accelerated it between two of those gleaming white fangs. And not a second too soon, for just as the *Falcon* flew from that living tunnel, the jaws clamped shut.

The *Falcon* sped through the rocky crevice of the asteroid, pursued by a titanic space slug. The enormous pink bulk didn't intend to lose its tasty meal and pushed itself out of its crater to swallow the escaping ship. But the monster was too slow. Within another moment the freighter had soared out, away from the slimy pursuer and into space. As it did so, the ship plunged into yet another danger: The *Millennium Falcon* had re-entered the deadly asteroid field.

Luke was panting, nearly out of breath in this, the latest of his endurance tests. His Jedi taskmaster had ordered him out on a marathon run through the dense growth of his planet's jungle. Not only had Yoda sent Luke on the exhausting run, but he had invited himself along for the ride. As the Jedi-in-training puffed and sweated his way on his rugged race, the little Jedi Master observed his progress from a pouch strapped to Luke's back.

Yoda shook his head and muttered to himself disparagingly about the youth's lack of endurance.

By the time they returned to the clearing where Artoo Detoo was patiently waiting, Luke's exhaustion had nearly overcome him. As he stumbled into the clearing, Yoda had yet another test planned for him.

Before Luke had caught his breath, the little Jedi on his back tossed a metal bar in front of Luke's eyes. In an instant Luke ignited his laser-sword and swung frantically at the bar. But he was not fast enough, and the bar fell – untouched – onto the ground with a thud. Luke collapsed on the wet earth in complete exhaustion. 'I can't,' he moaned, '. . . too tired.'

Yoda, who showed no sign of sympathy, retorted, 'It would be in seven pieces, were you a Jedi.'

But Luke knew that he was not a Jedi – not yet, anyway. And the rigorous training program devised by Yoda had left him nearly out of breath. 'I thought I was in good shape,' he gasped.

'Yes, but by what standard, ask I?' the little instructor quizzed. 'Forget your old measures. Unlearn, unlearn!'

Luke truly felt ready to unlearn all his old ways and willing to free himself to learn all this Jedi Master had to teach. It was rigorous training, but as time passed, Luke's strength and abilities increased and even his skeptical little master began to see hope. But it was not easy.

Yoda spent long hours lecturing his student about the ways of the Jedi. As they sat under the trees near Yoda's little house, Luke listened intently to all the master's tales and lessons. And as Luke listened, Yoda chewed on his Gimer Stick, a short twig with three small branches at the far end.

And there were physical tests of all kinds. In particular, Luke was working hard to perfect his leap. Once he felt ready to show Yoda his improvement. As the master sat on a log next to a wide pond, he heard the loud rustling of someone approaching through the vegetation.

Suddenly Luke appeared on the other side of the pond, coming toward the water at a run. As he approached the shore, he made a running leap toward Yoda, rising high above the water as he hurtled himself through the air. But he fell short of the other side and landed in the water with a loud splash, completely soaking Yoda.

Yoda's blue lips turned down in disappointment.

But Luke was not about to give up. He was determined to become a Jedi and, no matter how foolish he might feel in the attempt, would pass every test Yoda set for him. So he didn't complain when Yoda told him to stand on his head. A bit awkwardly at first, Luke inverted his body and, after a few wobbly moments, was standing firmly on his hands. It seemed he had been in this position for hours, but it was less difficult than it would have been before his training. His concentration had improved so much that he was able to maintain a perfect balance – even with Yoda perched on the soles of his feet.

But that was only part of the test. Yoda signaled Luke by tapping on his leg with his Gimer Stick. Slowly, carefully, and with full concentration, Luke raised one hand off the ground. His body wavered slightly with the weight shift – but Luke kept his balance, and, concentrating, started to lift a small rock in front of him. But suddenly a whistling and beeping R2 unit came rushing up to his youthful master.

Luke collapsed, and Yoda jumped clear of his falling body. Annoyed, the young Jedi student asked, 'Oh, Artoo, what is it?'

Artoo Detoo rolled about in frantic circles as he tried to communicate his message through a series of electronic chirps. Luke watched as the droid scooted to the edge of the swamp. He hurried to follow and then saw what it was the little robot was trying to tell him.

Standing at the water's edge, Luke saw that all but the tip of the X-wing's nose had disappeared beneath the water's surface.

'Oh, no,' moaned Luke. 'We'll never get it out now.'

Yoda had joined them, and stamped his foot in irritation at Luke's remark. 'So sure are you?' Yoda scolded. 'Tried have you? Always with you it can't be done. Hear you nothing that I say?' His little wrinkled face puckered with a furious scowl.

Luke glanced at his master, then looked doubtfully toward the sunken ship.

'Master,' he said skeptically, 'lifting rocks is one thing, but this is a little different.' Yoda was really angry now. 'No! No different!' he shouted. 'The differences are in your mind. Throw them out! No longer of use are they to you.'

Luke trusted his master. If Yoda said this could be done, then maybe he should try. He looked at the downed X-wing and readied himself for maximum concentration. 'Okay,' he said at last, 'I'll give it a try.'

Again he had spoken the wrong words. 'No,' Yoda said impatiently. 'Try not. *Do, do.* Or do not. There is no try.'

Luke closed his eyes. He tried to envision the contours, the shape, to feel the weight of his X-wing fighter. And he concentrated on the movement it would make as it rose from the murky waters.

As he concentrated, he began to hear the waters churn and gurgle, and then begin to bubble with the emerging nose of the X-wing. The tip of the fighter was slowly lifting from the water, and it hovered there for a moment, then sank back beneath the surface with a loud splash.

Luke was drained and had to gasp for breath. 'I can't,' he said dejectedly. 'It's too big.'

'Size has no meaning,' Yoda insisted. 'It matters not. Look at *me*. Judge me by my *size*, do you?'

Luke, chastened, just shook his head.

'And well you shouldn't,' the Jedi Master advised. 'For my ally is the Force. And a powerful ally it is. Life creates it and makes it grow. Its energy surrounds us and binds us. Luminous beings we are, not this crude matter,' he said as he pinched Luke's skin.

Yoda made a grand sweeping gesture to indicate the vastness of the universe about him. 'Feel it you must. Feel the flow. Feel the Force around you. Here,' he said, as he pointed, 'between you and me and that tree and that rock.'

While Yoda gave his explanation of the Force, Artoo spun his domed head around, trying without success to register this 'Force' on his scanners. He whistled and beeped in bafflement.

'Yes, everywhere,' Yoda continued, ignoring the little droid, 'waiting to be felt and used. Yes, even between this land and that ship!'

Then Yoda turned and looked at the swamp, and as he did the water began to swirl. Slowly, from the gently bubbling waters, the nose of the fighter appeared again.

Luke gasped in astonishment as the X-wing gracefully rose from its watery tomb and moved majestically toward the shore.

He silently vowed never to use the word 'impossible' again. For there, standing on his tree root pedestal, was tiny Yoda, effortlessly gliding the ship from the water onto the shore. It was a sight that Luke could scarcely believe. But he knew that it was a potent example of Jedi mastery over the Force.

Artoo, equally astounded but not so philosophical, issued a series of loud whistles, then bolted off to hide behind some giant roots.

The X-wing seemed to float onto the beach, and then gently came to a stop.

Luke was humbled by the feat he had witnessed and approached Yoda in awe. 'I . . .' he began, dazzled. 'I don't believe it.'

'That,' Yoda stated emphatically, 'is why you fail.'

Bewildered, Luke shook his head, wondering if he would ever rise to the station of a Jedi.

Bounty hunters! Among the most reviled of the galaxy's inhabitants, this class of amoral money-grubbers included members of every species. It was a repellent occupation, and it often attracted repellent creatures to its fold. Some of these creatures had been summoned by Darth Vader and now stood with him on the bridge of his Imperial Star Destroyer.

Admiral Piett observed this motley group from a distance as he stood with one of Vader's captains. They saw that the Dark Lord had invited a particularly bizarre assortment of fortune hunters, including Bossk, whose soft, baggy face gawked at Vader with huge bloodshot orbs. Next to Bossk stood Zuckuss and Dengar, two human types, battle-scarred by innumerable, unspeakable adventures. A battered and tarnished chromecolored droid named IG-88 was also with the group, standing next to the notorious Boba Fett. A human bounty hunter, Fett was known for his extremely ruthless methods. He was dressed in a weapon-covered, armored spacesuit, the kind worn by a group of evil warriors defeated by the Jedi Knights during the Clone Wars. A few braided scalps completed his unsavory image. The very sight of Boba Fett sent a shudder of revulsion through the admiral.

'Bounty hunters!' Piett said with disdain. 'Why should he bring them into this? The Rebels won't escape us.'

Before the captain could reply, a ship's controller rushed up to the admiral. 'Sir,' he said urgently, 'we have a priority signal from the Star Destroyer *Avenger*.'

Admiral Piett read the signal, then hurried to inform Darth Vader. As he approached the group, Piett heard the last of Vader's instructions to them. 'There will be a substantial reward for the one who finds the *Millennium Falcon*,' he was saying. 'You are free to use any methods necessary, but I want proof. No disintegrations.'

The Sith Lord stopped his briefing as Admiral Piett hurried to his side.

'My lord,' the admiral whispered ecstatically, 'we have them!'

X

THE *Avenger* had spotted the *Millennium Falcon* the moment the freighter shot out of the enormous asteroid.

From that moment, the Imperial ship renewed its pursuit of the freighter with a blinding barrage of fire. Undaunted by the steady rain of asteroids on its massive hull, the Star Destroyer relentlessly followed the smaller ship.

The *Millennium Falcon*, far more maneuverable than the other ship, darted around the larger asteroids as they came rocketing toward it. The *Falcon* was succeeding in holding its lead in front of the *Avenger*, but it was clear that the steadily pursuing ship was not about to abandon the chase.

Suddenly a gigantic asteroid appeared in the *Millennium Falcon*'s path, rushing toward the freighter at incredible speed. The ship quickly banked out of the way, and the asteroid hurtled past it, only to explode harmlessly against the *Avenger*'s hull.

Han Solo glimpsed the explosion's flare through the front window of his ship's cockpit. The craft that followed them seemed absolutely invulnerable; but he had no time to reflect on the differences between the ships. It took everything in his power to maintain control of the *Falcon* as it was pelted by Imperial cannon fire.

Princess Leia tensely watched the asteroids and cannon fire flaring in the blackness of space outside the cockpit windows. Her fingers had tightened on the arms of her chair. Silently she hoped against hope that they would emerge from this chase alive.

Carefully following the bleeping images on a tracking scope, See Threepio turned to Han. 'I can see the edge of the asteroid field, sir,' he reported.

'Good,' Han replied. 'Soon as we're clear, we'll kick this baby into hyperdrive.' He was confident that within moments the pursuing Star Destroyer would be left light-years behind. The repairs in the freighter's light-speed systems had been completed, and there was nothing left to do now but get the ship free of the asteroid field and into space, where it could blast away to safety.

There was an excited Wookiee bark as Chewbacca, looking out a cockpit window, saw that the asteroid density was already decreasing. But their escape could not yet be completed, for the *Avenger* was closing in, and the bolts from its laser cannons bombarded the *Falcon*, making it lurch and carom to one side.

Han rapidly adjusted the controls and brought his ship back on an even keel. And in the next instant, the *Falcon* zoomed out of the asteroid field and entered the peaceful, star-dotted silence of deep space. Chewbacca whined, joyful that they were at last out of the deadly field – but eager to leave the Star Destroyer far behind.

'I'm with you, Chewie,' Han responded. 'Let's vacate the area. Stand by for light-speed. This time *they* get the surprise. Hang on . . .'

Everyone braced themselves as Han pulled back on the light-speed throttle. But it was the crew of the *Millennium Falcon*, and most of all the captain himself, that got the surprise, once again—

—nothing happened.

Nothing!

Han frantically pulled back the throttle again.

The ship maintained its sublight speed.

'This isn't fair!' he exclaimed, beginning to panic.

Chewbacca was furious. It was rare that he lost his temper with his friend and captain. But now he was exasperated and roared his fury in angry Wookiee growls and barks.

'Couldn't be,' Han replied defensively, as he looked at his computer screens and quickly noted their readings. 'I checked the transfer circuits.'

Chewbacca barked again.

'I tell you, this time it's not my fault. I'm sure I checked it.'

Leia sighed deeply. 'No light-speed?' in a tone that indicated she had expected *this* catastrophe, too.

'Sir,' See Threepio interjected, 'we've lost the rear deflector shield. One more direct hit on the back quarter and we're done for.'

'Well,' Leia said, as she glared at the captain of the *Millennium Falcon*, 'what now?'

Han realized he had only one choice. There was no time to plan or to check computer readouts, not with the *Avenger* already out of the asteroid field and rapidly gaining on them. He had to make a decision based on instinct and hope. They really had no alternative.

'Sharp bank, Chewie,' he ordered and pulled back a lever as he looked at his copilot. 'Let's turn this bucket around.'

Not even Chewbacca could fathom what Han had in mind. He barked in bewilderment – perhaps he hadn't heard the order quite right.

'You heard me!' Han yelled. 'Turn around! Full power front shield!' This time there was no mistaking his command and, though Chewbacca couldn't comprehend the suicidal maneuver, he obeyed.

The princess was flabbergasted. 'You're going to attack them!' she stammered in disbelief. There wasn't a *chance* of survival now, she thought. Was it possible that Han really was crazy?

Threepio, after running some calculations through his computer brain, turned to Han Solo. 'Sir, if I might point out, the odds of surviving a direct assault on an Imperial Star Destroyer are—'

Chewbacca snarled at the golden droid, and Threepio immediately shut up. No one on board really wanted to hear the statistics, especially since the *Falcon* was already banking into a steep turn to begin its course into the erupting storm of Imperial cannon fire.

Solo concentrated intently on his flying. It was all he could do to avoid the barrage of flak bursts rocketing toward the *Falcon* from the Imperial ship. The freighter bobbed and weaved as Han, still heading directly for the Star Destroyer, steered to avoid the bolts.

No one on his tiny ship had the slightest idea what his plan might be.

'He's coming in too low!' the Imperial deck officer shouted, though he scarcely believed what he was seeing.

Captain Needa and the Star Destroyer crew rushed to the *Avenger*'s bridge to watch the suicidal approach of the *Millennium Falcon*, while alarms blared all over the vast Imperial ship. A small freighter could not do much damage if it collided against a Star Destroyer's hull; but if it smashed through the bridge windows, the control deck would be littered with corpses.

The panicked tracking officer reported his sighting. 'We're going to collide!'

'Shields up?' Captain Needa asked. 'He must be insane!'

'Look out!' the deck officer yelled.

The *Falcon* was headed straight for the bridge window and the *Avenger* crew and officers fell to the floor in terror. But at the last instant, the freighter veered up sharply. Then—

Captain Needa and his men slowly lifted their heads. All they saw outside the bridge windows was a peaceful ocean of stars.

'Track them,' Captain Needa ordered. 'They may come around for another pass.'

The tracking officer attempted to find the freighter on his scopes. But there was nothing to find.

'That's strange,' he muttered.

'What is it?' Needa asked, walking over to look at the tracking monitors for himself.

'The ship doesn't appear on any of our scopes.'

The captain was perplexed. 'It couldn't have disappeared. Could a ship that small have a cloaking device?'

'No, sir,' the deck officer answered. 'Maybe they went into light-speed at the last minute.'

Captain Needa felt his anger mounting at about the same rate as his befuddlement. 'Then why did they attack? They could have gone into hyperspace when they cleared the asteroid field.'

'Well, there's no trace of them, sir, no matter how they did it,' the tracking officer replied, still unable to locate the *Millennium Falcon* on his viewers. 'The only logical explanation is that they went into light-speed.'

The captain was staggered. How had that crate of a ship eluded him?

An aide approached. 'Sir, Lord Vader demands an update on the pursuit,' he reported. 'What should he be told?'

Needa braced himself. Letting the *Millennium Falcon* get away when it was so close was an unforgiveable error, and he knew he had to face Vader and report his failure. He felt resigned to whatever punishment waited in store for him.

'I am responsible for this,' he said. 'Get the shuttle ready. When we rendezvous with Lord Vader, I will apologize to him myself. Turn around and scan the area one more time.'

Then, like a living behemoth, the great *Avenger* slowly began to turn; but there was still no sign of the *Millennium Falcon*.

The two glowing balls hovered like alien fireflies above Luke's body lying motionless in the mud. Standing protectively next to his fallen master, a little barrel-shaped droid periodically extended a mechanical appendage to swat at the dancing objects as if they were mosquitoes. But the hovering balls of light leaped just out of the robot's reach.

Artoo Detoo leaned over Luke's inert body and whistled in an effort to revive him. But Luke, stunned unconscious by the charges of these energy balls, did not respond. The robot turned to Yoda, who was sitting calmly on a tree stump, and angrily began to beep and scold the little Jedi Master.

Getting no sympathy from him, Artoo turned back to Luke. His electronic circuits told him there was no use trying to wake Luke with his little noises. An emergency rescue system was activated within his metal hull and Artoo extended a small metal electrode and rested it on Luke's chest. Uttering a quiet beep of concern, Artoo generated a mild electrical charge, just strong enough to jolt Luke back to consciousness. The youth's chest heaved, and he awoke with a start.

Looking dazed, the young Jedi student shook his head clear. He looked around him, rubbing his shoulders to ease the ache from Yoda's seeker balls' attack. Glimpsing the seekers still suspended over him, Luke scowled. Then he heard Yoda chuckling merrily nearby, and turned his glare on him.

'Concentration, heh?' Yoda laughed, his lined face creased with enjoyment. 'Concentration!'

Luke was in no mood to return his smile. 'I thought those seekers were set for stun!' he exclaimed angrily.

'That they are,' the amused Yoda answered.

'They're a lot stronger than I'm used to.' Luke's shoulder ached painfully.

'That would not matter were the Force flowing through you,' Yoda reasoned. 'Higher you'd jump! Faster you'd move!' he exclaimed. 'Open yourself to the Force you must.'

The youth was beginning to feel exasperated with his arduous training, although he had only been at it a short time. He had felt very close to knowing the Force – but so many times he had failed and had realized how very far away it was from him still. But now Yoda's goading words made him spring to his feet. He was tired of waiting so long for this power, weary at his lack of success, and increasingly infuriated by Yoda's cryptic teachings.

Luke grabbed his laser sword from the mud and quickly ignited it.

Terrified, Artoo Detoo scurried away to safety.

'I'm open to it now!' Luke shouted. 'I feel it. Come on, you little flying blasters!' With fire in his eyes, Luke poised his weapon and moved toward the seekers. Immediately they zipped away and retreated to hover over Yoda.

'No, no,' the Jedi Master scolded, shaking his hoary head. 'This will not do. *Anger* is what you feel.'

'But I feel the Force!' Luke protested vehemently.

'Anger, anger, fear, aggression!' Yoda warned. 'The dark side of the Force are they. Easily *they* flow ... quick to join in a fight. Beware, beware, beware of them. A heavy price is paid for the power they bring.'

Luke lowered his sword and stared at Yoda in confusion. 'Price?' he asked. 'What do you mean?'

'The dark side beckons,' Yoda said dramatically. 'But if once start you down the dark path, forever will it dominate your destiny. Consume you it will ... as it did Obi-Wan's apprentice.'

Luke nodded. He knew who Yoda meant. 'Lord Vader,' he said. After he thought for a moment, Luke asked, 'Is the dark side stronger?'

'No, no. Easier, quicker, more seductive.'

'But how am I to know the good side from the bad?' he asked, puzzled.

'You will know,' Yoda answered. 'When you are at peace ... calm, passive. A Jedi uses the Force for knowledge. Never for attack.'

'But tell me why—' Luke began.

'No! There is no why. Nothing more will I tell you. Clear your mind of questions. Quiet now be – at peace . . .' Yoda's voice trailed off, but his words had a hypnotic effect on Luke. The young student stopped protesting and began to feel peaceful, his body and mind relaxing.

'Yes . . .' Yoda murmured, 'calm.'

Slowly Luke's eyes closed as he let his mind clear of distracting thoughts.

'Passive . . .'

Luke heard Yoda's soothing voice as it entered the receptive darkness of his mind. He willed himself to travel along with the master's words to wherever they might lead.

'Let yourself go . . .'

When Yoda perceived that Luke was as relaxed as the young student could be at this stage, he made the tiniest of gestures. As he did, the two seeker balls above his head shot toward Luke, firing stun bolts as they moved.

In that instant Luke sprang to life and ignited his laser sword. He leaped to his feet and, with pure concentration, began deflecting the bolts as they spun toward him. Fearlessly he faced the attack, and moved and dodged with extreme grace. His leaps into the air, as he jumped to meet the bolts, were higher than any he had achieved before. Luke wasted not a single motion as he concentrated only on every bolt as it sped his way.

Then, as suddenly as it had begun, the seeker attack was over. The glowing balls returned to hover on either side of their master's head.

Artoo Detoo, the ever-patient observer, let out an electronic sigh and shook his metal dome-head.

Grinning proudly, Luke looked toward Yoda.

'Much progress do you make, young one,' the Jedi Master confirmed. 'Stronger do you grow.' But the little instructor would not compliment him more than that.

Luke was full of pride at his marvelous achievement. He watched Yoda, expectantly waiting for further praise from him. But Yoda did not move or speak. He sat calmly – and then two more seeker balls floated up behind him and moved into formation with the first two.

Luke Skywalker's grin began to melt away.

*

A pair of white-armored stormtroopers lifted Captain Needa's lifeless form from the floor of Darth Vader's Imperial Star Destroyer.

Needa had known that death was the likely consequence of his failure to capture the *Millennium Falcon*. He had known, too, that he had to report the situation to Vader and make his formal apology. But there was no mercy for failure among the Imperial military. And Vader, in disgust, had signaled for the captain's death.

The Dark Lord turned, and Admiral Piett and two of his captains came to report their findings. 'Lord Vader,' Piett said, 'our ships have completed their scan of the area and found nothing. The *Millennium Falcon* definitely went into light-speed. It's probably somewhere on the other side of the galaxy by now.'

Vader hissed through his breath mask. 'Alert all commands,' he ordered. 'Calculate every possible destination along their last known trajectory and disburse the fleet to search for them. Don't fail me again, Admiral, I've had quite enough!'

Admiral Piett thought of the *Avenger*'s captain, whom he had just seen carried out of the room like a sack of grain. And he remembered the excruciating demise of Admiral Ozzel. 'Yes, my lord,' he answered, trying to hide his fear. 'We'll find them.'

Then the admiral turned to an aide. 'Deploy the fleet,' he instructed. As the aide moved to carry out his orders, a shadow of worry crossed the admiral's face. He was not at all certain that his luck would be any better than that of Ozzel or Needa.

Lord Vader's Imperial Star Destroyer regally moved off into space. Its protecting fleet of smaller craft hovered nearby as the Imperial armada left the Star Destroyer *Avenger* behind.

No one on the *Avenger* or in Vader's entire fleet had any idea how near they were to their prey. As the *Avenger* glided off into space to continue its search, it carried with it, clinging unnoticed to one side of the huge bridge tower, a saucer-shaped freighter ship – the *Millennium Falcon*.

Inside the *Falcon*'s cockpit all was quiet. Han Solo had stopped his ship and shut down all systems so quickly that even the customarily talkative See Threepio was silent. Threepio stood, not moving a rivet, a look of wonder frozen on his golden face.

'You could have warned him before you shut him off,' Princess Leia said, looking at the droid that stood motionless like a bronzed statue.

'Oh, so sorry!' Han said in mock concern. 'Didn't mean to offend your droid. You think braking and shutting everything down in that amount of time is easy?'

Leia was dubious about Han's entire strategy. 'I'm still not sure what you've accomplished.'

He shrugged off her doubt. She'll find out soon enough, he thought; there just wasn't any other choice. He turned to his copilot. 'Chewie, check the manual release on the landing claws.'

The Wookiee barked, then pulled himself out of his chair and moved toward the rear of the ship.

Leia watched as Chewbacca proceeded to disengage the landing claws so that the ship could take off without mechanical delay.

Shaking her head incredulously, she turned to Han. 'What do you have in mind for your *next* move?'

'The fleet is finally breaking up,' he answered as he pointed out a port window. 'I'm *hoping* they follow standard Imperial procedure and dump their garbage before they go into light-speed.'

The princess reflected on this strategy for a moment, and then began to smile. This crazy man might know what he was doing after all. Impressed, she patted him on the head. 'Not bad, hot shot, not bad. Then what?'

'Then,' Han said, 'we have to find a safe port around here. Got any ideas?'

'That depends. Where are we?'

'Here,' Han said, pointing to a configuration of small light points, 'near the Anoat system.'

Slipping out of her chair, Leia moved next to him for a better look at the screen.

'Funny,' Han said after thinking for a moment, 'I have the feeling I've been in this area before. Let me check my logs.'

'You keep logs?' Leia was more impressed by the minute. 'My, how organized,' she teased.

'Well, sometimes,' he answered as he hunted through the computer readout. 'Ah-ha, I knew it! Lando – now this should be interesting.'

'I never heard of that system,' said Leia.

'It's not a system. He's a man, Lando Calrissian. A gambler, con artist, all-around scoundrel ...' he paused long enough for the last word to sink in, and gave the princess a wink, 'your kind of guy. The

Bespin system. It's a fair distance but reachable.'

Leia looked at one of the computer monitor screens and read the data. 'A mining colony,' she noted.

'A Tibanna gas mine,' Han added. 'Lando won it in a sabacc match, or so he claims. Lando and I go way back.'

'Can you trust him?' Leia asked.

'No. But he has no love for the Empire, that much I know.'

The Wookiee barked over the intercom.

Quickly responding, Han flicked some switches to bring new information to the computer screens, and then stretched to look out the cockpit window. 'I see it, Chewie, I see it,' he said. 'Prepare for manual release.' Then, turning to the princess, Han said, 'Here goes nothing, sweetheart.' He leaned back in his chair and smiled invitingly at her.

Leia shook her head, then grinned shyly and gave him a quick kiss. 'You do have your moments,' she reluctantly admitted. 'Not many, but you have them.'

Han was getting used to the princess's back-handed compliments, and he couldn't say that he really minded them. More and more he was enjoying the fact that she shared his own sarcastic sense of humor. And he was fairly sure that she was enjoying it, too.

'Let 'er go, Chewie,' he shouted gleefully.

The hatch on the underbelly of the *Avenger* yawned open. And as the Imperial galactic cruiser zoomed into hyperspace, it spewed out its own belt of artificial asteroids – garbage and sections of irreparable machinery that scattered out into the black void of space. Hidden among that trail of refuse, the *Millennium Falcon* tumbled undetected off the side of the larger ship, and was left far behind as the *Avenger* streaked away.

Safe at last, Han Solo thought.

The *Millennium Falcon* ignited its ion engines, and raced off through the train of drifting space junk toward another system.

But concealed among that scattered debris was another ship.

And as the *Falcon* roared off to seek the Bespin system, this other ship ignited its own engines. Boba Fett, the most notorious and dreaded bounty hunter in the galaxy, turned his small, elephant's head-shaped craft, *Slave I*, to begin its pursuit. For Boba Fett had no intention of losing sight of the *Millennium Falcon*. Its pilot had too high a price on his head. And this was one reward that the fearsome bounty hunter was quite determined to collect.

Luke felt that he was definitely progressing.

He ran through the jungle – with Yoda perched on his neck – and leaped with gazellelike grace over the profusion of foliage and tree roots growing throughout the bog.

Luke had at last begun to detach himself from the emotion of pride. He felt unburdened, and was finally open to experience fully the flow of the Force.

When his diminutive instructor threw a silver bar above Luke's head, the young Jedi student reacted instantly. In a flash he turned to slice the bar into four shiny segments before it fell to the ground.

Yoda was pleased and smiled at Luke's accomplishment. 'Four this time! The Force you feel.'

But Luke was suddenly distracted. He sensed something dangerous, something evil. 'Something's not right,' he said to Yoda. 'I feel danger . . . death.'

He looked around him, trying to see what it was that emitted so powerful an aura. As he turned he saw a huge, tangled tree, its blackened bark dry and crumbling. The base of the tree was surrounded by a small pond of water, where the gigantic roots had grown to form the opening to a darkly sinister cave.

Luke gently lifted Yoda from his neck and set him on the ground. Transfixed, the Jedi student stared at the dark monstrosity. Breathing hard, he found himself unable to speak.

'You brought me here purposely,' Luke said at last.

Yoda sat on a tangled root and put his Gimer Stick in his mouth. Calmly looking at Luke, he said nothing.

Luke shivered. 'I feel cold,' he said, still gazing at the tree.

'This tree is strong with the dark side of the Force. A servant of evil it is. Into it you must go.'

Luke felt a tremor of apprehension. 'What's in there?'

'Only what you take with you,' Yoda said cryptically.

Luke looked warily at Yoda, and then at the tree. He silently resolved to take his courage, his willingness to learn, and step within that darkness to face whatever it was that awaited him. He would take nothing more than—

No. He would also bring his lightsaber.

Lighting his weapon, Luke stepped through the shallow waters of the pond and toward the dark opening between those great and foreboding roots.

But the Jedi Master's voice stopped him.

'Your weapon,' Yoda reproved. 'You won't need it.'

Luke paused and looked again at the tree. Go into that evil cave completely unarmed? As skilled as Luke was becoming, he did not feel quite equal to that test. He gripped his saber tighter and shook his head.

Yoda shrugged and placidly gnawed his Gimer Stick.

Taking a deep breath, Luke cautiously stepped into the grotesque tree cave.

The dark inside the cave was so thick that Luke could feel it against his skin, so black that the light thrown by his laser sword was quickly absorbed and illuminated scarcely more than a meter in front of him. As he slowly moved forward, slimy, dripping things brushed against his face and the moisture from the soggy cave floor began to seep into his boots.

As he pushed through the blackness, his eyes began to grow accustomed to the dark. He saw a corridor before him, but as he moved toward it, he was surprised by a thick, sticky membrane that completely enveloped him. Like the web of some gigantic spider, the mass clung tightly to Luke's body. Thrashing at it with his lightsaber, Luke finally managed to disentangle himself and clear a path ahead.

He held his glowing sword in front of him and noticed an object on the cave floor. Pointing his lightsaber downward, Luke illuminated a black, shiny beetle the size of his hand. In an instant, the thing scurried up the slimy wall to join a cluster of its mates.

Luke caught his breath and stepped back. At that moment he considered hunting for the exit – but he braced himself and ventured still deeper into the dark chamber.

He felt the space about him widen as he moved forward, using his lightsaber as a dim beacon. He strained to see in the darkness, trying his best to hear. But there was no sound at all. Nothing.

Then, a very loud *hiss*.

The sound was familiar. He froze where he stood. He had heard that hiss even in his nightmares; it was the labored breath of a thing that had once been a man.

Out of the darkness a light appeared – the blue flame of a just-ignited laser sword. In its illumination Luke saw the looming figure of Darth Vader raise his lighted weapon to attack, and then lunge.

Prepared by his disciplined Jedi training, Luke was ready. He raised his own lightsaber and perfectly side-stepped Vader's attack. In the same movement, Luke turned to Vader and, with his mind and body completely focused, the youth summoned the Force. Feeling its power within him, Luke raised his laser weapon and brought it crashing down on Vader's head.

With one powerful stroke, the Dark Lord's head was severed from his body. Head and helmet crashed to the ground and rolled about the cave floor with a loud metallic bang. As Luke watched in astonishment, Vader's body was completely swallowed up by the darkness. Then Luke looked down at the helmet that had come to rest directly in front of him. For a moment it was completely still. Then the helmet cracked in half and split open.

As Luke watched in shocked disbelief, the broken helmet fell aside to reveal, not the unknown, imagined face of Darth Vader, but Luke's own face, looking up at him.

He gasped, horrified at the sight. And then, as suddenly as it had appeared, the decapitated head faded away as if in a ghostly vision.

Luke stared at the dark space where the head and pieces of helmet had lain. His mind reeled, the emotions that raged inside of him were almost too much to bear.

The tree! he told himself. It was all some trick of this ugly cave, some charade of Yoda's, arranged because he had come into the tree carrying a weapon.

He wondered if he were really fighting himself, or if he had fallen prey to the temptations of the dark side of the Force. He might himself become a figure as evil as Darth Vader. And he wondered if there might be some even darker meaning behind the unsettling vision.

It was a long while before Luke Skywalker was able to move from that deep, dark cave.

Meanwhile, sitting on the root, the little Jedi Master calmly gnawed his Gimer Stick.

XI

IT was dawn on the gaseous Bespin planet.

As the *Millennium Falcon* began its approach through the planet's atmosphere, it soared past several of Bespin's many moons. The planet itself glowed with the same soft pink hue of dawn that tinted the hull of the powerful pirate starship. As the ship neared, it swerved to avoid a billowing canyon of clouds that swirled up around the planet.

When Han Solo finally lowered his ship through the clouds, he and his crew got their first glimpse of the gaseous world of Bespin. And as they maneuvered through the clouds, they noticed that they were being followed by some kind of flying vehicle. Han recognized the craft as a twin-pod cloud car but was surprised when the car began to bank close to his freighter. The *Falcon* suddenly lurched as a round of laser fire struck its hull. No one on the *Falcon* had expected *this* kind of greeting.

The other craft transmitted a static-obscured message over the *Falcon*'s radio system.

'No,' Han snarled in reply, 'I do not have a landing permit. My registration is—'

But his words were drowned out by a loud crackle of radio static.

The twin-pod car was apparently not willing to accept static for a reply. Again it opened up fire on the *Falcon*, shaking and rattling the ship with each strike.

A clear warning voice came over the freighter's speakers: 'Stand by. Any aggressive move will bring about your destruction.'

At this point Han had no intention of making any aggressive moves. Bespin was their only hope of sanctuary, and he didn't plan to alienate his prospective hosts.

'Rather touchy, aren't they?' the reactivated See Threepio asked.

'I thought you knew these people,' Leia chided, casting a suspicious look at Han.

'Well,' the Corellian hedged, 'it's been a while.'

Chewbacca growled and barked, shaking his head meaningfully at Han.

'That was a long time ago,' he answered sharply. 'I'm sure he's forgotten all about it.' But he began to wonder if Lando *had* forgotten the past . . .

'Permission granted to land on Platform 327. Any deviation of flight pattern will bring about your—'

Angrily, Han switched off the radio. Why was he being put through this harrassment? He was coming here peacefully; wasn't Lando going to let bygones be bygones? Chewbacca grunted and glanced at Solo, who turned to Leia and her worried robot. 'He'll help us,' he said, trying to reassure them all. 'We go way back . . . really. Don't worry.'

'Who's worried?' she lied unconvincingly.

By then they could clearly see the Cloud City of Bespin through the cockpit window. The city was immense and seemed to float in the clouds as it emerged through the white atmosphere. As the *Millennium Falcon* approached the city, it became evident that the expansive city structure was supported from below by a thin unipod. The base of this supporting stalk was a large round reactor that floated through its billowing sea of clouds.

The *Millennium Falcon* dipped closer to the huge city and veered in the direction of its landing platforms, flying past the rising towers and spires that dotted the city's landscape. In and about these structures cruised more of the twin-pod cloud cars, gliding effortlessly through the mists.

Han gently brought the *Falcon* in to land on Platform 327; and as the ship's ion engines whined to a stop, the captain and his crew could see the welcoming party moving toward the landing platform with weapons drawn. Like any cross-section of the citizenry of

Cloud City, this group included aliens, droids, and humans of all races and descriptions. One of these humans was the group's leader, Lando Calrissian.

Lando, a handsome black man perhaps the same age as Solo, was clad in elegant gray pants, blue shirt, and a flowing blue cape. He stood, unsmiling, on Landing Platform 327, waiting for the *Falcon*'s crew to disembark.

Han Solo and Princess Leia appeared at the open door of their ship, with blasters drawn. Standing behind them was the giant Wookiee, his gun in hand and a bandoleer of ammunition packs slung over his left shoulder.

Han didn't speak but quietly surveyed the menacing welcoming party that was marching across the platform toward them. An early morning wind began to sweep along the ground, making Lando's cloak fly up behind him like enormous deep blue wings.

'I don't like this,' Leia whispered to Han.

He didn't much like it either, but he wasn't going to let the princess know that. 'It'll be all right,' he said quietly. 'Trust me.' Then, cautioning her, he added, 'But keep your eyes open. Wait here.'

Han and Chewbacca left Leia guarding the *Falcon* and they walked down the ramp to face Calrissian and his motley army. The two parties moved toward each other until Han and Calrissian stopped, three meters apart, to face each other. For a long moment, each one eyed the other silently.

Finally Calrissian spoke, shaking his head and squinting at Han. 'Why, you slimy, double-crossing, no-good swindler,' he said grimly.

'I can explain everything, ol' buddy,' Han said quickly, 'if you'll just listen.'

Still unsmiling, Lando surprised alien and human alike when he said, 'Glad to see you.'

Han lifted an eyebrow skeptically. 'No hard feelings?'

'Are you kidding?' Lando asked coolly.

Han was becoming nervous. Had he been forgiven or not? The guards and aides still had not lowered their weapons, and Lando's attitude was mystifying. Trying to conceal his worry, Han remarked gallantly, 'I always said you were a gentleman.'

With that, the other man broke into a grin. 'I'll bet,' he chuckled.

Han laughed in relief, as the two old friends at last embraced each other like the long-lost accomplices they were.

Lando waved at the Wookiee, standing behind his boss. 'How you doing, Chewbacca?' he asked amiably. 'Still wasting your time with this clown, eh?'

The Wookiee growled a reserved greeting.

Calrissian was not certain what to make of that growl. 'Right,' he half-smiled, looking uncomfortable. But his attention was distracted from this shaggy mass of muscle and hair when he saw Leia beginning to walk down the ramp. This lovely vision was followed closely by her protocol droid, who cautiously glanced around as they walked toward Lando and Han.

'Hello! What have we here?' Calrissian welcomed her admiringly. 'I am Lando Calrissian, administrator of this facility. And who might you be?'

The princess remained coolly polite. 'You may call me Leia,' she replied.

Lando bowed formally and gently kissed the princess's hand.

'And I,' her robot companion said, introducing himself to the administrator, 'am See Threepio, human–cyborg relations, at your— '

But before Threepio could finish his little speech, Han draped one arm about Lando's shoulder and steered him away from the princess. 'She's travelling with me, Lando,' he advised his old friend, 'and I don't intend to gamble her away. So you might as well forget she exists.'

Lando looked longingly over his shoulder as he and Han began to walk across the landing platform, followed by Leia, Threepio, and Chewbacca. 'That won't be easy, my friend,' Lando said regretfully.

Then he turned to Han. 'What brings you here anyway?'

'Repairs.'

Mock panic spread across Lando's face. 'What have you done to my ship?'

Grinning, Han glanced back at Leia. 'Lando used to own the *Falcon*,' he explained. 'And he sometimes forgets that he lost her fair and square.'

Lando shrugged as he conceded to Han's boastful claim. 'That ship saved my life more than a few times. It's the fastest hunk of junk in the galaxy. What's wrong with her?'

'Hyperdrive.'

'I'll have my people get to work on it right away,' Lando said. 'I hate the thought of the *Millennium Falcon* without her heart.'

The group crossed the narrow bridge that joined the landing area to the city – and were instantly dazzled by its beauty. They saw numerous small plazas ringed by smooth-edged towers and spires and buildings. The structures that constituted Cloud City's business and residential sections were gleaming white, shining brightly in the morning sun. Numerous alien races made up the city's populace and many of these citizens leisurely walked through the spacious streets alongside the *Falcon* visitors.

'How's your mining operation going?' Han asked Lando.

'Not as well as I'd like,' Calrissian answered. 'We're a small outpost and not very self-sufficient. I've had supply problems of every kind and ...' The administrator noticed Han's amused grin. 'What's so funny?'

'Nothing.' Then Han chuckled. 'I never would have guessed that underneath that wild schemer I knew was a responsible leader and businessman.' Grudgingly, Han had to admit that he was impressed. 'You wear it well.'

Lando looked at his old friend reflectively. 'Seeing you sure brings back a few memories.' He shook his head, smiling. 'Yes, I'm *responsible* these days. It's the price of success. And you know what, Han? You were right all along. It's overrated.'

Both burst out laughing, causing a head or two to turn as the group moved through the city walkways.

See Threepio lagged a bit behind, fascinated by the bustling alien crowds in the Cloud City streets, the floating cars, the fabulous, fanciful buildings. He turned his head back and forth, trying to register it all in his computer circuits.

As the golden droid gawked at the new sights, he passed a door facing the walkway. Hearing it open, he turned to see a silver Threepio unit emerging and stopped to watch the other robot move away. While Threepio paused there, he heard a muffled beeping and whistling coming from behind the door.

He peeked in and saw a familiar-looking droid sitting in the anteroom. 'Oh, an R2 unit!' he chirped in delight. 'I'd almost forgotten what they sound like.'

Threepio moved through the doorway and walked into the room.

Instantly he sensed that he and the R2 unit were not alone. He threw his golden arms up in surprise, the expression of wonder on his gilded faceplate frozen in place. 'Oh, my!' he exclaimed. 'Those look like—'

As he spoke, a rocketing laser bolt crashed into his metal chest, sending him flying in twenty directions around the room. His bronzed arms and legs crashed against the walls and settled in a smoldering heap with the rest of his mechanical body.

Behind him, the door slammed shut.

Some distance away, Lando guided the small group into his hall of offices, pointing out objects of interest as they moved through the white corridors. None of them had noticed Threepio's absence as they walked along, discussing life in Bespin.

But Chewbacca suddenly stopped and curiously sniffed the air as he looked behind him. Then he shrugged his huge shoulders and continued to follow the others.

Luke was perfectly calm. Even his present position did not make him feel tense or strained or unsure, or any of the negative things he used to feel when he first attempted this feat. He stood, perfectly balanced on one hand. He knew the Force was with him.

His patient master, Yoda, sat calmly on the soles of Luke's upturned feet. Luke concentrated serenely on his task and all at once he lifted four fingers from the ground. His balance undisturbed, he held his upside-down position – on one thumb.

Luke's determination had made him a quick student. He was eager to learn and was undaunted by the tests Yoda had devised for him. And now he felt confident that when he finally left this planet, it would be as a full-fledged Jedi Knight prepared to fight only for the noblest of causes.

Luke was rapidly growing stronger with the Force and, indeed, was accomplishing miracles. Yoda grew more pleased with his apprentice's progress. Once, while Yoda stood watching nearby, Luke used the Force to lift two large equipment cases and suspend them in midair. Yoda was pleased, but noticed Artoo Detoo observing this apparent impossibility and emitting electronic beeps of disbelief. The Jedi Master raised his hand and, with the Force, lifted the little droid off the ground.

Artoo hovered, his baffled internal circuits and sensors trying to detect the unseen power that held him suspended in the air. And suddenly the invisible hand played still another joke on him: While hanging in midair, the little robot was abruptly turned upside down. His white legs kicked desperately and his dome head spun helplessly around. When Yoda finally lowered his hand, the droid, along with two supply cases, began to drop. But only the boxes smashed against the ground. Artoo remained suspended in space.

Turning his head, Artoo perceived his young master, standing with hand extended, preventing Artoo from a fatal tumble.

Yoda shook his head, impressed by his student's quick thinking and by his control.

Yoda sprang onto Luke's arm and the two of them turned back toward the house. But they had forgotten something: Artoo Detoo was still hanging in the air, beeping and whistling frantically, trying to get their attention. Yoda was merely playing another joke on the fretful droid, and as Yoda and Luke strolled away, Artoo heard the Jedi Master's bell-like laugh float in gay peals behind him as the droid slowly lowered to the ground.

Some time later, as dusk crept through the dense foliage of the bog, Artoo was cleaning the X-wing's hull. Through a hose that ran from the pond to an orifice in his side, the robot sprayed down the ship with a powerful stream of water. And while he worked, Luke and Yoda sat in the clearing, Luke's eyes closed in concentration.

'Be calm,' Yoda told him. 'Through the Force things you will see: other places, other thoughts, the future, the past, old friends long gone.'

Luke was losing himself as he concentrated on Yoda's words. He was becoming unaware of his body and let his consciousness drift with the words of his master.

'My mind fills with so many images.'

'Control, control you must learn of what you see,' the Jedi Master instructed. 'Not easy, not fast.'

Luke closed his eyes, relaxed, and began to free his mind, began to control the images. At last there was something, not clear at first, but something white, amorphous. Gradually the image cleared. It seemed to be that of a city, a city that perhaps floated in a billowing white sea.

'I see a city in the clouds,' he finally said.

'Bespin,' Yoda identified it. 'I see it, too. Friends you have there, heh? Concentrate and see them you will.'

Luke's concentration intensified. And the city in the clouds became clearer. As he concentrated he was able to see forms, familiar forms of people he knew.

'I see them!' Luke exclaimed, his eyes still shut. Then a sudden agony, of body and spirit, took hold of him. 'They're in pain. They're suffering.'

'It is the future you see,' the voice of Yoda explained.

The future, Luke thought. Then the pain he had felt had not yet been inflicted on his friends. So perhaps the future was not unchangeable.

'Will they die?' he asked his master.

Yoda shook his head and shrugged gently. 'Difficult to see. Always in motion is the future.'

Luke opened his eyes again. He stood up and quickly began to gather his equipment. 'They're my friends,' he said, guessing that the Jedi Master might try to dissuade him from doing what he knew he must.

'And therefore,' Yoda added, 'decide you must how to serve them best. If you leave now, help them you could. But you would destroy all for which they have fought and suffered.'

His words stopped Luke cold. The youth sank to the ground, feeling a shroud of gloom envelop him. Could he really destroy everything he had worked for and possibly also destroy his friends? But how could he *not* try to save them?

Artoo perceived his master's despair and rolled over to stand by him and provide what comfort he could.

Chewbacca, who had grown concerned about See Threepio, slipped away from Han Solo and the others and began hunting for the missing droid. All he had to follow were his keen Wookiee instincts as he wandered through the unfamiliar white passageways and corridors of Bespin.

Following his senses, Chewbacca finally came upon an enormous room in a corridor on the outside of the Cloud City. He approached the entrance to the room and heard the clamor of metallic objects clattering together. Along with the clanging, he heard the low grunting of creatures he had never encountered before.

The room he had found was a Cloud City junk room – the repository of all the city's broken machines and other discarded metal junk.

Standing amid the scattered pieces of metal and tangled wire were four hoglike creatures. White hair grew thickly on their heads and partially covered their wrinkled piggish faces. The humanoid beasts – called Ugnaughts on this planet – were busy separating the junked pieces of metal and casting them into a pit of molten metal.

Chewbacca entered the room and saw that one of the Ugnaughts held a familiar-looking piece of golden metal.

The piglike creature was already raising his arm to toss the severed metal leg into the sizzling pit when Chewbacca roared at him, barking desperately. The Ugnaught dropped the leg and ran, to cower in terror with his fellows.

The Wookiee grabbed the metal leg and inspected it closely. He hadn't been mistaken. And as he growled angrily at the huddled Ugnaughts, they shivered and grunted like a pack of frightened pigs.

Sunlight streamed into the circular lounge of the apartments assigned to Han Solo and his group. The lounge was white and furnished simply, with a couch and a table and little of anything else. Each of the four sliding doors, placed along the circular wall, led to an adjoining apartment.

Han leaned out the lounge's large bay window to take in the panoramic view of Cloud City. The sight was breathtaking, even to such a jaded star jockey. He watched the flying cloud cars weave between the towering buildings, then looked down to see the people moving through the networks of streets below. The cool, clean air swept against his face, and, at least for the present, he felt as if he didn't have a care in all the universe.

A door behind him opened, and he turned to see Princess Leia standing in the entranceway to her apartment. She was stunning. Dressed in red with a cloud-white cloak flowing to the floor, Leia looked more beautiful than Han had ever seen her. Her long, dark hair was tied with ribbons and it softly framed her oval face. And she was looking at him, smiling at his astounded expression.

'What are you staring at?' she asked, beginning to blush.

'Who's staring?'

'You look silly,' she said, laughing.

'You look great.'

Leia looked away in embarrassment. 'Has Threepio turned up yet?' she asked, trying to change the subject.

Solo was taken off guard. 'Huh? Oh. Chewie went to look for him. He's been gone too long just to be lost.' He patted the softly cushioned sofa. 'Come over here,' he beckoned. 'I want to check this out.'

She thought about his invitation for a moment, then walked over and sat next to him on the couch. Han was overjoyed at her apparent compliance and leaned over to put his arm around her. But just before he had quite succeeded, she spoke again. 'I hope Luke made it to the fleet all right.'

'Luke!' He was becoming exasperated. How hard did he have to play at this game of hard-to-get? It was her game, and her rules – but he *had* chosen to play. She was too lovely to resist. 'I'm sure he's fine,' Han said, soothingly. 'Probably sitting around wondering what we're doing right now.'

He moved closer and put his arm around her shoulders, pulling her closer to him. She gazed at him invitingly, and he moved to kiss her—

Just then one of the doors zapped open. Chewbacca lumbered in carrying a large packing case filled with disturbingly familiar metal parts – the remains, in bronzed bits and pieces, of See Threepio. The Wookiee dropped the case on the table. Gesturing toward Han, he barked and growled in distress.

'What happened?' Leia asked, moving closer to inspect the pile of disjointed parts.

'He found Threepio in a junk room.'

Leia gasped. 'What a mess! Chewie, do you think you can repair him?'

Chewbacca studied the collection of robot parts, then, looking back at the princess, shrugged his shoulders and howled. It looked to him like an impossible job.

'Why don't we just turn him over to Lando to fix?' Han suggested.

'No thanks,' Leia answered, with a cold look in her eyes. 'Something's wrong here. Your friend Lando is very charming, but I don't trust him.'

'Well, I do trust him,' Han argued, defending his host. 'Listen, sweetheart, I'm not going to have you accusing my friend of—'

But he was interrupted by a buzz as a door slid open, and Lando Calrissian entered the lounge. Smiling cordially, he walked toward the small group. 'Sorry, am I interrupting anything?'

'Not really,' the princess said distantly.

'My dear,' Lando said, ignoring her coldness toward him, 'your beauty is unparalleled. Truly you belong here with us among the clouds.'

She smiled icily. 'Thanks.'

'Would you care to join me for a little refreshment?'

Han had to admit that he was a bit hungry. But for some reason he could not quite name, he felt a wave of suspicion about his friend flood over him. He didn't remember Calrissian being quite so polite, quite so smooth. Perhaps Leia was correct in her suspicions . . .

His thoughts were interrupted by Chewbacca's enthusiastic bark at the mention of food. The big Wookiee was licking his lips at the prospect of a hearty meal.

'Everyone's invited, of course,' Lando said.

Leia took Lando's proffered arm and, as the group moved toward the door, Calrissian glimpsed the box of golden robot parts. 'Having problems with your droid?' he asked.

Han and Leia exchanged a quick glance. If Han was going to ask for Lando's help in repairing the droid, now was the moment. 'An accident,' he grunted. 'Nothing we can't handle.'

They left the lounge, leaving behind them the shattered remains of the protocol droid.

The group strolled through the long white corridors and Leia walked between Han and Lando. Han wasn't at all certain he liked the prospect of competing with Lando for Leia's affections – especially under the circumstances. But they were dependent on Lando's good graces now. They had no other choice.

Joining them as they walked was Lando's personal aide, a tall bald man dressed in a gray jacket with ballooning yellow sleeves. The aide wore a radio device that wrapped around the back of his head and covered both his ears. He walked along with Chewbacca a short distance behind Han, Leia, and Lando, and as they walked toward Lando's dining hall, the administrator described the status of his planet's government.

'So you see,' Lando explained, 'we are a free station and do not fall under the jurisdiction of the Empire.'

'You're part of the mining guild then?' Leia asked.

'Not actually. Our operation is small enough not to be noticed. Much of our trade is, well . . . unofficial.'

They stepped onto a veranda that overlooked the spiraled top of Cloud City. From here they saw several flying cloud cars gracefully swooping around the beautiful spired buildings of the city. It was a spectacular view, and the visitors were very impressed.

'It's a lovely outpost,' Leia marveled.

'Yes, we're proud of it,' Lando replied. 'You'll find the air quite special here . . . very stimulating.' He smiled at Leia meaningfully. 'You could grow to like it.'

Han didn't miss Lando's flirtatious glance – and he didn't like it, either. 'We don't plan on staying that long,' he said brusquely.

Leia raised an eyebrow and glanced mischievously at the now-fuming Han Solo. 'I find it most relaxing.'

Lando chuckled, and led them from the veranda. They approached the dining hall with its massive closed doors and, as they paused in front of them, Chewbacca lifted his head and sniffed the air curiously. He turned and barked urgently at Han.

'Not now, Chewie,' Han reproved, turning to Calrissian. 'Lando, aren't you afraid the Empire might eventually discover this little operation and shut you down?'

'That's always been the danger,' the administrator replied. 'It's loomed like a shadow over everything we've built here. But circumstances have developed which will insure security. You see, I've made a deal that will keep the Empire out of here forever.'

With that the mighty doors slid open – and immediately Han understood just what that 'deal' must have involved. At the far end of the huge banquet table stood the bounty hunter Boba Fett.

Fett stood next to a chair that held the black essence of evil itself – Darth Vader. Slowly the Dark Lord rose to his full, menacing two-meter height.

Han shot his meanest look at Lando.

'Sorry, friend,' Lando said, sounding mildly apologetic. 'I had no choice. They arrived right before you did.'

'I'm sorry, too,' Han snapped. In that instant, he cleared his blaster from its holster, aimed it directly at the figure in black, and began to pump laser bolts Vader's way.

But the man who may have been the fastest draw in the galaxy was not fast enough to surprise Vader. Before those bolts zipped halfway across the table, the Dark Lord had lifted a gauntlet-protected hand and effortlessly deflected them so they exploded against the wall in a harmless spray of flying white shards.

Astounded by what he had just seen, Han tried firing again. But before he could discharge another laser blast, something – something unseen yet incredibly strong – yanked the weapon from his hand and sent it flying into Vader's grip. The raven figure calmly placed the weapon on top of the dining table.

Hissing through his obsidian mask, the Dark Lord addressed his would-be assailant. 'We would be honored if you joined us.'

Artoo Detoo felt the rain plunking on top of his metal dome as he trudged through the muddy puddles of the bog. He was headed for the sanctuary of Yoda's little hut, and soon his optical sensors picked up the golden glow shining through its windows. As he neared the inviting house, he felt a robot's relief that at last he would get out of this annoying, persistent rain.

But when he tried to pass through the entrance he discovered that his inflexible droid body just could not get in; he tried from one angle, then from another. At last the perception that he was simply the wrong shape to get in seeped into his computer mind.

He could scarcely believe his sensors. As he peered into the house, he scanned a busy figure, bustling about the kitchen, stirring steaming pots, chopping this and that, running back and forth. But the figure in Yoda's tiny kitchen, doing Yoda's kitchen tasks, was not the Jedi Master – but his apprentice.

Yoda, it appeared from Artoo's scan, was simply sitting back observing his young pupil from the adjacent room, and quietly smiling. Then suddenly, in the midst of all his kitchen activity, Luke paused, as if a painful vision had appeared before him.

Yoda noticed Luke's troubled look. As he watched his student, three glow-ball seekers appeared from behind Yoda and noiselessly shot through the air to attack the young Jedi from behind. Instantly Luke turned to face them, a pot lid in one hand and a spoon in the other.

The seekers sent one rocketing bolt after another directly at Luke.

But, with astounding skill, he warded off every one. He knocked one of the seekers toward the open door where Artoo stood watching his master's performance. But the faithful droid saw the shining ball too late to avoid the bolt it shot at him. The impact knocked the shrieking robot onto the ground with a *clunk* that nearly shook loose his electronic insides.

Later that evening, after the student had successfully passed a number of his teacher's tests, a weary Luke Skywalker finally fell asleep on the ground outside Yoda's house. He slept fitfully, tossing and softly moaning. His concerned droid stood by him, reaching out an extension arm and covering Luke with the blanket that had slipped halfway off. But when Artoo started to roll away, Luke began to groan and shudder as if in the grip of some horrible nightmare.

Inside the house, Yoda heard the groans and hurried to his doorway.

Luke awoke from his sleep with a start. Dazed, he looked about him, then saw his teacher worriedly watching him from his house. 'I can't keep the vision out of my head,' Luke told Yoda. 'My friends . . . they're in trouble . . . and I feel that—'

'Luke, you must not go,' Yoda warned.

'But Han and Leia will die if I don't.'

'You don't know that.' It was the whispered voice of Ben, who was beginning to materialize before them. The dark-robed figure stood, a shimmering image, and told Luke, 'Even Yoda cannot see their fate.'

But Luke was deeply worried about his friends and was determined to do something. 'I can help them!' he insisted.

'You're not ready yet,' Ben said gently. 'You still have much to learn.'

'I feel the Force,' Luke said.

'But you cannot control it. This is a dangerous stage for you, Luke. You are now most susceptible to the temptations of the dark side.'

'Yes, yes,' Yoda added. 'To Obi-Wan you listen, young one. The tree. Remember your failure at the tree! Heh?'

Painfully, Luke remembered, though he felt he had gained a great deal of strength and understanding in that experience. 'I've learned much since then. And I'll return to finish. I promise that, master.'

'You underestimate the Emperor,' Ben told him gravely. 'It is you he wants. That is why your friends suffer.'

'And that,' Luke said, 'is why I must go.'

Kenobi was firm. 'I will not lose you to the Emperor as I once lost Vader.'

'You won't.'

'Only a fully trained Jedi Knight, with the Force as his ally, will conquer Vader and his Emperor,' Ben emphasized. 'If you end your training now, if you choose the quick and easy path – as Vader did – you will become an agent of evil, and the galaxy will be plunged deeper into the abyss of hate and despair.'

'Stopped they must be,' Yoda interjected. 'Do you hear? On this *all* depends.'

'You are the last Jedi, Luke. You are our only hope. Be patient.'

'And sacrifice Han and Leia?' the youth asked incredulously.

'If you honor what they fight for,' Yoda said, pausing for a long moment, '. . . yes!'

Great anguish overcame Luke. He wasn't certain that he could reconcile the advice of these two great mentors with his own feelings. His friends were in terrible danger, and of course he must save them. But his teachers thought he was not ready, that he might be too vulnerable to the powerful Vader and his Emperor, that he might bring harm to his friends and himself – and possibly be lost forever on the path of evil.

Yet how could he fear these abstract things when Han and Leia were real and were suffering? How could he permit himself to fear possible danger to himself when his friends were presently in real danger of death?

There was no longer any question in his mind as to what he had to do.

It was dusk the next day on the bog planet when Artoo Detoo settled himself into his nook behind the cockpit of Luke's X-wing fighter.

Yoda stood on one of the storage cases, watching Luke load the cases one by one into the fighter's underbelly as he worked in the glow of the X-wing's lights.

'I cannot protect you, Luke,' the voice of Ben Kenobi came, as his robed figure took solid form. 'If you choose to face Vader, you will do it alone. Once you've made this decision, I cannot interfere.'

'I understand,' Luke replied calmly. Then, turning to his droid, he said, 'Artoo, fire up the power converters.'

Artoo, who had already unfastened the power couplings on the ship, whistled happily, grateful to be leaving this dismal bog world, which was certainly no place for a droid.

'Luke,' Ben advised, 'use the Force only for knowledge and for defense, not as a weapon. Don't give in to hate or anger. They lead the way to the dark side.'

Luke nodded, only half-listening. His mind was on the long journey and on the difficult tasks ahead of him. He must save his friends, whose lives were in danger because of him. He climbed into the cockpit, then looked at his little Jedi Master.

Yoda was deeply concerned about his apprentice. 'Strong is Vader,' he warned ominously. 'Clouded is your fate. Mind what you have learned. Notice *everything*, everything! It can save you.'

'I will, Master Yoda,' Luke assured him. 'I will and I'll be back to finish what I have begun. I give you my word!'

Artoo closed the cockpit and Luke started the engines.

Yoda and Obi-Wan Kenobi watched the X-wing gear its engines and begin to move away for take-off.

'Told you, I did,' Yoda said sorrowfully, as the sleek fighter craft began to lift into the misty heavens. 'Reckless is he. Now things are going to worse.'

'That boy is our last hope,' Ben Kenobi said, his voice heavy with emotion.

'No,' Kenobi's former teacher corrected with a knowing gleam in his large eyes, 'there is another.'

Yoda lifted his head toward the darkening sky where Luke's ship was already a barely distinguishable point of light among the flickering stars.

XII

CHEWBACCA thought he was going mad!

The prison cell was flooded with hot, blinding light that seared his sensitive Wookiee eyes. Not even his huge hands and hairy arms, thrust up over his face, could entirely protect him from the glare. And to add to his misery, a high-pitched whistle blared into the cubicle, tormenting his keen sense of hearing. He roared in agony, but his guttural roars were drowned out by the piercing, screeching noise.

The Wookiee paced back and forth within the confines of the cell. Moaning pitifully, he pounded at the thick walls in desperation, wanting someone, anyone, to come and free him. While he pounded, the whistle that had nearly exploded his eardrums suddenly stopped and the deluge of light flickered and went out.

Chewbacca staggered back a step with the sudden absence of torture, and then moved to one of the cell walls to try to detect whether anyone was approaching to release him. But the thick walls revealed nothing and, maddened to a fury, Chewbacca slammed a giant fist against the wall.

But the wall stood undamaged and as impenetrable as before, and Chewbacca realized it would take more than Wookiee brute strength to topple it. Despairing of his chances of breaking through the cell to freedom, Chewbacca shuffled toward the bed, where the box of 3PO parts had been placed.

Idly at first, and then with more interest, the Wookiee began poking through the box. It dawned on him that it might be possible to repair the disjointed droid. Not only would doing so pass the time, but it might be helpful to have Threepio back in working condition.

He picked up the golden head and gazed into its darkened eyes. He held the head and barked a few soliloquizing words as if to prepare the robot for the joy of re-entry into activity – or for the disappointment of Chewbacca's possible failure to reconstruct him properly.

Then, quite delicately for a creature of his size and strength, the giant Wookiee placed the staring head atop the bronzed torso. Tentatively he began experimenting with Threepio's tangle of wires and circuits. His mechanical skills had previously only been tested in repairs on the *Millennium Falcon*, so he wasn't at all certain he could complete the delicate task. Chewbacca jiggled and fiddled with the wires, baffled by this intricate mechanism, when suddenly Threepio's eyes lit up.

A whine came from inside the robot. It sounded vaguely like Threepio's normal voice, but was so low and so slow that the words were unintelligible.

'Imm-peeeeer-eee-all-storr-mmm-trppp . . .'

Bewildered, Chewbacca scratched his furry head and studied the broken robot intently. An idea came to him, and he tried switching one wire to another plug. Instantly Threepio began speaking in his normal voice. What he had to say sounded like words from a bad dream.

'Chewbacca!' the head of See Threepio cried. 'Watch out, there are Imperial stormtroopers hidden in—' He paused, as if reliving the whole traumatic experience, and then he cried, 'Oh, no! I've been shot!'

Chewbacca shook his head in sympathy. All he could do at this point was try to put the rest of See Threepio back together again.

Quite possibly it was the first time Han Solo had ever screamed. Never had he endured such excruciating torment. He was strapped to a platform that angled away from the floor at approximately forty-five degrees. While he was strapped there, electric currents of searing power shot through his body at short intervals, each jolt more painfully powerful than the last. He squirmed to free himself but his agony was so severe that it was all he could do just to remain conscious.

Standing near the torture rack, Darth Vader silently watched Han Solo's ordeal. Seeming neither pleased nor displeased, he watched until he had seen enough, and then the Dark Lord turned his back on the writhing figure and left the cell, the door sliding behind him to muffle Solo's anguished screams.

Outside the torture chamber, Boba Fett waited for Lord Vader with Lando Calrissian and the administrator's aide.

With obvious disdain, Vader turned to Fett. 'Bounty hunter,' Vader addressed the man in the black-marked silver helmet, 'if you are waiting for your reward, you will wait until I have Skywalker.'

The self-assured Boba Fett appeared unruffled by this news. 'I am in no hurry, Lord Vader. My concern is that Captain Solo not be damaged. The reward from Jabba the Hut is double if he's alive.'

'His pain is considerable, bounty hunter,' Vader hissed, 'but he will not be harmed.'

'What about Leia and the Wookiee?' Lando asked with some concern.

'You will find them well enough,' Vader answered. 'But,' he added with unmistakable finality, 'they must never again leave this city.'

'That was never a condition of our agreement,' Calrissian urged. 'Nor was giving Han to this bounty hunter.'

'Perhaps you think you're being treated unfairly,' Vader said sarcastically.

'No,' Lando said, glancing at his aide.

'Good,' Vader continued, adding a veiled threat. 'It would be most unfortunate if I had to leave a permanent garrison here.'

Bowing his head reverently, Lando Calrissian waited until Darth Vader had turned and swept into a waiting elevator with the silver-armored bounty hunter. Then, taking his aide with him, the administrator of Cloud City strode swiftly down a white-walled corridor.

'This deal's becoming worse all the time,' Lando complained.

'Maybe you should have tried to negotiate with him,' the aide suggested.

Lando looked at his aide grimly. He was beginning to realize that the deal with Darth Vader was giving nothing to him. And, beyond that, it was bringing harm to people he might have called friends. Finally, he said, low enough not to be heard by any of Vader's spies, 'I've got a bad feeling about this.'

See Threepio was at last beginning to feel something like his old self.

The Wookiee had been busily working on reconnecting the droid's many wires and internal circuits, and just now was beginning to figure out how to attach the limbs. So far he had reattached the head to the torso and had successfully completed connecting an arm. The rest of Threepio's parts still lay on the table with wires and circuits hanging out of the severed joints.

But, though the Wookiee was diligently working to complete his task, the golden droid began to complain vociferously. 'Well, something's not right,' he fussed, 'because now I can't see.'

The patient Wookiee barked, and adjusted a wire in Threepio's neck. At last the robot could see again and he breathed a little mechanical sigh of relief. 'There now, that's better.'

But it wasn't *much* better. When he cast his newly activated sensor gaze toward where his chest should be he saw – his back! 'Wait— Oh, my. What have you done? I'm backwards!' Threepio sputtered. 'You flea-bitten furball! Only an overgrown mophead like you would be stupid enough to put my head—'

The Wookiee growled menacingly. He had forgotten what a complainer this droid was. And this cell was too small for him to listen to any more of that! Before Threepio knew what was happening to him, the Wookiee lumbered over and pulled a wire. Instantly the grumbling ceased, and the room became quiet again.

Then there was a familiar scent nearing the cell.

The Wookiee sniffed the air and hurried to the door.

The cell door buzzed open and a ragged, exhausted Han Solo was shoved in by two Imperial stormtroopers. The troopers left and Chewbacca quickly moved to his friend, embracing him with relief. Han's face was pale, with dark circles under his eyes. It seemed that he was on the verge of collapse, and Chewbacca barked his concern to his long-time companion.

'No,' Han said wearily, 'I'm all right. I'm all right.'

The door opened once again, and Princess Leia was thrown into the cell by the stormtroopers. She was still dressed in her elegant cloak but, like Han, she looked tired and disheveled.

When the stormtroopers left and the door slid shut behind them, Chewbacca helped Leia over to Han. The two gazed at one another with great emotion, then reached out and tightly embraced. After a moment they kissed tenderly.

While Han still held her, Leia weakly asked him, 'Why are they doing this? I can't understand what they're up to.'

Han was as puzzled as she. 'They had me howling on the scan grid, but they never asked me any questions.'

Then the door slid open again, admitting Lando and two of his Cloud City guards.

'Get out of here, Lando!' Han snarled. If he had felt stronger, he would have leaped up to attack his traitorous friend.

'Shut up a minute and listen,' Lando snapped. 'I'm doing what I can to make this easier for you.'

'This ought to be good,' Han remarked caustically.

'Vader has agreed to turn Leia and Chewie over to me,' explained Lando. 'They'll have to stay here, but at least they'll be safe.'

Leia gasped. 'What about Han?'

Lando looked solemnly at his friend. 'I didn't know you had a price on your head. Vader has given you to the bounty hunter.'

The princess quickly looked at Han, concern flooding her eyes.

'You don't know much about much,' Han said to Calrissian, 'if you think Vader won't want us dead before all this is over.'

'He doesn't want you at all,' Lando said. 'He's after someone called Skywalker.'

The two prisoners caught their breath at the casual mention of that name.

Han seemed puzzled. 'Luke? I don't get it.'

The princess's mind was racing. All the facts were beginning to fit together into a terrible mosaic. In the past, Vader had wanted Leia because of her political importance in the war between Empire and Rebel Alliance. Now she was almost beneath his notice, useful only for one possible function.

'Lord Vader has set a trap for him,' Lando added, 'and—'

Leia finished his statement. 'We're the bait.'

'All this just to get the kid?' Han asked. 'What's so important about him?'

'Don't ask me, but he's on his way.'

'Luke's coming here?'

Lando Calrissian nodded.

'You fixed us all pretty good,' Han growled, spitting his words at Lando, ' – friend!'

As he snarled that last, accusing word, Han Solo's strength returned in a rush. He put all of his might into a punch that sent Lando reeling. Instantly the two former friends were engaged in a furious, close-quarters battle. Lando's two guards moved closer to the two grappling opponents and began striking at Han with the butts of their laser rifles. One powerful blow struck Han on the chin and sent him flying across the room, blood streaming from his jaw.

Chewbacca began to growl savagely and started for the guards. As they raised their laser weapons, Lando shouted, 'Don't shoot!'

Bruised and winded, the administrator turned to Han. 'I've done what I can for you,' he said. 'I'm sorry it's not better, but I've got my own problems.' Then turning to leave the cell, Lando Calrissian added, 'I've already stuck my neck out farther than I should.'

'Yeah,' Han Solo retorted, regaining his composure, 'you're a real hero.'

When Lando had left with his guards, Leia and Chewbacca helped Han back to his feet and led him to one of the bunks. He eased his weary, battered body onto the bunk, and Leia took a piece of her cloak and began gently dabbing at his chin, cleaning off the oozing blood.

As she did so, she started to chuckle softly. 'You certainly have a way with people,' she teased.

Artoo Detoo's head swiveled atop his barrel-like body as his scanners perceived the star-studded void of the Bespin system.

The speeding X-wing had just entered the system, and was swooping through black space like a great white bird.

The R2 unit had a lot to communicate to his pilot. His electronic thoughts were tumbling out, one on top of the other, and were translated on the cockpit scope.

The grim-faced Luke quickly responded to the first of Artoo's urgent questions. 'Yes,' Luke replied. 'I'm sure Threepio is with them.'

The little robot whistled an excited exclamation.

'Just hold on,' Luke said patiently, 'we'll be there soon.'

Artoo's turning head perceived the regal clusters of stars, his innards warm and cheerful, as the X-wing continued like a celestial arrow toward a planet with a city in the clouds.

Lando Calrissian and Darth Vader stood near the hydraulic platform that dominated the huge carbon-freezing chamber. The Dark Lord was quiet while aides hurried to prepare the room.

The hydraulic platform was housed within a deep pit in the center of the chamber and was surrounded by countless steam pipes and enormous chemical tanks of varying shapes.

Standing guard with laser rifles clutched in their hands were four armor-suited Imperial stormtroopers.

Darth Vader turned to Calrissian after appraising the chamber. 'The facility is crude,' he remarked, 'but it should suit our needs.'

One of Vader's officers rushed to the Sith Lord's side. 'Lord Vader,' he reported, 'ship approaching – X-wing class.'

'Good,' Vader said coldly. 'Monitor Skywalker's progress and allow him to land. We'll have the chamber ready for him shortly.'

'We only use this facility for carbon-freezing,' the administrator of Cloud City said nervously. 'If you put him in there, it might kill him.'

But Vader had already considered that possibility. He knew a way to find out just how powerful this freezing unit was. 'I don't wish the Emperor's prize to be damaged. We'll test it first.' He caught the attention of one of his stormtroopers. 'Bring in Solo,' the Dark Lord commanded.

Lando quickly glanced at Vader. He hadn't been prepared for the pure evil that was manifested in this terrifying being.

The X-wing speedily made its descent, and began to pierce the dense cloud blanket enveloping the planet.

Luke checked his monitor screens with growing concern. Maybe Artoo had more information than he was getting on his own panel. He tapped out a question to the robot.

'You haven't picked up any patrol ships?'

Artoo Detoo's reply was negative.

And so Luke, thoroughly convinced that his arrival was thus far undetected, pressed his ship onward, toward the city of his troubled vision.

*

Six of the piglike Ugnaughts frantically prepared the carbon-freezing chamber for use, while Lando Calrissian and Darth Vader – now the true master of Cloud City – observed the hasty activity.

As they scurried about the carbon-freezing platform, the Ugnaughts lowered a network of pipes – resembling some alien giant's circulatory system – into the pit. They raised the carbonite hoses and hammered them into place. Then the six humanoids lifted the heavy coffinlike container and set it securely onto the platform.

Boba Fett rushed in, leading a squad of six Imperial stormtroopers. The troopers shoved and pulled Han, Leia, and the Wookiee in front of them, forcing them to hurry into the chamber. Strapped to the Wookiee's broad back was the partially reassembled See Threepio, whose unattached arm and legs were roughly bundled against his gilded torso. The droid's head, facing the opposite direction from Chewbacca's, frantically turned around to try to see where they were going and what lay in store for them.

Vader turned to the bounty hunter. 'Put him in the carbon-freezing chamber.'

'What if he doesn't survive?' the calculating Boba Fett asked. 'He is worth a lot to me.'

'The Empire will compensate you for the loss,' Vader said succinctly.

Anguished, Leia protested, 'No!'

Chewbacca threw back his maned head and gave out a bellowing Wookiee howl. Then he charged directly at the line of stormtroopers guarding Han.

Screaming in panic, See Threepio raised his one functioning arm to protect his face.

'Wait!' the robot yelled. 'What are you doing?'

But the Wookiee wrestled and grappled with the troopers, undaunted by their number or by Threepio's frightened shrieks.

'Oh, no ... Don't hit me!' the droid begged, trying to protect his disassembled parts with his arm. 'No! He doesn't mean it! Calm down, you hairy fool!'

More stormtroopers had come into the room and joined the fight. Some of the troopers began to club the Wookiee with the butts of their rifles, banging against Threepio in the process.

'Ouch!' the droid screamed. '*I* didn't do anything!'

The stormtroopers had begun to overpower Chewbacca, and were about to smash him in the face with their weapons when, over the sounds of the fray, Han shouted, 'Chewie, no! Stop it, Chewbacca!'

Only Han Solo could deflect the maddened Wookiee from his battle. Straining against the hold of his guards, Han broke away from them and rushed over to break up the fight.

Vader signaled his guards to let Han go and signaled the battling stormtroopers to stop the fight.

Han gripped the massive forearms of his hairy friend to calm him down, then gave him a stern look.

The flustered Threepio was still fussing and fuming. 'Oh, yes ... stop, stop.' Then, with a robotic sigh of relief, he said, 'Thank heavens!'

Han and Chewbacca faced each other, the former looking grimly into his friend's eyes. For a moment they embraced tightly, then Han told the Wookiee, 'Save your strength for another time, pal, when the odds are better.' He mustered a reassuring wink, but the Wookiee was grief-stricken and barked a mournful wail.

'Yeah,' Han said, trying his best to crack a grin, 'I know. I feel the same way. Keep well.' Han Solo turned to one of the guards. 'You'd better chain him until it's over.'

The subdued Chewbacca did not resist as the stormtrooper guards placed restraining bands around his wrists. Han gave his partner a final farewell hug, then turned to Princess Leia. He took her in his arms and they embraced as if they would never let go.

Then Leia pressed her lips to his in a lingering kiss of passion. When their kiss ended, tears were in her eyes. 'I love you,' she said softly. 'I couldn't tell you before, but it's true.'

He smiled his familiar cocky smile. 'Just remember that, because I'll be back.' Then his face grew tender and he kissed her gently on the forehead.

Tears began to roll down her cheeks as Han turned away from her and walked quietly and fearlessly toward the waiting hydraulic platform.

The Ugnaughts rushed to his side and positioned him on the platform, binding his arms and legs tightly onto the hydraulic deck. He stood alone and helpless, and gazed one last time at his friends.

Chewbacca looked at his friend mournfully, Threepio's head peek-ing over the Wookiee's shoulder to get one last look at the brave man. The administrator, Calrissian, watched this ordeal, a solemn look of regret etched deeply into his face. And then there was Leia. Her face was contorted with the pain of her grief as she stood regally trying to be strong.

Leia's was the last face Han saw when he felt the hydraulic platform suddenly drop. As it dropped, the Wookiee bellowed a final, baleful farewell.

In that terrible moment, the grieving Leia turned away, and Lando grimaced in sorrow.

Instantly fiery liquid began to pour down into the pit in a great cascading shower of fluid and sparks.

Chewbacca half-turned from the horrifying spectacle, giving Threepio a better view of the process.

'They're encasing him in carbonite,' the droid reported. 'It's high-quality alloy. Much better than my own. He should be quite well protected . . . That is, if he survived the freezing process.'

Chewbacca quickly glanced over his shoulder at Threepio, silencing his technical description with an angry bark.

When the liquid finally solidified, huge metal tongs lifted the smoldering figure from the pit. The figure, which was cooling rapidly, had a recognizably human shape, but was featureless and rocky like an unfinished sculpture.

Some of the hogmen, their hands protected by thick black gloves, approached the metal-encased body of Han Solo and shoved the block over. After the figure crashed to the platform with a loud, metallic *clang*, the Ugnaughts hoisted it into the casket-shaped container. They then attached a boxlike electronic device to its side and stepped away.

Kneeling, Lando turned some knobs on the device and checked the gauge measuring the temperature of Han's body. He sighed with relief and nodded his head. 'He's alive,' he informed Han Solo's anxious friends, 'and in perfect hibernation.'

Darth Vader turned to Boba Fett. 'He's all yours, bounty hunter,' he hissed. 'Reset the chamber for Skywalker.'

'He's just landed, my lord,' an aide informed him.

'See to it that he finds his way here.'

Indicating Leia and Chewbacca, Lando told Vader, 'I'll take what is mine now.' He was determined to whisk them out of Vader's clutches before the Dark Lord reneged on their contract.

'Take them,' Vader said, 'but I'm keeping a detachment of troops here to watch over them.'

'That wasn't part of the bargain,' Lando protested hotly. 'You said the Empire wouldn't interfere in—'

'I'm altering the bargain. Pray I don't alter it any further.'

A sudden tightness grasped Lando's throat, a threatening sign of what would happen to him if he gave Vader any difficulty. Lando's hand automatically went to his neck, but in the next moment the unseen hold was released and the administrator turned to face Leia and Chewbacca. The look in his eyes might have expressed despair, but neither of them cared to look at him at all.

Luke and Artoo moved cautiously through a deserted corridor.

It concerned Luke that thus far they had not been stopped for questioning. No one had asked them for landing permits, identification papers, purpose of visit. No one in Cloud City seemed at all curious about who this young man and his little droid might be – or what they were doing there. It all seemed rather ominous, and Luke was beginning to feel very uneasy.

Suddenly he heard a sound at the far end of the corridor. Luke halted, pressing himself close against the corridor wall. Artoo, thrilled to think that they might be back among familiar droids and humans, began to whistle and beep excitedly. Luke glanced at him to be still, and the little robot emitted one last, feeble squeak. Luke then peered around a corner and saw a group approaching from a side hallway. Leading the group was an imposing figure in battered armor and helmet. Behind him, two Cloud City armed guards pushed a transparent case down the corridor. From where Luke stood it appeared the case contained a floating, statuelike human figure. Following the case were two Imperial stormtroopers, who spotted Luke.

Instantly, the troopers took aim and began to fire.

But Luke dodged their laser bolts and, before they could shoot another round, the youth fired his blaster, ripping two sizzling holes into the stormtroopers' armored chests.

As the troopers fell, the two guards quickly whisked the encased figure into another hallway and the armor-clad figure leveled his laser blaster at Luke, sending a deadly bolt at him. The beam just missed the youth, and nicked a large chunk out of the wall next to him, shattering it into a shower of dustlike particles. When the particles had cleared, Luke peeked back around the corner and saw that the nameless attacker, the guards, and the case had all disappeared behind a thick metal door.

Hearing sounds behind him, Luke turned to see Leia, Chewbacca, See Threepio, and an unfamiliar man in a cloak moving down yet another hallway, and guarded by a small band of Imperial stormtroopers.

He gestured to catch the princess's attention.

'Leia!' he shouted.

'Luke, no!' she exclaimed, her voice charged with fear. 'It's a trap!'

Leaving Artoo trailing behind, Luke ran off to follow them. But when he reached a small anteroom, Leia and the others had disappeared. Luke heard Artoo whistling frantically as he scooted toward the anteroom. Yet, as the youth swiftly turned, he saw a mammoth metal door crash down in front of the startled robot with a thundering *clang*.

With the slamming of that door, Luke was cut off from the main corridor. And, when he turned to find another way out, he saw more metal doors bang shut in the other doorways of the chamber.

Meanwhile, Artoo stood somewhat dazed by the shock of his close call. If he had rolled just a tiny bit farther into the anteroom, that door would have squashed him into scrap metal. He pressed his metal nose against the door, then gave out a whistle of relief and wandered off in the opposite direction.

The anteroom was full of hissing pipes and steam that belched from the floor. Luke began to explore the room and noticed an opening above his head, leading to a place he could not even imagine. He moved forward to get a better look, and as he did, the section of floor he stood on began to rise slowly upward. Luke rode up with the lifting platform, determined to face the foe he had traveled so far to meet.

Keeping his blaster clutched in his hand, Luke rose into the carbon-freezing chamber. The room was deathly quiet, except for the hissing of steam escaping some of the pipes in the room. It appeared to Luke that he was the only living creature in this chamber of strange machinery and chemical containers, but he sensed that he was not alone.

'Vader . . .'

He spoke the name to himself as he looked around the chamber.

'Lord Vader. I feel your presence. Show yourself,' Luke taunted his unseen enemy, 'or do you fear me?'

While Luke spoke, the escaping steam began to billow out in great clouds. Then, unaffected by the searing heat, Vader appeared and strode through the hissing vapors, stepping onto the narrow walkway above the chamber, his black cloak trailing behind him.

Luke took a cautious step toward the demonic figure in black and holstered his blaster. He experienced a surge of confidence and felt completely ready to face the Dark Lord as one Jedi against another. There was no need for his blaster. He sensed that the Force was with him and that, at last, he was ready for this inevitable battle. Slowly he began to mount the stairs toward Vader.

'The Force is with you, young Skywalker,' Darth Vader said from above, 'but you are not a Jedi yet.'

Vader's words had a chilling effect. Briefly Luke hesitated, recalling the words of another former Jedi Knight; '*Luke, use the Force only for knowledge and for defense, not as a weapon. Don't give in to hate or anger. They lead the way to the dark side.*'

But throwing aside any fragment of doubt, Luke gripped the smoothly finished handle of his lightsaber and quickly ignited the laser blade.

At the same instant, Vader ignited his own laser sword and quietly waited for the young Skywalker to attack.

His great hatred for Vader impelled Luke to lunge at him savagely, bringing his sizzling blade down upon Vader's. But effortlessly, the Dark Lord deflected the blow with a defensive turn of his own weapon.

Again Luke attacked. Once again their energy blades clashed.

And then they stood, staring at one another for an endless moment through their crossed lightsabers.

XIII

SIX Imperial stormtroopers guarded Lando, Leia, and Chewbacca as they marched through the inner corridor of Cloud City. They reached an intersection when twelve of Lando's guards, and his aide, arrived to block their path.

'Code Force Seven,' Lando commanded as he stopped in front of his aide.

At that moment the twelve guards aimed their laser weapons at the startled stormtroopers, and Lando's aide calmly took the six troopers' weapons from them. He handed one of the guns to Leia and one to Lando, then waited for the next order.

'Hold them in the security tower,' the Cloud City administrator said. 'Quietly! No one must know.'

The guards and Lando's aide, carrying the extra weapons, marched the stormtroopers away to the tower.

Leia had watched this rapid turn of events in confusion. But her confusion turned to astonishment when Lando, the man who had betrayed Han Solo, began removing Chewbacca's bonds.

'Come on,' he urged. 'We're getting out of here.'

The Wookiee's giant hands were freed at last. Not caring to wait for explanations, Chewbacca turned toward the man who had freed him, and with a blood-curdling roar, lunged at Lando and began to throttle him.

'After what you did to Han,' Leia said, 'I wouldn't trust you to—'

Lando, desperately trying to free himself from Chewbacca's ferocious grip, tried to explain. 'I had no choice,' he began – but the Wookiee interrupted him with an angry bark.

'There's still a chance to save Han,' Lando gasped. 'They're at the East Platform.'

'Chewie,' Leia said at last, 'let go!'

Still fuming, Chewbacca released Lando and glared at him as Calrissian fought to regain his breath.

'Keep your eyes on him, Chewie,' Leia cautioned as the Wookiee growled threateningly.

'I have a feeling,' Lando muttered under his breath, 'that I'm making another big mistake.'

The stout little R2 unit meandered up and down the corridor, sending his scanners in every possible direction as he tried to detect some sign of his master – or of *any* kind of life. He realized he was dreadfully turned around and had lost track of how many meters he had traveled.

As Artoo Detoo turned a corner he spotted a number of forms moving up the corridor. Beeping and whistling droid greetings, he hoped that these were friendly sorts.

His tooting was detected by one of the creatures, who began to call out to him.

'Artoo . . . Artoo . . .' It was Threepio!

Chewbacca, still carrying the semiassembled See Threepio, quickly turned around to see the stubby R2 droid rolling their way. But as the Wookiee turned, Threepio was spun out of sight of his friend.

'Wait!' the aggravated Threepio demanded. 'Turn around, you woolly . . . Artoo, hurry! We're trying to save Han from the bounty hunter.'

Artoo scooted forward, beeping all the way, and Threepio patiently replied to his frantic questions.

'I know. But Master Luke can take care of himself.' At least that was what See Threepio kept telling himself as the group continued its search for Han.

On the East Landing Platform of Cloud City, two guards shoved the

frozen body of Han Solo through a side hatchway of the *Slave I.*
Boba Fett climbed up a ladder next to the opening and boarded his
ship, ordering it sealed as soon as he entered the cockpit.

Fett ignited his ship's engines and the craft began rolling across
the platform for takeoff.

Lando, Leia, and Chewbacca raced onto the platform in time only
to see the *Slave I* lifting off and soaring into the orange and purple
of the Cloud City sunset. Raising his blaster, Chewbacca howled and
fired the weapon at the departing spaceship.

'It's no use,' Lando told him. 'They're out of range.'

All but Threepio gazed at the departing craft. Still strapped to
Chewbacca's back, he saw something that the others had not yet
noticed.

'Oh, my, no!' he exclaimed.

Charging the group was a squad of Imperial stormtroopers, blasts
already issuing from their drawn blasters. The first bolt narrowly
missed Princess Leia. Lando responded quickly in returning the
enemy fire, and the air was ablaze with a brilliant criss-cross of red
and green laser bolts.

Artoo scooted over to the platform's elevator and hid inside,
peeking out to see the fury of the battle from a safe distance.

Lando shouted above the sounds of the blasters. 'Come on, let's
move!' he called, breaking for the open elevator and blasting at the
stormtroopers as he ran.

But Leia and Chewbacca did not move. They stood their ground
and kept up a steady fire against the assault of the stormtroopers.
Troopers groaned and dropped as their chests, arms, and stomachs
erupted under the fatally accurate aim of this one female human
and one male Wookiee.

Lando, sticking his head out of the elevator, tried to get their
attention, motioning them to run. But the two seemed possessed as
they blasted away, getting retaliation for all of their anger and
captivity and the loss of one they both loved. They were determined
to extinguish the lives of these minions of the Galactic Empire.

Threepio would gladly have been *anywhere* else. Unable to get
away, all he could do was frantically yell for help. 'Artoo, help me!'
he screamed. 'How did I get into this? What a fate worse than death
it is to be strapped to the back of a Wookiee!'

'Get in here!' Lando shouted again. 'Hurry up! Hurry up!'

Leia and Chewbacca began to move toward him, evading the erupting rain of laser fire as they rushed inside the waiting elevator. As the elevator doors closed, they glimpsed the remaining troopers racing at them.

Lightsabers clashed in Luke Skywalker and Darth Vader's battle on the platform above the carbon-freezing chamber.

Luke felt the shaking platform shudder with every blow and parry and thrust of their weapons. But he was undaunted, for with every thrust of his sword he drove the evil Darth Vader back.

Vader, using his lightsaber to ward off Luke's aggressive lunges, spoke calmly as they fought. 'The fear does not reach you. You have learned more than I anticipated.'

'You'll find I'm full of surprises,' the confident youth retorted, threatening Vader with yet another thrust.

'And I, too,' was the calm, portentous reply.

With two graceful moves, the Dark Lord hooked Luke's weapon out of his hands and sent it flying away. A slash of Vader's energy blade at Luke's feet made the youth jump back in an effort to protect himself. But he stumbled backward, and tumbled down the stairs.

Sprawled on the platform, Luke gazed up and saw the ominous dark figure looming above him at the top of the stairs. Then the figure flew right at him, its sable cloak billowing out in the air like the wings of a monstrous bat.

Quickly Luke rolled to one side, not taking his eyes off Vader, as the vast black figure landed soundlessly next to him.

'Your future lies with me, Skywalker,' Vader hissed, looming over the crouching youth. 'Now you will embrace the dark side. Obi-Wan knew this to be true.'

'No!' Luke yelled, trying to fight off the evil presence.

'There is much Obi-Wan did not tell you,' Vader continued. 'Come, I will complete your training.'

Vader's influence was incredibly strong; it seemed to Luke like a thing alive.

Don't listen to him, Luke told himself. *He is trying to trick me, to lead me astray, to lead me to the dark side of the Force, just like Ben warned me!*

Luke began to back away from the advancing Sith Lord. Behind the youth, the hydraulic elevator cover silently opened, ready to receive him.

'I'll die first,' Luke proclaimed.

'That won't be necessary.' The Dark Lord suddenly lunged at Luke with his lightsaber, so forcefully that the youth lost his balance and tumbled into the gaping opening.

Vader turned away from the freezing-pit and casually deactivated his lightsaber. 'All too easy,' he shrugged. 'Perhaps you are not as strong as the Emperor thought.'

As he spoke, molten metal began to pour into the opening behind him. And, while his back was still turned, something rose in a blur upward.

'Time will tell,' Luke quietly replied to Vader's remark.

The Dark Lord spun around. At this point in the freezing process, the subject certainly shouldn't be able to speak! Vader glanced around the room and then turned his helmeted head up toward the ceiling.

Hanging from some hoses draped across the ceiling, Luke was suspended, having leaped some five meters into the air to escape the carbonite.

'Impressive,' Vader admitted, 'your agility is impressive.'

Luke dropped back to the platform on the other side of the steaming pit. He reached his hand out and his sword, lying on another part of the platform, flew back into his grip. Immediately the lightsaber ignited.

Vader's sword sprang to life at the very same moment. 'Ben has taught you well. You have controlled your fear. Now release your anger. I destroyed your family. Take your revenge.'

But this time Luke was cautious and more controlled. If he could subdue his anger, as he had finally controlled his fear, he would not be swayed.

Remember the training, Luke cautioned himself. *Remember what Yoda taught! Cast out all hatred and anger and receive the Force!*

Gaining control over his negative feelings, Luke began to advance, ignoring Vader's goading. He lunged at Vader and, after a quick exchange, began to force him back.

'Your hatred can give you the power to destroy me,' Vader tempted. 'Use it.'

Luke began to realize just how awesomely powerful his dark enemy was, and softly told himself, 'I will not become a slave to the dark side of the Force,' and moved cautiously toward Vader.

As Luke approached, Vader slowly moved backward in retreat. Luke lunged at him with a powerful swing. But when Vader blocked it, he lost his balance and fell into the outer rim of steaming pipes.

Luke's knees nearly buckled with the exhaustion of battling his fearsome opponent. He gathered his strength and cautiously moved to the edge and looked down. But he saw no sign of Vader. Switching off his lightsaber and hooking it into his belt, Luke lowered himself into the pit.

He dropped to the floor of the pit and found himself in a large control and maintenance room that overlooked the reactor powering the entire city. Looking around the chamber, he noticed a large window; standing silhouetted in front of it was the unmoving figure of Darth Vader.

Luke slowly moved closer to the window and reignited his lightsaber.

But Vader did not light his own sword, nor did he make any effort to defend himself as Luke drew nearer. The Dark Lord's only weapon, in fact, was his tempting voice. 'Attack,' he goaded the young Jedi. 'Destroy me.'

Confused by Vader's ploy, Luke hesitated.

'Only by taking your revenge can you save yourself . . .'

Luke stood locked in place. Should he act on Vader's words and thus use the Force as a tool of revenge? Or should he step away from this battle now, hoping for another chance to fight Vader when he had gained better control?

No, how could he delay the opportunity to destroy this evil being? Here was his chance, now, and he must not delay . . .

There might never again be such an opportunity!

Luke grasped his deadly lightsaber in both hands, tightly gripping the smooth handle like an ancient broadsword and raising the weapon to deliver the blow that would slay this masked horror.

But before he could swing, a large piece of machinery detached itself from the wall behind him and came hurtling at his back. Turning instantly, Luke flashed his lightsaber and cut the thing in half, and the two massive pieces crashed to the floor.

A second piece of machinery sped toward the youth, and again he used the Force to deflect it. The weighty object bounced away as if it had struck an unseen shield. Then a large pipe came tumbling toward him through the air. But even as Luke repelled that enormous object, tools and pieces of machinery came flying at him from all directions. Then wires, that pulled themselves out of the walls, came twisting and sparking and whipping at him.

Bombarded on all sides, Luke did what he could to deflect the assault; but he was beginning to get bloodied and bruised in the attempt.

Another large piece of machinery glanced off Luke's body and crashed out the large window, letting in the screaming wind. Suddenly everything in the room was blown about, and the fierce wind lashed Luke's body and filled the room with a bansheelike howl.

And in the very center of the room, standing still and triumphant, was Darth Vader.

'You are beaten,' the Dark Lord of the Sith gloated. 'It is useless to resist. You will join me or you will join Obi-Wan in death!'

As Vader spoke those words, a final piece of heavy machinery soared through the air, striking the young Jedi and knocking him through the broken window. Everything became a great blur as the wind carried him, tossing and rolling, until he managed to grab hold of a beam with one hand.

When the wind subsided a bit and his vision cleared, Luke realized that he was hanging from the gantry of the reactor shaft outside the control room. When he gazed down he saw what appeared to be an endless abyss. A wave of dizziness swept over him and he squeezed his eyes closed in an effort to keep from panicking.

Compared to the podlike reactor from which he hung, Luke was no more than a speck of squirming matter, while the pod itself – just one of many jutting from the circular, light-dotted inner wall – was no more than a speck itself in comparison with the rest of the immense chamber.

Grasping the beam firmly with only one hand, Luke managed to hook his lightsaber on to his belt and then grab the beam with both hands. Hoisting himself up, he scrambled onto the gantry and stood on it, just in time to see Darth Vader walking toward him down the shaft.

As Vader approached Luke, the public address system began to blare, echoing through the cavernous rooms: 'Fugitives heading toward Platform 327. Secure all transports. All security forces on alert.'

Walking menacingly toward Luke, Vader predicted, 'Your friends will never escape and neither will you.'

Vader took another step, and Luke immediately raised his sword, ready to renew the battle.

'You are beaten,' Vader stated with horrifying certainty and finality. 'It is useless to resist.'

But Luke did resist. He lunged at the Dark Lord with a vicious blow, bringing his sizzling laser blade to crash onto Vader's armor and sear through to the flesh. Vader staggered from the blow, and it seemed to Luke that he was in pain. But only for a moment. Then, once again, Vader began to move toward him.

Taking another step, the Dark Lord warned, 'Don't let yourself be destroyed as Obi-Wan was.'

Luke was breathing hard, cold sweat dropping from his forehead. But the sound of Ben's name instilled a sudden resolve in him.

'Calm—' he reminded himself. 'Be calm.'

But the grimly cloaked specter stalked toward him along the narrow gantry, and it seemed he wanted the young Jedi's life.

Or worse, his fragile soul.

Lando, Leia, Chewbacca, and the droids hurried down a corridor. They turned a corner and saw the door to the landing platform standing open. Through it they glimpsed the *Millennium Falcon* waiting for their escape. But suddenly the door slammed shut. Ducking into an alcove, the group saw a squad of stormtroopers charging them, their laser guns blasting as they ran. Chunks of wall and floor shattered and flew into the air with the impact of the ricocheting energy beams.

Chewbacca growled, returning the stormtroopers' fire with savage Wookiee rage. He covered Leia, who punched desperately at the door's control panel. But the door failed to budge.

'Artoo!' Threepio called. 'The control panel. You can override the alert system.'

Threepio gestured at the panel, urging the little robot to hurry, and pointing out a computer socket on the control board.

Artoo Detoo scooted toward the control panel, beeping and whistling as he scurried to help.

Twisting his body to avoid the burning laser bolts, Lando feverishly worked to connect his com-link to the panel's intercom.

'This is Calrissian,' he broadcast over the system. 'The Empire is taking control of the city. I advise you to leave before more Imperial troops arrive.'

He switched off the communicator. Lando knew that he had done what he could to warn his people; his job now was to get his friends safely off the planet.

Meanwhile, Artoo removed a connector cover and inserted an extended computer arm into the waiting socket. The droid issued a short beep that suddenly turned into a wild robot scream. He began to quiver, his circuits lighting up in a mad display of flashing brilliance, and every orifice in his hull spewing smoke. Lando quickly pulled Artoo away from the power socket. As the droid began to cool off, he directed a few wilted beeps Threepio's way.

'Well, next time *you* pay more attention,' Threepio replied defensively. 'I'm not supposed to know power sockets from computer feeds. I'm an interpreter—'

'Anybody else got any ideas?' Leia shouted as she stood firing at the attacking stormtroopers.

'Come on,' Lando answered over the din of the battle, 'we'll try another way.'

The wind that shrieked though the reactor shaft entirely absorbed the sounds of the clashing lightsabers.

Luke moved agilely across the gantry and took refuge beneath a huge instrument panel to evade his pursuing foe. But Vader was there in an instant, his lightsaber thrashing down like a pulsating guillotine blade, cutting the instrument complex loose. The complex began to fall, but was abruptly caught by the wind and blown upward.

An instant of distraction was all Vader needed. As the instrument panel floated away, Luke involuntarily glanced at it. At that second, the Dark Lord's laser blade came slashing down across Luke's hand, cutting it, and sending the youth's lightsaber flying.

The pain was excruciating. Luke smelled the terrible odor of his own seared flesh and squeezed his forearm beneath his armpit to try to stop the agony. He stepped backward along the gantry until he reached its extreme end, stalked all the while by the black-garbed apparition.

Abruptly, ominously, the wind subsided. And Luke realized he had nowhere else to go.

'There is no escape,' the Dark Lord of the Sith warned, looming over Luke like a black angel of death. 'Don't make me destroy you. You are strong with the Force. Now you must learn to use the dark side. Join me and together we will be more powerful than the Emperor. Come, I will complete your training and we will rule the galaxy together.'

Luke refused to give in to Vader's taunts. 'I will never join you!'

'If you only knew the power of the dark side,' Vader continued. 'Obi-Wan never told you what happened to your father, did he?'

Mention of his father aroused Luke's anger. 'He told me enough!' he yelled. 'He told me you killed him.'

'No,' Vader replied calmly. 'I am your father.'

Stunned, Luke stared with disbelief at the black-clad warrior and then pulled away at this revelation. The two warriors stood staring at one another, father and son.

'No, no! That's not true ...' Luke said, refusing to believe what he had just heard. 'That's impossible.'

'Search your feelings,' Vader said, sounding like an evil version of Yoda, 'you know it to be true.'

Then Vader turned off the blade of his lightsaber and extended a steady and inviting hand.

Bewildered and horror-stricken at Vader's words, Luke shouted, 'No! No!'

Vader continued persuasively. 'Luke, you can destroy the Emperor. He has foreseen this. It is your destiny. Join me and together we can rule the galaxy as father and son. Come with me. It is the only way.'

Luke's mind whirled with those words. Everything was finally beginning to coalesce in his brain. Or was it? He wondered if Vader were telling him the truth – if the training of Yoda, the teaching of saintly old Ben, his own strivings for good and his abhorrence of evil, if everything he had fought for were no more than a lie.

He didn't want to believe Vader, tried convincing himself that it was Vader who lied to him – but somehow he could *feel* the truth in the Dark Lord's words. But, if Darth Vader did speak the truth, why, he wondered, had Ben Kenobi lied to him? *Why?* His mind screamed louder than any wind the Dark Lord could ever summon against him.

The answers no longer seemed to matter.

His Father.

With the calmness that Ben himself and Yoda, the Jedi Master, had taught him, Luke Skywalker made, perhaps, what might be his final decision of all. 'Never,' Luke shouted as he stepped out into the empty abyss beneath him. For all its unperceived depth, Luke might have been falling to another galaxy.

Darth Vader moved to the end of the gantry to watch as Luke tumbled away. A strong wind began to blow, billowing Vader's black cloak out behind him as he stood looking over the edge.

Skywalker's body quickly plunged downward. Toppling head over foot, the wounded Jedi desperately reached out to grab at something to stop his fall.

The Dark Lord watched until he saw the youth's body sucked into a large exhaust pipe in the side of the reactor shaft. When Luke vanished, Vader quickly turned and hurried off the platform.

Luke sped through the exhaust shaft trying to grab the sides to slow his fall. But the smooth, shiny sides of the pipe had no hand-holes or ridges for Luke to grasp.

At last he came to the end of the tunnellike pipe, his feet striking hard against a circular grill. The grill, which opened over an apparently bottomless drop, was knocked out by the impact of Luke's momentum, and he felt his body start to slide out through the opening. Frantically clawing at the smooth interior of the pipe, Luke began to call out for assistance.

'Ben . . . Ben, help me,' he pleaded desperately.

Even at he called out, he felt his fingers slip along the inside of the pipe, while his body inched ever closer to the yawning opening.

Cloud City was in chaos.

As soon as Lando Calrissian's broadcast was heard throughout the city, its residents began to panic. Some of them packed a few belongings, others just rushed out into the streets seeking escape. Soon the streets were filled with running humans and aliens, rushing chaotically through the city. Imperial stormtroopers charged after the fleeing inhabitants, exchanging laser fire with them in a raging, clamorous battle.

In one of the city's central corridors, Lando, Leia, and Chewbacca held off a squad of stormtroopers by blasting heavy rounds of laser bolts at the Imperial warriors. It was urgent that Lando and the others hold their ground, for they had come upon another entrance that would lead them to the landing platform. If only Artoo succeeded in opening the door.

Artoo was trying to remove the plate from this door's control panel. But because of the noise and distraction of the laser fire blasting around him, it was difficult for the little droid to concentrate on his work. He beeped to himself as he worked, sounding a bit befuddled to Threepio.

'What are you talking about?' Threepio called to him. 'We're not interested in the hyperdrive on the *Millennium Falcon*. It's fixed. Just tell the computer to open the door.'

Then, as Lando, Leia, and the Wookiee edged toward the door, dodging heavy Imperial laser fire, Artoo beeped triumphantly and the door snapped open.

'Artoo, you did it!' Threepio exclaimed. The droid would have applauded had his other arm been attached. 'I never doubted you for a second.'

'Hurry,' Lando shouted, 'or we'll never make it.'

The helpful R2 unit came through once again. As the others dashed through the entrance, the stout robot sprayed out a thick fog – as dense as the clouds surrounding this world – that obscured his friends from the encroaching stormtroopers. Before the cloud had cleared, Lando and the others were racing toward Platform 327.

The stormtroopers followed, blasting at the small band of fugitives bolting toward the *Millennium Falcon*. Chewbacca and the robots boarded the freighter while Lando and Leia covered them with their blasters, cutting down still more of the Emperor's warriors.

When the low-pitched roar of the *Falcon*'s engines started and then rose to an ear-battering whine, Lando and Leia discharged a few more bolts of brilliant energy. Then they sprinted up the ramp. They entered the pirate ship and the main hatchway closed behind them. And as the ship began to move, they heard a barrage of Imperial laser fire that sounded as if the entire planet were splitting apart at its foundations.

*

Luke could no longer slow his inexorable slide out the exhaust pipe.

He slid the final few centimeters and then dropped through the cloudy atmosphere, his body spinning and his arms flailing to grip on to something solid.

After what seemed like forever, he caught hold of an electronic weather vane that jutted out from the bowllike underside of Cloud City. Winds buffeted him and clouds swirled around him as he held on tightly to the weather vane. But his strength was beginning to fail; he didn't think he could hang like this – suspended above the gaseous surface – for very much longer.

All was very quiet in the *Millennium Falcon* cockpit.

Leia, just catching her breath from their close escape, sat in Han Solo's chair. Thoughts of him rushed to her mind, but she tried not to worry about him, tried not to miss him.

Behind the princess, looking over her shoulder out the front windscreen, stood a silent and exhausted Lando Calrissian.

Slowly the ship began to move, picking up speed as it coursed along the landing platform.

The giant Wookiee, in his old copilot's chair, threw a series of switches that brought a dancing array of lights across the ship's main control panel. Pulling the throttle, Chewbacca began to guide the ship upward, to freedom.

Clouds rushed by the cockpit windows and everyone finally breathed with relief as the *Millennium Falcon* soared into a red-orange twilight sky.

Luke managed to hook one of his legs over the electronic weather vane, which continued to support his weight. But air from the exhaust pipe rushed at him, making it difficult for him to keep from slipping off the vane.

'Ben . . .' he moaned in agony. '. . . Ben.'

Darth Vader strode onto the empty landing platform and watched the speck that was the *Millennium Falcon* disappear in the far distance.

He turned to his two aides. 'Bring my ship in!' he commanded. And then he left, black robes flowing behind him, to prepare for his journey.

*

Somewhere near the supporting stalk of Cloud City, Luke spoke again. Concentrating his mind on one whom he thought cared for him and might somehow come to his aid, he called, 'Leia, hear me.' Pitifully he cried out once again. 'Leia.'

Just then, a large piece of the weather vane broke off and went hurtling off into the clouds far below. Luke tightened his grip on what remained of the vane, and strained to hold on in the blast of air rushing at him from the pipe above.

'It looks like three fighters,' Lando said to Chewbacca as they watched the computer-screen configurations. 'We can outdistance them easily,' he added, knowing the capabilities of the freighter as well as Han Solo did.

Looking at Leia, he mourned the passing of his administratorship. 'I knew that setup was too good to last,' he moaned. 'I'm going to miss it.'

But Leia seemed to be in a daze. She didn't acknowledge Lando's comments, but stared straight ahead of her as if transfixed. Then, out of her dreamlike trance, she spoke. 'Luke,' she said, as if responding to something she heard.

'What?' Lando asked.

'We've got to go back,' she said urgently. 'Chewie, head for the bottom of the city.'

Lando looked at her in astonishment. 'Wait a minute. We're not going back there!'

The Wookiee barked, for once in agreement with Lando.

'No argument,' Leia said firmly, assuming the dignity of one accustomed to having her orders obeyed. 'Just do it. That's a command!'

'What about those fighters?' Lando argued as he pointed to the three TIE fighters closing in on them. He looked to Chewbacca for support.

But, growling menacingly, Chewbacca conveyed that he knew who was in command now.

'Okay, okay,' Lando quietly acquiesced.

With all the grace and speed for which the *Millennium Falcon* was famed, the ship banked through the clouds and turned back toward the city. And, as the freighter continued on what could become a suicide run, the three pursuing TIE fighters matched its turn.

Luke Skywalker was unaware of the *Millennium Falcon*'s approach. Barely conscious, he somehow maintained his hold on the creaking and swaying weather vane. The device bent under the weight of his body, then completely broke off from its foundation, and sent Luke tumbling helplessly through the sky. And this time, he knew, there would be nothing for him to cling to as he fell.

'Look!' Lando exclaimed, indicating a figure plunging in the distance. 'Someone's falling ...'

Leia managed to remain calm; she knew that panic now would doom them all. 'Get under him, Chewie,' she told the pilot. 'It's Luke.'

Chewbacca immediately responded and carefully eased the *Millennium Falcon* on a descent trajectory.

'Lando,' Leia called, turning to him, 'open the top hatch.'

As he rushed out of the cockpit, Lando thought it a strategy worthy of Solo himself.

Chewbacca and Leia could see Luke's plunging body more clearly, and the Wookiee guided the ship toward him. As Chewie retarded the ship's speed drastically, the plummeting form skimmed the windscreen and then landed with a *thud* against the outer hull.

Lando opened the upper hatch. In the distance he glimpsed the three TIE fighters approaching the *Falcon*, their laser guns brightening the twilight sky with streaks of hot destruction. Lando stretched his body out of the hatch and reached to grasp the battered warrior and pull him inside the ship. Just then the *Falcon* lurched as a bolt exploded near it, and almost threw Luke's body overboard. But Lando caught his hand and held on tightly.

The *Millennium Falcon* veered away from Cloud City and soared through the thick billowing cloud cover. Swerving to avoid the blinding flak from the TIE fighters, Princess Leia and the Wookiee pilot struggled to keep their ship skyborne. But explosions burst all around the cockpit, the din competing with Chewbacca's howl as he frantically worked the controls.

Leia switched on the intercom. 'Lando, is he all right?' she shouted over the noise in the cockpit. 'Lando, do you hear me?'

From the rear of the cockpit, she heard a voice that wasn't Lando's. 'He'll survive,' Luke replied faintly.

Leia and Chewbacca turned to see Luke, battered and bloodied and wrapped in a blanket, being helped into the cockpit by Lando. The princess jumped up from her chair and hugged him ecstatically. Chewbacca, still trying to guide the ship out of the TIE fighters' range of fire, threw back his head and barked in jubilation.

Behind the *Millennium Falcon*, the planet of clouds was receding farther in the distance. But the TIE fighters kept up their close pursuit, firing their laser weapons and rocking the pirate craft with each on-target hit.

Working diligently in the *Falcon's* hold, Artoo Detoo struggled against the constant lunging and tossing to reassemble his golden friend. Meticulously trying to undo the mistakes of the well-intentioned Wookiee, the little droid beeped as he performed the intricate task.

'Very good,' the protocol droid praised. His head was on properly and his second arm was nearly completely reattached. 'Good as new.'

Artoo beeped apprehensively.

'No, Artoo, don't worry. I'm sure we'll make it this time.'

But in the cockpit, Lando was not so optimistic. He saw the warning lights on the control panel begin to flash; suddenly alarms all over the ship went on. 'The deflector shields are going,' he reported to Leia and Chewbacca.

Leia looked over Lando's shoulder and noticed another blip, ominously large, that had appeared on the radarscope. 'There's another ship,' she said, 'much bigger, trying to cut us off.'

Luke quietly gazed out the cockpit window toward the starry void. Almost to himself, he said, 'It's Vader.'

Admiral Piett approached Vader, who stood on the bridge of this, the greatest of all Imperial Star Destroyers, and stared out the windows.

'They'll be in range of the tractor beam in moments,' the admiral reported confidently.

'And their hyperdrive has been deactivated?' Vader asked.

'Right after they were captured, sir.'

'Good,' the giant black-robed figure said. 'Prepare for the boarding and set your weapons for stun.'

The *Millennium Falcon* so far had managed to evade its TIE fighter pursuers. But could it escape attack from the ominous Star

Destroyer that pressed toward it, ever closer?

'We don't have any room for mistakes,' Leia said tensely, watching the large blip on the monitors.

'If my men said they fixed this baby, they fixed it,' Lando assured her. 'We've got nothing to worry about.'

'Sounds familiar,' Leia mused to herself.

The ship was rocked again by the concussion of another laser explosion, but at that moment a green light began flashing on the control panel.

'The coordinates are set, Chewie,' Leia said. 'It's now or never.'

The Wookiee barked in agreement. He was ready for the hyperdrive escape.

'Punch it!' Lando yelled.

Chewbacca shrugged as if to say it was worth a try. He pulled back on the light-speed throttle, suddenly altering the sound of the ion engines. All on board were praying in human and droid fashion that the system would work; they had no other hope of escape. But abruptly the sound choked and died and Chewbacca roared a howl of desperate frustration.

Again the hyperdrive system had failed them.

And still the *Millennium Falcon* lurched with the TIE fighters' fire.

From his Imperial Star Destroyer, Darth Vader watched in fascination as the TIE fighters relentlessly fired at the *Millennium Falcon*. Vader's ship was closing in on the fleeing *Falcon* – it would not be long before the Dark Lord had Skywalker completely in his power.

And Luke sensed it, too. Quietly he gazed out, knowing that Vader was near, that his victory over the weakened Jedi would soon be complete. His body was battered, was exhausted; his spirit was prepared to succumb to his fate. There was no reason to fight any more – there was nothing left to believe in.

'Ben,' he whispered in utter despair, 'why didn't you tell me?'

Lando tried to adjust some controls, and Chewbacca leaped from his chair to race to the hold. Leia took Chewbacca's seat and helped Lando as they flew the *Falcon* through the exploding flak.

As the Wookiee ran into the hold, he passed Artoo, who was still working on Threepio. The R2 unit began to beep in great consternation as he scanned the Wookiee frantically trying to fix the hyperdrive system.

'I said we're doomed!' the panicked Threepio told Artoo. 'The light-speed engines are malfunctioning again.'

Artoo beeped as he connected a leg.

'How could you know what's wrong?' the golden droid scoffed. 'Ouch! Mind my foot! And stop chattering on so.'

Lando's voice sounded in the hold through the intercom. 'Chewie, check the secondary deviation controls.'

Chewbacca dropped into the hold's pit. He fought to loosen a section of the paneling with an enormous wrench. But it failed to budge. Roaring in frustration, he gripped the tool like a club and bashed the panel with all his strength.

Suddenly the cockpit control panel sprayed Lando and the princess with a shower of sparks. They jumped back in their seats in surprise, but Luke didn't seem to notice anything happening around him. His head hung in discouragement and deep pain.

'I won't be able to resist him,' he muttered softly.

Again Lando banked the *Millennium Falcon*, trying to shed the pursuers. But the distance between freighter and TIE fighters was narrowing by the moment.

In the *Millennium Falcon*'s hold, Artoo raced to a control panel, leaving an outraged Threepio to stand sputtering in place on his one attached leg. Artoo worked swiftly, relying only on mechanical instinct to reprogram the circuit board. Lights flashed brightly with each of Artoo's adjustments, when suddenly, from deep within the *Falcon*'s hyperspeed engines, a new and powerful hum resonated throughout the ship.

The freighter tilted suddenly, sending the whistling R2 droid rolling across the floor into the pit to land on the startled Chewbacca.

Lando, who had been standing near the control panel, tumbled back against the cockpit wall. But as he fell back, he saw the stars outside become blinding, infinite streaks of light.

'We did it!' Lando yelled triumphantly.

The *Millennium Falcon* had shot victoriously into hyperdrive.

Darth Vader stood silently. He gazed at the black void where, a moment before, the *Millennium Falcon* had been. His deep, black silence brought terror to the two men standing near him. Admiral Piett and his captain waited, chills of fear coursing through their bodies, and wondered how soon they would feel the invisible, viselike talons around their throats.

But the Dark Lord did not move. He stood, silently contemplative, with his hands behind his back. Then he turned and slowly walked off the bridge, his ebony cloak billowing behind him.

XIV

THE *Millennium Falcon* was at last safely docked on a huge Rebel cruiser. Gleaming in the distance was a glorious red glow that radiated from a large red star – a glow that shed its crimson light on the battered hull of the small freighter craft.

Luke Skywalker rested in the medical center of the Rebel Star Cruiser, where he was attended by the surgeon droid called Too-Onebee. The youth sat quietly, thoughtfully, while Too-Onebee gently began to look at his wounded hand.

Gazing up, Luke saw Leia, followed by See Threepio and Artoo Detoo, entering the medical center to check his progress, and, perhaps, bring him a little cheer. But Luke knew that the best therapy he had received yet aboard this cruiser was in the radiant image before him.

Princess Leia was smiling. Her eyes were wide and sparkling with a wondrous glow. She looked just as she had that first time he saw her – a lifetime ago, it seemed – when Artoo Detoo first projected her holographic image. And, in her floor-length, high-necked gown of purest white, she looked angelic.

Raising his hand, Luke offered it to the expert service of Too-Onebee. The surgeon droid examined the bionic hand that was skillfully fused to Luke's arm. Then the robot wrapped a soft metalized strip about the hand and attached a small electronic unit to the strip, tightening it slightly. Luke made a fist with his new hand and felt the healing pulsations imparted by Too-Onebee's apparatus. Then he let his hand and arm relax.

Leia and the two droids moved closer to Luke as a voice came over an intercom loudspeaker. It was Lando: 'Luke ...' the voice blared, 'we're ready for takeoff.'

Lando Calrissian sat in the *Millennium Falcon*'s pilot's chair. He had missed his old freighter, but now that he was once again its captain, he felt quite uncomfortable. In his copilot's chair, the great Wookiee Chewbacca noticed his new captain's discomfort while he began to throw the switches to ready the ship for takeoff.

Luke's voice came over Lando's comlink speaker: 'I'll meet you on Tatooine.'

Again Lando spoke into his comlink microphone, but this time he spoke to Leia: 'Don't worry, Leia,' he said with emotion, 'we'll find Han.'

And leaning over, Chewbacca barked his farewell into the microphone – a bark that may have transcended the limits of time and space to be heard by Han Solo, wherever the bounty hunter had taken him.

It was Luke who spoke the final farewell, though he refused to say good-bye. 'Take care, my friends,' he said with a new maturity in his voice. 'May the Force be with you.'

Leia stood alone at the great circular window of the Rebel Star Cruiser, her slim white-draped form dwarfed by the vast canopy of stars and the drifting ships of the fleet. She watched the majestic scarlet star that burned in the infinite black sea.

Luke, with Threepio and Artoo tagging along, moved to stand next to her. He understood what she was feeling for he knew how terrible such a loss could be.

Standing together, the group faced the inviting heavens and saw the *Millennium Falcon* moving into view, then veering off in another direction to soar with great dignity through the Rebel fleet. Soon the *Millennium Falcon* had left the fleet in its wake.

They needed no words in this moment. Luke knew that Leia's mind and heart were with Han, no matter where he was or what his fate might be. As to his own destiny, he was now more uncertain about himself than he had ever been – even before this simple farm boy on a distant world first learned of the intangible something called the Force. He only knew he had to return to Yoda and finish his training before he set off to rescue Han.

Slowly he put his arm around Leia and together with Threepio and Artoo, they faced the heavens bravely, each of them gazing at the same crimson star.

EPISODE

VI

STAR WARS®:

Return of the Jedi®

by **James Kahn**
Screenplay by
Lawrence Kasdan and **George Lucas**

Story by **George Lucas**

A long time ago, in a galaxy far, far away . . .

Prologue

THE very depth of space. There was the length, and width, and height; and then these dimensions curved over on themselves into a bending blackness measurable only by the glinting stars that tumbled through the chasm, receding to infinity. To the very depth.

These stars marked the moments of the universe. There were aging orange embers, blue dwarfs, twin yellow giants. There were collapsing neutron stars, and angry supernovae that hissed into the icy emptiness. There were borning stars, breathing stars, pulsing stars, and dying stars. There was the Death Star.

At the feathered edge of the galaxy, the Death Star floated in stationary orbit above the green moon Endor – a moon whose mother planet had long since died of unknown cataclysm and disappeared into unknown realms. The Death Star was the Empire's armored battle station, nearly twice as big as its predecessor, which Rebel forces had destroyed so many years before – nearly twice as big, but more than twice as powerful. Yet it was only half complete.

Half a steely dark orb, it hung above the green world of Endor, tentacles of unfinished superstructure curling away toward its living companion like the groping legs of a deadly spider.

An Imperial Star Destroyer approached the giant space station at cruising speed. It was massive – a city itself – yet it moved with deliberate grace, like some great sea dragon. It was accompanied by dozens of Twin Ion Engine fighters – black insectlike combat flyers that zipped back and forth around the battleship's perimeter: scouting, sounding, docking, regrouping.

Soundlessly the main bay of the ship opened. There was a brief ignition-flash, as an Imperial shuttle emerged from the darkness of the hold, into the darkness of space. It sped toward the half-completed Death Star with quiet purpose.

In the cockpit the shuttle captain and his copilot made final readings, monitored descent functions. It was a sequence they'd each performed a thousand times, yet there was an unusual tension in the air now. The captain flipped the transmitter switch, and spoke into his mouthpiece.

'Command Station, this is ST321. Code Clearance Blue. We're starting our approach. Deactivate the security shield.'

Static filtered over the receiver; then the voice of the port controller: 'The security deflector shield will be deactivated when we have confirmation of your code transmission. Stand by . . .'

Once more silence filled the cockpit. The shuttle captain bit the inside of his cheek, smiled nervously at his copilot, and muttered, 'Quick as you can, please – this better not take long. He's in no mood to wait . . .'

They refrained from glancing back into the passenger section of the shuttle, now under lights-out for landing. The unmistakable sound of the mechanical breathing coming from the chamber's shadow filled the cabin with a terrible impatience.

In the control room of the Death Star below, operators moved along the bank of panels, monitoring all the space traffic in the area, authorizing flight patterns, accessing certain areas to certain vehicles. The shield operator suddenly checked his monitor with alarm; the view-screen depicted the battle station itself, the moon Endor, and a web of energy – the deflector shield – emanating from the green moon, encompassing the Death Star. Only now, the security web was beginning to separate, to retract and form a clear channel – a channel through which the dot that was the Imperial shuttle sailed, unimpeded, toward the massive space station.

The shield operator quickly called his control officer over to the view-screen, uncertain how to proceed.

'What is it?' the officer demanded.

'That shuttle has a class-one priority ranking.' He tried to replace the fear in his voice with disbelief.

The officer glanced at the view-screen for only a moment before realizing who was on the shuttle and spoke to himself: 'Vader!'

He strode past the view port, where the shuttle could be seen already making its final approach, and headed toward the docking bay. He turned to the controller.

'Inform the commander that Lord Vader's shuttle has arrived.'

The shuttle sat quietly, dwarfed by the cavernous reaches of the huge docking bay. Hundreds of troops stood assembled in formation, flanking the base of the shuttle ramp – white-armored Imperial stormtroopers, gray-suited officers, and the elite, red-robed Imperial Guard. They snapped to attention as Moff Jerjerrod entered.

Jerjerrod – tall, thin, arrogant – was the Death Star commander. He walked without hurry up the ranks of soldiers, to the ramp of the shuttle. Hurry was not in Jerjerrod, for hurry implied a wanting to be elsewhere, and he was a man who distinctively *was* exactly where he wanted to be. Great men never hurried (he was fond of saying); great men caused *others* to hurry.

Yet Jerjerrod was not blind to ambition; and a visit by such a one as this great Dark Lord could not be taken too lightly. He stood at the shuttle mouth, therefore, waiting – with respect, but not hurry.

Suddenly the exit hatch of the shuttle opened, pulling the troops in formation to even tauter attention. Only darkness glowed from the exit at first; then footsteps; then the characteristic electrical respirations, like the breathing of a machine; and finally Darth Vader, Lord of the Sith, emerged from the void.

Vader strode down the ramp, looking over the assemblage. He stopped when he came to Jerjerrod. The commander bowed from the neck, and smiled.

'Lord Vader, this is an unexpected pleasure. We are honored by your presence.'

'We can dispense with the pleasantries, Commander.' Vader's words echoed as from the bottom of a well. 'The Emperor is concerned with your progress. I am here to put you back on schedule.'

Jerjerrod turned pale. This was news he'd not expected. 'I assure you, Lord Vader, my men are working as fast as they can.'

'Perhaps I can encourage their progress in ways you have not considered,' Vader growled. He had ways, of course; this was known. Ways, and ways again.

Jerjerrod kept his tone even, though deep inside, the ghost of hurry began to scrabble at his throat. 'That won't be necessary, my Lord. I tell you, without question this station will be operational as planned.'

'I'm afraid the Emperor does not share your optimistic appraisal of the situation.'

'I fear he asks the impossible,' the commander suggested.

'Perhaps you could explain that to him when he arrives.' Vader's face remained invisible behind the deathly black mask that protected him; but the malice was clear in the electronically modified voice.

Jerjerrod's pallor intensified. 'The Emperor is coming here?'

'Yes, Commander. And he will be quite displeased if you are still behind schedule when he arrives.' He spoke loudly, to spread the threat over all who could hear.

'We shall double our efforts, Lord Vader.' And he meant it. For sometimes didn't even great men hurry, in time of great need?

Vader lowered his voice again. 'I hope so, Commander, for your sake. The Emperor will tolerate no further delay in the final destruction of the outlaw Rebellion. And we have secret news now' – he included Jerjerrod, only, in this intimate detail – 'The Rebel fleet has gathered all its forces into a single giant armada. The time is at hand when we can crush them, without mercy, in a single blow.'

For the briefest second, Vader's breathing seemed to quicken, then resumed its measured pace, like the rising of a hollow wind.

I

OUTSIDE the small adobe hut, the sandstorm wailed like a beast in agony, refusing to die. Inside, the sounds were muted.

It was cooler in this shelter, more hushed, and darker. While the beast without howled, in this place of nuance and shadow a shrouded figure worked.

Tanned hands, holding arcane tools, extended from the sleeves of a caftanlike robe. The figure crouched on the ground, working. Before him lay a discoid device of strange design, wires trailing from it at one end, symbols etched into its flat surface. He connected the wired end to a tubular, smooth handle, pulled through an organic-looking connector, locked it in place with another tool. He motioned to a shadow in the corner; the shadow moved toward him.

Tentatively, the obscure form rolled closer to the robed figure. 'Vrrrr-dit dweet?' the little R2 unit questioned timidly as it approached, pausing when it was just a foot from the shrouded man with the strange device.

The shrouded man motioned the droid nearer still. Artoo Detoo scooted the last distance, blinking; and the hands raised toward his domed little head.

The fine sand blew hard over the dunes of Tatooine. The wind seemed to come from everywhere at once, typhooning in spots, swirling in devil-winds here, hovering in stillness there, without pattern or meaning.

A road wound across the desert plain. Its nature changed constantly, at one moment obscured by drifts of ochre sand, the next moment swept clean, or distorted by the heat of the shimmering air above it. A road more ephemeral than navigable; yet a road to be followed, all the same. For it was the only way to reach the palace of Jabba the Hutt.

Jabba was the vilest gangster in the galaxy. He had his fingers in smuggling, slave-trading, murder; his minions scattered across the stars. He both collected and invented atrocities, and his court was a den of unparalleled decay. It was said by some that Jabba had chosen Tatooine as his place of residence because only in this arid crucible of a planet could he hope to keep his soul from rotting away altogether – here the parched sun might bake his humor to a festering brine.

In any case, it was a place few of kind spirit even knew of, let alone approached. It was a place of evil, where even the most courageous felt their powers wilt under the foul gaze of Jabba's corruption.

'Poot-wEEt beDOO gung ooble DEEp!' vocalized Artoo Detoo.

'Of course I'm worried,' See Threepio fussed. 'And you should be too. Poor Lando Calrissian never returned from this place. Can you imagine what they've done to him?'

Artoo whistled timidly.

The golden droid waded stiffly through a shifting sand hill, then stopped short, as Jabba's palace suddenly loomed, suddenly dark, in the near distance. Artoo almost bumped into him, quickly skidding to the side of the road.

'Watch where you're going, Artoo.' See Threepio resumed walking, but more slowly, his little friend rolling along at his side. And as they went, he chattered on. 'Why couldn't Chewbacca have delivered this message? No, whenever there's an impossible mission, they turn to us. No one worries about droids. Sometimes I wonder why we put up with it all.'

On and on he rambled, over the desolate final stretch of road, until at last they reached the gates to the palace: massive iron doors, taller than Threepio could see – part of a series of stone and iron walls, forming several gigantic cylindrical towers that seemed to rise out of a mountain of packed sand.

The two droids fearfully looked around the ominous door for signs of life, or welcome, or some sort of signaling device with which to make their presence known. Seeing nothing in any of those categories, See Threepio mustered his resolve (which function had been programmed into him quite a long time earlier), knocked softly three times on the thick metal grate, then quickly turned around and announced to Artoo, 'There doesn't seem to be anyone here. Let's go back and tell Master Luke.'

Suddenly a small hatch opened in the center of the door. A spindly mechanical arm popped out, affixed to which a large electronic eyeball peered unabashedly at the two droids. The eyeball spoke.

'Tee chuta hhat yudd!'

Threepio stood erect, proud though his circuits quivered a bit. He faced the eye, pointed to Artoo, and then to himself. 'Artoo Detoowha bo Seethreepiosha ey toota odd mischka Jabba du Hutt.'

The eye looked quickly from one robot to the other, then retracted back through the little window and slammed the hatch shut.

'Boo-dEEp gaNOOng,' whispered Artoo with concern.

Threepio nodded. 'I don't think they're going to let us in, Artoo. We'd better go.' He turned to leave, as Artoo beeped a reluctant four-tone.

At that, a horrific, grinding screech erupted, and the massive iron door slowly began to rise. The two droids looked at each other skeptically, and then into the yawning black cavity that faced them. They waited, afraid to enter, afraid to retreat.

From the shadows, the strange voice of the eye screamed at them: 'Nudd chaa!'

Artoo beeped and rolled forward into the gloom. Threepio hesitated, then rushed after his stubby companion with a start. 'Artoo wait for me!' They stopped together in the gaping passageway, as Threepio scolded: 'You'll get lost.'

The great door slammed shut behind them with a monumental crash that echoed through the dark cavern. For a moment the two frightened robots stood there without moving; then, haltingly, they stepped forward.

They were immediately joined by three large Gamorrean guards – powerful piglike brutes whose racial hatred of robots was well known. The guards ushered the two droids down the dark corridor without so much as a nod. When they reached the first half-lit hallway, one of them grunted an order. Artoo beeped a nervous query at Threepio.

'You don't want to know,' the golden droid responded apprehensively. 'Just deliver Master Luke's message and get us out of here quick.'

Before they could take another step, a form approached them from the obscurity of a cross-corridor: Bib Fortuna, the inelegant major-domo of Jabba's degenerate court. He was a tall, humanoid creature with eyes that saw only what was necessary, and a robe that hid all. Protruding from the back of his skull were two fat, tentacular appendages that exhibited prehensile, sensual, and cognitive functions at various times – which he wore either draped over his shoulders for decorative effect or, when the situation called for balance, hanging straight down behind him as if they were twin tails.

He smiled thinly as he stopped before the two robots. 'Die wanna wanga.'

Threepio spoke up officially. 'Die wanna wanaga. We bring a message to your master, Jabba the Hutt.' Artoo beeped a postscript, upon which Threepio nodded and added: 'And a gift.' He thought about this a moment, looked as puzzled as it was possible for a droid to look, and whispered loudly to Artoo, 'Gift, what gift?'

Bib shook his head emphatically. 'Nee Jabba no badda. Me chaade su goodie.' He held out his hand toward Artoo.

The small droid backed up meekly, but his protest was lengthy. 'bDooo EE NGrwrrr Op dbooDEEop!'

'Artoo, give it to him!' Threepio insisted. Sometimes Artoo could be so binary.

At this, though, Artoo became positively defiant, beeping and tooting at Fortuna and Threepio as if they'd *both* had their programs erased.

Threepio nodded finally, hardly happy with Artoo's answer. He smiled apologetically at Bib. 'He says our master's instructions are to give it only to Jabba himself.' Bib considered the problem a moment, as Threepio went on explaining. 'I'm terribly sorry. I'm afraid he's ever so stubborn about these things.' He managed to throw a disparaging yet loving tone into his voice, as he tilted his head toward his small associate.

Bib gestured for them to follow. 'Nudd chaa.' He walked back into the darkness, the droids following close behind, the three Gamorrean guards lumbering along at the rear.

As See Threepio descended into the belly of the shadow, he muttered quietly to the silent R2 unit, 'Artoo, I have a bad feeling about this.'

See Threepio and Artoo Detoo stood at the entrance of the throne room, looking in. 'We're doomed,' whimpered Threepio, wishing for the thousandth time that he could close his eyes.

The room was filled, wall to cavernous wall, with the animate dregs of the universe. Grotesque creatures from the lowest star systems, drunk on spiced liquor and their own fetid vapors. Gamorreans, twisted humans, jawas – all reveling in base pleasures, or raucously comparing mean feats. And in the front of the room, reclining on a daïs that overlooked the debauchery, was Jabba the Hutt.

His head was three times human size, perhaps four. His eyes were yellow, reptilian – his skin was like a snake's, as well, except covered with a fine layer of grease. He had no neck, but only a series of chins that expanded finally into a great bloated body, engorged to bursting with stolen morsels. Stunted, almost useless arms sprouted from his upper torso, the sticky fingers of his left hand languidly wrapped around the smoking-end of his water-pipe. He had no hair – it had fallen out from a combination of diseases. He had no legs – his trunk simply tapered gradually to a long, plump snake-tail that stretched along the length of the platform like a tube of yeasty dough. His lipless mouth was wide, almost ear to ear, and he drooled continuously. He was quite thoroughly disgusting.

Chained to him, chained at the neck, was a sad, pretty dancing-girl, a member of Fortuna's species, with two dry, shapely tentacles sprouting from the back of her head, hanging suggestively down her bare, muscled back. Her name was Oola. Looking forlorn, she sat as far away as her chain would allow, at the other end of the daïs.

And sitting near Jabba's belly was a small monkey-like reptile named Salacious Crumb, who caught all the food and ooze that spilled out of Jabba's hands or mouth and ate it with a nauseating cackle.

Shafts of light from above partially illuminated the drunken courtiers as Bib Fortuna crossed the floor to the daïs. The room was composed of an endless series of alcoves within alcoves, so that much of what went on was, in any case, visible only as shadow and movement. When Fortuna reached the throne, he delicately leaned forward and whispered into the slobbering monarch's ear. Jabba's eyes became slits . . . then with a maniacal laugh he motioned for the two terrified droids to be brought in.

'Bo shuda,' wheezed the Hutt, and lapsed into a fit of coughing. Although he understood several languages, as a point of honor he only spoke Huttese. His only such point.

The quaking robots scooted forward to stand before the repulsive ruler, though he grossly violated their most deeply programmed sensibilities. 'The message, Artoo, the message,' Threepio urged.

Artoo whistled once, and a beam of light projected from his domed head, creating a hologram of Luke Skywalker that stood before them on the floor. Quickly the image grew to over ten feet tall, until the young Jedi warrior towered over the assembled throng. All at once the room grew quiet, as Luke's giant presence made itself felt.

'Greetings, Exalted One,' the hologram said to Jabba. 'Allow me to introduce myself. I am Luke Skywalker, Jedi Knight and friend of Captain Solo. I seek an audience with Your Greatness, to bargain for his life.' At this, the entire room burst into laughter which Jabba instantly stopped with a hand motion. Luke didn't pause long. 'I know that you are powerful, mighty Jabba, and that your anger with Solo must be equally powerful. But I'm sure we can work out an arrangement which will be mutually beneficial. As a token of my good will, I present to you a gift – these two droids.'

Threepio jumped back as if stung. 'What! What did he say?'

Luke continued. '. . . Both are hardworking and will serve you well.' With that, the hologram disappeared.

Threepio wagged his head in despair. 'Oh no, this can't be. Artoo, you must have played the wrong message.'

Jabba laughed and drooled.

Bib spoke in Huttese. 'Bargain rather than fight? He is no Jedi.'

Jabba nodded in agreement. Still grinning, he rasped at Threepio, 'There will be no bargain. I have no intention of giving up my favorite decoration.' With a hideous chuckle he looked toward the dimly lit alcove beside the throne; there, hanging flat against the wall, was the carbonized form of Han Solo, his face and hands emerging out of the cold hard slab, like a statue reaching from a sea of stone.

Artoo and Threepio marched dismally through the dank passage-way at the prodding of a Gamorrean guard. Dungeon cells lined both walls. The unspeakable cries of anguish that emanated from within as the droids passed echoed off the stone and down the endless catacombs. Periodically a hand or claw or tentacle would reach through the bars of a door to grab at the hapless robots.

Artoo beeped pitifully. Threepio only shook his head. 'What could have possibly come over Master Luke? Was it something I did? He never expressed any unhappiness with my work . . .'

They approached a door at the end of the corridor. It slid open automatically, and the Gamorrean shoved them forward. Inside, their ears were assaulted by deafening machine sounds – wheels creaking, piston-heads slamming, water-hammers, engine hums – and a continuously shifting haze of steam made visibility short. This was either the boiler room, or programmed hell.

An agonized electronic scream, like the sound of stripping gears, drew their attention to the corner of the room. From out of the mist walked EV-9D9, a thin humanlike robot with some disturbingly human appetites. In the dimness behind Ninedenine, Threepio could see the legs being pulled off a droid on a torture rack, while a second droid, hanging upside down, was having red-hot irons applied to its feet; it had emitted the electronic scream Threepio heard a few moments earlier, as the sensor circuits in its metal skin melted in agony. Threepio cringed at the sound, his own wiring sympathetically crackling with static electricity.

Ninedenine stopped in front of Threepio, raising her pincer hands expansively. 'Ah, new acquisitions,' she said with great satisfaction. 'I am Eve-Ninedenine, Chief of Cyborg Operations. You're a protocol droid, aren't you?'

'I am See Threepio, human-cyborg re—'

'Yes or no will do,' Ninedenine said icily.

'Well, yes,' Threepio replied. This robot was going to be trouble, that much was obvious – one of those droids who always had to prove she was more-droid-than-thou.

'How many languages do you speak?' Ninedenine continued.

Well, two can play at that game, thought Threepio. He ran his most dignified, official introductory tape. 'I am fluent in over six million forms of communication, and can—'

'Splendid!' Ninedenine interrupted gleefully. 'We have been without an interpreter since the master got angry with something our last protocol droid said and disintegrated him.'

'Disintegrated!' Threepio wailed. Any semblance of protocol left him.

Ninedenine spoke to a pig guard who suddenly appeared. 'This one will be quite useful. Fit him with a restraining bolt, then take him back up to the main audience chamber.'

The guard grunted and roughly shoved Threepio toward the door.

'Artoo, don't leave me!' Threepio called out, but the guard grabbed him and pulled him away; and he was gone.

Artoo let out a long, plaintive cry as Threepio was removed. Then he turned to Ninedenine and beeped in outrage, and at length.

Ninedenine laughed. 'You're a feisty little one, but you'll soon learn some respect. I have need for you on the master's Sail Barge. Several of our astrodroids have been disappearing recently – stolen for spare parts, most likely. I think you'll fill in nicely.'

The droid on the torture rack emitted a high-frequency wail, then sparked briefly and was silent.

The court of Jabba the Hutt roiled in malignant ecstasy. Oola, the beautiful creature chained to Jabba, danced in the center of the floor, as the inebriated monsters cheered and heckled. Threepio hovered warily near the back of the throne, trying to keep the lowest profile possible. Periodically he had to duck to avoid a fruit hurled in his direction or to sidestep a rolling body. Mostly, he just laid low. What else was a protocol droid to do, in a place of so little protocol?

Jabba leered through the smoke of his hooka and beckoned the creature Oola to come sit beside him. She stopped dancing instantly, a fearful look in her eye, and backed up, shaking her head. Apparently she had suffered such invitations before.

Jabba became angry. He pointed unmistakably to a spot beside him on the daïs. 'Da eitha!' he growled.

Oola shook her head more violently, her face a mask of terror. 'Na chuba negatorie. Na! Na! Natoota . . .'

Jabba became livid. Furiously he motioned to Oola. 'Boscka!'

Jabba pushed a button as he released Oola's chain. Before she could flee, a grating trap door in the floor dropped open, and she tumbled into the pit below. The door snapped shut instantly. A moment of silence, followed by a low, rumbling roar, followed by a terrified shriek was followed once more by silence.

Jabba laughed until he slobbered. A dozen revelers hurried over to peer through the grate, to observe the demise of the nubile dancer.

Threepio shrank even lower and looked for support to the carbonite form of Han Solo, suspended in bas relief above the floor. Now *there* was a human without a sense of protocol, thought Threepio wistfully.

His reverie was interrupted by an unnatural quiet that suddenly fell over the room. He looked up to see Bib Fortuna making his way through the crowd, accompanied by two Gamorrean guards, and followed by a fierce-looking cloaked-and-helmeted bounty hunter who led his captive prize on a leash: Chewbacca, the Wookiee.

Threepio gasped, stunned. 'Oh, no! Chewbacca!' The future was looking very bleak indeed.

Bib muttered a few words into Jabba's ear, pointing to the bounty hunter and his captive. Jabba listened intently. The bounty hunter was humanoid, small and mean: a belt of cartridges was slung across his jerkin and an eye-slit in his helmet-mask gave the impression of his being able to see through things. He bowed low, then spoke in fluent Ubese. 'Greetings, Majestic One. I am Boushh.' It was a metallic language, well-adapted to the rarefied atmosphere of the home planet from which this nomadic species arose.

Jabba answered in the same tongue, though his Ubese was stilted and slow. 'At last someone has brought me the mighty Chewbacca . . .' He tried to continue, but stuttered on the word he wanted. With a roaring laugh, he turned toward Threepio. 'Where's my talkdroid?' he boomed, motioning Threepio to come closer. Reluctantly, the courtly robot obeyed.

Jabba ordered him congenially. 'Welcome our mercenary friend and ask his price for the Wookiee.'

Threepio translated the message to the bounty hunter. Boushh listened carefully, simultaneously studying the feral creatures around the room, possible exits, possible hostages, vulnerable points. He particularly noticed Boba Fett – standing near the door – the steel-masked mercenary who had caught Han Solo.

Boushh assessed this all in a moment's moment, then spoke evenly in his native tongue to Threepio. 'I will take fifty thousand, no less.'

Threepio quietly translated for Jabba, who immediately became enraged and knocked the golden droid off the raised throne with a sweep of his massive tail. Threepio clattered in a heap on the floor, where he rested momentarily, uncertain of the correct protocol in this situation.

Jabba raved on in guttural Huttese, Boushh shifted his weapon to a more usable position. Threepio sighed, struggled back onto the throne, composed himself, and translated for Boushh – loosely – what Jabba was saying.

'Twenty-five thousand is all he'll pay . . .' Threepio instructed.

Jabba motioned his pig guards to take Chewbacca, as two jawas covered Boushh. Boba Fett also raised his weapon. Jabba added, to Threepio's translation: 'Twenty-five thousand, plus his life.'

Threepio translated. The room was silent, tense, uncertain. Finally Boushh spoke, softly, to Threepio.

'Tell that swollen garbage bag he'll have to do better than that, or they'll be picking his smelly hide out of every crack in this room. I'm holding a thermal detonator.'

Threepio suddenly focused on the small silver ball Boushh held partially concealed in his left hand. It could be heard humming a quiet, ominous hum. Threepio looked nervously at Jabba, then back at Boushh.

Jabba barked at the droid. 'Well? What did he say?'

Threepio cleared his throat. 'Your Grandness, he, uh ; . . He—'

'Out with it, droid!' Jabba roared.

'Oh, dear,' Threepio fretted. He inwardly prepared himself for the worst, then spoke to Jabba in flawless Huttese. 'Boushh respectfully disagrees with Your Exaltedness, and begs you to reconsider the amount . . . or he will release the thermal detonator he is holding.'

Instantly a disturbed murmuring circled in the room. Everyone backed up several feet, as if that would help. Jabba stared at the ball clenched in the bounty hunter's hand. It was beginning to glow.

Another tense hush came over the onlookers.

Jabba stared malevolently at the bounty hunter for several long seconds. Then, slowly, a satisfied grin crept over his vast, ugly mouth. From the bilious pit of his belly, a laugh rose like gas in a mire. 'This bounty hunter is my kind of scum. Fearless and inventive. Tell him thirty-five, no more – and warn him not to press his luck.'

Threepio felt greatly relieved by this turn of events. He translated for Boushh. Everyone studied the bounty hunter closely for his reaction; guns were readied.

Then Boushh released a switch on the thermal detonator, and it went dead. 'Zeebuss,' he nodded.

'He agrees,' Threepio said to Jabba.

The crowd cheered; Jabba relaxed. 'Come, my friend, join our celebration. I may find other work for you.' Threepio translated, as the party resumed its depraved revelry.

Chewbacca growled under his breath, as he was led away by the Gamorreans. He might have cracked their heads just for being so ugly, or to remind everyone present what a Wookiee was made of – but near the door he spotted a familiar face. Hidden behind a half-mask of pit-boar teeth was a human in the uniform of a skiff guard – Lando Calrissian. Chewbacca gave no sign of recognition; nor did he resist the guard who now escorted him from the room.

Lando had managed to infiltrate this nest of maggots months earlier to see if it was possible to free Solo from Jabba's imprisonment. He'd done this for several reasons.

First, because he felt (correctly) that it was his fault Han was in this predicament, and he wanted to make amends – provided, of course, he could do so without getting hurt. Blending in here, like just one of the pirates, was no problem for Lando, though – mistaken identity was a way of life with him.

Second, he wanted to join forces with Han's buddies at the top of the Rebel Alliance. They were out to beat the Empire, and he wanted nothing more in his life now than to do just that. The Imperial police had moved in on his action once too often; so this was a grudge match, now. Besides, Lando liked being part of Solo's crowd, since they seemed to be right up at the business end of all the action against the Empire.

Third, Princess Leia had asked him to help, and he just never could refuse a princess asking for help. Besides, you never knew how she might thank you some day.

Finally, Lando would have bet anything that Han simply could not be rescued from this place – and Lando just plain couldn't resist a bet.

So he spent his days watching a lot. Watching and calculating. That's what he did now, as Chewie was led away – he watched, and then he faded into the stonework.

The band started playing, led by a blue, flop-eared jizz-wailer named Max Rebo. Dancers flooded the floor. The courtiers hooted, and brewed their brains a bit more.

Boushh leaned against a column, surveying the scene. His gaze swept coolly over the court, taking in the dancers, the smokers, the rollers, the gamblers . . . until it came to rest squarely on an equally unflappable stare from across the room. Boba Fett was watching him.

Boushh shifted slightly, posturing with his weapon cradled like a loving child. Boba Fett remained motionless, an arrogant sneer all but visible behind his ominous mask.

Pig guards led Chewbacca through the unlit dungeon corridor. A tentacle coiled out one of the doors to touch the brooding Wookiee.

'Rheeaaahhr!' he screamed, and the tentacle shot back into its cell.

The next door was open. Before Chewie fully realized what was happening, he was hurled forcefully into the cell by all the guards. The door slammed shut, locking him in darkness.

He raised his head and let out a long, pitiful howl that carried through the entire mountain of iron and sand up to the infinitly patient sky.

The throne room was quiet, dark and empty, as night filled its littered corners. Blood, wine, and saliva stained the floor, shreds of tattered clothing hung from the fixtures, unconscious bodies curled under broken furniture. The party was over.

A dark figure moved silently among the shadows, pausing behind a column here, a statue there. He made his way stealthily along the perimeter of the room, stepping once over a snoring Yak Face. He never made a sound. This was Boushh, the bounty hunter.

He reached the curtained alcove beside which the slab that was Han Solo hung suspended by a force field on the wall. Boushh looked around furtively, then flipped a switch near the side of the carbonite coffin. The humming of the force field wound down, and the heavy monolith slowly lowered to the floor.

Boushh stepped up and studied the frozen face of the space pirate. He touched Solo's carbonized cheek, curiously, as if it were a rare, precious stone. Cold and hard as diamond.

For a few seconds he examined the controls at the side of the slab, then activated a series of switches. Finally, after one last, hesitant glance at the living statue before him, he slid the decarbonization lever into place.

The casing began to emit a high-pitched sound. Anxiously Boushh peered all around again, making certain no one heard. Slowly, the hard shell that was covering the contours of Solo's face started to melt away. Soon, the coating was gone from the entire front of Solo's body, freeing his upraised hands – so long frozen in protest – to fall slackly to his sides. His face relaxed into what looked like nothing so much as a death-mask. Boushh extracted the lifeless body from its casing and lowered it gently to the floor.

He leaned his gruesome helmet close to Solo's face, listening closely for signs of life. No breath. No pulse. With a start, Han's eyes suddenly snapped open, and he began to cough. Boushh steadied him, tried to quiet him – there were still guards who might hear.

'Quiet!' he whispered. 'Just relax.'

Han squinted up at the dim form above him. 'I can't see ... What's happening?' He was, understandably, disoriented, after having been in suspended animation for six of this desert planet's months – a period that was, to him, timeless. It had been a grim sensation – as if for an eternity he'd been trying to draw breath, to move, to scream, every moment in conscious, painful asphyxiation – and now suddenly he was dumped into a loud, black, cold pit.

His senses assaulted him all at once. The air bit at his skin with a thousand icy teeth; the opacity of his sight was impenetrable; wind seemed to rush around his ears at hurricane volumes; he couldn't feel which way was up; the myriad smells filling his nose made him nauseous, he couldn't stop salivating, all his bones hurt – and then came the visions.

Visions from his childhood, from his last breakfast, from twenty-seven piracies ... as if all the images and memories of his life had been crammed into a balloon, and the balloon popped and they all came bursting out now, randomly, in a single moment. It was nearly overwhelming, it was sensory overload; or more precisely, memory overload. Men had gone mad, in these first minutes following decarbonization, hopelessly, utterly mad – unable ever again to reorganize the ten-billion individual images that comprised a lifespan into any kind of coherent, selective order.

Solo wasn't that susceptible. He rode the surge of this tide of impressions until it settled down to a churning backwash, submerging the bulk of his memories, leaving only the most recent flotsam to foam on the surface; his betrayal by Lando Calrissian, whom he'd once called friend; his ailing ship; his last view of Leia; his capture by Boba Fett, the iron-masked bounty hunter who ...

Where was he now? What had happened? His last image was of Boba Fett watching him turn into carbonite. Was this Fett again now, come to thaw him for more abuse? The air roared in his ears, his breathing felt irregular, unnatural. He batted his hand in front of his face.

Boushh tried to reassure him. 'You're free of the carbonite and have hibernation sickness. Your eyesight will return in time. Come, we must hurry if we're to leave this place.'

Reflexively Han grabbed the bounty hunter, felt at the grated face-mask, then drew back. 'I'm not going anywhere – I don't even know where I am.' He began sweating profusely as his heart once again churned blood, and his mind groped for answers. 'Who are you, anyway?' he demanded suspiciously. Perhaps it was Fett after all.

The bounty hunter reached up and pulled the helmet away from his head revealing, underneath, the beautiful face of Princess Leia.

'One who loves you,' she whispered, taking his face tenderly in her still-gloved hands and kissing him long on the lips.

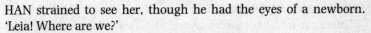

HAN strained to see her, though he had the eyes of a newborn. 'Leia! Where are we?'

'Jabba's palace. I've got to get you out of here quick.'

He sat up shakily. 'Everything's a blur ... I'm not going to be much help ...'

She looked at him a long moment, her blinded love – she'd traveled light-years to find him, risked her life, lost hard-won time needed sorely by the Rebellion, time she couldn't really afford to throw away on personal quests and private desires ... but she loved him.

Tears filled her eyes. 'We'll make it,' she whispered.

Impulsively, she embraced him and kissed him again. He, too, was flooded with emotion all at once – back from the dead, the beautiful princess filling his arms, snatching him from the teeth of the void. He felt overwhelmed. Unable to move, even to speak, he held her tightly, his blind eyes closed fast against all the sordid realities that would come rushing in soon enough.

Sooner than that, as it happened. A repulsive squishing sound suddenly became all too obvious behind them. Han opened his eyes, but could still see nothing. Leia looked up to the alcove beyond, and her gaze turned to an expression of horror. For the curtain had been drawn away, and the entire area, floor to ceiling, was composed of a gallery of the most disgusting miscreants of Jabba's court – gawking, salivating, wheezing.

Leia's hand shot up to her mouth.

'What is it?' Han pressed her. Something obviously was terribly wrong. He stared into his own blackness.

An obscene cackle rose from the other side of the alcove. A Huttese cackle.

Han held his head, closed his eyes again, as if to keep away the inevitable for just one more moment. 'I know that laugh.'

The curtain on the far side was suddenly drawn open. There sat Jabba, Ishi Tib, Bib, Boba, and several guards. They all laughed, kept laughing, laughed to punish.

'My, my, what a touching sight,' Jabba purred. 'Han, my boy, your taste in companions has improved, even if your luck has not.'

Even blind, Solo could slide into smooth talk easier than a spice-eater. 'Listen, Jabba, I was on my way back to pay you when I got a little side-tracked. Now I know we've had our differences, but I'm sure we can work this out . . .'

This time Jabba genuinely chuckled. 'It's too late for that, Solo. You may have been the best smuggler in the business, but now you're Bantha fodder.' He cut short his smile and gestured to his guards. 'Take him.'

Guards grabbed Leia and Han. They dragged the Corellian pirate off, while Leia continued struggling where she was.

'I will decide how to kill him later,' Jabba muttered.

'I'll pay you triple,' Solo called out. 'Jabba, you're throwing away a fortune. Don't be a fool.' Then he was gone.

From the rank of guards, Lando quickly moved forward, took hold of Leia, and attempted to lead her away.

Jabba stopped them. 'Wait! Bring her to me.'

Lando and Leia halted in mid-stride. Lando looked tense, uncertain what to do. It wasn't quite time to move yet. The odds still weren't just right. He knew he was the ace-in-the-hole, and an ace-in-the-hole was something you had to know how to play to win.

'I'll be all right,' Leia whispered.

'I'm not so sure,' he replied. But the moment was past; there was nothing else to be done now. He and Ishi Tib, the Birdlizard, dragged the young princess to Jabba.

Threepio, who'd been watching everything from his place behind

Jabba, could watch no more. He turned away in dread.

Leia, on the other hand, stood tall before the loathsome monarch. Her anger ran high. With all the galaxy at war, for her to be detained on this dustball of a planet by this petty scumdealer was more outrageous than she could tolerate. Still, she kept her voice calm; for she was, in the end, a princess. 'We have powerful friends Jabba. You will soon regret this . . .'

'I'm sure, I'm sure,' the old gangster rumbled with glee, 'but in the meantime, I will thoroughly enjoy the pleasure of your company.'

He pulled her eagerly to him until their faces were mere inches apart, her belly pressed to his oily snake skin. She thought about killing him outright, then and there. But she held her ire in check, since the rest of these vermin might have killed her before she could escape with Han. Better odds were sure to come later. So she swallowed hard and, for the time being, put up with this slimepot as best she could.

Threepio peeked out momentarily, then immediately withdrew again. 'Oh no, I can't watch.'

Foul beast that he was, Jabba poked his fat, dripping tongue out to the princess, and slopped a beastly kiss squarely on her mouth.

Han was thrown roughly into the dungeon cell; the door crashed shut behind him. He fell to the floor in the darkness, then picked himself up and sat against the wall. After a few moments of pounding the ground with his fist, he quieted down and tried to organize his thoughts.

Darkness. Well, blast it, blind is blind. No use wishing for moondew on a meteorite. Only it was so frustrating, coming out of deep-freeze like that, saved by the one person who . . .

Leia! The star captain's stomach dropped at the thought of what must be happening to her now. If only he knew where he was. Tentatively he knocked on the wall behind him. Solid rock.

What could he do? Bargain, maybe. But what did he have to bargain with? Dumb question, he thought – when did I ever have to *have* something before I could *bargain* with it?

What, though? Money? Jabba had more than he could ever count. Pleasures? Nothing could give Jabba more pleasure than to defile the princess and kill Solo. No, things were bad – in fact, it didn't look like they could get much worse.

Then he heard the growl. A low, formidable snarl from out of the dense blackness at the far corner of the cell, the growl of a large and angry beast.

The hair on Solo's arms stood on end. Quickly he rose, his back to the wall. 'Looks like I've got company,' he muttered.

The wild creature bellowed out an insane '*Groawwwwr!*' and raced straight at Solo, grabbing him ferociously around the chest, lifting him several feet into the air, squeezing off his breathing.

Han was totally motionless for several long seconds – he couldn't believe his ears. 'Chewie, is that you!?'

The giant Wookiee barked with joy.

For the second time in an hour, Solo was overcome with happiness; but this was an entirely different matter. 'All right, all right, wait a second, you're crushing me.'

Chewbacca put his friend down. Han reached up and scratched his partner's chest; Chewie cooed like a pup.

'Okay, what's going on around here, anyway?' Han was instantly back on track. Here was unbelievably good fortune – here was someone he could make a plan *with*. And not only someone, but his most loyal friend in the galaxy.

Chewie filled him in at length. 'Arh arhaghh shpahrgh rahr aurowwwrahrah grop rahp rah.'

'Lando's plan? What is *he* doing here?'

Chewie barked extensively.

Han shook his head. 'Is Luke crazy? Why'd you listen to him? That kid can't even take care of himself, let alone rescue anyone.'

'Rowr ahrgh awf ahraroww rowh rohngr grgrff rf rf.'

'A Jedi Knight? Come on. I'm out of it for a little while and everybody gets delusions . . .'

Chewbacca growled insistently.

Han nodded dubiously in the blackness. 'I'll believe it when I see it—' he commented, walking stoutly into the wall. 'If you'll excuse the expression.'

The iron main gate of Jabba's palace scraped open harshly, oiled only with sand and time. Standing outside in the dusty gale, staring into the black cavernous entranceway, was Luke Skywalker.

He was clad in the robe of the Jedi Knight – a cassock, really – but bore neither gun nor lightsaber. He stood loosely, without bravado, taking a measure of the place before entering. He was a man now. Wiser, like a man – older more from loss than from years. Loss of illusions, loss of dependency. Loss of friends, to war. Loss of sleep, to stress. Loss of laughter. Loss of his hand.

But of all his losses, the greatest was that which came from knowledge, and from the deep recognition that he could never un-know what he knew. So many things he wished he'd never learned. He had aged with the weight of this knowledge.

Knowledge brought benefits, of course. He was less impulsive now. Manhood had given him perspective, a framework in which to fit the events of his life – that is, a lattice of spatial and time coordinates spanning his existence, back to earliest memories, ahead to a hundred alternative futures. A lattice of depths, and conundrums, and interstices, through which Luke could peer at any new event in his life, peer at it with perspective. A lattice of shadows and corners, rolling back to the vanishing point on the horizon of Luke's mind. And all these shadow boxes that lent such *perspective* to things ... well, this lattice gave his life a certain darkness.

Nothing of substance, of course – and in any case, some would have said this shading gave a depth to his personality, where before it had been thin, without dimension – though such a suggestion probably would have come from jaded critics, reflecting a jaded time. Nonetheless, there was a certain darkness, now.

There were other advantages to knowledge: rationality, etiquette, choice. Choice, of them all, was a true double-edged sword; but it did have its advantages.

Furthermore he was skilled in the craft of the Jedi now, where before he'd been merely precocious.

He was more aware now.

These were all desirable attributes, to be sure; and Luke knew as well as anyone that all things alive must grow. Still, it carried a certain sadness, the sum of all this knowledge. A certain sense of regret. But who could afford to be a boy in times such as these?

Resolutely, Luke strode into the arching hallway.

Almost immediately two Gamorreans stepped up, blocking his path. One spoke in a voice that did not invite debate. 'No chuba!'

Luke raised his hand and pointed at the guards. Before either could draw a weapon, they were both clutching their own throats, choking, gasping. They fell to their knees.

Luke lowered his hand and walked on. The guards, suddenly able to breathe again, slumped to the sanddrifted steps. They didn't follow.

Around the next corner Luke was met by Bib Fortuna. Fortuna began speaking as he approached the young Jedi, but Luke never broke stride, so Bib had to reverse his direction in mid-sentence and hurry along with Skywalker in order to carry on a conversation.

'You must be the one called Skywalker. His Excellency will not see you.'

'I will speak to Jabba, now,' Luke spoke evenly, never slowing. They passed several more guards at the next crossing, who fell in behind them.

'The great Jabba is asleep,' Bib explained. 'He has instructed me to tell you there will be no bargains—'

Luke stopped suddenly, and stared at Bib. He locked eyes with the major-domo, raised his hand slightly, took a minutely inward turn. 'You will take me to Jabba, now.'

Bib paused, tilted his head a fraction. What were his instructions? Oh, yes, now he remembered. 'I will take you to Jabba now.'

He turned and walked down the twisting corridor that led to the throne chamber. Luke followed him into the gloom.

'You serve your master well,' he whispered in Bib's ear.

'I serve my master well,' Bib nodded with conviction.

'You are sure to be rewarded,' Luke added.

Bib smiled smugly. 'I am sure to be rewarded.'

As Luke and Bib entered Jabba's court, the level of tumult dropped precipitously as if Luke's presence had a cooling effect. Everyone felt the change.

The lieutenant and the Jedi Knight approached the throne. Luke saw Leia seated there, now, by Jabba's belly. She was chained at the neck and dressed in the skimpy costume of a dancing girl. He could feel her pain immediately, from across the room – but he said nothing, didn't even look at her, shut her anguish completely out of his mind. For he needed to focus his attention entirely on Jabba.

Leia, for her part, sensed this at once. She closed her mind to Luke, to keep herself from distracting him; yet at the same time she kept it open, ready to receive any sliver of information she might need to act. She felt charged with possibilities.

Threepio peeked out from behind the throne as Bib walked up. For the first time in many days, he scanned his hope program. 'Ah! At last Master Luke's come to take me away from all this,' he beamed.

Bib stood proudly before Jabba. 'Master, I present Luke Sky-walker, Jedi Knight.'

'I told you not to admit him,' the gangster-slug growled in Huttese.

'I must be allowed to speak,' Luke spoke quietly, though his words were heard throughout the hall.

'He must be allowed to speak,' Bib concurred thoughtfully.

Jabba, furious, bashed Bib across the face and sent him reeling to the floor. 'You weak-minded fool! He's using an old Jedi mind trick!'

Luke let all the rest of the motley horde that surrounded him melt into the recesses of his consciousness, to let Jabba fill his mind totally. 'You will bring Captain Solo and the Wookiee to me.'

Jabba smiled grimly. 'Your mind powers will not work on me, boy. I am not affected by your human thought pattern.' Then, as an after thought: 'I was killing your kind when being a Jedi meant something.'

Luke altered his stance somewhat, internally and externally. 'Nevertheless, I am taking Captain Solo and his friends. You can either profit from this ... or be destroyed. It's your choice, but I warn you not to underestimate my powers.' He spoke in his own language, which Jabba well understood.

Jabba laughed the laugh of a lion cautioned by a mouse.

Threepio, who had been observing this interplay intently, leaned forward to whisper to Luke: 'Master, you're standing—' A guard abruptly restrained the concerned droid, though, and pulled him back to his place.

Jabba cut short his laugh with a scowl. 'There will be no bargain, young Jedi. I shall enjoy watching you die.'

Luke raised his hand. A pistol jumped out of the holster of a nearby guard and landed snugly in the Jedi's palm. Luke pointed the weapon at Jabba.

Jabba spat. 'Boscka!'

The floor suddenly dropped away, sending Luke and his guard crashing into the pit below. The trap door immediately closed again.

All the beasts of the court rushed to the floor-grating and looked down.

'Luke!' yelled Leia. She felt part of her self torn away, pulled down into the pit with him. She started forward, but was held in check by the manacle around her throat. Raucous laughter crowded in from everywhere at once, set her on edge. She poised to flee.

A human guard touched her shoulder. She looked. It was Lando. Imperceptibly, he shook his head. No. Imperceptibly, her muscles relaxed. This wasn't the right moment, he knew – but it was the right hand. All the cards were here, now – Luke, Han, Leia, Chewbacca . . . and old Wild Card Lando. He just didn't want Leia revealing the hand before all the bets were out. The stakes were just too high.

In the pit below, Luke picked himself up off the floor. He found he was now in a large cavelike dungeon, the walls formed of craggy boulders pocked with lightless crevices. The half-chewed bones of countless animals were strewn over the floor, smelling of decayed flesh and twisted fear.

Twenty-five feet above him, in the ceiling, he saw the iron grating through which Jabba's repugnant courtiers peered.

The guard beside him suddenly began to scream uncontrollably, as a door in the side of the cave slowly rumbled open. With infinite calm, Luke surveyed his surroundings as he removed his long robe down to his Jedi tunic, to give him more freedom of movement. He backed quickly to the wall and crouched there, watching.

Out of the side passage emerged the giant Rancor. The size of an elephant, it was somehow reptilian, somehow as unformed as a nightmare. Its huge screeching mouth was asymmetrical in its head, its fangs and claws set all out of proportion. It was clearly a mutant, and wild as all unreason.

The guard picked up the pistol from the dirt where it had fallen and began firing laser bursts at the hideous monster. This only made the beast angrier. It lumbered toward the guard.

The guard kept firing. Ignoring the laser blasts, the beast grabbed the hysterical guard, popped him into its slavering jaws, and swallowed him in a gulp. The audience above cheered, laughed, and threw coins.

The monster then turned and started for Luke. But the Jedi Knight leaped eight meters straight up and grabbed onto the overhead grate. The crowd began to boo. Hand over hand, Luke traversed the grating toward the corner of the cave, struggling to maintain his grip as the audience jeered his efforts. One hand slipped on the oily grid, and he dangled precariously over the baying mutant.

Two jawas ran across the top of the grate. They mashed Luke's fingers with their rifle butts; once again, the crowd roared its approval.

The Rancor pawed at Luke from below, but the Jedi dangled just out of reach. Suddenly Luke released his hold and dropped directly onto the eye of the howling monster; he then tumbled to the floor.

The Rancor screamed in pain and stumbled, swatting its own face to knock away the agony. It ran in circles a few times, then spotted Luke again and came at him. Luke stooped down to pick up the long bone of an earlier victim. He brandished it before him. The gallery above thought this was hilarious and hooted in delight.

The monster grabbed Luke and brought him up to its salivating mouth. At the last moment, though, Luke wedged the bone deep in the Rancor's mouth and jumped to the floor as the beast began to gag. The Rancor bellowed and flailed about, running headlong into a wall. Several rocks were dislodged, starting an avalanche that nearly buried Luke, as he crouched deep in a crevice near the floor. The crowd clapped in unison.

Luke tried to clear his mind. Fear is a great cloud, Ben used to tell him. It makes the cold colder and the dark darker; but let it rise and it will dissolve. So Luke let it rise past the clamor of the beast above him, and examined ways he might turn the sad creature's rantings on itself.

It was not an evil beast, that much was clear. Had it been purely malicious, its wickedness could easily have been turned on itself – for pure evil, Ben had said, was always self-destructive in the end. But this monster wasn't bad – merely dumb and mistreated. Hungry and in pain, it lashed out at whatever came near. For Luke to have looked on that as evil would only have been a projection of Luke's own darker aspects – it would have been false, and it certainly wouldn't have helped him out of this situation.

No, he was going to have to keep his mind clear – that was all – and just outwit the savage brute, to put it out of its misery.

Most preferable would have been to set it loose in Jabba's court, but that seemed unlikely. He considered, next, giving the creature the means to do itself in – to end its own pain. Unfortunately, the creature was far too angered to comprehend the solace of the void. Luke finally began studying the specific contours of the cave, to try to come up with a specific plan.

The Rancor, meanwhile, had knocked the bone from its mouth and, enraged, was scrabbling through the rubble of fallen rocks, searching for Luke. Luke, though his vision was partially obscured by the pile that still sheltered him, could see now past the monster, to a holding cave beyond – and beyond that, to a utility door. If only he could get to it.

The Rancor knocked away a boulder and spotted Luke recoiling in the crevice. Voraciously, it reached in to pluck the boy out. Luke grabbed a large rock and smashed it down on the creature's finger as hard as he could. As the Rancor jumped, howling in pain once more, Luke ran for the holding cave.

He reached the doorway and ran in. Before him, a heavy barred gate blocked the way. Beyond this gate, the Rancor's two keepers sat eating dinner. They looked up as Luke entered, then stood and walked toward the gate.

Luke turned around to see the monster coming angrily after him. He turned back to the gate and tried to open it. The keepers poked at him with their two-pronged spears, jabbed at him through the bars, laughing and chewing their food, as the Rancor drew closer to the young Jedi.

Luke backed against the side wall, as the Rancor reached in the room for him. Suddenly he saw the restraining-door control panel halfway up the opposite wall. The Rancor began to enter the holding room, closing for the kill, when all at once Luke picked up a skull off the floor and hurled it at the panel.

The panel exploded in a shower of sparks, and the giant iron overhead restraining door came crashing down on the Rancor's head, crushing it like an axe smashing through a ripe watermelon.

Those in the audience above gasped as one, then were silent. They were all truly stunned at this bizarre turn of events. They all looked to Jabba, who was apoplectic with rage. Never had he felt such fury. Leia tried to hide her delight, but was unable to keep from smiling, and this increased Jabba's anger even further. Harshly he snapped at his guards: 'Get him out of there. Bring me Solo and the

Wookiee. They will all suffer for this outrage.'

In the pit below, Luke stood calmly as several of Jabba's henchmen ran in, clapped him in bonds, and ushered him out.

The Rancor keeper wept openly and threw himself down on the body of his dead pet. Life would be a lonely proposition for him from that day.

Han and Chewie were led before the steaming Jabba. Han still squinted and stumbled every few feet. Threepio stood behind the Hutt, unbearably apprehensive. Jabba kept Leia on a short tether, stroking her hair to try to calm himself. A constant murmuring filled the room, as the rabble speculated on what was going to happen to whom.

With a flurry, several guards – including Lando Calrissian – dragged Luke in across the room. To give them passage, the courtiers parted like an unruly sea. When Luke, too, was standing before the throne, he nudged Solo with a smile. 'Good to see you again, old buddy.'

Solo's face lit up. There seemed to be no end to the number of friends he kept bumping into. 'Luke! Are you in this mess now, too?'

'Wouldn't miss it,' Skywalker smiled. For just a moment, he almost felt like a boy again.

'Well, how we doing?' Han raised his eyebrows.

'Same as always,' said Luke.

'Oh-oh,' Solo replied under his breath. He felt one hundred percent relaxed. Just like old times – but a second later, a bleak thought chilled him.

'Where's Leia? Is she . . .'

Her eyes had been fixed on him from the moment he'd entered the room, though – guarding his spirit with her own. When he spoke of her now, she responded instantly, calling from her place on Jabba's throne. 'I'm all right, but I don't know how much longer I can hold off your slobbering friend, here.' She was intentionally cavalier, to put Solo at ease. Besides, the sight of all of her friends there at once made her feel nearly invincible. Han, Luke, Chewie, Lando – even Threepio was skulking around somewhere, trying to be forgotten. Leia almost laughed out loud, almost punched Jabba in the nose. She could barely restrain herself. She wanted to hug them all.

Suddenly Jabba shouted; the entire room was immediately silent. 'Talkdroid!'

Timidly, Threepio stepped forward and with an embarrassed, self-effacing head gesture, addressed the captives. 'His High Exaltedness, the great Jabba the Hutt, has decreed that you are to be terminated immediately.'

Solo said loudly, 'That's good, I hate long waits . . .'

'Your extreme offense against His Majesty,' Threepio went on, 'demands the most torturous form of death . . .'

'No sense in doing things halfway,' Solo cracked. Jabba could be so pompous, sometimes, and now with old Goldenrod, there, making his pronouncements . . .

No matter what else, Threepio simply *hated* being interrupted. He collected himself, nonetheless, and continued. 'You will be taken to the Dune Sea, where you will be thrown into the Great Pit of Carkoon—'

Han shrugged, then turned to Luke. 'That doesn't sound too bad.'

Threepio ignored the interruption. '. . . the resting place of the all-powerful Sarlacc. In his belly you will find a new definition of pain and suffering, as you slowly digest for a thousand years.'

'On second thought we could pass on that,' Solo reconsidered. A thousand years was a bit much.

Chewie barked his whole-hearted agreement.

Luke only smiled. 'You should have bargained, Jabba. This is the last mistake you'll ever make.' Luke was unable to suppress the satisfaction in his voice. He found Jabba despicable – a leech of the galaxy, sucking the life from whatever he touched. Luke wanted to burn the villain, and so was actually rather glad Jabba had refused to bargain – for now Luke would get his wish precisely. Of course, his primary objective was to free his friends, whom he loved dearly; it was this concern that guided him now, above all else. But in the process, to free the universe of this gangster slug – this was a prospect that tinted Luke's purpose with an ever-so-slightly dark satisfaction.

Jabba chortled evilly. 'Take them away.' At last, a bit of pure pleasure on an otherwise dreary day – feeding the Sarlacc was the only thing he enjoyed as much as feeding the Rancor. Poor Rancor.

A loud cheer rose from the crowd as the prisoners were carried off. Leia looked after them with great concern; but when she caught a glimpse of Luke's face she was stirred to see it still fixed in a broad, genuine smile. She sighed deeply, to expel her doubts.

Jabba's giant antigravity Sail Barge glided slowly over the endless Dune Sea. Its sand-blasted iron hull creaked in the slight breeze, each puff of wind coughing into the two huge sails as if even nature suffered some terminal malaise wherever it came near Jabba. He was belowdecks, now, with most of his court, hiding the decay of his spirit from the cleansing sun.

Alongside the barge, two small skiffs floated in formation – one an escort craft, bearing six scruffy soldiers; the other, a gun skiff, containing the prisoners: Han, Chewie, Luke. They were all in bonds, and surrounded by armed guards – Barada, two Weequays. And Lando Calrissian.

Barada was the no-nonsense sort, and not likely to let anything get out of hand. He carried a long-gun as if he wanted nothing more than to hear it speak.

The Weequays were an odd sort. They were brothers, leathery and bald save for a tribal top-knot, braided and worn to the side. No one was certain whether Weequay was the name of their tribe, or their species; or whether all in their tribe were brothers, or all were named Weequays. It was known only that these two were called by this name, and that they treated all other creatures indifferently. With each other they were gentle, even tender; but like Barada, they seemed anxious for the prisoners to misbehave.

And Lando, of course, remained silent, ready – waiting for an opportunity. This reminded him of the lithium scam he'd run on Pesmenben IV – they'd salted the dunes there with lithium carbonate, to con the Imperial governor into leasing the planet. Lando, posing as a nonunion mine guard, had made the governor lie face down in the bottom of the boat and throw his bribe overboard when the 'union officials' raided them. They'd gotten away scot-free on that one; Lando expected this job would go much the same, except they might have to throw the guards overboard as well.

Han kept his ear tuned, for his eyes were still useless. He spoke with reckless disregard, to put the guards at ease – to get them used to his talking and moving, so when the time came for him *really* to move, they'd be a critical fraction behind his mark. And, of course – as always – he spoke just to hear himself speak.

'I think my sight is getting better,' he said, squinting over the sand. 'Instead of a big dark blur, I see a big bright blur.'

'Believe me, you're not missing anything.' Luke smiled. 'I grew up here.'

Luke thought of his youth on Tatooine, living on his uncle's farm, cruising in his souped-up landspeeder with his few friends – sons of other settlers, sitting their own lonely outposts. Nothing ever to do here, really, for man or boy, but cruise the monotonous dunes and try to avoid the peevish Tusken Raiders who guarded the sand as if it were gold-dust. Luke knew this place.

He'd met Obi-Wan Kenobi, here – old Ben Kenobi, the hermit who'd lived in the wilderness since nobody knew when. The man who'd first shown Luke the way of the Jedi.

Luke thought of him now with great love, and great sorrow. For Ben was, more than anyone, the agent of Luke's discoveries and losses – and discoveries of losses.

Ben had taken Luke to Mos Eisley, the pirate city on the western face of Tatooine, to the cantina where they'd first met Han Solo, and Chewbacca the Wookiee. Taken him there after Imperial stormtroopers had murdered Uncle Owen and Aunt Beru, searching for the fugitive droids, Artoo and Threepio.

That's how it had all started for Luke, here on Tatooine. Like a recurring dream he knew this place; and he had sworn then that he would never return.

'I grew up here,' he repeated softly.

'And now we're going to die here,' Solo replied.

'I wasn't planning on it,' Luke shook himself out of his reverie.

'If this is your big plan, so far I'm not crazy about it.'

'Jabba's palace was too well guarded. I had to get you out of there. Just stay close to Chewie and Lando. We'll take care of everything.'

'I can hardly wait.' Solo had a sinking feeling this grand escape depended on Luke's thinking he was a Jedi – a questionable premise at best, considering it was an extinct brotherhood that had used a Force he didn't really believe in anyway. A fast ship and a good blaster are what Han believed in, and he wished he had them now.

*

Jabba sat in the main cabin of the Sail Barge, surrounded by his entire retinue. The party at the palace was simply continuing, in motion – the result being a slightly wobblier brand of carousing – more in the nature of a prelynching celebration. So blood lust and belligerence were testing new levels.

Threepio was way out of his depth. At the moment, he was being forced to translate an argument between Ephant Mon and Ree-Yees, concerning a point of quark warfare that was marginally beyond him. Ephant Mon, a bulky upright pachydermoid with an ugly, betusked snout, was taking (to Threepio's way of thinking) an untenable position. However, on his shoulder sat Salacious Crumb, the insane little reptilian monkey who had the habit of repeating verbatim everything Ephant said, thereby effectively doubling the weight of Ephant's argument.

Ephant concluded the oration with a typically bellicose avowal. 'Woossie jawamba boog!'

To which Salacious nodded, then added, 'Woossie jawamba boog!'

Threepio didn't really want to translate this to Ree-Yees, the three-eyed goat-face who was already drunk as a spicer, but he did.

All three eyes dilated in fury. 'Backawa! Backawa!' Without further preamble, he punched Ephant Mon in the snout, sending him flying into a school of Squid Heads.

See Threepio felt this response needed no translation, and took the opportunity to slip to the rear – where he promptly bumped into a small droid serving drinks. The drinks spilled everywhere.

The stubby little droid let out a fluent series of irate beeps, toots, and whistles – recognizable to Threepio instantly. He looked down in utter relief. 'Artoo! What are you doing here?'

'dooo WEEp chWHRrrrree bedzhng.'

'I can see you're serving drinks. But this place is dangerous. They're going to execute Master Luke, and if we're not careful, us too!'

Artoo whistled – a bit nonchalantly, as far as Threepio was concerned. 'I wish I had your confidence,' he replied glumly.

Jabba chuckled to see Ephant Mon go down – he loved a good beating. He especially loved to see strength crumble, to see the proud fall.

He tugged, with his swollen fingers, on the chain attached to

Princess Leia's neck. The more resistance he met with, the more he drooled – until he'd drawn the struggling, scantily-clad princess close to him once more.

'Don't stray too far, my lovely. Soon you will begin to appreciate me.' He pulled her very near and forced her to drink from his glass.

Leia opened her mouth and she closed her mind. It was disgusting, of course; but there were worse things, and in any case, this wouldn't last.

The worse things she knew well. Her standard of comparison was the night she'd been tortured by Darth Vader. She had almost broken. The Dark Lord never knew how close he'd come to extracting the information he wanted from her, the location of the Rebel base. He had captured her just after she'd managed to send Artoo and Threepio for help – captured her, taken her to the Death Star, injected her with mind-weakening chemicals . . . and tortured her.

Tortured her body first, with his efficient pain-droids. Needles, pressure points, fire-knives, electrojabbers. She'd endured these pains, as she now endured Jabba's loathsome touch – with a natural, inner strength.

She slid a few feet away from Jabba, now, as his attention was distracted – moved to peer out the slats in the louvered windows, to squint through the dusty sunlight at the skiff on which her rescuers were being carried.

It was stopping.

The whole convoy was stopping, in fact, over a huge sand pit. The Sail Barge moved to one side of the giant depression, with the escort skiff. The prisoners' skiff hovered directly over the pit, though, perhaps twenty feet in the air.

At the bottom of the deep cone of sand, a repulsive, mucus-lined, pink, membranous hole puckered, almost unmoving. The hole was eight feet in diameter, its perimeter clustered with three rows of inwardly-directed needle-sharp teeth. Sand stuck to the mucus that lined the sides of the opening, occasionally sliding into the black cavity at the center.

This was the mouth of the Sarlacc.

An iron plank was extended over the side of the prisoners' skiff. Two guards untied Luke's bonds and shoved him gruffly out onto the plank, straight above the orifice in the sand, now beginning to undulate in peristaltic movement and salivate with increased mucus secretion as it smelled the meat it was about to receive.

Jabba moved his party up to the observation deck.

Luke rubbed his wrists to restore circulation. The heat shimmering off the desert warmed his soul – for finally, this would always be his home. Born and bred in a Bantha patch. He saw Leia standing at the rail of the big barge, and winked. She winked back.

Jabba motioned Threepio to his side, then mumbled orders to the golden droid. Threepio stepped up to the comlink. Jabba raised his arm, and the whole motley array of intergalactic pirates fell silent. Threepio's voice arose, amplified by the loudspeaker.

'His Excellency hopes you will die honorably,' Threepio announced. This did not scan at all. Someone had obviously mislaid the correct program. Nonetheless, *he* was only a *droid*, his functions well delineated. Translation only, no free will *please*. He shook his head and continued. 'But should any of you wish to beg for mercy, Jabba will now listen to your pleas.'

Han stepped forward to give the bloated slime pot his last thoughts, in case all else failed. 'You tell that slimy piece of worm-ridden filth—'

Unfortunately, Han was facing into the desert, away from the Sail Barge. Chewie reached over and turned Solo around, so he was now properly facing the piece of worm-ridden filth he was addressing.

Han nodded, without stopping. ' – worm-ridden filth he'll get no such pleasure from us.'

Chewie made a few growly noises of general agreement.

Luke was ready. 'Jabba, this is your last chance,' he shouted. 'Free us or die.' He shot a quick look to Lando, who moved unobtrusively toward the back of the skiff. This was it, Lando figured – they'd just toss the guards overboard and take off under everyone's nose.

The monsters on the barge roared with laughter. Artoo, during this commotion, rolled silently up the ramp to the side of the upper deck.

Jabba raised his hand, and his minions were quiet. 'I'm sure you're right, my young Jedi friend,' he smiled. Then he turned his thumb down. 'Put him in.'

The spectators cheered, as Luke was prodded to the edge of the plank by Weequay. Luke looked up at Artoo, standing alone by the rail, and flipped the little droid a jaunty salute. At that prearranged signal, a flap slid open in Artoo's domed head, and a projectile shot high into the air and curved in a gentle arc over the desert.

Luke jumped off the plank; another bloodthirsty cheer went up. In less than a second, though, Luke had spun around in freefall, and caught the end of the plank with his fingertips. The thin metal bent wildly from his weight, paused near to snapping, then catapulted him up. In mid-air he did a complete flip and dropped down in the middle of the plank – the spot he'd just left, only now behind the confused guards. Casually, he extended his arm to his side, palm up – and suddenly, his lightsaber, which Artoo had shot sailing toward him, dropped neatly into his open hand.

With Jedi speed, Luke ignited his sword and attacked the guard at the skiff-edge of the plank, sending him, screaming, overboard into the twitching mouth of the Sarlacc.

The other guards swarmed toward Luke. Grimly he waded into them, lightsaber flashing.

His own lightsaber – not his father's. He had lost his father's in the duel with Darth Vader in which he'd lost his hand as well. Darth Vader, who had told Luke *he* was his father.

But this lightsaber Luke had fashioned himself, in Obi-Wan Kenobi's abandoned hut on the other side of Tatooine – made with the old Master Jedi's tools and parts, made with love and craft and dire need. He wielded it now as if it were fused to his hand; as if it were an extension of his own arm. This lightsaber, truly, was Luke's.

He cut through the onslaught like a light dissolving shadows.

Lando grappled with the helmsman, trying to seize the controls of the skiff. The helmsman's laser pistol fired, blasting the nearby panel; and the skiff lurched to the side, throwing another guard into the pit, knocking everyone else into a pile on the deck. Luke picked himself up and ran toward the helmsman, lightsaber raised. The creature retreated at the overpowering sight, stumbled . . . and he, too, went over the edge, into the maw.

The bewildered guard landed in the soft, sandy slope of the pit and began an inexorable slide down toward the toothy, viscous opening. He clawed desperately at the sand, screaming. Suddenly a muscled tentacle oozed out of the Sarlacc's mouth, slithered up the caked sand, coiled tightly around the helmsman's ankle, and pulled him into the hole with a grotesque slurp.

All this happened in a matter of seconds. When he saw what was happening, Jabba exploded in a rage, and yelled furious commands at those around him. In a moment, there was general uproar, with creatures running through every door. It was during this direction-less confusion that Leia acted.

She jumped onto Jabba's throne, grabbed the chain which enslaved her, and wrapped it around his bulbous throat. Then she dove off the other side of the support, pulling the chain violently in her grasp. The small metal rings buried themselves in the loose folds of the Hutt's neck, like a garrote.

With a strength beyond her own strength, she pulled. He bucked with his huge torso, nearly breaking her fingers, nearly yanking her arms from their sockets. He could get no leverage, his bulk was too unwieldy. But just his sheer mass was almost enough to break any mere physical restraint.

Yet Leia's hold was not merely physical. She closed her eyes, closed out the pain in her hands, focused all of her life-force – and all it was able to channel – into squeezing the breath from the horrid creature.

She pulled, she sweated, she visualized the chain digging millimeter by millimeter deeper into Jabba's windpipe – as Jabba wildly thrashed, frantically twisted from this least expected of foes.

With a last gasping effort, Jabba tensed every muscle and lurched forward. His reptilian eyes began to bulge from their sockets as the chain tightened; his oily tongue flopped from his mouth. His thick tail twitched in spasms of effort, until he finally lay still – deadweight.

Leia set about trying to free herself from the chain at her neck, while outside, the battle began to rage.

Boba Fett ignited his rocket pack, leaped into the air, and with a single effort flew down from the barge to the skiff just as Luke finished freeing Han and Chewie from their bonds. Boba aimed his laser gun at Luke, but before he could fire, the young Jedi spun around, sweeping his lightsword in an arc that sliced the bounty hunter's gun in half.

A series of blasts suddenly erupted from the large cannon on the upper deck of the barge, hitting the skiff broadside, and rocking it forty degrees askew. Lando was tossed from the deck, but at the last moment he grabbed a broken strut and dangled desperately above the Sarlacc. This development was definitely not in his game plan, and he vowed to himself never again to get involved in a con that he didn't run from start to finish.

The skiff took another direct hit from the barge's deck gun, throwing Chewie and Han against the rail. Wounded, the Wookiee howled in pain. Luke looked over at his hairy friend; whereupon Boba Fett, taking advantage of that moment of distraction, fired a cable from out of his armored sleeve.

The cable wrapped itself several times around Luke, pinning his arms to his sides, his sword arm now free only from the wrist down. He bent his wrist, so the lightsaber pointed straight up ... and then spun toward Boba along the cable. In a moment, the lightsaber touched the end of the wire lasso, cutting through it instantly. Luke shrugged the cable away, just as another blast hit the skiff, knocking Boba unconscious to the deck. Unfortunately this explosion also dislodged the strut from which Lando was hanging, sending him careening into the Sarlacc pit.

Luke was shaken by the explosion, but unhurt. Lando hit the sandy slope, shouted for help, and tried to scramble out. The loose sand only tumbled him deeper toward the gaping hole. Lando closed his eyes and tried to think of all the ways he might give the Sarlacc a thousand years of indigestion. He bet himself three to two he could outlast anybody else in the creature's stomach. Maybe if he talked that last guard out of his uniform ...

'Don't move!' Luke screamed, but his attention was immediately diverted by the incoming second skiff, full of guards firing their weapons.

It was a Jedi rule-of-thumb, but it took the soldiers in the second skiff by surprise: when outnumbered, attack. This drives the force of the enemy in toward himself. Luke jumped directly into the center of the skiff and immediately began decimating them in their midst with lightning sweeps of his lightsaber.

Back in the other boat, Chewie tried to untangle himself from the wreckage, as Han struggled blindly to his feet. Chewie barked at him, trying to direct him toward a spear lying loose on the deck.

Lando screamed, starting to slide closer to the glistening jaws. He was a gambling man, but he wouldn't have taken long odds on his chances of escape right now.

'Don't move, Lando!' Han called out. 'I'm coming!' Then, to Chewie: 'Where is it, Chewie?' He swung his hands frantically over the deck as Chewie growled directions, guiding Solo's movements. At last, Han locked onto the spear.

Boba Fett stumbled up just then, still a little dizzy from the exploding shell. He looked over at the other skiff, where Luke was in a pitched battle with six guards. With one hand Boba steadied himself on the rail; with the other he aimed his weapon at Luke.

Chewie barked at Han.

'Which way?' shouted Solo. Chewie barked.

The blinded space pirate swung his long spear in Boba's direction. Instinctively, Fett blocked the blow with his forearm; again, he aimed at Luke. 'Get out of my way, you blind fool,' he cursed Solo.

Chewie barked frantically. Han swung his spear again, this time in the opposite direction, landing the hit squarely in the middle of Boba's rocket pack.

The impact caused the rocket to ignite. Boba blasted off unexpectedly, shooting over the second skiff like a missile and ricocheting straight down into the pit. His armored body slid quickly past Lando and rolled without pause into the Sarlacc's mouth.

'Rrgrrowrrbroo fro bo,' Chewie growled.

'He did?' Solo smiled. 'I wish I could have seen that—'

A major hit from the barge deck gun flipped the skiff on its side, sending Han and almost everything else overboard. His foot caught on the railing, though, leaving him swinging precariously above the Sarlacc. The wounded Wookiee tenaciously held on to the twisted debris astern.

Luke finished going through his adversaries on the second skiff, assessed the problem quickly, and leaped across the chasm of sand to the sheer metal side of the huge barge. Slowly, he began a hand-over-hand climb up the hull, toward the deck gun.

Meanwhile, on the observation deck, Leia had been intermittently struggling to break the chain which bound her to the dead gangster, and hiding behind his massive carcass whenever some guard ran by. She stretched her full length, now, trying to retrieve a discarded laser pistol – to no avail. Fortunately, Artoo at last came to her rescue, after having first lost his bearings and rolled down the wrong plank.

He zipped up to her finally, extended a cutting appendage from the side of his casing, and sliced through her bonds.

'Thanks, Artoo, good work. Now let's get out of here.'

They raced for the door. On the way, they passed Threepio, lying on the floor, screaming, as a giant, tuberous hulk named Hermi Odle sat on him. Salacious Crumb, the reptilian monkey-monster, crouched by Threepio's head, picking out the golden droid's right eye.

'No! No! Not my eyes!' Threepio screamed.

Artoo sent a bolt of charge into Hermi Odle's backside, sending him wailing through a window. A similar flash blasted Salacious to the ceiling, from which he didn't come down. Threepio quickly rose, his eye dangling from a sheaf of wires; then he and Artoo hurriedly followed Leia out the back door.

The deck gun blasted the tilting skiff once more, shaking out virtually everything that remained inside except Chewbacca. Desperately holding on with his injured arm, he was stretching over the rail, grasping the ankle of the dangling Solo, who was, in turn, sightlessly reaching down for the terrified Calrissian. Lando had managed to stop his slippage by lying very still. Now, every time he reached up for Solo's outstretched arm, the loose sand slid him a fraction closer to the hungry hole. He sure hoped Solo wasn't still holding that silly business back on Bespin against him.

Chewie barked another direction at Han.

'Yeah, I know, I can see a lot better now – it must be all the blood rushing to my head.'

'Great,' Lando called up. 'Now could you just grow a few inches taller?'

The deck gunners on the barge were lining up this human chain in their sights for the coup de grace, when Luke stepped in front of them, laughing like a pirate king. He lit his lightsaber before they could squeeze off a shot; a moment later they were smoking corpses.

A company of guards suddenly rushed up the steps from the lower decks, firing. One of the blasts shot Luke's lightsaber from his hand. He ran down the deck, but was quickly surrounded. Two of the soldiers manned the deck gun again. Luke looked at his hand; the mechanism was exposed – the complex steel-and-circuit construction that replaced his real hand, which Vader had cut off in their last encounter.

He flexed the mechanism; it still worked.

The deck gunners fired at the skiff below. It hit to the side of the small boat. The shock wave almost knocked Chewie loose, but in tipping the boat further, Han was able to grab onto Lando's wrist.

'Pull!' Solo yelled at the Wookiee.

'I'm caught!' screamed Calrissian. He looked down in panic to see one of the Sarlacc's tentacles slowly wrap around his ankle. Talk about a wild card – they kept changing the rules every five minutes in this game. Tentacles! What kind of odds was anybody gonna give on tentacles? Very long, he decided with a fatalistic grunt; long, and sticky.

The deck gunners realigned their sights for the final kill, but it was all over for them before they could fire – Leia had commandeered the second deck gun, at the other end of the ship. With her first shot she blasted the rigging that stood between the two deck guns. With her second shot she wiped out the first deck gun.

The explosions rocked the great barge, momentarily distracting the five guards who surrounded Luke. In that moment he reached out his hand, and the lightsaber, lying on the deck ten feet away, flew into it. He leaped straight up as two guards fired at him – their laser bolts killed each other. He ignited his blade in the air and, swinging it as he came down, mortally wounded the others.

He yelled to Leia across the deck. 'Point it down!'

She tilted the second deck gun into the deck and nodded to Threepio at the rail.

Artoo, beside him, beeped wildly.

'I can't, Artoo!' Threepio cried. 'It's too far to jump . . . aaahhh!'

Artoo butted the golden droid over the edge, and then stepped off himself, tumbling head over wheels toward the sand.

Meanwhile, the tug-of-war was continuing between the Sarlacc and Solo, with Baron Calrissian as the rope and the prize. Chewbacca held Han's leg, braced himself on the rail, and succeeded in pulling a laser pistol out of the wreckage with his other hand. He aimed the gun toward Lando, then lowered it, barking his concern.

'He's right!' Lando called out. 'It's too far!'

Solo looked up. 'Chewie, give me the gun.'

Chewbacca gave it to him. He took it with one hand, still holding on to Lando with the other.

'Now, wait a second, pal,' Lando protested, 'I thought you were blind.'

'I'm better, trust me,' Solo assured him.

'Do I have a choice? Hey! A little higher, please.' He lowered his head.

Han squinted ... pulled the trigger ... and scored a direct hit on the tentacle. The wormy thing instantly released its grip, slithering back into its own mouth.

Chewbacca pulled mightily, drawing first Solo back into the boat – and then Lando.

Luke, meantime, gathered Leia up in his left arm; with his right he grabbed a hold of a rope from the rigging of the half blown-down mast, and with his foot kicked the trigger of the second deck gun – and jumped into the air as the cannon exploded into the deck.

The two of them swung on the swaying rope, all the way down to the empty, hovering escort skiff. Once there, Luke steered it over to the still-listing prison skiff, where he helped Chewbacca, Han, and Lando on board.

The Sail Barge continued exploding behind them. Half of it was now on fire.

Luke guided the skiff around beside the barge, where See Threepio's legs could be seen sticking straight up out of the sand. Beside them, Artoo Detoo's periscope was the only part of his anatomy visible above the dune. The skiff stopped just above them and lowered a large electromagnet from its compartment in the boat's helm. With a loud clang, the two droids shot out of the sand and locked to the magnet's plate.

'Ow,' groaned Threepio.

'beeeDOO dwEET!' Artoo agreed.

In a few minutes, they were all in the skiff together, more or less in one piece; and for the first time, they looked at one another and realized they were all in the skiff together, more or less in one piece. There was a great, long moment of hugging, laughing, crying, and beeping. Then someone accidentally squeezed Chewbacca's wounded arm, and he bellowed; and then they all ran about, securing the boat, checking the perimeters, looking for supplies – and sailing away.

The great Sail Barge settled slowly in a chain of explosions and violent fires, and – as the little skiff flew quietly off across the desert – disappeared finally in a brilliant conflagration that was only partially diminished by the scorching afternoon light of Tatooine's twin suns.

III

THE sandstorm obscured everything – sight, breath, thought, motion. The roar of it alone was disorienting, sounding like it came from everywhere at once, as if the universe were composed of noise, and this was its chaotic center.

The seven heroes walked step by step through the murky gale, holding on to one another so as not to get lost. Artoo was first, following the signal of the homing device which sang to him in a language not garbled by the wind. Threepio came next, then Leia guiding Han, and finally Luke and Lando, supporting the hobbling Wookiee.

Artoo beeped loudly, and they all looked up: vague, dark shapes could be seen through the typhoon.

'I don't know,' shouted Han. 'All I can see is a lot of blowing sand.'

'That's all any of us can see,' Leia shouted back.

'Then I guess I'm getting better.'

For a few steps, the dark shapes grew darker; and then out of the darkness, the *Millennium Falcon* appeared, flanked by Luke's X-wing and a two-seater Y-wing. As soon as the group huddled under the bulk of the *Falcon*, the wind died down to something more describable as a severe weather condition. Threepio hit a switch, and the gangplank lowered with a hum.

Solo turned to Skywalker. 'I've got to hand it to you, kid, you were pretty good out there.'

Luke shrugged it off. 'I had a lot of help.' He started toward his X-wing.

Han stopped him, his manner suddenly quieter, even serious. 'Thanks for coming after me, Luke.'

Luke felt embarrassed for some reason. He didn't know how to respond to anything but a wisecrack from the old pirate. 'Think nothing of it,' he finally said.

'No, I'm thinkin' a lot about it. That carbon freeze was the closest thing to dead there is. And it wasn't just sleepin', it was a big, wide awake Nothin'.'

A Nothing from which Luke and the others had saved him – put their own lives in great peril at his expense, for no other reason than that . . . he was their friend. This was a new idea for the cocky Solo – at once terrible and wonderful. There was jeopardy in this turn of events. It made him feel somehow blinder than before, but visionary as well. It was confusing. Once, he was alone; now he was a part.

That realization made him feel indebted, a feeling he'd always abhorred; only now the debt was somehow a new kind of bond, a bond of brotherhood. It was even freeing, in a strange way.

He was no longer so alone.

No longer alone.

Luke saw a difference had come over his friend, like a sea change. It was a gentle moment; he didn't want to disturb it. So he only nodded.

Chewie growled affectionately at the young Jedi warrior, mussing his hair like a proud uncle. And Leia warmly hugged him.

They all had great love for Solo, but somehow it was easier to show it by being demonstrative to Luke.

'I'll see you back at the fleet,' Luke called, moving toward his ship.

'Why don't you leave that crate and come with us?' Solo nudged.

'I have a promise I have to keep first . . . to an old friend.' A *very* old friend, he smiled to himself in afterthought.

'Well, hurry back,' Leia urged. 'The entire Alliance should be assembled by now.' She saw something in Luke's face; she couldn't put a name to it, but it scared her, and simultaneously made her feel closer to him. 'Hurry back,' she repeated.

'I will,' he promised. 'Come on, Artoo.'

Artoo rolled toward the X-wing, beeping a farewell to Threepio.

'Good-bye, Artoo,' Threepio called out fondly. 'May the Maker bless you. You will watch out for him, won't you, Master Luke?'

But Luke and the little droid were already gone, on the far side of the flyer.

The others stood without moving for a moment, trying to see their futures in the swirling sand.

Lando jarred them awake. 'Come on, let's get off this miserable dirt ball.' His luck here had been abominable; he hoped to fare better in the next game. It would be house rules for a while, he knew; but he might be able to load a few dice along the way.

Solo clapped him on the back. 'Guess I owe you some thanks too, Lando.'

'Figured if I left you frozen like that you'd just give me bad luck the rest of my life, so I might as well get you unfrozen sooner, as later.'

'He means "you're welcome."' Leia smiled. 'We all mean you're welcome.' She kissed Han on the cheek to say it personally one more time.

They all headed up the ramp of the *Falcon*. Solo paused just before going inside and gave the ship a little pat. 'You're lookin' good, old girl. I never thought I'd live to see you again.'

He entered at last, closing the hatch behind him.

Luke did the same in the X-wing. He strapped himself into the cockpit, started up the engines, felt the comfortable roar. He looked at his damaged hand: wires crossed aluminum bones like spokes in a puzzle. He wondered what the solution was. Or the puzzle, for that matter. He pulled a black glove over the exposed infrastructure, set the X-wing's controls, and for the second time in his life, he rocketed off his home planet, into the stars.

The Super Star Destroyer rested in space above the half-completed Death Star battle station and its green neighbor, Endor. The Destroyer was a massive ship, attended by numerous smaller warships of various kinds, which hovered or darted around the great mother ship like children of different ages and temperaments: medium range fleet cruisers, bulky cargo vessels, TIE fighter escorts.

The main bay of the Destroyer opened, space-silent. An Imperial shuttle emerged and accelerated toward the Death Star, accompanied by four squads of fighters.

Darth Vader watched their approach on the view-screen in the control room of the Death Star. When docking was imminent, he marched out of the command center, followed by Commander Jerjerrod and a phalanx of Imperial stormtroopers, and headed toward the docking bay. He was about to welcome his master.

Vader's pulse and breathing were machine-regulated, so they could not quicken; but something in his chest became more electric around his meetings with the Emperor; he could not say how. A feeling of fullness, of power, of dark and demon mastery – of secret lusts, unrestrained passion, wild submission – all these things were in Vader's heart as he neared his Emperor. These things and more.

When he entered the docking bay, thousands of Imperial troops snapped to attention with a momentous clap. The shuttle came to rest on the pod. Its ramp lowered like a dragon jaw, and the Emperor's royal guard ran down, red robes flapping, as if they were licks of flame shooting out the mouth to herald the angry roar. They poised themselves at watchful guard in two lethal rows beside the ramp. Silence filled the great hall. At the top of the ramp, the Emperor appeared.

Slowly, he walked down. A small man was he, shriveled with age and evil. He supported his bent frame on a gnarled cane and covered himself with a long, hooded robe – much like the robe of the Jedi, only black. His shrouded face was so thin of flesh it was nearly a skull; his piercing yellow eyes seemed to burn through all at which they stared.

When the Emperor reached the bottom of the ramp, Commander Jerjerrod, his generals, and Lord Vader all kneeled before him. The Supreme Dark Ruler beckoned to Vader, and began walking down the row of troops.

'Rise, my friend, I would talk with you.'

Vader rose, and accompanied his master. They were followed in procession by the Emperor's courtiers, the royal guard, Jerjerrod, and the Death Star elite guard, with mixed reverence and fear.

Vader felt complete at the Emperor's side. Though the emptiness at his core never left him, it became a glorious emptiness in the glare of the Emperor's cold light, an exalted void that could encompass the universe. And someday *would* encompass the universe . . . when the Emperor was dead.

For that was Vader's final dream. When he'd learned all he could of the dark power from this evil genius, to take that power from him, seize it and keep its cold light at his own core – kill the Emperor and devour his darkness, and rule the universe. Rule with his son at his side.

For that was his other dream – to reclaim his boy, to show Luke the majesty of this shadow force: why it was so potent, why he'd chosen rightly to follow its path. And Luke would come with him, he knew. That seed was sown. They would rule together, father and son.

His dream was very close to realization, he could feel it; it was near. Each event fell into place, as he'd nudged it, with Jedi subtlety; as he'd pressed, with delicate dark strength.

'The Death Star will be completed on schedule, my master,' Vader breathed.

'Yes, I know,' replied the Emperor. 'You have done well, Lord Vader . . . and now I sense you wish to continue your search for the young Skywalker.'

Vader smiled beneath his armored mask. The Emperor always knew the sense of what was in his heart; even if he didn't know the specifics. 'Yes, my master.'

'Patience, my friend,' the Supreme Ruler cautioned. 'You always had difficulty showing patience. In time, *he* will seek *you* out . . . and when he does, you must bring him before me. He has grown strong. Only together can we turn him to the dark side of the Force.'

'Yes, my master.' Together, they would corrupt the boy – the child of the father. Great, dark glory. For soon, the old Emperor would die – and though the galaxy would bend from the horror of that loss, Vader would remain to rule, with young Skywalker at his side. As it was always meant to be.

The Emperor raised his head a degree, scanning all the possible futures. 'Everything is proceeding as I have foreseen.'

He, like Vader, had plans of his own – plans of spiritual violation, the manipulation of lives and destinies. He chuckled to himself, savoring the nearness of his conquest: the final seduction of the young Skywalker.

Luke left his X-wing parked at the edge of the water and carefully picked his way through the adjoining swamp. A heavy mist hung in layers about him. Jungle steam. A strange insect flew at him from out of a cluster of hanging vines, fluttered madly about his head, and vanished. In the undergrowth, something snarled. Luke concentrated momentarily. The snarling stopped. Luke walked on.

He had terribly ambivalent feelings about this place. Dagobah. His place of tests, of training to be a Jedi. This was where he'd truly learned to use the Force, to let it flow through him to whatever end he directed it. So he'd learned how caretaking he must be in order to use the Force well. It was walking on light; but to a Jedi it was as stable as an earthen floor.

Dangerous creatures lurked in this swamp; but to a Jedi, none were evil. Voracious quicksand mires waited, still as pools; tentacles mingled with the hanging vines. Luke knew them all, now, they were all part of the living planet, each integral to the Force of which he, too, was a pulsing aspect.

Yet there were dark things here, as well – unimaginably dark, reflections of the dark corners of his soul. He'd seen these things here. He'd run from them, he'd struggled with them; he'd even faced them. He'd vanquished some of them.

But some still cowered here. These dark things.

He climbed around a barricade of gnarled roots, slippery with moss. On the other side, a smooth, unimpeded path led straight in the direction he wanted to go; but he did not take it. Instead, he plunged once more into the undergrowth.

High overhead, something black and flapping approached, then veered away. Luke paid no attention. He just kept walking.

The jungle thinned a bit. Beyond the next bog, Luke saw it – the small, strangely-shaped dwelling, its odd little windows shedding a warm yellow light in the damp rain-forest. He skirted the mire, and crouching low, entered the cottage.

Yoda stood smiling inside, his small green hand clutching his walking stick for support. 'Waiting for you I was,' he nodded.

He motioned Luke to sit in a corner. The boy was struck by how much more frail Yoda's manner seemed – a tremor to the hand, a weakness to the voice. It made Luke afraid to speak, to betray his shock at the old master's condition.

'That face you make,' Yoda crinkled his tired brow cheerfully. 'Look I so bad to young eyes?'

He tried to conceal his woeful countenance, shifting his position in the cramped space. 'No, Master ... of course not.'

'I do, yes, I do!' the tiny Jedi Master chuckled gleefully. 'Sick I've become. Yes. Old and weak.' He pointed a crooked finger at his young pupil. 'When nine hundred years old you reach, look as good you will not.'

The creature hobbled over to his bed, still chuckling and, with great effort, lay down. 'Soon will I rest. Yes, forever sleep. Earned it, I have.'

Luke shook his head. 'You can't die, Master Yoda – I won't let you.'

'Trained well, and strong with the Force are you – but not that strong! Twilight is upon me, and soon night must fall. That is the way of things ... the way of the Force.'

'But I need your help,' Luke insisted. 'I want to complete my training.' The great teacher couldn't leave him now – there was too much, still, to understand. And he'd taken so much from Yoda already, and as yet given back nothing. He had much he wanted to share with the old creature.

'No more training do you require,' Yoda assured him. 'Already know you that which you need.'

'Then I am a Jedi?' Luke pressed. No. He knew he was not, quite. Something still lacked.

Yoda wrinkled up his wizened features. 'Not yet. One thing remains. Vader ... Vader you must confront. Then, only then, a full Jedi you'll be. And confront him you will, sooner or later.'

Luke knew this would be his test, it could not be otherwise. Every quest had its focus, and Vader was inextricably at the core of Luke's struggle. It was agonizing for him to put the question to words; but after a long silence, he again spoke to the old Jedi. 'Master Yoda – is Darth Vader my father?'

Yoda's eyes filled with a weary compassion. This boy was not yet a man complete. A sad smile creased his face, he seemed almost to grow smaller in his bed. 'A rest I need. Yes. A rest.'

Luke stared at the dwindling teacher, trying to give the old one strength, just by the force of his love and will. 'Yoda, I must know,' he whispered.

'Your father he is,' Yoda said simply.

Luke closed his eyes, his mouth, his heart, to keep away the truth of what he knew was true.

'Told you, did he?' Yoda asked.

Luke nodded, but did not speak. He wanted to keep the moment frozen, to shelter it here, to lock time and space in this room, so it could never escape into the rest of the universe with this terrible knowledge, this unrelenting truth.

A look of concern filled Yoda's face. 'Unexpected this is, and unfortunate—'

'Unfortunate that I know the truth?' A bitterness crept into Luke's voice, but he couldn't decide if it was directed at Vader, Yoda, himself, or the universe at large.

Yoda gathered himself up with an effort that seemed to take all his strength. 'Unfortunate that you rushed to face him – that incomplete your training was . . . that not ready for the burden were you. Obi-Wan would have told you long ago, had I let him . . . now a great weakness you carry. Fear for you, I do. Fear for you, yes.' A great tension seemed to pass out of him and he closed his eyes.

'Master Yoda, I'm sorry.' Luke trembled to see the potent Jedi so weak.

'I know, but face Vader again you must, and sorry will not help.' He leaned forward, and beckoned Luke close to him. Luke crawled over to sit beside his master. Yoda continued, his voice increasingly frail. 'Remember, a Jedi's strength flows from the Force. When you rescued your friends, you had revenge in your heart. Beware of anger, fear, and aggression. The dark side are they. Easily they flow, quick to join you in a fight. Once you start down the dark path, forever will it dominate your destiny.'

He lay back in bed, his breathing became shallow. Luke waited quietly, afraid to move, afraid to distract the old one an iota, lest it jar his attention even a fraction from the business of just keeping the void at bay.

After a few minutes, Yoda looked at the boy once more, and with a maximum effort, smiled gently, the greatness of his spirit the only thing keeping his decrepit body alive. 'Luke – of the Emperor beware. Do not underestimate his powers, or suffer your father's fate you will. When gone I am . . . last of the Jedi will you be. Luke, the Force is strong in your family. Pass on what you . . . have . . . learned . . .' He began to falter, he closed his eyes. 'There . . . is . . . another . . . sky . . .'

He caught his breath, and exhaled, his spirit passing from him like a sunny wind blowing to another sky. His body shivered once; and he disappeared.

Luke sat beside the small, empty bed for over an hour, trying to fathom the depth of this loss. It was unfathomable.

His first feeling was one of boundless grief. For himself, for the universe. How could such a one as Yoda be gone forever? It felt like a black, bottomless hole had filled his heart, where the part that was Yoda had lived.

Luke had known the passing of old mentors before. It was helplessly sad; and inexorably, a part of his own growing. Is this what coming of age was, then? Watching beloved friends grow old and die? Gaining a new measure of strength or maturity from their powerful passages?

A great weight of hopelessness settled upon him, just as all the lights in the little cottage flickered out. For several more minutes he sat there, feeling it was the end of everything, that all the lights in the universe had flickered out. The last Jedi, sitting in a swamp, while the entire galaxy plotted the last war.

A chill came over him, though, disturbing the nothingness into which his consciousness had lapsed. He shivered, looked around. The gloom was impenetrable.

He crawled outside and stood up. Here in the swamp, nothing had changed. Vapor congealed, to drip from dangling roots back into the mire, in a cycle it had repeated a million times, would repeat forever. Perhaps *there* was his lesson. If so, it cut his sadness not a whit.

Aimlessly he made his way back to where his ship rested. Artoo rushed up, beeping his excited greeting; but Luke was disconsolate, and could only ignore the faithful little droid. Artoo whistled a brief condolence, then remained respectfully silent.

Luke sat dejectedly on a log, put his head in his hands, and spoke softly to himself. 'I can't do it. I can't go on alone.'

A voice floated down to him on the dim mist. 'Yoda and I will be with you always.' It was Ben's voice.

Luke turned around swiftly to see the shimmering image of Obi-Wan Kenobi standing behind him. 'Ben!' he whispered. There were so many things he wanted to say, they rushed through his mind all in a whirl, like the churning, puffed cargo of a ship in a maelstrom. But one question rose quickly to the surface above all the others.

'Why, Ben? Why didn't you tell me?'

It was not an empty question. 'I was going to tell you when you had completed your training,' the vision of Ben answered. 'But you found it necessary to rush off unprepared. I warned you about your impatience.' His voice was unchanged, a hint of scolding, a hint of love.

'You told me Darth Vader betrayed and murdered my father.' The bitterness he'd felt earlier, with Yoda, had found its focus now on Ben.

Ben absorbed the vitriol undefensively, then padded it with instruction. 'Your father, Anakin, was seduced by the dark side of the Force – he ceased to be Anakin Skywalker, and became Darth Vader. When that happened, he betrayed everything that Anakin Skywalker believed in. The good man who was your father was destroyed. So what I told you was true ... from a certain point of view.'

'A certain point of view!' Luke rasped derisively. He felt betrayed – by life more than anything else, though only poor Ben was available to take the brunt of his conflict.

'Luke,' Ben spoke gently, 'you're going to find that many of the truths we cling to depend greatly on our point of view.'

Luke turned unresponsive. He wanted to hold onto his fury, to guard it like a treasure. It was all he had, he would not let it be stolen from him, as everything else had been stolen. But already he felt it slipping, softened by Ben's compassionate touch.

'I don't blame you for being angry,' Ben coaxed. 'If I was wrong in what I did, it certainly wouldn't have been for the first time. You see, what happened to your father was my fault ...'

Luke looked up with sudden acute interest. He'd never heard this and was rapidly losing his anger to fascination and curiosity – for knowledge was an addictive drug, and the more he had the more he wanted.

As he sat on his stump, increasingly mesmerized, Artoo pedaled over, silent, just to offer a comforting presence.

'When I first encountered your father,' Ben continued, 'he was already a great pilot. But what amazed me was how strongly the Force was with him. I took it upon myself to train Anakin in the ways of the Jedi. My mistake was thinking I could be as good a teacher as Yoda. I was not. Such was my foolish pride. The Emperor sensed Anakin's power, and he lured him to the dark side.' He paused sadly and looked directly into Luke's eyes, as if he were asking for the boy's forgiveness. 'My pride had terrible consequences for the galaxy.'

Luke was entranced. That Obi-Wan's hubris could have caused his father's fall was horrible. Horrible because of what his father had needlessly become, horrible because Obi-Wan wasn't perfect, wasn't even a perfect Jedi, horrible because the dark side could strike so close to home, could turn such right so wrong. Darth Vader must yet have a spark of Anakin Skywalker deep inside. 'There is still good in him,' he declared.

Ben shook his head remorsefully. 'I also thought he could be turned back to the good side. It couldn't be done. He is more machine, now, than man – twisted, and evil.'

Luke sensed the underlying meaning in Kenobi's statement, he heard the words as a command. He shook his head back at the vision. 'I can't kill my own father.'

'You should not think of that machine as your father.' It was the teacher speaking again. 'When I saw what had become of him, I tried to dissuade him, to draw him back from the dark side. We fought ... your father fell into a molten pit. When your father clawed his way out of that fiery pool, the change had been burned into him forever – he was Darth Vader, without a trace of Anakin Skywalker. Irredeemably dark. Scarred. Kept alive only by machinery and his own black will ...'

Luke looked down at his own mechanical right hand. 'I tried to stop him once. I couldn't do it.' He would not challenge his father again. He could not.

'Vader humbled you when first you met him, Luke – but that experience was *part* of your training. It taught you, among other things, the value of patience. Had you not been so impatient to defeat Vader *then*, you could have finished your training here with Yoda. You would have been prepared.'

'But I had to help my friends.'

'And did you help them? It was *they* who had to save *you*. You achieved little by rushing back prematurely, I fear.'

Luke's indignation melted, leaving only sadness in its wake. 'I found out Darth Vader was my father,' he whispered.

'To be a Jedi, Luke, you must confront and then go beyond the dark side – the side your father couldn't get past. Impatience is the easiest door – for you, like your father. Only, your father was seduced by what he found on the other side of the door, and you have held firm. You're no longer so reckless now, Luke. You are strong and patient. And you are ready for your final confrontation.'

Luke shook his head again, as the implications of the old Jedi's speech became clear. 'I can't do it, Ben.'

Obi-Wan Kenobi's shoulders slumped in defeat. 'Then the Emperor has already won. You were our only hope.'

Luke reached for alternatives. 'Yoda said I could train another to . . .'

'The other he spoke of is your twin sister,' the old man offered a dry smile. 'She will find it no easier than you to destroy Darth Vader.'

Luke was visibly jolted by this information. He stood up to face this spirit. 'Sister? I don't have a sister.'

Once again Obi-Wan put a gentle inflection in his voice, to soothe the turmoil brewing in his young friend's soul. 'To protect you both against the Emperor, you were separated when you were born. The Emperor knew, as I did, that one day, with the Force on their side, Skywalker's offspring would be a threat to him. For that reason, your sister has remained safely anonymous.'

Luke resisted this knowledge at first. He neither needed nor wanted a twin. He was unique! He had no missing parts – save the hand whose mechanical replacement he now flexed tightly. Pawn in a castle conspiracy? Cribs mixed, siblings switched and parted and whisked away to different secret lives? Impossible. He knew who he was! He was Luke Skywalker, born to a Jedi-turned-Sithlord, raised on a Tatooine sandfarm by Uncle Owen and Aunt Beru, raised in a life without frills, a hardworking honest pauper – because his mother . . . his mother . . . What was it about his mother? What had she said? Who was she? What had she told him? He turned his mind inward, to a place and time far from the damp soil of Dagobah, to his mother's chamber, his mother and his . . . sister. His sister . . .

'Leia! Leia is my sister,' he exclaimed, nearly falling over the stump.

'Your insight serves you well,' Ben nodded. He quickly became stern, though. 'Bury your feelings deep down, Luke. They do you credit, but they could be made to serve the Emperor.'

Luke tried to comprehend what his old teacher was saying. So much information, so fast, so vital . . . it almost made him swoon.

Ben continued his narrative. 'When your father left, he didn't know your mother was pregnant. Your mother and I knew he would find out eventually, but we wanted to keep you both as safe as possible, for as long as possible. So I took you to live with my brother Owen, on Tatooine . . . and your mother took Leia to live as the daughter of Senator Organa, on Alderaan.'

Luke settled down to hear this tale, as Artoo nestled up beside him, humming in a subaudible register to comfort.

Ben, too, kept his voice even, so that the sounds could give solace when the words did not. 'The Organa family was high-born and politically quite powerful in that system. Leia became a princess by virtue of lineage – no one knew she'd been adopted, of course. But it was a title without real power, since Alderaan had long been a democracy. Even so, the family continued to be politically powerful, and Leia, following in her foster father's path, became a senator as well. That's not all she became, of course – she became the leader of her cell in the Alliance against the corrupt Empire. And because she had diplomatic immunity, she was a vital link for getting information to the Rebel cause.

'That's what she was doing when her path crossed yours – for her foster parents had always told her to contact *me* on Tatooine, if her troubles became desperate.'

Luke tried sorting through his multiplicity of feelings – the love he'd always felt for Leia, even from afar, now had a clear basis. But suddenly he was feeling protective toward her as well, like an older brother – even though, for all he knew, she might have been his elder by several minutes.

'But you can't let her get involved now, Ben,' he insisted. 'Vader will destroy her.' Vader. Their father. Perhaps Leia *could* resurrect the good in him.

'She hasn't been trained in the ways of the Jedi the way you have, Luke – but the Force is strong with her, as it is with all of your family. That is why her path crossed mine – because the Force in her must be nourished by a Jedi. You're the last Jedi, now, Luke . . . but she returned to us – to me – to learn, and grow. Because it was her destiny to learn and grow; and mine to teach.'

He went on more slowly, each word deliberate, each pause emphatic. 'You cannot escape your destiny, Luke.' He locked his eyes on Luke's eyes, and put as much of his spirit as he could into the gaze, to leave it forever imprinted on Luke's mind. 'Keep your sister's identity secret, for if you fail she is truly our last hope. Gaze on me now, Luke – the coming fight is yours alone, but much will depend on its outcome, and it may be that you can draw some strength from my memory. There is no avoiding the battle, though – you can't escape your destiny. You will have to face Darth Vader again . . .'

DARTH Vader stepped out of the long, cylindrical elevator into what had been the Death Star control room, and now was the Emperor's throne room. Two royal guards stood either side of the door, red robes from neck to toe, red helmets covering all but eyeslits that were actually electrically modified view-screens. Their weapons were always drawn.

The room was dim except for the light cables running either side of the elevator shaft, carrying power and information through the space station. Vader walked across the sleek black steel floor, past the humming giant converter engines, up the short flight of steps to the platform level upon which sat the Emperor's throne. Beneath this platform, off to the right, was the mouth of the shaft that delved deeply into the pit of the battle station, down to the very core of the power unit. The chasm was black, and reeked of ozone, and echoed continuously in a low, hollow rumble.

At the end of the overhanging platform was a wall, in the wall, a huge, circular observation window. Sitting in an elaborate control-chair before the window, staring out into space, was the Emperor.

The uncompleted half of the Death Star could be seen immediately beyond the window, shuttles and transports buzzing around it, men with tight-suits and rocket-packs doing exterior construction or surface work. In the near-distance beyond all this activity was the jade green moon Endor, resting like a jewel on the black velvet of space – and scattered to infinity, the gleaming diamonds that were the stars.

The Emperor sat, regarding this view, as Vader approached from behind. The Lord of the Sith kneeled and waited. The Emperor let him wait. He perused the vista before him with a sense of glory beyond all reckoning: this was all his. And more glorious still, all his by his own hand.

For it wasn't always so. Back in the days when he was merely Senator Palpatine, the galaxy had been a Republic of stars, cared for and protected by the Jedi Knighthood that had watched over it for centuries. But inevitably it had grown too large – too massive a bureaucracy had been required, over too many years, in order to maintain the Republic. Corruption had set in.

A few greedy senators had started the chain reaction of malaise, some said; but who could know? A few perverted bureaucrats, arrogant, self-serving – and suddenly a fever was in the stars. Governor turned on governor, values eroded, trusts were broken – fear had spread like an epidemic in those early years, rapidly and without visible cause, and no one knew what was happening, or why.

And so Senator Palpatine had seized the moment. Through fraud, clever promises, and astute political maneuvering, he'd managed to get himself elected head of the Council. And then through sub-terfuge, bribery and terror, he'd named himself Emperor.

Emperor. It had a certain ring to it. The Republic had crumbled, the Empire was resplendent with its own fires, and would always be so – for the Emperor knew what others refused to believe: the dark forces were the strongest.

He'd known this all along, in his heart of hearts – but relearned it every day: from traitorous lieutenants who betrayed their superiors for favors; from weak-principled functionaries who gave him the secrets of local star systems' governments; from greedy landlords, and sadistic gangsters, and power-hungry politicians. No one was immune, they all craved the dark energy at their core. The Emperor had simply recognized this truth, and utilized it – for his own aggrandizement, of course.

For his soul was the black center of the Empire.

He contemplated the dense impenetrability of the deep space beyond the window. Densely black as his soul – as if he *were*, in some real way, this blackness; as if his inner spirit was itself this void over which he reigned. He smiled at the thought: he *was* the Empire; he *was* the Universe.

Behind him, he sensed Vader still waiting in genuflection. How long had the Dark Lord been there? Five minutes? Ten? The Emperor was uncertain. No matter. The Emperor had not quite finished his meditation.

Lord Vader did not mind waiting, though, nor was he even aware of it. For it was an honor, and a noble activity, to kneel at his ruler's feet. He kept his eyes inward, seeking reflection in his own bottomless core. His power was great, now, greater than it had ever been. It shimmered from within, and resonated with the waves of darkness that flowed from the Emperor. He felt engorged with this power; it surged like black fire, demon electrons looking for ground ... but he would wait. For his Emperor was not ready; and his son was not ready, and the time was not yet. So he waited.

Finally the chair slowly rotated until the Emperor faced Vader.

Vader spoke first. 'What is thy bidding, my master?'

'Send the fleet to the far side of Endor. There it will stay until called for.'

'And what of the reports of the Rebel fleet massing near Sullust?'

'It is of no concern. Soon the Rebellion will be crushed and young Skywalker will be one of us. Your work here is finished, my friend. Go out to the command ship and await my orders.'

'Yes, my master.' He hoped he would be given command over the destruction of the Rebel Alliance. He hoped it would be soon.

He rose and exited, as the Emperor turned back to the galactic panorama beyond the window, to view his domain.

In a remote and midnight vacuum beyond the edge of the galaxy, the vast Rebel fleet stretched, from its vanguard to its rear echelon, past the range of human vision. Corellian battle ships, cruisers, destroyers, carriers, bombers, Sullustian cargo freighters, Calamarian tankers, Alderaanian gunships, Kesselian blockade runners, Bestinian sky-hoppers, X-wing, Y-wing, and A-wing fighters, shuttles, transport vehicles, manowars. Every Rebel in the galaxy, soldier and civilian alike, waited tensely in these ships for instructions. They were led by the largest of the Rebel Star Cruisers, the *Headquarters Frigate*.

Hundreds of Rebel commanders, of all species and lifeforms, assembled in the war room of the giant Star Cruiser, awaiting orders from the High Command. Rumors were everywhere, and an air of excitement spread from squadron to squadron.

At the center of the briefing room was a large, circular light-table, projected above which a holographic image of the unfinished Imperial Death Star hovered beside the Moon of Endor, whose scintillating protective deflector shield encompassed them both.

Mon Mothma entered the room. A stately, beautiful woman of middle age, she seemed to walk above the murmurs of the crowd. She wore white robes with gold braiding, and her severity was not without cause – for she was the elected leader of the Rebel Alliance.

Like Leia's adopted father – like Palpatine the Emperor himself – Mon Mothma had been a senior senator of the Republic, a member of the High Council. When the Republic had begun to crumble, Mon Mothma had remained a senator until the end, organizing dissent, stabilizing the increasingly ineffectual government.

She had organized cells, too, toward the end. Pockets of resistance, each of which was unaware of the identity of the others – each of which was responsible for inciting revolt against the Empire when it finally made itself manifest.

There had been other leaders, but many were killed when the Empire's first Death Star annihilated the planet Alderaan. Leia's adopted father died in that calamity.

Mon Mothma went underground. She joined her political cells with the thousands of guerrillas and insurgents the Empire's cruel dictatorship had spawned. Thousands more joined this Rebel Alliance. Mon Mothma became the acknowledged leader of all the galaxy's creatures who had been left homeless by the Emperor. Homeless, but not without hope.

She traversed the room, now, to the holographic display where she conferred with her two chief advisors, General Madine and Admiral Ackbar. Madine was Corellian – tough, resourceful, if a bit of a martinet. Ackbar was pure Calamarian – a gentle, salmon-colored creature, with huge, sad eyes set in a high-domed head, and webbed hands that made him more at home in water or free space than on board a ship. But if the humans were the arm of the Rebellion, the Calamarians were the soul – which isn't to say they couldn't fight with the best, when pushed to the limit. And the evil Empire had reached that limit.

Lando Calrissian made his way through the crowd, now, scanning faces. He saw Wedge, who was to be his wing pilot – they nodded at each other, gave the thumbs-up sign; but then Lando moved on. Wedge wasn't the one he was looking for. He made it to a clearing near the center, peered around, finally saw his friends standing by a side door. He smiled and wandered over.

Han, Chewie, Leia, and the two droids greeted Lando's appearance with a cacophony of cheers, laughs, beeps, and barks.

'Well, look at you,' Solo chided, straightening the lapel of Calrissian's new uniform and pulling on the insignias: 'A general!'

Lando laughed affectionately. 'I'm a man of many faces and many costumes. Someone must have told them about my little maneuver at the battle of Taanab.' Taanab was an agrarian planet raided seasonally by bandits from Norulac. Calrissian – before his stint as governor of Cloud City – had wiped out the bandits against all odds, using legendary flying and unheard of strategies. And he'd done it on a bet.

Han opened his eyes wide with sarcasm. 'Hey, don't look at me. I just told them you were a "fair" pilot. I had no idea they were looking for someone to lead this crazy attack.'

'That's all right, I asked for it. I *want* to lead this attack.' For one thing, he *liked* dressing up like a general. People gave him the respect he deserved, and he didn't have to give up flying circles around some pompous Imperial military policeman. And that was the other thing – he was finally going to stick it to this Imperial navy, stick it so it hurt, for all the times he'd been stuck. Stick it and leave his signature on it. *General* Calrissian, thank you.

Solo looked at his old friend, admiration combined with disbelief. 'Have you ever seen one of those Death Stars? You're in for a very short generalship, old buddy.'

'I'm surprised they didn't ask you to do it,' Lando smiled.

'Maybe they did,' Han intimated. 'But I'm not crazy. You're the respectable one, remember? Baron-Administrator of the Bespin Cloud City?'

Leia moved closer to Solo and took his arm protectively. 'Han is going to stay on the command ship with me ... we're both very grateful for what you're doing, Lando. And proud.'

Suddenly, at the center of the room, Mon Mothma signaled for attention. The room fell silent. Anticipation was keen.

'The data brought to us by the Bothan spies have been confirmed,' the supreme leader announced. 'The Emperor has made a critical error, and the time for our attack has come.'

This caused a great stir in the room. As if her message had been a valve letting off pressure, the air hissed with comment. She turned to the hologram of the Death Star, and went on. 'We now have the exact location of the Emperor's new battle station. The weapon systems on this Death Star are not yet operational. With the Imperial fleet spread throughout the galaxy in a vain effort to engage us, it is relatively unprotected.' She paused here, to let her next statement register its full effect. 'Most important, we have learned the Emperor himself is personally overseeing the construction.'

A volley of spirited chatter erupted from the assembly. This was it. The chance. The hope no one could hope to hope for. A shot at the Emperor.

Mon Mothma continued when the hubbub died down slightly. 'His trip was undertaken in the utmost secrecy, but he underestimated our spy network. Many Bothans died to bring us this information.' Her voice turned suddenly stern again to remind them of the price of this enterprise.

Admiral Ackbar stepped forward. His specialty was Imperial defense procedures. He raised his fin and pointed at the holographic model of the force field emanating from Endor. 'Although uncompleted, the Death Star is not entirely without a defense mechanism,' he instructed in soothing Calamarian tones. 'It is protected by an energy shield which is generated by the nearby Moon of Endor, here. No ship can fly through it, no weapon can penetrate it.' He stopped for a long moment. He wanted the information to sink in. When he thought it had, he spoke more slowly. 'The shield must be deactivated if *any* attack is to be attempted. Once the shield is down, the cruisers will create a perimeter while the fighters fly into the superstructure, here ... and attempt to hit the main reactor ...' he pointed to the unfinished portion of the Death Star '... somewhere in here.'

Another murmur swept over the room of commanders, like a swell in a heavy sea.

Ackbar concluded. 'General Calrissian will lead the fighter attack.'

Han turned to Lando, his doubts gilded with respect. 'Good luck, buddy.'

'Thanks,' said Lando simply.

'You're gonna need it.'

Admiral Ackbar yielded the floor to General Madine, who was in charge of covert operations. 'We have acquired a small Imperial shuttle,' Madine declared smugly. 'Under this guise, a strike team will land on the moon and deactivate the shield generator. The control bunker is well guarded, but a small squad should be able to penetrate its security.'

This news stimulated another round of general mumbling.

Leia turned to Han and said under her breath, 'I wonder who they found to pull that one off?'

Madine called out: 'General Solo, is your strike team assembled?'

Leia looked up at Han, shock quickly melting to joyous admiration. She knew there was a reason she loved him – in spite of his usual crass insensitivity and oafish bravado. Beneath it all, he had heart.

Moreover, a change *had* come over him since he emerged from carbonization. He wasn't just a loner anymore, only in this for the money. He had lost his selfish edge and had somehow, subtly, become part of the whole. He was actually doing something for someone else, now, and that fact moved Leia greatly. Madine had called him *General*; that meant Han had let himself officially become a member of the army. A part of the whole.

Solo responded to Madine. 'My squad is ready, sir, but I need a command crew for the shuttle.' He looked questioningly at Chewbacca, and spoke in a lower voice. 'It's gonna be rough, old pal. I didn't want to speak for you.'

'Roo roowfl,' Chewie shook his head with gruff love, and raised his hairy paw.

'That's one,' Han called.

'Here's two!' Leia shouted, sticking her arm in the air. Then softly, to Solo: 'I'm not letting you out of my sight again, Your Generalship.'

'And I'm with you, too!' a voice was raised from the back of the room.

They all turned their heads to see Luke standing at the top of the stairs.

Cheers went up for the last of the Jedi.

And though it wasn't his style, Han was unable to conceal his joy. 'That's three,' he smiled.

Leia ran up to Luke and hugged him warmly. She felt a special closeness to him all of a sudden, which she attributed to the gravity of the moment, the import of their mission. But then she sensed a change in him, too, a difference of substance that seemed to radiate from his very core – something that she alone could see.

'What is it, Luke?' she whispered. She suddenly wanted to hold him; she could not have said why.

'Nothing. I'll tell you someday,' he murmured quietly. It was distinctly not nothing, though.

'All right,' she answered, not pushing. 'I'll wait.' She wondered. Maybe he was just dressed differently – that was probably it. Suited up all in black now – it made him look older. Older, that was it.

Han, Chewie, Lando, Wedge, and several others crowded around Luke all at once, with greetings and diverse sorts of hubbub. The assembly as a whole broke up into multiple such small groups. It was a time for last farewells and good graces.

Artoo beeped a singsong little observation to a somewhat less sanguine Threepio.

'I don't think "exciting" is the right word,' the golden droid answered. Being a translator in his master program, of course, Threepio was most concerned with locating the right word to describe the present situation.

The *Millennium Falcon* rested in the main docking bay of the Rebel Star Cruiser, getting loaded and serviced. Just beyond it sat the stolen Imperial shuttle, looking anomalous in the midst of all the Rebel X-wing fighters.

Chewie supervised the final transfer of weapons and supplies to the shuttle and oversaw the placement of the strike team. Han stood with Lando between the two ships, saying good-bye – for all they knew, forever.

'I mean it, take her!' Solo insisted, indicating the *Falcon*. 'She'll bring you luck. You *know* she's the fastest ship in the whole fleet, now.' Han had really souped her up after winning her from Lando. She'd always been fast, but now she was much faster. And the modifications Solo added had really made the *Falcon* a part of him

– he'd put his love and sweat into it. His spirit. So giving her to Lando now was truly Solo's final transformation – as selfless a gift as he'd ever given.

And Lando understood. 'Thanks, old buddy. I'll take good care of her. *You* know I always flew her better than you did, anyway. She won't get a scratch on her, with me at the stick.'

Solo looked warmly at the endearing rogue. 'I've got your word – not a scratch.'

'Take off, you pirate – next thing you'll have me putting down a security deposit.'

'See you soon, pal.'

They parted without their true feelings expressed aloud, as was the way between men of deeds in those times; each walked up the ramp into a different ship.

Han entered the cockpit of the Imperial shuttle as Luke was doing some fine tuning on a rear navigator panel. Chewbacca, in the copilot's seat, was trying to figure out the Imperial controls. Han took the pilot's chair, and Chewie growled grumpily about the design.

'Yeah, yeah,' Solo answered, 'I don't think the Empire designed it with a Wookiee in mind.'

Leia walked in from the hold, taking her seat near Luke. 'We're all set back there.'

'Rrrwfr,' said Chewie, hitting the first sequence of switches. He looked over at Solo, but Han was motionless, staring out the window at something. Chewie and Leia both followed his gaze to the object of his unyielding attention – the *Millennium Falcon*.

Leia gently nudged the pilot. 'Hey, you awake up there?'

'I just got a funny feeling,' Han mused. 'Like I'm not going to see her again.' He thought of the times she'd saved him with her speed, of the times he'd saved her with his cunning, or his touch. He thought of the universe they'd seen together, of the shelter she'd given him; of the way he knew her, inside and out. Of the times they'd slept in each other's embrace, floating still as a quiet dream in the black silence of deep space.

Chewbacca, hearing this, took his own longing look at the *Falcon*. Leia put her hand on Solo's shoulder. She knew he had special love for his ship and was reluctant to interrupt this last communion. But time was dear, and becoming dearer. 'Come on, Captain,' she whispered. 'Let's move.'

Han snapped back to the moment. 'Right. Okay, Chewie, let's find out what this baby can do.'

They fired up the engines in the stolen shuttle, eased out of the docking bay, and banked off into the endless night.

Construction on the Death Star proceeded. Traffic in the area was thick with transport ships, TIE fighters and equipment shuttles. Periodically, the Super Star Destroyer orbited the area, surveying progress on the space station from every angle.

The bridge of the Star Destroyer was a hive of activity. Messengers ran back and forth along a string of controllers studying their tracking screens, monitoring ingress and egress of vehicles through the deflector shield. Codes were sent and received, orders given, diagrams plotted. It was an operation involving a thousand scurrying ships, and everything was proceeding with maximum efficiency, until Controller Jhoff made contact with a shuttle of the Lambda class, approaching the shield from Sector Seven.

'Shuttle to Control, please come in,' the voice broke into Jhoff's headset with the normal amount of static.

'We have you on our screen now,' the controller replied into his comlink. 'Please identify.'

'This is Shuttle *Tydirium*, requesting deactivation of the deflector shield.'

'Shuttle *Tydirium*, transmit the clearance code for shield passage.'

Up in the shuttle, Han threw a worried look at the others and said into his comlink, 'Transmission commencing.'

Chewie flipped a bank of switches, producing a syncopated series of high-frequency transmission noises.

Leia bit her lip, bracing herself for fight or flight. 'Now we find out if that code was worth the price we paid.'

Chewie whined nervously.

Luke stared at the huge Super Star Destroyer that loomed everywhere in front of them. It fixed his eye with its glittering darkness, filled his vision like a malignant cataract – but it made more than his vision opaque. It filled his mind with blackness, too; and his heart. Black fear, and a special knowing. 'Vader is on that ship,' he whispered.

'You're just jittery, Luke,' Han reassured them all. 'There are lots of command ships. But, Chewie,' he cautioned, 'let's keep our distance, without looking like we're keeping our distance.'

'Awroff rwrgh rrfrough?'

'I don't know – fly casual,' Han barked back.

'They're taking a long time with that code clearance,' Leia said tightly. What if it didn't work? The Alliance could do nothing if the Empire's deflector shield remained functioning. Leia tried to clear her mind, tried to focus on the shield generator she wanted to reach, tried to weed away all feelings of doubt or fear she may have been giving off.

'I'm endangering the mission,' Luke spoke now, in a kind of emotional resonance with his secret sister. His thoughts were of Vader, though: their father. 'I shouldn't have come.'

Han tried to buoy things up. 'Hey, why don't we try to be optimistic about this?' He felt beleaguered by negativity.

'He knows I'm here,' Luke avowed. He kept staring at the command ship out the view-window. It seemed to taunt him. It awaited.

'Come on, kid, you're imagining things.'

'Ararh gragh,' Chewie mumbled. Even he was grim.

Lord Vader stood quite still, staring out a large view-screen at the Death Star. He thrilled to the sight of this monument to the dark side of the Force. Icily he caressed it with his gaze.

Like a floating ornament, it sparkled for him. A magic globe. Tiny specks of light raced across its surface, mesmerizing the Dark Lord as if he were a small child entranced by a special toy. It was a transcendant state he was in, a moment of heightened perceptions.

And then, all at once, in the midst of the stillness of his contemplation, he grew absolutely motionless: not a breath, not even a heartbeat stirred to mar his concentration. He strained his every sense into the ether. What had he felt? His spirit tilted its head to listen. Some echo, some vibration apprehended only by him, had passed – no, had not passed. Had swirled the moment and altered the very shape of things. Things were no longer the same.

He walked down the row of controllers until he came to the spot where Admiral Piett was leaning over the tracking screen of Controller Jhoff. Piett straightened at Vader's approach, then bowed stiffly, at the neck.

'Where is that shuttle going?' Vader demanded quietly, without preliminary.

Piett turned back to the view-screen and spoke into the comlink. 'Shuttle *Tydirium*, what is your cargo and destination?'

The filtered voice of the shuttle pilot came back over the receiver. 'Parts and technical personnel for the Sanctuary Moon.'

The bridge commander looked to Vader for a reaction. He hoped nothing was amiss. Lord Vader did not take mistakes lightly.

'Do they have a code clearance?' Vader questioned.

'It's an older code, but it checks out,' Piett replied immediately. 'I was about to clear them.' There was no point in lying to the Lord of the Sith. He always knew if you lied; lies sang out to the Dark Lord.

'I have a strange feeling about that ship,' Vader said more to himself than to anyone else.

'Should I hold them?' Piett hurried, anxious to please his master.

'No, let them pass, I will deal with this myself.'

'As you wish, my Lord.' Piett bowed, partly to hide his surprise. He nodded at Controller Jhoff, who spoke into the comlink, to the Shuttle *Tydirium*.

In the Shuttle *Tydirium*, the group waited tensely. The more questions they were asked about things like cargo and destination, the more likely it seemed they were going to blow their cover.

Han looked fondly at his old Wookiee partner. 'Chewiee, if they don't go for this, we're gonna have to beat it quick.' It was a good-bye speech, really; they all knew this pokey shuttle wasn't about to outrun anything in the neighborhood.

The static voice of the controller broke up, and then came in clearly over the comlink. 'Shuttle *Tydirium*, deactivation of the shield will commence immediately. Follow your present course.'

Everyone but Luke exhaled in simultaneous relief; as if the trouble were all over now, instead of just beginning. Luke continued to stare at the command ship, as if engaged in some silent, complex dialogue.

Chewiee barked loudly.

'Hey, what did I tell you?' Han grinned. 'No sweat.'

Leia smiled affectionately. 'Is that what you told us?'

Solo pushed the throttle forward, and the stolen shuttle moved smoothly toward the green Sanctuary Moon.

Vader, Piett, and Jhoff watched the view-screen in the control room, as the weblike deflector grid read-out parted to admit the Shuttle *Tydirium*, which moved slowly toward the center of the web – to Endor.

Vader turned to the deck officer and spoke with more urgency in his voice than was usually heard. 'Ready my shuttle. I must go to the Emperor.'

Without waiting for response, the Dark Lord strode off, clearly in the thrall of a dark thought.

THE trees of Endor stood a thousand feet tall. Their trunks, covered with shaggy, rust bark, rose straight as a pillar, some of them as big around as a house, some thin as a leg. Their foliage was spindly, but lush in color, scattering the sunlight in delicate blue-green patterns over the forest floor.

Distributed thickly among these ancient giants was the usual array of woodsy flora – pines of several species, various deciduous forms, variously gnarled and leafy. The groundcover was primarily fern, but so dense in spots as to resemble a gentle green sea that rippled softly in the forest breeze.

This was the entire moon: verdant, primeval, silent. Light filtered through the sheltering branches like golden ichor, as if the very air were alive. It was warm, and it was cool. This was Endor.

The stolen Imperial shuttle sat in a clearing many miles from the Imperial landing port, camouflaged with a blanket of dead branches, leaves, and mulch. In addition the little ship was thoroughly dwarfed by the towering trees. Its steely hull might have looked incongruous here, had it not been so totally inconspicuous.

On the hill adjacent to the clearing, the Rebel contingent was just beginning to make its way up a steep trail. Leia, Chewie, Han, and Luke led the way, followed in single file by the raggedy, helmeted squad of the strike team. This unit was composed of the elite groundfighters of the Rebel Alliance. A scruffy bunch in some ways, they'd each been hand-picked for initiative, cunning, and ferocity. Some were trained commandos, some paroled criminals – but they all hated the Empire with a passion that exceeded self-preservation. And they all knew this was the crucial raid. If they failed to destroy the shield generator here, the Rebellion was doomed. No second chances.

Consequently, no one had to tell them to be alert as they made their way silently up the forest path. They were, every one, more alert than they had ever been.

Artoo Detoo and See Threepio brought up the rear of the brigade. Artoo's domed pate swiveled round and round as he went, blinking his sensor lights at the infinitely tall trees which surrounded them.

'Beee-doop!' he commented to Threepio.

'No, I don't think it's pretty here,' his golden companion replied testily. 'With our luck, it's inhabited solely by droid-eating monsters.'

The trooper just ahead of Threepio turned around and gave them a harsh 'Shush!'

Threepio turned back to Artoo, and whispered, 'Quiet, Artoo.'

They were all a bit nervous.

Up ahead, Chewie and Leia reached the crest of the hill. They dropped to the ground, crawled the last few feet, and peered over the edge. Chewbacca raised his great paw, signaling the rest of the group to stop. All at once, the forest seemed to become much more silent.

Luke and Han crawled forward on their bellies, to view what the others were observing. Pointing through the ferns, Chewie and Leia cautioned stealth. Not far below, in a glen beside a clear pool, two Imperial scouts had set up temporary camp. They were fixing a meal of rations and were preoccupied warming it over a portable cooker. Two speeder bikes were parked nearby.

'Should we try to go around?' whispered Leia.

'It'll take time,' Luke shook his head.

Han peeked from behind a rock. 'Yeah, and if they catch sight of us and report, this whole party's for nothing.'

'Is it just the two of them?' Leia still sounded skeptical.

'Let's take a look,' smiled Luke, with a sigh of tension about to be released; they all responded with a similar grin. It was beginning.

Leia motioned the rest of the squad to remain where they were; then she, Luke, Han, and Chewbacca quietly edged closer to the scout camp.

When they were quite near the clearing, but still covered by underbrush, Solo slid quickly to the lead position. 'Stay here,' he rasped, 'Chewie and I will take care of this.' He flashed them his most roguish smile.

'Quietly,' warned Luke, 'there might be—'

But before he could finish, Han jumped up with his furry partner and rushed into the clearing.

' – more out there,' Luke finished speaking to himself. He looked over at Leia.

She shrugged. 'What'd you expect?' Some things never changed.

Before Luke could respond, though, they were distracted by a loud commotion in the glen. They flattened to the ground and watched.

Han was engaged in a rousing fist fight with one of the scouts – he hadn't looked so happy in days. The other scout jumped on his speeder bike to escape. But by the time he'd ignited the engines, Chewie was able to get off a few shots from his crossbow laser. The ill-fated scout crashed instantly against an enormous tree; a brief, muffled explosion followed.

Leia drew her laser pistol and raced into the battle zone, followed closely by Luke. As soon as they were running clear, though, several large laser blasts went off all around them, tumbling them to the ground. Leia lost her gun.

Dazed, they both looked up to see two more Imperial scouts emerge from the far side of the clearing, heading for their speeder bikes hidden in the peripheral foliage. The scouts holstered their pistols as they mounted the bikes and fired up the engines.

Leia staggered to her feet, 'Over there, two more of them!'

'I see 'em,' answered Luke, rising. 'Stay here.'

But Leia had ideas of her own. She ran to the remaining rocket speeder, charged it up, and took off in pursuit of the fleeing scouts. As she tore past Luke, he jumped up behind her on the bike, and off they flew.

'Quick, center switch,' he shouted to her over her shoulder, over the roar of the rocket engines. 'Jam their comlinks!'

As Luke and Leia soared out of the clearing after the Imperials,

Han and Chewie were just subduing the last scout. 'Hey, wait!' Solo shouted; but they were gone. He threw his weapon to the ground in frustration, and the rest of the Rebel commando squad poured over the rise into the clearing.

Luke and Leia sped through the dense foliage, a few feet off the ground, Leia at the controls, Luke grabbing on behind her. The two escaping Imperial scouts had a good lead, but at two hundred miles per hour, Leia was the better pilot – the talent ran in her family.

She let off a burst from the speeder's laser cannon periodically, but was still too far behind to be very accurate. The explosions hit away from the moving targets, splintering trees and setting the shrubbery afire, as the bikes weaved in and out between massive, imposing branches.

'Move closer!' Luke shouted.

Leia opened the throttle, closed the gap. The two scouts sensed their pursuer gaining and recklessly veered this way and that, skimming through a narrow opening between two trees. One of the bikes scraped the bark, tipping the scout almost out of control, slowing him significantly.

'Get alongside!' Luke yelled into Leia's ear.

She pulled her speeder so close to the scout's, their steering vanes scraped hideously against each other. Luke suddenly leaped from the back of Leia's bike to the back of the scout's, grabbed the Imperial warrior around the neck, and flipped him off. The white-armored trooper smashed into a thick trunk with a bone-shattering crunch, and settled forever into the sea of ferns.

Luke scooted forward to the driver's seat of the speeder bike, played with the controls a few seconds, and lurched forward, following Leia, who'd pulled ahead. The two of them now tore after the remaining scout.

Over hill and under stonebridge they flew, narrowly avoiding collision, flaming dry vines in their afterburn. The chase swung north and passed a gully where two more Imperial scouts were resting. A moment later, *they* swung into pursuit, now hot on Luke and Leia's tail, blasting away with laser cannon. Luke, still behind Leia, took a glancing blow.

'Keep on that one!' he shouted up at her, indicating the scout in the lead. 'I'll take the two behind us!'

Leia shot ahead. Luke, at the same instant, flared up his

retrorockets, slamming the bike into rapid deceleration. The two scouts on his tail zipped past him in a blur on either side, unable to slow their momentum. Luke immediately roared into high velocity again, firing with his blasters, suddenly in pursuit of his pursuers.

His third round hit its mark: one of the scouts, blown out of control, went spinning against a boulder in a rumble of flame.

The scout's cohort took a single glance at the flash, and put his bike into supercharge mode, speeding even faster. Luke kept pace.

Far ahead, Leia and the first scout continued their own high-speed slalom through the barricades of impassive trunks and low-slung branches. She had to brake through so many turns, in fact, Leia seemed unable to draw any closer to her quarry. Suddenly she shot into the air, at an unbelievably steep incline, and quickly vanished from sight.

The scout turned in confusion, uncertain whether to relax or cringe at his pursuer's sudden disappearance. Her whereabouts became clear soon enough. Out of the tree-tops, Leia dove down on him, cannon blasting from above. The scout's bike took the shock wave from a near hit. Her speed was even greater than she'd anticipated, and in a moment she was racing alongside him. But before she knew what was happening, he reached down and drew a handgun from his holster – and before she could react, he fired.

Her bike spun out of control. She jumped free just in time – the speeder exploded on a giant tree, as Leia rolled clear into a tangle of matted vines, rotting logs, shallow water. The last thing she saw was the orange fireball through a cloud of smoking greenery; and then blackness.

The scout looked behind him at the explosion, with a satisfied sneer. When he faced forward again, though, the smug look faded, for he was on a collision course with a fallen tree. In a moment it was all over but the flaming.

Meanwhile, Luke was closing fast on the last scout. As they wove from tree to tree, Luke eased up behind and then drew even with the Imperial rider. The fleeing soldier suddenly swerved, slamming his bike into Luke's – they both tipped precariously, barely missing a large fallen trunk in their path. The scout zoomed under it, Luke over it – and when he came down on the other side, he crashed directly on top of the scout's vehicle. Their steering vanes locked.

The bikes were shaped more or less like one-man sleds, with long thin rods extending from their snouts, and fluttery ailerons for guidance at the tip of the rods. With these vanes locked, the bikes flew as one, though either rider could steer.

The scout banked hard right, to try to smash Luke into an onrushing grove of saplings on the right. But at the last second Luke leaned all his weight left, turning the locked speeders actually horizontal, with Luke on top, the scout on the bottom.

The biker scout suddenly stopped resisting Luke's leftward leaning and threw his own weight in the same direction, resulting in the bikes flipping over three hundred sixty degrees and coming to rest exactly upright once more ... but with an enormous tree looming immediately in front of Luke.

Without thinking, he leaped from his bike. A fraction of a second later, the scout veered steeply left – the steering vanes separated – and Luke's riderless speeder crashed explosively into the redwood.

Luke rolled, decelerating, up a moss-covered slope. The scout swooped high, circled around, and came looking for him.

Luke stumbled out of the bushes as the speeder was bearing down on him full throttle, laser cannon firing. Luke ignited his lightsaber and stood his ground. His weapon deflected every bolt the scout fired at Luke; but the bike kept coming. In a few moments, the two would meet; the bike accelerated even more, intent on bodily slicing the young Jedi in half. At the last moment, though, Luke stepped aside – with perfect timing, like a master matador facing a rocket-powered bull – and chopped off the bike's steering vanes with a single mighty slash of his lightsaber.

The bike quickly began to shudder; then pitch and roll. In a second it was out of control entirely, and in another second it was a rumbling billow of fire on the forest floor.

Luke snuffed out his lightsaber and headed back to join the others.

Vader's shuttle swung around the unfinished portion of the Death Star and settled fluidly into the main docking bay. Soundless bearings lowered the Dark Lord's ramp; soundless were his feet as they glided down the chilly steel. Chill with purpose were his strides, and swift.

The main corridor was filled with courtiers, all awaiting an audience with the Emperor. Vader curled his lip at them – fools, all.

Pompous toadys in their velvet robes and painted faces; perfumed bishops passing notes and passing judgments among themselves – for who else cared; oily favor-merchants, bent low from the weight of jewelry still warm from a previous owner's dying flesh; easy, violent men and women, lusting to be tampered with.

Vader had no patience for such petty filth. He passed them without a nod, though many of them would have paid dearly for a felicitous glance from the high Dark Lord.

When he reached the elevator to the Emperor's tower, he found the door closed. Red-robed, heavily armed royal guards flanked the shaft, seemingly unaware of Vader's presence. Out of the shadow, an officer stepped forward, directly in Lord Vader's path, preventing his further approach.

'You may not enter,' the officer said evenly.

Vader did not waste words. He raised his hand, fingers outstretched, toward the officer's throat. Ineffably, the officer began to choke. His knees started buckling, his face turned ashen.

Gasping for air, he spoke again. 'It is the ... Emperor's ... command.'

Like a spring, Vader released the man from his remote grip. The officer, breathing again, sank to the floor, trembling. He rubbed his neck gently.

'I will await his convenience,' Vader said. He turned and looked out the view-window. Leaf-green Endor glowed there, floating in black space, almost as if it were radiant from some internal source of energy. He felt its pull like a magnet, like a vacuum, like a torch in the dead night.

Han and Chewie crouched opposite each other in the forest clearing, being quiet, being near. The rest of the strike squad relaxed – as much as was possible – spread out around them in groups of twos and threes. They all waited.

Even Threepio was silent. He sat beside Artoo, polishing his fingers for lack of anything better to do. The others checked their watches, or their weapons, as the afternoon sunlight ticked away.

Artoo sat, unmoving except for the little radar screen that stuck out the top of his blue and silver dome, revolving, scanning the forest. He exuded the calm patience of a utilized function, a program being run.

Suddenly, he beeped.

Threepio ceased his obsessive polishing and looked apprehensively into the forest. 'Someone's coming,' he translated.

The rest of the squad faced out; weapons were raised. A twig cracked beyond the western perimeter. No one breathed.

With a weary stride, Luke stepped out of the foliage, into the clearing. All relaxed, lowered their guns. Luke was too tired to care. He plopped down on the hard dirt beside Solo and lay back with an exhausted groan.

'Hard day, huh kid?' Han commented.

Luke sat up on one elbow, smiling. It seemed like an awful lot of effort and noise just to nail a couple of Imperial scouts; and they hadn't even gotten to the really tough part yet. But Han could still maintain his light tone. It was a state of grace, his particular brand of charm. Luke hoped it never vanished from the universe. 'Wait'll we get to that generator,' he retorted in kind.

Solo looked around, into the forest Luke had just come from. 'Where's Leia?'

Luke's face suddenly turned to one of concern. 'She didn't come back?'

'I thought she was with you,' Han's voice marginally rose in pitch and volume.

'We got split up,' Luke explained. He exchanged a grim look with Solo, then both of them slowly stood. 'We better look for her.'

'Don't you want to rest a while?' Han suggested. He could see the fatigue in Luke's face and wanted to spare him for the coming confrontation, which would surely take more strength than any of them had.

'I want to find Leia,' he said softly.

Han nodded, without argument. He signaled to the Rebel officer who was second in command of the strike squad. The officer ran up and saluted.

'Take the squad ahead,' ordered Solo. 'We'll rendezvous at the shield generator at 0-30.'

The officer saluted again and immediately organized the troops. Within a minute they were filing silently into the forest, greatly relieved to be moving at last.

Luke, Chewbacca, General Solo, and the two droids faced in the opposite direction. Artoo led the way, his revolving scanner sensing for all the parameters that described his mistress; and the others followed him into the woods.

The first thing Leia was aware of was her left elbow. It was wet. It was lying in a pool of water, getting quite soaked.

She moved the elbow out of the water with a little splash, revealing something else: pain – pain in her entire arm when it moved. For the time being, she decided to keep it still.

The next thing to enter her consciousness were sounds. The splash her elbow had made, the rustle of leaves, an occasional bird chirp. Forest sounds. With a grunt, she took a short breath and noted the grunting sound.

Smells began to fill her nostrils next: humid mossy smells, leafy oxygen smells, the odor of a distant honey, the vapor of rare flowers.

Taste came with smell – the taste of blood on her tongue. She opened and closed her mouth a few times, to localize where the blood was coming from; but she couldn't. Instead, the attempt only brought the recognition of new pains – in her head, in her neck, in her back. She started to move her arms again, but this entailed a whole catalogue of new pains; so once again, she rested.

Next she allowed temperature to waft into her sensorium. Sun warmed the fingers of her right hand, while the palm, in shadow, stayed cool. A breeze drafted the back of her legs. Her left hand, pressed against the skin of her belly, was warm.

She felt . . . awake.

Slowly – reticent actually to witness the damage, since seeing things made them real, and seeing her own broken body was not a reality she wanted to acknowledge – slowly, she opened her eyes. Things were blurry here at ground level. Hazy browns and grays in the foreground, becoming progressively brighter and greener in the distance. Slowly, things came into focus.

Slowly, she saw the Ewok.

A strange, small, furry creature, he stood three feet from Leia's face and no more than three feet tall. He had large, dark, curious, brownish eyes, and stubby little finger-paws. Completely covered, head to foot, with soft, brown fur, he looked like nothing so much as the stuffed baby Wookiee doll Leia remembered playing with as a child. In fact, when she first saw the creature standing before her, she thought it merely a dream, a childhood memory rising out of her addled brain.

But this wasn't a dream. It was an Ewok. And his name was Wicket.

Nor was he exclusively cute – for as Leia focused further, she could see a knife strapped to his waist. It was all he wore, save for a thin leather mantle only covering his head.

They watched each other, unmoving, for a long minute. The Ewok seemed puzzled by the princess; uncertain of what she was, or what she intended. At the moment, Leia intended to see if she could sit up.

She sat up, with a groan.

The sound apparently frightened the little fluffball; he rapidly stumbled backward, tripped, and fell. 'Eeeeep!' he squeaked.

Leia scrutinized herself closely, looking for signs of serious damage. Her clothes were torn; she had cuts, bruises, and scrapes everywhere – but nothing seemed to be broken or irreparable. On the other hand, she had no idea where she was. She groaned again.

That did it for the Ewok. He jumped up, grabbed a four-foot-long spear, and held it defensively in her direction. Warily, he circled, poking the pointed javelin at her, clearly more fearful than aggressive.

'Hey, cut that out,' Leia brushed the weapon away with annoyance. That was all she needed now – to be skewered by a teddy bear. More gently, she added: 'I'm not going to hurt you.'

Gingerly, she stood up, testing her legs. The Ewok backed away with caution.

'Don't be afraid,' Leia tried to put reassurance into her voice. 'I just want to see what happened to my bike here.' She knew the more she talked in this tone, the more at ease it would put the little creature. Moreover, she knew if she was talking, she was doing okay.

Her legs were a little unsteady, but she was able to walk slowly over to the charred remains of the speeder, now lying in a half-melted pile at the base of the partially blackened tree.

Her movement was away from the Ewok, who, like a skittish puppy, took this as a safe sign and followed her to the wreckage. Leia picked the Imperial scout's laser pistol off the ground; it was all that was left of him.

'I think I got off at the right time,' she muttered.

The Ewok appraised the scene with his big, shiny eyes, nodded, shook his head, and squeaked vociferously for several seconds.

Leia looked all around her at the dense forest, then sat down, with a sigh, on a fallen log. She was at eyelevel with the Ewok, now, and they once again regarded each other, a little bewildered, a little concerned. 'Trouble is, I'm sort of stuck here,' she confided. 'And I don't even know where here is.'

She put her head in her hands, partly to mull over the situation, partly to rub some of the soreness from her temples. Wicket sat down beside her and mimicked her posture exactly – head in paws, elbows on knees – then let out a little sympathetic Ewok sigh.

Leia laughed appreciatively and scratched the small creature's furry head, between the ears. He purred like a kitten.

'You wouldn't happen to have a comlink on you by any chance?' Big joke – but she hoped maybe talking about it would give her an idea. The Ewok blinked a few times – but he only gave her a mystified look. Leia smiled. 'No, I guess not.'

Suddenly Wicket froze; his ears twitched, and he sniffed the air. He tilted his head in an attitude of keen attention.

'What is it?' Leia whispered. Something was obviously amiss. Then she heard it: a quiet snap in the bushes beyond, a tentative rustling.

All at once the Ewok let out a loud, terrified screech. Leia drew her pistol, jumping behind the log; Wicket scurried beside her and squeezed under it. A long silence followed. Tense, uncertain, Leia trained her senses on the near underbrush. Ready to fight.

For all her readiness, she hadn't expected the laser bolt to come from where it did – high, off to the right. It exploded in front of the log with a shower of light and pine needles. She returned the fire quickly – two short blasts – then just as quickly sensed something behind her. Slowly she swiveled, to find an Imperial scout standing over her, his weapon leveled at her head. He reached out his hand for the pistol she held.

'I'll take that,' he ordered.

Without warning, a furry hand came out from under the log and jabbed the scout in the leg with a knife. The man howled in pain, began jumping about on one foot.

Leia dove for his fallen laser pistol. She rolled, fired and hit the scout squarely in the chest, flash-burning his heart.

Quickly the forest was quiet once more, the noise and light swallowed up as if they had never been. Leia lay still where she was, panting softly, waiting for another attack. None came.

Wicket poked his fuzzy head up from under the log, and looked around. 'Eeep rrp scrp ooooh,' he mumbled in a tone of awe.

Leia hopped up, ran all about the area, crouched, turned her head from side to side. It seemed safe for the time being. She motioned to her chubby new friend. 'Come on, we'd better get out of here.'

As they moved into the thick flora, Wicket took the lead. Leia was unsure at first, but he shrieked urgently at her and tugged her sleeve. So she relinquished control to the odd little beast and followed him.

She cast her mind adrift for a while, letting her feet carry her nimbly along among the gargantuan trees. She was struck, suddenly, not by the smallness of the Ewok who guided her, but by her own smallness next to these trees. They were ten thousand years old, some of them, and tall beyond sight. They were temples to the life-force she championed; they reached out to the rest of the universe. She felt herself part of their greatness, but also dwarfed by it.

And lonely. She felt lonely here, in this forest of giants. All her life she'd lived among giants of her own people: her father, the great Senator Organa; her mother, then Minister of Education; her peers and friends, giants all . . .

But these trees. They were like mighty exclamation points, announcing their own preeminence. They were here! They were older than time! They would be here long after Leia was gone, after the Rebellion, after the Empire . . .

And then she didn't feel lonely again, but felt a part again, of these magnificent, poised beings. A part of them across time, and space, connected by the vibrant, vital force, of which . . .

It was confusing. A part, and apart. She couldn't grasp it. She felt large and small, brave and timid. She felt like a tiny, creative spark, dancing about in the fires of life . . . dancing behind a furtive, pudgy midget bear, who kept beckoning her deeper into the woods.

It was this, then, that the Alliance was fighting to preserve – furry creatures in mammoth forests helping scared, brave princesses to safety. Leia wished her parents were alive, so she could tell them.

*

Lord Vader stepped out of the elevator and stood at the entrance to the throne room. The light-cables hummed either side of the shaft, casting an eerie glow on the royal guards who waited there. He marched resolutely down the walkway, up the stairs, and paused subserviently behind the throne. He kneeled, motionless.

Almost immediately, he heard the Emperor's voice. 'Rise. Rise and speak, my friend.'

Vader rose, as the throne swiveled around, and the Emperor faced him.

They made eye contact from light-years and a soul's breath away. Across that abyss, Vader responded. 'My master, a small Rebel force has penetrated the shield and landed on Endor.'

'Yes, I know.' There was no hint of surprise in his tone; rather, fulfillment.

Vader noted this, then went on. 'My son is with them.'

The Emperor's brow furrowed less than a millimeter. His voice remained cool, unruffled, slightly curious. 'Are you sure?'

'I felt him, my master.' It was almost a taunt. He knew the Emperor was frightened of young Skywalker, afraid of his power. Only together could Vader and the Emperor hope to pull the Jedi Knight over to the dark side. He said it again, emphasizing his own singularity. 'I felt him.'

'Strange, that I have not,' the Emperor murmured, his eyes becoming slits. They both knew the Force wasn't all-powerful – and no one was infallible with its use. It had everything to do with awareness, with vision. Certainly, Vader and his son were more closely linked than was the Emperor with young Skywalker – but, in addition, the Emperor was now aware of a cross-current he hadn't read before, a buckle in the Force he couldn't quite understand. 'I wonder if your feelings on this matter are clear, Lord Vader.'

'They are clear, my master.' He knew his son's presence, it galled him and fueled him and lured him and howled in a voice of its own.

'Then you must go to the Sanctuary Moon and wait for him,' Emperor Palpatine said simply. As long as things were clear, things were clear.

'He will come to me?' Vader asked skeptically. This was not what he felt. He felt drawn.

'Of his own free will,' the Emperor assured him. It must be of his own free will, else all was lost. A spirit could not be coerced into corruption, it had to be seduced. It had to participate actively. It had to crave. Luke Skywalker knew these things, and still he circled the black fire, like a cat. Destinies could never be read with absolute certainty – but Skywalker would come, that was clear. 'I have foreseen it. His compassion for you will be his undoing.' Compassion had always been the weak belly of the Jedi, and forever would be. It was the ultimate vulnerability. The Emperor had none. 'The boy will come to you, and you will then bring him before me.'

Vader bowed low. 'As you wish.'

With casual malice, the Emperor dismissed the Dark Lord. With grim anticipation, Vader strode out of the throne room, to board the shuttle for Endor.

Luke, Chewie, Han, and Threepio picked their way methodically through the undergrowth behind Artoo, whose antenna continued to revolve. It was remarkable the way the little droid was able to blaze a trail over jungle terrain like this, but he did it without fuss, the miniature cutting tools on his walkers and dome slicing neatly through anything too dense to push out of the way.

Artoo suddenly stopped, causing some consternation on the part of his followers. His radar screen spun faster, he clicked and whirred to himself, then darted forward with an excited announcement. 'Vrrr dEEP dWP booooo dWEE op!'

Threepio raced behind him. 'Artoo says the rocket bikes are right up – oh, dear.'

They broke into the clearing just ahead of the others, but all stopped in a clump on entering. The charred debris of three speeder bikes was strewn around the area – not to mention the remains of some Imperial scouts.

They spread out to inspect the rubble. Little of note was evident, except a torn piece of Leia's jacket. Han held it soberly, thinking.

Threepio spoke quietly. 'Artoo's sensors find no other trace of Princess Leia.'

'I hope she's nowhere near here, now,' Han said to the trees. He didn't want to imagine her loss. After all that had happened, he simply couldn't believe it would end this way for her.

'Looks like she ran into two of them,' Luke said, just to say something. None of them wanted to draw any conclusions.

'She seems to have done all right,' Han responded somewhat tersely. He was addressing Luke, but speaking to himself.

Only Chewbacca seemed uninterested in the clearing in which they were standing. He stood facing the dense foliage beyond, then wrinkled his nose, sniffing.

'Rahrr!' he shouted, plunging into the thicket. The others rushed after him.

Artoo whistled softly, nervously.

'Picking up what?' Threepio snapped. 'Try to be more specific, would you?'

The trees became significantly taller as the group pushed on. Not that it was possible to see any higher, but the girth of the trunks was increasingly massive. The rest of the forest was thinning a bit in the process, making passage easier, but giving them the distinct sense that they were shrinking. It was an ominous feeling.

All at once the undergrowth gave way again, to yet another open space. At the center of this clearing, a single tall stake was planted in the ground, from which hung several shanks of raw meat. The searchers stared, then cautiously walked to the stake.

'What's this?' Threepio voiced the collective question.

Chewbacca's nose was going wild, in some kind of olfactory delirium. He held himself back as long as he could, but was finally unable to resist: he reached out for one of the slabs of meat.

'No wait!' shouted Luke. 'Don't—'

But it was too late. The moment the meat was pulled from the stake, a huge net sprang up all around the adventurers, instantly hoisting them high above the ground, in a twisting jumble of arms and legs.

Artoo whistled wildly – he was programmed to hate being upside-down – as the Wookiee bayed his regret.

Han peeled a hairy paw away from his mouth, spitting fur. 'Great, Chewie. Nice work. Always thinking with your stomach—'

'Take it easy,' called Luke. 'Let's just figure out how to get out of this thing.' He tried, but was unable, to free his arms; one locked behind him through the net, one pinned to Threepio's leg. 'Can anyone reach my lightsaber?'

Artoo was bottommost. He extended his cutting appendage and began clipping the loops of the viney net.

Solo, meantime, was trying to squeeze his arm past Threepio, trying to stretch to reach the lightsaber hanging at Luke's waist. They settled, jerkily, as Artoo cut through another piece of mesh, leaving Han pressed face to face with the protocol droid.

'Out of the way, Goldenrod – unh – get off of—'

'How do you think I feel?' Threepio charged. There was no protocol in a situation like this.

'I don't really—' Han began, but suddenly Artoo cut through the last link, and the entire group crashed out of the net, to the ground. As they gradually regained their senses, sat up, checked to make certain the others were all safe, one by one they realized they were surrounded by twenty furry little creatures, all wearing soft leather hoods, or caps; all brandishing spears.

One came close to Han, pushing a long spear in his face, screeching 'eeee wk!'

Solo knocked the weapon aside, with a curt directive. 'Point that thing somewhere else.'

A second Ewok became alarmed, and lunged at Han. Again, he deflected the spear, but in the process got cut on the arm.

Luke reached for his lightsaber, but just then a third Ewok ran forward, pushing the more aggressive ones out of the way, and shrieked a long string of seeming invective at them, in a decidedly scolding tone. At this, Luke decided to hold off on his lightsaber.

Han was wounded and angry, though. He started to draw his pistol. Luke stopped him before he cleared his holster, with a look. 'Don't – it'll be all right,' he added. Never confuse ability with appearance, Ben used to tell him – or actions with motivations. Luke was uncertain of these little furries, but he had a feeling.

Han held his arm, and held his peace, as the Ewoks swarmed around, confiscating all their weapons. Luke even relinquished his lightsaber. Chewie growled suspiciously.

Artoo and Threepio were just extracting themselves from the collapsed net, as the Ewoks chattered excitedly to each other.

Luke turned to the golden droid. 'Threepio, can you understand what they're saying?'

Threepio rose from the mesh trap, feeling himself for dents or rattles. 'Oh, my head,' he complained.

At the sight of his fully upright body, the Ewoks began squeaking among themselves, pointing and gesticulating.

Threepio spoke to the one who appeared to be the leader. 'Chree breeb a shurr du.'

'Bloh wreee dbleeop weeschhreee!' answered the fuzzy beast.

'Du wee sheess?'

'Reeop glwah wrrripsh.'

'Shreee?'

Suddenly one of the Ewoks dropped his spear with a little gasp and prostrated himself before the shiny droid. In another moment, all the Ewoks followed suit. Threepio looked at his friends with a slightly embarrassed shrug.

Chewie let out a puzzled bark. Artoo whirred speculatively. Luke and Han regarded the battalion of kow-towing Ewoks in wonder.

Then, at some invisible signal from one of their group, the small creatures began to chant in unison: 'Eekee whoh, eekee whoh, Rheakee rheekee whoh . . .'

Han looked at Threepio with total disbelief. 'What'd you *say* to them?'

'"Hello," I think,' Threepio replied almost apologetically. He hastened to add, 'I could be mistaken, they're using a very primitive dialect . . . I believe they think I'm some sort of god.'

Chewbacca and Artoo thought that was very funny. They spent several seconds hysterically barking and whistling before they finally managed to quiet down. Chewbacca had to wipe a tear from his eye.

Han just shook his head with a galaxy-weary look of patience. 'Well how about using your divine influence to get us out of this?' he suggested solicitously.

Threepio pulled himself up to his full height, and spoke with unrelenting decorum. 'I beg your pardon, Captain Solo, but that wouldn't be proper.'

'Proper!?' Solo roared. He always knew this pompous droid was going to go too far with him one day – and this might well be the day.

'It's against my programming to impersonate a deity,' he replied to Solo, as if nothing so obvious needed explanation.

Han moved threateningly toward the protocol droid, his fingers itching to pull a plug. 'Listen, you pile of bolts, if you don't—' He got no farther, as fifteen Ewok spears were thrust menacingly in his face. 'Just kidding,' he smiled affably.

*

The procession of Ewoks wound its way slowly into the ever-darkening forest – tiny, somber creatures, inching through a giant's maze. The sun had nearly set, now, and the long criss-crossing shadows made the cavernous domain even more imposing than before. Yet the Ewoks seemed well at home, turning down each dense corridor of vines with precision.

On their shoulders they carried their four prisoners – Han, Chewbacca, Luke, Artoo – tied to long poles, wrapped around and around with vines, immobilizing them as if they were wriggling larvae in coarse, leafy cocoons.

Behind the captives, Threepio, borne on a litter – rough-hewn of branches in the shape of a chair – was carried high upon the shoulders of the lowly Ewoks. Like a royal potentate, he perused the mighty forest through which they carried him – the magnificent lavender sunset glowing between the vinery, the exotic flowers starting to close, the ageless trees, the glistening ferns – and knew that no one before him had ever appreciated these things in just precisely the manner he was now. No one else had his sensors, his circuits, his programs, his memory banks – and so in some real way, he *was* the creator of this little universe, its images, and colors.

And it was good.

VI

THE starry sky seemed very near the treetops to Luke as he and his friends were carried into the Ewok village. He wasn't even aware it was a village at first – the tiny orange sparks of light in the distance he thought initially to be stars. This was particularly true when – dangling on his back, strapped to the pole as he was – the fiery bright points flickered directly above him, between the trees.

But then he found himself being hoisted up intricate stairways and hidden ramps *around* the immense trunks; and gradually, the higher they went, the bigger and cracklier the lights became. When the group was hundreds of feet up in the trees, Luke finally realized the lights were bonfires – *among* the treetops.

They were finally taken out onto a rickety wooden walkway, far too far off the ground to be able to see anything below them but the abysmal drop. For one bleak moment Luke was afraid they were simply going to be pitched over the brink to test their knowledge of forest lore. But the Ewoks had something else in mind.

The narrow platform ended midway between two trees. The first creature in line grabbed hold of a long vine and swung across to the far trunk – which Luke could see, by twisting his head around, had a large cavelike opening carved into its titanic surface. Vines were quickly tossed back and forth across the chasm, until soon a kind of lattice was constructed – and Luke found himself being pulled across it, on his back, still tied to the wooden poles. He looked down once, into nothingness. It was an unwelcome sensation.

On the other side they rested on a shaky, narrow platform until everyone was across. Then the diminutive monkey-bears dismantled the webbing of vines and proceeded into the tree with their captives. It was totally black inside, but Luke had the impression it was more of a tunnel through the wood than an actual cavern. The impression of dense, solid walls was everywhere, like a burrow in a mountain. When they emerged, fifty yards beyond, they were in the village square.

It was a series of wooden platforms, planks, and walkways connecting an extensive cluster of enormous trees. Supported by this scaffolding was a village of huts, constructed of an odd combination of stiffened leather, daub and wattle, thatched roofs, mud floors. Small campfires burned before many of the huts – the sparks were caught by an elaborate system of hanging vines, which funneled them to a smothering point. And everywhere, were hundreds of Ewoks.

Cooks, tanners, guards, grandfathers. Mother Ewoks gathered up squealing babies at the sight of the prisoners and scurried into their huts or pointed or murmured. Dinner smoke filled the air; children played games; minstrels played strange, resonant music on hollow logs, windy reeds.

There was vast blackness below, vaster still, above; but here in this tiny village suspended between the two, Luke felt warmth and light, and special peace.

The entourage of captors and captives stopped before the largest hut. Luke, Chewie, and Artoo were leaned, on their poles, against a nearby tree. Han was tied to a spit, and balanced above a pile of kindling that looked suspiciously like a barbecue pit. Dozens of Ewoks gathered around, chattering curiously in animated squeals.

Teebo emerged from the large structure. He was slightly bigger than most of the others, and undeniably fiercer. His fur was a pattern of light and dark gray stripes. Instead of the usual leathery hood, he wore a horned animal half-skull atop his head, which he'd further adorned with feathers. He carried a stone hatchet, and even for someone as small as an Ewok, he walked with a definite swagger.

He examined the group cursorily, then seemed to make some kind of pronouncement. At that, a member of the hunting party stepped forward – Paploo, the mantled Ewok who seemed to have taken a more protective view toward the prisoners.

Teebo conferred with Paploo for a short time. The discussion soon turned into a heated disagreement, however, with Paploo apparently taking the Rebels' side, and Teebo seemingly dismissing whatever considerations arose. The rest of the tribe stood around watching the debate with great interest, occasionally shouting comments or squeaking excitedly.

Threepio, whose litter/throne had been set down in a place of honor near the stake to which Solo was tied, followed the ongoing argument with rapt fascination. He began to translate once or twice for Luke and the others – but stopped after only a few words, since the debaters were talking so fast, he didn't want to lose the gist of what was being said. Consequently, he didn't transmit any more information than the names of the Ewoks involved.

Han looked over at Luke with a dubious frown. 'I don't like the looks of this.'

Chewie growled his wholehearted agreement.

Suddenly Logray exited from the large hut, silencing everyone with his presence. Shorter than Teebo, he was nonetheless clearly the object of greater general respect. He, too, wore a half-skull on his head – some kind of great bird skull, a single feather tied to its crest. His fur was striped tan, though, and his face wise. He carried no weapon; only a pouch at his side, and a staff topped by the spine of a once-powerful enemy.

One by one, he carefully appraised the captives, smelling Han, testing the fabric of Luke's clothing between his fingers. Teebo and Paploo babbled their opposing points of view at him, but he seemed supremely uninterested, so they soon stopped.

When Logray came to Chewbacca, he became fascinated, and poked at the Wookiee with his staff of bones. Chewie took exception to this, though: he growled dangerously at the tiny bear-man. Logray needed no further coaching and did a quick back-step – at the same time reaching into his pouch and sprinkling some herbs in Chewie's direction.

'Careful, Chewie,' Han cautioned from across the square. 'He must be the head honcho.'

'No,' Threepio corrected, 'actually I believe he's their Medicine Man.'

Luke was about to intervene, then decided to wait. It would be better if this serious little community came to its own conclusions about them, in its own way. The Ewoks seemed curiously grounded for a people so airborne.

Logray wandered over to examine Artoo Detoo, a most wondrous creature. He sniffed, tapped, and stroked the droid's metal shell, then scrunched up his face in a look of consternation. After a few moments of thought, he ordered the small robot cut down.

The crowd murmured excitedly and backed off a few feet. Artoo's vine binders were slashed by two knife-wielding guards, causing the droid to slide down his pole and crash unceremoniously to the ground.

The guards set him upright. Artoo was instantly furious. He zeroed in on Teebo as the source of his ignominy, and beeping a blue streak, began to chase the terrified Ewok in circles. The crowd roared – some cheering on Teebo, some squeaking encouragement to the deranged droid.

Finally Artoo got close enough to Teebo to zing him with an electric charge. The shocked Ewok jumped into the air, squealed raucously, and ran away as fast as his stubby little legs could carry him. Wicket slipped surreptitiously into the big hut, as the onlookers screeched their indignation or delight.

Threepio was incensed. 'Artoo, stop that! You're only going to make matters worse.'

Artoo scooted over directly in front of the golden droid, and began beeping a vehement tirade. 'Wreee op doo rhee vrrr gk gdk dk whoo dop dhop vree doo dweet . . .'

This outburst miffed Threepio substantially. With a haughty tilt he sat up straight in his throne. 'That's no way to speak to someone in my position.'

Luke was afraid the situation was well on its way to getting out of control. He called with the barest hint of impatience to his faithful droid. 'Threepio, I think it's time you spoke on our behalf.'

Threepio – rather ungraciously, actually – turned to the assemblage of fuzzy creatures and made a short speech, pointing from time to time to his friends tied to the stakes.

Logray became visibly upset by this. He waved his staff, stamped his feet, shrieked at the golden droid for a full minute. At the conclusion of his statement, he nodded to several attentive fellows, who nodded back and began filling the pit under Han with firewood.

'Well, what did he say?' Han shouted with some concern.

Threepio wilted with chagrin. 'I'm rather embarrassed, Captain Solo, but it appears you are to be the main course at a banquet in my honor. He is quite offended that I should suggest otherwise.'

Before another word could be said, log-drums began beating in ominous syncopation. As one, all the furry heads turned toward the mouth of the large hut. Out of it came Wicket; and behind him, Chief Chirpa.

Chirpa was gray of fur, strong of will. On his head he bore a garland woven of leaves, teeth, and the horns of great animals he'd bested in the hunt. In his right hand he carried a staff fashioned from the longbone of a flying reptile, in his left he held an iguana, who was his pet and advisor.

He surveyed the scene in the square at a glance, then turned to wait for the guest who was only now emerging from the large hut behind him.

The guest was the beautiful young Princess of Alderaan.

'Leia!' Luke and Han shouted together.

'Rahrhah!'

'Boo dEEdwee!'

'Your Highness!'

With a gasp she rushed toward her friends, but a phalanx of Ewoks blocked her way with spears. She turned to Chief Chirpa, then to her robot interpreter.

'Threepio, tell them these are my friends. They must be set free.'

Threepio looked at Chirpa and Lograd. 'Eep sqee rheeow,' he said with much civility. 'Sqeeow roah meep meeb eerah.'

Chirpa and Logray shook their heads with a motion that was unequivocally negative. Logray chattered an order at his helpers, who resumed vigorously piling wood under Solo.

Han exchanged helpless looks with Leia. 'Somehow I have a feeling that didn't do us much good.'

'Luke, what can we do?' Leia urged. She hadn't expected this at all. She'd expected a guide back to her ship, or at worst a short supper and lodging for the night. She definitely didn't understand these creatures. 'Luke?' she questioned.

Han was about to offer a suggestion when he paused, briefly taken aback by Leia's sudden intense faith in Luke. It was something he hadn't really noted before; he merely noted it now.

Before he could speak up with his plan, though, Luke chimed in.

'Threepio, tell them if they don't do as you wish, you'll become angry and use your magic.'

'But Master Luke, what magic?' the droid protested. 'I couldn't—'

'Tell them!' Luke ordered, uncharacteristically raising his voice. There were times when Threepio could test even the patience of a Jedi.

The interpreter-droid turned to the large audience, and spoke with great dignity. 'Eemeeblee screesh oahr aish sh sheestee meep eep eep.'

The Ewoks seemed greatly disturbed by this proclamation. They all backed up several steps, except for Logray, who took two steps forward. He shouted something at Threepio – something that sounded very in the nature of a challenge.

Luke closed his eyes with absolute concentration. Threepio began rattling on in a terribly unsettled manner, as if he'd been caught falsifying his own program. 'They don't believe me, Master Luke, just as I told you . . .'

Luke wasn't listening to the droid, though; he was visualizing him. Seeing him sitting shiny and golden on his throne of twigs, nodding this way and that, prattling on about the most incon-sequential of matters, sitting there in the black void of Luke's consciousness . . . and slowly beginning to rise.

Slowly, Threepio began to rise.

At first, he didn't notice; at first, nobody did. Threepio just went right on talking, as his entire litter steadily elevated off the ground. '. . . told you, I told you, I told you they wouldn't. I don't know why you – wha – wait a minute . . . what's happening here? . . .'

Threepio and the Ewoks all realized what was happening at just about the same moment. The Ewoks silently fell back in terror from the floating throne. Threepio now began to spin, as if he were on a revolving stool. Graceful, majestic spinning.

'Help,' he whispered. 'Artoo, help me.'

Chief Chirpa shouted orders to his cowering minions. Quickly they ran forward and released the bound prisoners. Leia, Han, and Luke enfolded each other in a long, powerful embrace. It seemed, to all of them, a strange setting in which to gain the first victory of this campaign against the Empire.

Luke was aware of a plaintive beeping behind him, and turned to see Artoo staring up at a still-spinning Threepio. Luke lowered the golden droid slowly to the ground.

'Thanks, Threepio,' the young Jedi patted him gratefully on the shoulder.

Threepio, still a bit shaken, stood with a wobbly, amazed smile. 'Why – why – I didn't know I had it in me.'

The hut of Chief Chirpa was large, by Ewok standards – though Chewbacca, sitting cross-legged, nearly scraped the ceiling with his head. The Wookiee hunched along one side of the dwelling with his Rebel comrades, while the Chief and ten Elders sat on the other side facing them. In the center, between the two groups, a small fire warmed the night air, casting ephemeral shadows on the earthen walls.

Outside, the entire village awaited the decisions this council would arrive at. It was a pensive, clear night, charged with high moment. Though it was quite late, not an Ewok slept.

Inside, Threepio was speaking. Positive and negative feedback loops had already substantially increased his fluency in this squeaky language; he was now in the midst of an animated history of the Galactic Civil War – replete with pantomime, elocution, explosive sound effects, and editorial commentary. He even mimicked an Imperial Walker at one point.

The Ewok Elders listened carefully, occasionally murmuring comments to each other. It was a fascinating story, and they were thoroughly absorbed – at times, horrified; at times, outraged. Logray conferred with Chief Chirpa once or twice, and several times asked Threepio questions, to which the golden droid responded quite movingly – once Artoo even whistled, probably for emphasis.

In the end, though, after a rather brief discussion among the Elders, the Chief shook his head negatively, with an expression of rueful dissatisfaction. He spoke finally to Threepio, and Threepio interpreted for his friends.

'Chief Chirpa says it's a very moving story,' the droid explained. 'But it really has nothing to do with Ewoks.'

A deep and pressing silence filled the small chamber. Only the fire softly crackled its bright but darkling soliloquy.

It was finally Solo – of all people – who opened his mouth to speak for the group. For the Alliance.

'Tell them this, Goldenrod—' he smiled at the droid, with

conscious affection for the first time. 'Tell them it's hard to translate a rebellion, so maybe a translator shouldn't tell the story. So *I'll* tell 'em.

'They shouldn't help us 'cause we're asking 'em to. They shouldn't even help us 'cause it's in their own interest to – even though it *is*, you know – just for one example, the Empire's tappin' a *lot* of energy out of this moon to generate its deflector shield, and that's a lot of energy you guys are gonna be *without* come winter, and I mean you're gonna be hurtin' ... but never mind that. Tell 'em, Threepio.'

Threepio told them. Han went on.

'But that's not why they should help us. That's why I used to do stuff, because it was in my interest. But not anymore. Well, not so much, anyway. Mostly I do things for my *friends*, now – 'cause what else is so important? Money? Power? Jabba had that, and you know what happened to him. Okay, okay, the point is – your friends are ... your *friends*. You know?'

This was one of the most inarticulate pleas Leia had ever heard, but it made her eyes fill with tears. The Ewoks, on the other hand, remained silent, impassive. Teebo and the stoic little fellow named Paploo traded a few muttered words; the rest were motionless, their expressions unreadable.

After another protracted pause, Luke cleared his throat. 'I realize this concept may be abstract – may be difficult to draw these connections,' he started slowly, 'but it's terribly important for the entire galaxy, for our Rebel force to destroy the Imperial presence here on Endor. Look up, there, through the smoke hole in the roof. Just through that tiny hole, you can count a hundred stars. In the whole sky there are millions, and billions more you can't even see. And they all have planets, and moons, and happy people just like you. And the Empire is destroying all that. You can ... you could get dizzy just lying on your back and staring up at all the starshine. You could almost ... explode, it's so beautiful sometimes. And you're part of the beauty, it's all part of the same Force. And the Empire is trying to turn out the lights.'

It took a while for Threepio to finish translating this – he wanted to get all the words just right. When he did eventually stop talking, there was an extensive squeaking among the Elders, rising and falling in volume, ceasing and then resuming again.

Leia knew what Luke was trying to say, but she feared greatly that the Ewoks wouldn't see the connection. It was connected intimately, though, if she could only bridge the gap for them. She thought of her experience in the forest earlier – her sense of oneness with the trees, whose outstretched limbs seemed to touch the very stars; the stars, whose light filtered down like cascading magic. She felt the power of the magic within her, and it resonated around the hut, from being to being, flowing through her again, making her stronger, still; until she felt one with these Ewoks, nearly – felt as if she understood them, knew them; conspired with them, in the primary sense of the word: they breathed together.

The debate wound down, leaving finally another quiet moment in the hut. Leia's respirations quieted, too, in resonance; and with an air of confident serenity, she made her appeal to the council.

'Do it because of the trees,' she said.

That's all she said. Everyone expected more, but there was no more; only this short, oblique outburst.

Wicket had been observing these proceedings with increasing concern, from the sidelines. On several occasions it was apparent he was restraining himself with great difficulty from entering the council's discourse – but now he jumped to his feet, paced the width of the hut several times, finally faced the Elders, and began his own impassioned speech.

'Eep eep, meep eek squee . . .'

Threepio translated for his friends: 'Honorable Elders, we have this night received a perilous, wondrous gift. The gift of freedom. This golden god . . .' – here Threepio paused in his translation just long enough to savor the moment; then went on – '. . . This golden god, whose return to us has been prophesied since the First Tree, tells us now he will not be our Master, tells us we are free to choose as we will – that we *must* choose; as all living things must choose their own destiny. He has come, Honorable Elders, and he will go; no longer may we be slaves to his divine guidance. We are free.

'Yet how must we comport ourselves? Is an Ewok's love of the wood any less because he can leave it? No – his love is more, because he can leave it, yet he stays. So is it with the voice of the Golden One: we can close our eyes; yet we listen.

'His friends tell us of a Force, a great living spirit, of which we are all part, even as the leaves are things separate yet part of the tree.

We know this spirit, Honorable Elders, though we call it not the Force. The friends of the Golden One tell us this Force is in great jeopardy, here and everywhere. When the fire reaches the forest, who is safe? Not even the Great Tree of which all things are part; nor its leaves, nor its roots, nor its birds. All are in peril, forever and ever.

'It is a brave thing to confront such a fire, Honorable Elders. Many will die, that the forest lives on.

'But the Ewoks are brave.'

The little bear-creature fixed his gaze on the others in the hut. Not a word was spoken; nonetheless, the communication was intense. After a minute like this, he concluded his statement.

'Honorable Elders, we must aid this noble party not less for the trees, but more for the sake of the *leaves* on the trees. These Rebels are like the Ewoks, who are like the leaves. Battered by the wind, eaten without thought by the tumult of locusts that inhabit the world – yet do we throw ourselves on smoldering fires, that another may know the warmth of light; yet do we make a soft bed of ourselves, that another may know rest; yet do we swirl in the wind that assails us, to send the fear of chaos into the hearts of our enemies; yet do we change color, even as the season calls upon us to change. So must we help our Leafbrothers, these Rebels – for so has come a season of change upon us.'

He stood, still, before them, the small fire dancing in his eye. For a timeless moment, all the world seemed still.

The Elders were moved. Without saying another word, they nodded in agreement. Perhaps they were telepathic.

In any case, Chief Chirpa stood and, without preface, made a brief pronouncement.

All at once drums began to beat throughout the entire village. The Elders jumped up – no longer at all so serious – and ran across the tent to hug the Rebels. Teebo even began to hug Artoo, but thought better of it as the little droid backed off with a low warning whistle. Teebo scurried over to hop playfully on the Wookiee's back instead.

Han smiled uncertainly. 'What's going on?'

'I'm not sure,' Leia answered out the side of her mouth, 'But it doesn't look too bad.'

Luke, like the others, was sharing the joyous occasion –

whatever it meant – with a pleasant smile and diffuse good will, when suddenly a dark cloud filled his heart, hovered there, nestled a clammy chill into the corners of his soul. He wiped its traces from his visage, made his face a mask. Nobody noticed.

Threepio finally nodded his understanding to Wicket, who was explaining the situation to him. He turned, with an expansive gesture, to the Rebels. 'We are now part of the tribe.'

'Just what I've always wanted,' said Solo.

Threepio continued talking to the others, trying to ignore the sarcastic Star Captain. 'The Chief has vowed to help us in any way to rid their land of the evil ones.'

'Well, short help is better than no help, I always say,' Solo chuckled.

Threepio was once again rapidly overheating his circuits toward the Corellian ingrate. 'Teebo says his chief scouts, Wicket and Paploo, will show us the fastest way to the shield generator.'

'Tell him thanks, Goldenrod.' He just loved irking Threepio. He couldn't help himself.

Chewie let out a righteous bark, happy to be on the move again. One of the Ewoks thought he was asking for food, though, and brought the Wookiee a large slab of meat. Chewbacca didn't refuse. He downed the meat in a single gulp, as several Ewoks gathered, watching in amazement. They were so incredulous at this feat, in fact, they began giggling furiously; and the laughter was so infectious, it started the Wookiee chortling. His gruff guffaws were *really* hilarious to the chuckling Ewoks, so – as was their custom – they jumped on him in a frenzy of tickling, which he returned threefold, until they all lay in a puddle, quite exhausted. Chewie wiped his eyes and grabbed another piece of meat, which he gnawed at a more leisurely pace.

Solo, meanwhile, began organizing the expedition. 'How far is it? We'll need some fresh supplies. There's not much time, you know. Give me some of that, Chewie . . .'

Chewie snarled.

Luke drifted to the back of the hut and then slipped outside during the commotion. Out in the square, a great party was going on – dancing, squealing, tickling – but Luke avoided this, too. He wandered away from the bonfires, away from the gaiety, to a secluded walkway on the dark side of a colossal tree.

Leia followed him.

The sounds of the forest filled the soft night air, here. Crickets, skittering rodents, desolate breezes, anguished owls. The perfumes were a mixture of night-blooming jasmine, and pine; the harmonies were strictly ethereal. The sky was crystal black.

Luke stared at the brightest star in the heavens. It looked to be fired from deep within its core by raging elemental vapors. It was the Death Star.

He couldn't take his eyes from it. Leia found him like that.

'What's wrong?' she whispered.

He smiled wearily. 'Everything, I'm afraid. Or nothing, maybe. Maybe things are finally going to be as they were meant to be.'

He felt the presence of Darth Vader very near.

Leia took his hand. She felt so close to Luke, yet ... she couldn't say how. He seemed so lost now, so alone. So distant. She almost couldn't feel his hand in hers. 'What is it, Luke?'

He looked down at their intertwined fingers. 'Leia ... do you remember your mother? Your real mother?'

The question took her totally by surprise. She'd always felt so close to her adopted parents, it was as if they *were* her real parents. She almost never thought of her *real* mother – that was like a dream.

Yet now Luke's question made her start. Flashes from her infancy assaulted her – distorted visions of running ... a beautiful woman ... hiding in a trunk. The fragments suddenly threatened to flood her with emotion.

'Yes,' she said, pausing to regain her composure. 'Just a little bit. She died when I was very young.'

'What do you remember?' he pressed. 'Tell me.'

'Just feelings, really ... images.' She wanted to let it slide, it was so out of the blue, so far from her immediate concerns ... but somehow so loud inside, all of a sudden.

'Tell me,' Luke repeated.

She felt surprised by his insistence, but decided to follow him with it, at least for the time being. She trusted him, even when he frightened her. 'She was very beautiful,' Leia remembered aloud. 'Gentle and kind – but sad.' She looked deeply into his eyes, seeking his intentions. 'Why are you asking me this?'

He turned away, peering back up at the Death Star, as if he'd been on the verge of opening up; then something scared him, and he pulled it all in once more. 'I have no memory of my mother,' he claimed. 'I never knew her.'

'Luke, tell me what's troubling you.' She wanted to help, she knew she could help.

He stared at her a long moment, estimating her abilities, gauging her need to know, her desire to know. She was strong. He felt it, unwaveringly. He could depend on her. They all could. 'Vader is here . . . now. On this moon.'

She felt a chill, like a physical sensation, as if her blood had actually congealed. 'How do you know?'

'I can feel his presence. He's come for me.'

'But how could he know we were here? Was it the code, did we leave out some password?' She knew it was none of these things.

'No, it's me. He can feel it when I'm near.' He held her by the shoulders. He wanted to tell her everything, but now as he tried, his will was starting to fail. 'I must leave you, Leia. As long as I'm here, I endanger the whole group and our mission here.' His hands trembled. 'I have to face Vader.'

Leia was fast becoming distraught, confused. Intimations were rushing at her like wild owls out of the night, their wings brushing her cheek, their talons catching her hair, their harsh whispers thrilling her ear: 'Who? Who? Who?'

She shook her head hard. 'I don't understand, Luke. What do you mean, you have to face Vader?'

He pulled her to him, his manner suddenly gentle; abidingly calm. To say it, just to say it, in some basic way released him. 'He's my father, Leia.'

'Your father!?' She couldn't believe it; yet of course it was true.

He held her steady, to be a rock for her. 'Leia, I've found something else out. It's not going to be easy for you to hear it, but you have to. You have to know before I leave here because I might not be back. And if I don't make it, you're the only hope for the Alliance.'

She looked away, she shook her head, she wouldn't look at him. It was terribly disturbing, what Luke was saying, though she couldn't imagine why. It was nonsense, of course; *that* was why. To call her the only hope for the Alliance if he should die – why, it was absurd. Absurd to think of Luke dying, and to think of her being the only hope.

Both thoughts were out of the question. She moved away from him, to deny his words; at least to give them distance, to let her breathe. Flashes of her mother came again, in this breathing space. Parting embraces, flesh torn from flesh . . .

'Don't talk that way, Luke. You have to survive. I do what I can – we all do – but I'm of no importance. Without you . . . I can do nothing. It's you, Luke. I've seen it. You have a power I don't understand . . . and could never have.'

'You're wrong, Leia.' He held her at arm's length. 'You have that power, too. The Force is strong in you. In time you'll learn to use it as I have.'

She shook her head. She couldn't hear this. He was lying. She had no power, the power was elsewhere, she could only help and succor and support. What was he saying? Was it possible?

He brought her closer still, held her face in his hands.

He looked so tender now, so giving. Was he giving her the power? Could she truly hold it? What was he saying? 'Luke, what's come over you?'

'Leia, the Force is strong in my family. My father has it, I have it, and . . . my sister has it.'

Leia stared full into his eyes again. Darkness whirled there. And truth. What she saw frightened her . . . but now, this time, she didn't draw away. She stood close to him. She started to understand.

'Yes,' he whispered, seeing her comprehension. 'Yes. It's you, Leia.' He held her in his arms.

Leia closed her eyes tightly against his words, against her tears. To no avail. It all washed over her, now, and through her. 'I know,' she nodded. Openly she wept.

'Then you know I must go to him.'

She stood back, her face hot, her mind swimming in a storm. 'No, Luke, no. Run away, far away. If he can feel your presence, go away from this place.' She held his hands, put her cheek on his chest. 'I wish I could go with you.'

He stroked the back of her head. 'No, you don't. You've never faltered. When Han and I and the others have doubted, you've always been strong. You've never turned away from your responsibility. I can't say the same.' He thought of his premature flight from Dagobah, racing to risk everything before his training had been completed, almost destroying everything because of it. He looked down at the black, mechanical hand he had to show for it. How much more would be lost to his weakness? 'Well,' he choked, 'now we're both going to fulfill our destinies.'

'Luke, why? Why must you confront him?'

He thought of all the reasons – to win, to lose, to join, to struggle, to kill, to weep, to walk away, to accuse, to ask why, to forgive, to not forgive, to die – but knew, in the end, there was only one reason, now and always. Only one reason that could ever matter. 'There's good in him, I've felt it. He won't give me over to the Emperor. I can save him, I can turn him back to the good side.' His eyes became wild for just a moment, torn by doubts and passions. 'I have to try, Leia. He's our father.'

They held each other close. Tears streamed silently down her face.

'Goodbye, dear sister – lost, and found. Goodbye, sweet, sweet Leia.'

She cried openly, now – they both did – as Luke held her away and moved slowly back along the planking. He disappeared into the darkness of the tree-cave that led out of the village.

Leia watched him go, quietly weeping. She gave free vent to her feelings, did not try to stop the tears – tried, instead, to feel them, to feel the source they came from, the path they took, the murky corners they cleansed.

Memories poured through her, now, clues, suspicions, half-heard mutterings when they'd thought she was asleep. Luke, her brother! And Vader, her father. This was too much to assimilate all at once, it was information overload.

She was crying and trembling and whimpering all at once, when suddenly Han stepped up and embraced her from behind. He'd gone looking for her, and heard her voice, and came around just in time to see Luke leaving – but only now, when Leia jumped at his touch and he turned her around, did he realize she was sobbing.

His quizzical smile turned to concern, tempered by the heart-fear of the would-be lover. 'Hey, what's going on here?'

She stifled her sobs, wiped her eyes. 'It's nothing, Han. I just want to be alone for a while.'

She was hiding something, that much was plain, and that much was unacceptable. 'It's not nothing!' he said angrily. 'I want to know what's going on. Now you tell me what it is.' He shook her. He'd never felt like this before. He wanted to know, but he didn't want to know what he thought he knew. It made him sick at heart to think of Leia ... with Luke ... he couldn't even bring himself to imagine what it was he didn't want to imagine.

He'd never been out of control like this, he didn't like it, he couldn't stop it. He realized he was still shaking her, and stopped.

'I can't, Han ...' Her lip began to tremble again.

'You can't! You can't tell *me*? I thought we were closer than that, but I guess I was wrong. Maybe you'd rather tell Luke. Sometimes I—'

'Oh, Han!' she cried, and burst into tears once more. She buried herself in his embrace.

His anger turned slowly to confusion and dismay, as he found himself wrapping his arms around her, caressing her shoulders, comforting her. 'I'm sorry,' he whispered into her hair. 'I'm sorry.' He didn't understand, not an iota – didn't understand her, or himself, or his topsy-turvy feelings, or women, or the universe. All he knew was that he'd just been furious, and now he was affectionate, protective, tender. Made no sense.

'Please ... just hold me,' she whispered. She didn't want to talk. She just wanted to be held.

He just held her.

Morning mist rose off dewy vegetation as the sun broke the horizon over Endor. The lush foliage of the forest's edge had a moist, green odor; in that dawning moment the world was silent, as if holding its breath.

In violent contrast, the Imperial landing platform squatted over the ground. Harsh, metallic, octagonal, it seemed to cut like an insult into the verdant beauty of the place. The bushes at its perimeter were singed black from repeated shuttle landings; the flora beyond that was wilting – dying from refuse disposal, trampling feet, chemical exhaust fumes. Like a blight was this outpost.

Uniformed troops walked continuously on the platform and in the area – loading, unloading, surveilling, guarding. Imperial Walkers were parked off to one side – square, armored, two-legged war machines, big enough for a squad of soldiers to stand inside, firing laser cannon in all directions. An Imperial shuttle took off for the Death Star, with a roar that made the trees cringe. Another walker emerged from the timber on the far side of the platform, returning from a patrol mission. Step by lumbering step, it approached the loading dock.

Darth Vader stood at the rail of the lower deck, staring mutely into the depths of the lovely forest. Soon. It was coming soon; he could feel it. Like a drum getting louder, his destiny approached. Dread was all around, but fear like this excited him, so he let it bubble quietly within. Dread was a tonic, it heightened his senses, honed a raw edge to his passions. Closer, it came.

Victory, too, he sensed. Mastery. But laced with something else ... what was it? He couldn't see it, quite. Always in motion, the future; difficult to see. Its apparitions tantalized him, swirling specters, always changing. Smoky was his future, thunderous with conquest and destruction.

Very close, now. Almost here.

He purred, in the pit of his throat, like a wild cat smelling game on the air.

Almost here.

The Imperial Walker docked at the opposite end of the deck, and opened its doors. A phalanx of stormtroopers marched out in tight circular formation. They lock-stepped toward Vader.

He turned around to face the oncoming troopers, his breathing even, his black robes hanging still in the windless morning. The stormtroopers stopped when they reached him, and at a word from their captain, parted to reveal a bound prisoner in their midst. It was Luke Skywalker.

The young Jedi gazed at Vader with complete calm, with many layers of vision.

The stormtrooper captain spoke to Lord Vader. 'This is the Rebel that surrendered to us. Although he denies it, I believe there may be more of them, and I request permission to conduct a wider search of the area.' He extended his hand to the Dark Lord; in it, he held Luke's lightsaber. 'He was armed only with this.'

Vader looked at the lightsaber a moment, then slowly took it from the captain's hand. 'Leave us. Conduct your search, and bring his companions to me.'

The officer and his troops withdrew back to the walker.

Luke and Vader were left standing alone facing each other, in the emerald tranquillity of the ageless forest. The mist was beginning to burn off. Long day ahead.

VII

'SO,' the Dark Lord rumbled. 'You have come to me.'

'And you to me.'

'The Emperor is expecting you. He believes you will turn to the dark side.'

'I know . . . Father.' It was a momentous act for Luke – to address his father, as his father. But he'd done it, now, and kept himself under control, and the moment was past. It was done. He felt stronger for it. He felt potent.

'So, you have finally accepted the truth,' Vader gloated.

'I have accepted the truth that you were once Anakin Skywalker, my father.'

'That name no longer has meaning for me.' It was a name from long ago. A different life, a different universe. Could he truly once have been that man?

'It is the name of your true self,' Luke's gaze bore steadily down on the cloaked figure. 'You have only forgotten. I know there is good in you. The Emperor hasn't driven it fully away.' He molded with his voice, tried to form the potential reality with the strength of his belief. 'That's why you could not destroy me. That's why you won't take me to your Emperor now.'

Vader seemed almost to smile through his mask at his son's use of Jedi voice-manipulation. He looked down at the lightsaber the captain had given him – Luke's lightsaber. So the boy was truly a Jedi now. A man grown. He held the lightsaber up. 'You have constructed another.'

'This one is mine,' Luke said quietly. 'I no longer use yours.'

Vader ignited the blade, examined its humming, brilliant light, like an admiring craftsman. 'Your skills are complete. Indeed, you are as powerful as the Emperor has foreseen.'

They stood there for a moment, the lightsaber between them. Sparks dove in and out of the cutting edge: photons pushed to the brink by the energy pulsing between these two warriors.

'Come with me, Father.'

Vader shook his head. 'Ben once thought as you do—'

'Don't blame Ben for your fall—' Luke took a step closer, then stopped.

Vader did not move. 'You don't know the power of the dark side. I must obey my master.'

'I will not turn – you will be forced to destroy me.'

'If that is your destiny.' This was not his wish, but the boy was strong – if it came, at last, to blows, yes, he would destroy Luke. He could no longer afford to hold back, as he once had.

'Search your feelings, Father. You can't do this. I feel the conflict within you. Let go of your hate.'

But Vader hated no one; he only lusted too blindly. 'Someone has filled your mind with foolish ideas, young one. The Emperor will show you the true nature of the Force. *He* is your master, now.'

Vader signaled to a squad of distant stormtroopers as he extinguished Luke's lightsaber. The guards approached. Luke and the Dark Lord faced one another for a long, searching moment. Vader spoke just before the guards arrived.

'It is too late for me, Son.'

'Then my father is truly dead,' answered Luke. So what was to stop him from killing the Evil One who stood before him now? he wondered.

Nothing, perhaps.

The vast Rebel fleet hung poised in space, ready to strike. It was hundreds of light-years from the Death Star – but in hyperspace, all time was a moment, and the deadliness of an attack was measured not in distance but in precision.

Ships changed in formation from corner to side, creating a faceted diamond shape to the armada – as if, like a cobra, the fleet was spreading its hood.

The calculations required to launch such a meticulously coordinated offensive at lightspeed made it necessary to fix on a stationary point – that is, stationary relative to the point of reentry from hyperspace. The point chosen by the Rebel command was a small, blue planet of the Sullust system. The armada was positioned around it, now, this unblinking cerulean world. It looked like the eye of the serpent.

The *Millennium Falcon* finished its rounds of the fleet's perimeter, checking final positions, then pulled into place beneath the flagship. The time had come.

Lando was at the controls of the *Falcon*. Beside him, his copilot, Nien Nunb – a jowled, mouse-eyed creature from Sullust – flipped switches, monitored readouts, and made final preparations for the jump to hyperspace.

Lando set his comlink to war channel. Last hand of the night, his deal, a table full of high rollers – his favorite kind of game. With dry mouth, he made his summary report to Ackbar on the command ship. 'Admiral, we're in position. All fighters are accounted for.'

Ackbar's voice crackled back over the headset. 'Proceed with the countdown. All groups assume attack coordinates.'

Lando turned to his copilot with a quick smile. 'Don't worry, my friends are down there, they'll have that shield down on time . . .' He turned back to his instruments, saying under his breath: 'Or this will be the shortest offensive of all time.'

'Gzhung Zhgodio,' the copilot commented.

'All right,' Lando grunted. 'Stand by, then.' He patted the control panel for good luck, even though his deepest belief was that a good gambler made his own luck. Still, that's what Han's job was this time, and Han had almost never let Lando down. Just once – and that was a long time ago, in a star system far, far away.

This time was different. This time they were going to redefine luck, and call it Lando. He smiled, and patted the panel one more time . . . just right.

Up on the bridge of the Star Cruiser command ship, Ackbar paused, looked around at his generals: all was ready.

'Are all groups in their attack coordinates?' he asked. He knew they were.

'Affirmative, Admiral.'

Ackbar gazed out his view-window meditatively at the starfield, for perhaps the last reflective moment he would ever have. He spoke finally into the comlink war channel. 'All craft will begin the jump to hyperspace on my mark. May the Force be with us.'

He reached forward to the signal button.

In the *Falcon*, Lando stared at the identical galactic ocean, with the same sense of grand moment; but also with foreboding. They were doing what a guerrilla force must never do: engage the enemy like a traditional army. The Imperial army, fighting the Rebellion's guerrilla war, was always losing – unless it won. The Rebels, by contrast, were always winning – unless they lost. And now, here was the most dangerous situation – the Alliance drawn into the open, to fight on the Empire's terms: if the Rebels lost this battle, they lost the war.

Suddenly the signal light flashed on the control panel: Ackbar's mark. The attack was commenced.

Lando pulled back the conversion switch and opened up the throttle. Outside the cockpit, the stars began streaking by. The streaks grew brighter, and longer, as the ships of the fleet roared, in large segments, at lightspeed, keeping pace first with the very photons of the radiant stars in the vicinity, and then soaring through the warp into hyperspace itself – and disappearing in the flash of a muon.

The blue crystal planet hovered in space alone, once again; staring; unseeing, into the void.

The strike squad crouched behind a woodsy ridge overlooking the Imperial outpost. Leia viewed the area through a small electronic scanner.

Two shuttles were being off-loaded on the landing platform docking ramp. Several walkers were parked nearby. Troops stood around, helped with construction, took watch, carried supplies. The massive shield generator hummed off to the side.

Flattened down in the bushes on the ridge with the strike force were several Ewoks, including Wicket, Paploo, Teebo, and War-wick. The rest stayed lower, behind the knoll, out of sight.

Leia put down the scanner and scuttled back to the others. 'The entrance is on the far side of that landing platform. This isn't going to be easy.'

'Ahrck grah rahr hrowrowhr,' Chewbacca agreed.

'Oh, come on, Chewie,' Han gave the Wookiee a pained look. 'We've gotten into more heavily guarded places than that—'

'Frowh rahgh rahrahraff vrawgh gr,' Chewie countered with a dismissing gesture.

Han thought for a second. 'Well, the spice vaults of Gargon, for one.'

'Krahghrowf,' Chewbacca shook his head.

'Of course I'm right – now if I could just remember how I did it . . .' Han scratched his head, poking his memory.

Suddenly Paploo began chattering away, pointing, squealing. He garbled something to Wicket.

'What's he saying, Threepio?' Leia asked.

The golden droid exchanged a few terse sentences with Paploo; then Wicket turned to Leia with a hopeful grin.

Threepio, too, now looked at the Princess. 'Apparently Wicket knows about a back entrance to this installation.'

Han perked up at that. 'A back door? That's it! That's how we did it!'

Four Imperial scouts kept watch over the entrance to the bunker that half-emerged from the earth far to the rear of the main section of the shield generator complex. Their rocket bikes were parked nearby.

In the undergrowth beyond, the Rebel strike squad lay in wait.

'Grrr, rowf rrrhl brhnnnh,' Chewbacca observed slowly.

'You're right, Chewie,' Solo agreed, 'with just those guards this should be easier than breaking a Bantha.'

'It only takes one to sound the alarm,' Leia cautioned.

Han grinned, a bit overselfconfidently. 'Then we'll have to do this real quietlike. If Luke can just keep Vader off our backs, like you said he said he would, this oughta be no sweat. Just gotta hit those guards fast and quiet . . .'

Threepio whispered to Teebo and Paploo, explaining the problem and the objective. The Ewoks babbled giddily a moment, then Paploo jumped up and raced through the underbrush.

Leia checked the instrument on her wrist. 'We're running out of time. The fleet's in hyperspace by now.'

Threepio muttered a question to Teebo and received a short reply. 'Oh, dear,' Threepio replied, starting to rise, to look into the clearing beside the bunker.

'Stay down!' rasped Solo.

'What is it, Threepio?' Leia demanded.

'I'm afraid our furry companion has gone and done something rash.' The droid hoped he wasn't to be blamed for this.

'What are you talking about?' Leia's voice cut with an edge of fear.

'Oh, no. Look.'

Paploo had scampered down through the bushes to where the scouts' bikes were parked. Now, with the sickening horror of inevitability, the Rebel leaders watched the little ball of fur swing his pudgy body up onto one of the bikes, and begin flipping switches at random. Before anyone could do anything, the bike's engines ignited with a rumbling roar. The four scouts looked over in surprise. Paploo grinned madly, and continued flipping switches.

Leia held her forehead. 'Oh, no, no, no.'

Chewie barked. Han nodded. 'So much for our surprise attack.'

The Imperial scouts raced toward Paploo just as the forward drive engaged, zooming the little teddy bear into the forest. He had all he could do just to hang on to the handlebar with his stubby paws. Three of the guards jumped on their own bikes, and sped off in pursuit of the hotrod Ewok. The fourth scout stayed at his post, near the door of the bunker.

Leia was delighted, if a bit incredulous.

'Not bad for a ball of fuzz,' Han admired. He nodded at Chewie, and the two of them slipped down toward the bunker.

Paploo, meanwhile, was sailing through the trees, more lucky than in control. He was going at fairly low velocity for what the bike could do – but in Ewok-time, Paploo was absolutely dizzy with speed and excitement. It was terrifying; but he loved it. He would talk about this ride until the end of his life, and then his children would tell their children, and it would get faster with each generation.

For now, though, the Imperial scouts were already pulling in sight behind him. When, a moment later, they began firing laser bolts at him, he decided he'd finally had enough. As he rounded the next tree, just out of their sight, he grabbed a vine and swung up into the branches. Several seconds later the three scouts tore by underneath him, pressing their pursuit to the limit. He giggled furiously.

Back at the bunker, the last scout was undone. Subdued by Chewbacca, bound, stripped of his suit, he was being carried into the woods now by two other members of the strike team. The rest of the squad silently crouched, forming a perimeter around the entrance.

Han stood at the door, checking the stolen code against the digits on the bunker's control panel. With natural speed he punched a series of buttons on the panel. Silently, the door opened.

Leia peeked inside. No sign of life. She motioned the others, and entered the bunker. Han and Chewie followed close on her heels. Soon the entire team was huddled inside the otherwise empty steel corridor, leaving one lookout outside, dressed in the unconscious scout's uniform. Han pushed a series of buttons on the inner panel, closing the door behind them.

Leia thought briefly of Luke – she hoped he could detain Vader at least long enough to allow her to destroy this shield generator; she hoped even more dearly he could avoid such a confrontation altogether. For she feared Vader was the stronger of the two.

Furtively she led the way down the dark and low-beamed tunnel.

Vader's shuttle settled onto the docking bay of the Death Star, like a black, wingless carrion-eating bird; like a nightmare insect. Luke and the Dark Lord emerged from the snout of the beast with a small escort of stormtroopers, and walked rapidly across the cavernous main bay to the Emperor's tower elevator.

Royal guards awaited them there, flanking the shaft, bathed in a carmine glow. They opened the elevator door. Luke stepped forward.

His mind was buzzing with what to do. It was the Emperor he was being taken to, now. The Emperor! If Luke could but focus, keep his mind clear to see what must be done – and do it.

A great noise filled his head, though, like an underground wind.

He hoped Leia deactivated the deflector shield quickly, and destroyed the Death Star – now, while all three of them were here. Before anything else happened. For the closer Luke came to the

Emperor, the more *anythings* he feared *would* happen. A black storm raged inside him. He wanted to kill the Emperor, but then what? Confront Vader? What would his father do? And what if Luke faced his father first, faced him and – destroyed him. The thought was at once repugnant and compelling. Destroy Vader – and then what? For the first time, Luke had a brief murky image of himself, standing on his father's body, holding his father's blazing power, and sitting at the Emperor's right hand.

He squeezed his eyes shut against this thought, but it left a cold sweat on his brow, as if Death's hand had brushed him there and left its shallow imprint.

The elevator door opened. Luke and Vader walked out into the throne room alone, across the unlit ante-chamber, up the grated stairs, to stand before the throne: father and son, side by side, both dressed in black, one masked and one exposed, beneath the gaze of the malignant Emperor.

Vader bowed to his master. The Emperor motioned him to rise, though; the Dark Lord did his master's bidding.

'Welcome, young Skywalker,' the Evil One smiled graciously. 'I have been expecting you.'

Luke stared back brazenly at the bent, hooded figure. Defiantly. The Emperor's smile grew even softer, though; even more fatherly. He looked at Luke's manacles.

'You no longer need these,' he added with *noblesse oblige* – and made the slightest motion with his finger in the direction of Luke's wrists. At that, Luke's binders simply fell away, clattering noisily to the floor.

Luke looked at his own hands – free, now, to reach out for the Emperor's throat, to crush his windpipe in an instant . . .

Yet the Emperor seemed gentle. Had he not just let Luke free? But he was devious, too, Luke knew. Do not be fooled by appearances, Ben had told him. The Emperor was unarmed. He could still strike. But wasn't aggression part of the dark side? Mustn't he avoid that at all costs? Or could he use darkness judiciously, and then put it away? He stared at his free hands . . . he could have ended it all right there – or could he? He had total freedom to choose what to do now; yet he could not choose. Choice, the double-edge sword. He could kill the Emperor, he could succumb to the Emperor's arguments. He could kill Vader . . . and then he could even become Vader. Again this thought laughed at him like a broken clown, until he pushed it back into a black corner of his brain.

The Emperor sat before him, smiling. The moment was convulsive with possibilities . . .

The moment passed. He did nothing.

'Tell me, young Skywalker,' the Emperor said when he saw Luke's first struggle had taken its course. 'Who has been involved in your training until now?' The smile was thin, open-mouthed, hollow.

Luke was silent. He would reveal nothing.

'Oh, I know it was Obi-Wan Kenobi at first,' the wicked ruler continued, rubbing his fingers together as if trying to remember. Then pausing, his lips creased into a sneer. 'Of course, we are familiar with the talent Obi-Wan Kenobi had, when it came to training Jedi.' He nodded politely in Vader's direction, indicating Obi-Wan's previous star pupil. Vader stood without responding, without moving.

Luke tensed with fury at the Emperor's defamation of Ben – though, of course, to the Emperor it was praise. And he bridled even more, knowing the Emperor was so nearly right. He tried to bring his anger under control, though, for it seemed to please the malevolent dictator greatly.

Palpatine noted the emotions on Luke's face and chuckled. 'So, in your early training you have followed your father's path, it would seem. But alas, Obi-Wan is now dead, I believe; his elder student, here, saw to that—' again, he made a hand motion toward Vader. 'So tell me, young Skywalker – who continued your training?'

That smile, again, like a knife. Luke held silent, struggling to regain his composure.

The Emperor tapped his fingers on the arm of the throne, recalling. 'There was one called . . . Yoda. An aged Master Jed . . . Ah, I see by your countenance I have hit a chord, a resonant chord indeed. Yoda, then.'

Luke flashed with anger at himself, now, to have revealed so much, unwillingly, unwittingly. Anger and self-doubt. He strove to calm himself – to see all, to show nothing; only to be.

'This Yoda,' the Emperor mused. 'Lives he still?'

Luke focused on the emptiness of space beyond the window behind the Emperor's chair. The deep void, where nothing was.

Nothing. He filled his mind with this black nothing. Opaque, save for the occasional flickering of starlight that filtered through the ether.

'Ah,' cried Emperor Palpatine. 'He lives not. Very good, young Skywalker, you almost hid this from me. But you could not. And you can not. Your deepest flickerings are to me apparent. Your nakedest soul. That is my first lesson to you.' He beamed.

Luke wilted – but a moment. In the very faltering, he found strength. Thus had Ben and Yoda both instructed him: when you are attacked, fall. Let your opponent's power buffet you as a strong wind topples the grass. In time, he will expend himself, and you will still be upright.

The Emperor watched Luke's face with cunning. 'I'm sure Yoda taught you to use the Force with great skill.'

The taunt had its desired effect – Luke's face flushed, his muscles flexed.

He saw the Emperor actually lick his lips at the sight of Luke's reaction. Lick his lips and laugh from the bottom of his throat, the bottom of his soul.

Luke paused, for he saw something else, as well; something he hadn't seen before in the Emperor. Fear.

Luke saw fear in the Emperor – fear of Luke. Fear of Luke's power, fear that this power could be turned on him – on the Emperor – in the same way Vader had turned it on Obi-Wan Kenobi. Luke saw this fear in the Emperor – and he knew, now, the odds had shifted slightly. He had glimpsed the Emperor's nakedest self.

With sudden absolute calm, Luke stood upright. He stared directly into the malign ruler's hood.

Palpatine said nothing for a few moments, returning the young Jedi's gaze, assessing his strengths and weaknesses. He sat back at last, pleased with this first confrontation. 'I look forward to completing your training, young Skywalker. In time, you will call *me* Master.'

For the first time, Luke felt steady enough to speak. 'You're gravely mistaken. You will not convert me as you did my father.'

'No, my young Jedi,' the Emperor leaned forward, gloating, 'you will find that it is *you* who are mistaken ... about a great many things.'

Palpatine suddenly stood, came down from his throne, walked up very close to Luke, stared venomously into the boy's eyes. At last, Luke saw the entire face within the hood: eyes, sunken like tombs; the flesh decayed beneath skin weathered by virulent storms, lined by holocaust; the grin, a death's-grin; the breath, corrupt.

Vader extended a gloved hand toward the Emperor, holding out Luke's lightsaber. The Emperor took it with a slow sort of glee, then walked with it across the room to the huge circular view-window. The Death Star had been revolving slowly, so the Sanctuary Moon was now visible at the window's curving margin.

Palpatine looked at Endor, then back at the lightsaber in his hand. 'Ah, yes, a Jedi's weapon. Much like your father's.' He faced Luke directly. 'By now you must know your father can never be turned from the dark side. So will it be with you.'

'Never. Soon I will die, and you with me.' Luke was confident of that now. He allowed himself the luxury of a boast.

The Emperor laughed, a vile laugh. 'Perhaps you refer to the imminent attack of your Rebel fleet.' Luke had a thick, reeling moment, then steadied himself. The Emperor went on. 'I assure you, we are quite safe from your friends here.'

Vader walked toward the Emperor, stood at his side, looking at Luke.

Luke felt increasingly raw. 'Your overconfidence is your weakness,' he challenged them.

'Your faith in your friends is yours.' The Emperor began smiling; but then his mouth turned down, his voice grew angry. 'Everything that has transpired has done so according to *my* design. Your friends up there on the Sanctuary Moon – they're walking into a trap. And so is your Rebel fleet!'

Luke's face twitched visibly. The Emperor saw this, and really began to foam. 'It was *I* who allowed the Alliance to know the location of the shield generator. It is quite safe from your pitiful little band – an entire legion of my troops awaits them there.'

Luke's eyes darted from the Emperor, to Vader, and finally to the lightsaber in the Emperor's hand. His mind quivered with alternatives; suddenly everything was out of control again. He could count on nothing but himself. And on himself, his hold was tenuous.

The Emperor kept rattling on imperiously. 'I'm afraid the deflector shield will be quite operational when your fleet arrives.

And that is only the beginning of my surprise – but of course I don't wish to spoil it for you.'

The situation was degenerating fast, from Luke's perspective. Defeat after defeat was being piled on his head. How much could he take? And now another surprise coming? There seemed to be no end to the rank deeds Palpatine could carry out against the galaxy. Slowly, infinitesimally, Luke raised his hand in the direction of the lightsaber.

The Emperor continued. 'From here, young Skywalker, you will witness the final destruction of the Alliance – and the end of your insignificant rebellion.'

Luke was in torment. He raised his hand further. He realized both Palpatine and Vader were watching him. He lowered his hand, lowered his level of anger, tried to restore his previous calm, to find his center to see what it was he needed to do.

The Emperor smiled, a thin dry smile. He offered the lightsaber to Luke. 'You want this, don't you? The hate is swelling in you, now. Very good, take your Jedi weapon. Use it. I am unarmed. Strike me down with it. Give in to your anger. With each passing moment you make yourself more my servant.'

His rasping laughter echoed off the walls like desert wind. Vader continued staring at Luke.

Luke tried to hide his agony. 'No, never.' He thought desperately of Ben and Yoda. They were part of the Force, now, part of the energy that shaped it. Was it possible for them to distort the Emperor's vision by their presence? No one was infallible, Ben had told him – surely the Emperor couldn't see everything, couldn't know every future, twist every reality to suit his gluttony. *Ben*, thought Luke, *if ever I needed your guidance, it is now. Where can I take this, that it will not lead me to ruin?*

As if in answer, the Emperor leered, and put the lightsaber down on the control chair near Luke's hand. 'It is unavoidable,' the Emperor said quietly. 'It is your destiny. You, like your father, are now . . . mine.'

Luke had never felt so lost.

Han, Chewie, Leia, and a dozen commandos made their way down the labyrinthine corridors toward the area where the shield generator room was marked on the stolen map. Yellow lights illuminated the low rafters, casting long shadows at each inter-section. At the first three turnings, all remained quiet; they saw no guard or worker.

At the fourth cross-corridor, six Imperial stormtroopers stood a wary watch.

There was no way around; the section had to be traversed. Han and Leia looked at each other and shrugged; there was nothing for it but to fight.

With pistols drawn, they barged into the entryway. Almost as if they'd been expecting an attack, the guards instantly crouched and began firing their own weapons. A barrage of laserbolts followed, ricocheting from girder to floor. Two stormtroopers were hit immediately. A third lost his gun; pinned behind a refrigerator console, he was unable to do much but stay low.

Two more stood behind a fire door, though, and blasted each commando who tried to get through. Four went down. The guards were virtually impregnable behind their vulcanized shield – but *virtually* didn't account for Wookiees.

Chewbacca rushed the door, physically dislodging it on top of the two stormtroopers. They were crushed.

Leia shot the sixth guard as he stood to draw a bead on Chewie. The trooper who'd been crouching beneath the refrigeration unit suddenly bolted, to go for help. Han raced after him a few long strides and brought him down with a flying tackle. He was out cold.

They checked themselves over, accounted for casualties. Not too bad – but it had been noisy. They'd have to hurry now, before a general alarm was set. The power center that controlled the shield generator was very near. And there would be no second chances.

The Rebel fleet broke out of hyperspace with an awesome roar. Amid glistening streamers of light, battalion after battalion emerged in formation, to fire off toward the Death Star and its Sanctuary Moon hovering brightly in the close distance. Soon the entire navy was bearing down on its target, the *Millennium Falcon* in the lead.

Lando was worried from the moment they came out of hyper-space. He checked his screen, reversed polarities, queried the computer.

The copilot was perplexed, as well. 'Zhng ahzi gngnohzh. Dzhy lyhz!'

'But how could that be?' Lando demanded. 'We've got to be able to get *some* kind of reading on the shield, up or down.' Who was conning whom on this raid?

Nien Nunb pointed at the control panel, shaking his head. 'Dzhmbd.'

'Jammed? How could they be jamming us if they don't know we're . . . coming.'

He grimaced at the onrushing Death Star, as the implications of what he'd just said sank in. This was not a surprise attack, after all. It was a spider web.

He hit the switch on his comlink. 'Break off the attack! The shield's still up!'

Red Leader's voice shouted back over the headphones. 'I get no reading, are you sure?'

'Pull up!' Lando commanded. 'All craft pull up!'

He banked hard to the left, the fighters of the Red Squad veering close on his tail.

Some didn't make it. Three flanking X-wings nicked the invisible deflector shield, spinning out of control, exploding in flames along the shield surface. None of the others paused to look back.

On the Rebel Star Cruiser bridge, alarms were screaming, lights flashing, klaxons blaring, as the mammoth space cruiser abruptly altered its momentum, trying to change course in time to avoid collision with the shield. Officers were running from battle stations to navigation controls; other ships in the fleet could be seen through the view-screens, careening wildly in a hundred directions, some slowing, some speeding up.

Admiral Ackbar spoke urgently but quietly into the comlink. 'Take evasive action. Green Group steer course for Holding Sector. MG-7 Blue group—'

A Mon Calamari controller, across the bridge, called out to Ackbar with grave excitement. 'Admiral, we have enemy ships at Sector RT-23 and PB-4.'

The large central view-screen was coming alive. It was no longer just the Death Star and the green moon behind it, floating isolated in space. Now the massive Imperial fleet could be seen flying in perfect, regimental formation, out from behind Endor in two behemoth flanking waves – heading to surround the Rebel fleet from both sides, like the pincers of a deadly scorpion.

And the shield barricaded the Alliance in front. They had nowhere to go.

Ackbar spoke desperately into the comlink. 'It's a trap. Prepare for attack.'

An anonymous fighter pilot's voice came back over the radio. 'Fighters coming in! Here we go!'

The attack began. The battle was joined.

TIE fighters, first – they were much faster than the bulky Imperial Cruisers, so they were the first to make contact with the Rebel invaders. Savage dogfights ensued, and soon the black sky was aglow with ruby explosions.

An aide approached Ackbar. 'We've added power to the forward shield, Admiral.'

'Good. Double power on the main battery, and—'

Suddenly the Star Cruiser was rocked by thermonuclear fireworks outside the observation window.

'Gold Wing is hit hard!' another officer shouted, stumbling up to the bridge.

'Give them cover!' Ackbar ordered. 'We must have time!' He spoke again into the comlink, as yet another detonation rumbled the frigate. 'All ships, stand your position. Wait for my command to return!'

It was far too late for Lando and his attack squadrons to heed that order, though. They were already way ahead of the pack, heading straight for the oncoming Imperial fleet.

Wedge Antilles, Luke's old buddy from the first campaign, led the X-wings that accompanied the *Falcon*. As they drew near the Imperial defenders, his voice came over the comlink, calm and experienced. 'Lock X-foils in attack positions.'

The wings split like dragonfly gossamers, poised for increased maneuvering and power.

'All wings report in,' said Lando.

'Red Leader standing by,' Wedge replied.

'Green Leader standing by.'

'Blue Leader standing by.'

'Gray Leader—'

This last transmission was interrupted by a display of pyrotechnics that completely disintegrated Gray Wing.

'Here they come,' Wedge commented.

'Accelerate to attack speed,' Lando ordered. 'Draw fire away from our cruisers as long as possible.'

'Copy, Gold Leader,' Wedge responded. 'We're moving to point three across the axis—'

'Two of them coming in at twenty degrees—' someone advised.

'I see them,' noted Wedge. 'Cut left, I'll take the leader.'

'Watch yourself, Wedge, three from above.'

'Yeah, I—'

'I'm on it, Red Leader.'

'There's too many of them—'

'You're taking a lot of fire, back off—'

'Red Four, watch out!'

'I'm hit!'

The X-wing spun, sparking, across the starfield, out of power, into the void.

'You've picked one up, watch it!' Red Six yelled at Wedge.

'My scope's negative, where is he?'

'Red Six, a squadron of fighters has broken through—'

'They're heading for the Medical Frigate! After them!'

'Go ahead,' Lando agreed. 'I'm going in. There're four marks at point three five. Cover me!'

'Right behind you, Gold Leader. Red Two, Red Three, pull in—'

'Hang on, back there.'

'Close up formations, Blue Group.'

'Good shooting, Red Two.'

'Not bad,' said Lando. 'I'll take out the other three . . .'

Calrissian steered the *Falcon* into the complete flip, as his crew fired at the Imperial fighters from the belly guns. Two were direct hits, the third a glancing blow that caused the TIE fighter to tumble into another of its own squads. The heavens were absolutely thick with them, but the *Falcon* was faster by half than anything else that flew.

Within a matter of minutes, the battlefield was a diffuse red glow, spotted with puffs of smoke, blazing fireballs, whirling spark showers, spinning debris, rumbling implosions, shafts of light, tumbling machinery, space-frozen corpses, wells of blackness, electron storms.

It was a grim and dazzling spectacle. And only beginning.

Nien Nunb made a guttural aside to Lando.

'You're right,' the pilot frowned. 'Only their fighters are attacking. What are those Star Destroyers waiting for?' Looked like the Emperor was trying to get the Rebels to buy some real estate he wasn't intending to sell.

'Dzhng zhng,' the copilot warned, as another squadron of TIE fighters swooped down from above.

'I see 'em. We're sure in the middle of it, now.' He took a second to glance at Endor, floating peacefully off to his right. 'Come on, Han old buddy, don't let me down.'

Han pressed the button on his wrist-unit and covered his head: the reinforced door to the main control room blew into melted pieces. The Rebel squad stormed through the gaping portal.

The stormtroopers inside seemed taken completely by surprise. A few were injured by the exploding door; the rest gawked in dismay as the Rebels rushed them with guns drawn. Han took the lead, Leia right behind; Chewie covered the rear.

They herded all the personnel into one corner of the bunker. Three commandos guarded them there, three more covered the exits. The rest began placing the explosive charges.

Leia studied one of the screens on the control panel. 'Hurry, Han, look! The fleet's being attacked!'

Solo looked over at the screen. 'Blast it! With the shield still up, they're backed against the wall.'

'That is correct,' came a voice from the rear of the room. 'Just as *you* are.'

Han and Leia spun around to find dozens of Imperial guns trained on them; an entire legion had been hiding in the wall compartments of the bunker. Now, in a single moment, the Rebels were surrounded – nowhere to run, far too many stormtroopers to fight. Completely surrounded.

More Imperial troops charged through the door, roughly disarming the stunned commandos.

Han, Chewie, and Leia exchanged helpless, hopeless looks. They'd been the Rebellion's last chance.

They'd failed.

Some distance from the main area of battle, coasting safely in the center of the blanket of ships that constituted the Imperial fleet, was the flagship Super Star Destroyer. On the bridge, Admiral Piett watched the war through the enormous observation window – curious, as if viewing an elaborate demonstration, or an entertainment.

Two fleet captains stood behind him, respectfully silent; also learning the elegant designs of their Emperor.

'Have the fleet hold here,' Admiral Piett ordered.

The first captain hurried to carry out the order. The second stepped up to the window, beside the admiral. 'We aren't going to attack?'

Piett smirked. 'I have my orders from the Emperor himself. He has something special planned for this Rebel scum.' He accented the specialness with a long pause, for the inquisitive captain to savor. 'We are only to keep them from escaping.'

The Emperor, Lord Vader, and Luke watched the aerial battle rage from the safety of the throne room in the Death Star.

It was a scene of pandemonium. Silent, crystalline explosions surrounded by green, violet, or magenta auras. Wildly vicious dogfights. Gracefully floating crags of melted steel; icicle sprays that might have been blood.

Luke watched in horror, as another Rebel ship toppled against the unseeable deflector shield, exploding in a fiery concussion.

Vader watched Luke. His boy was powerful, stronger than he'd imagined. And still pliable. Not lost yet – either to the sickening, weakly side of the Force, that had to beg for everything it received; or to the Emperor, who feared Luke with reason.

There was yet time to take Luke for his own – to retake him. To join with him in dark majesty. To rule the galaxy together. It would only take patience and a little wizardry to show Luke the exquisite satisfactions of the dark way and to pry him from the Emperor's terrified clutch.

Vader knew Luke had seen it, too – the Emperor's fear. He was a clever boy, young Luke, Vader smiled grimly to himself. He was his father's son.

The Emperor interrupted Vader's contemplation with a cackled remark to Luke. 'As you can see, my young apprentice, the deflector shield is still in place. Your friends have failed! And now ...' he raised his spindly hand above his head to mark this moment:

'Witness the power of this fully armed and operational battle station.' He walked over to the comlink and spoke in a gravelly whisper, as if to a lover. 'Fire at will, Commander.'

In shock, and in foreknowledge, Luke looked out across the surface of the Death Star, to the space battle beyond and to the bulk of the Rebel fleet beyond that.

Down in the bowels of the Death Star, Commander Jerjerrod gave an order. It was with mixed feelings that he issued the command, because it meant the final destruction of the Rebel insurrectionists – which meant an end to the state of war, which Jerjerrod cherished above all things. But second to ongoing war itself Jerjerrod loved total annihilation; so while tempered with regret, this order was not entirely without thrill.

At Jerjerrod's instruction, a controller pulled a switch, which ignited a blinking panel. Two hooded Imperial soldiers pushed a series of buttons. A thick beam of light slowly pulsed from a long, heavily blockaded shaft. On the outer surface of the completed half of the Death Star, a giant laser dish began to glow.

Luke watched in impotent horror, as the unbelievably huge laser beam radiated out from the muzzle of the Death Star. It touched – for only an instant – one of the Rebel Star Cruisers that was surging in the midst of the heaviest fighting. And in the next instant, the Star Cruiser was vaporized. Blown to dust. Returned to its most elemental particles, in a single burst of light.

In the numbing grip of despair, with the hollowest of voids devouring his heart, Luke's eyes, alone, glinted – for he saw, again, his lightsaber, lying unattended on the throne. And in this bleak and livid moment, the dark side was much with him.

VIII

ADMIRAL Ackbar stood on the bridge in stunned disbelief, looking out the observation window at the place where, a moment before, the Rebel Star Cruiser *Liberty* had just been engaged in a furious long-range battle. Now, there was nothing. Only empty space, powdered with a fine dust that sparkled in the light of more distant explosions. Ackbar stared in silence.

Around him, confusion was rampant. Flustered controllers were still trying to contact the *Liberty*, while fleet captains ran from screen to port, shouting, directing, misdirecting.

An aide handed Ackbar the comlink. General Calrissian's voice was coming through.

'Home-one, this is Gold Leader. That blast came from the Death Star! Repeat, the Death Star is operational!'

'We saw it,' Ackbar answered wearily. 'All craft prepare to retreat.'

'I'm not going to give up and run!' Lando shouted back. He'd come a long way to be in this game.

'We have no choice, General Calrissian. Our cruisers can't repel firepower of that magnitude!'

'You won't get a second chance at this, Admiral. Han will have that shield down – we've got to give him more time. Head for those Star Destroyers.'

Ackbar looked around him. A huge charge of flak rumbled the ship, painting a brief, waxen light over the window. Calrissian was right: there would be no second chance. It was now, or it was the end.

He turned to his First Star captain. 'Move the fleet forward.'

'Yes, sir.' The man paused. 'Sir, we don't stand much of a chance against those Star Destroyers. They out-gun us, and they're more heavily armored.'

'I know,' Ackbar said softly.

The captain left. An aide approached.

'Forward ships have made contact with the Imperial fleet, sir.'

'Concentrate your fire on their power generators. If we can knock out their shields, our fighters might stand a chance against them.'

The ship was rocked by another explosion – a laserbolt hit to one of the aft gyrostabilizers.

'Intensify auxiliary shields!' someone yelled.

The pitch of the battle augmented another notch.

Beyond the window of the throne room, the Rebel fleet was being decimated in the soundless vacuum of space, while inside, the only sound was the Emperor's thready cackle. Luke continued his spiral into desperation as the Death Star laser beam incinerated ship after ship.

The Emperor hissed. 'Your fleet is lost – and your friends on the Endor Moon will not survive . . .' He pushed a comlink button on the arm of his throne and spoke into it with relish. 'Commander Jerjerrod, should the Rebels manage to blow up the shield generator, you will turn this battle station onto the Endor Moon and destroy it.'

'Yes, Your Highness,' came the voice over the receiver, 'but we have several battalions stationed on—'

'You will destroy it!' the Emperor's whisper was more final than any scream.

'Yes, Your Highness.'

Palpatine turned back to Luke – the former, shaking with glee; the latter, with outrage.

'There is no escape, my young pupil. The Alliance will die – as will your friends.'

Luke's face was contorted, reflecting his spirit. Vader watched him carefully, as did the Emperor. The lightsaber began to shake on its resting place. The young Jedi's hand was trembling, his lips pulled back in grimace, his teeth grinding.

The Emperor smiled. 'Good. I can feel your anger. I am defenseless – take your weapon. Strike me down with all of your hatred, and your journey toward the dark side will be complete.' He laughed, and laughed.

Luke was able to resist no longer. The lightsaber rattled violently on the throne a moment, then flew into his hand, impelled by the Force. He ignited it a moment later and swung it with his full weight downward toward the Emperor's skull.

In that instant, Vader's blade flashed into view, parrying Luke's attack an inch above the Emperor's head. Sparks flew like forging steel, bathing Palpatine's grinning face in a hellish glare.

Luke jumped back, and turned, lightsaber upraised, to face his father. Vader extended his own blade, poised to do battle.

The Emperor sighed with pleasure and sat in his throne, facing the combatants – the sole audience to this dire, aggrieved contest.

Han, Leia, Chewbacca, and the rest of the strike team were escorted out of the bunker by their captors. The sight that greeted them was substantially different from the way the grassy area had appeared when they'd entered. The clearing was now filled with Imperial troops.

Hundreds of them, in white or black armor – some standing at ease, some viewing the scene from atop their two-legged walkers, some leaning on their speeder bikes. If the situation had appeared hopeless inside the bunker, it looked even worse now.

Han and Leia turned to each other full of feeling. All they'd struggled for, all they'd dreamed of – gone, now. Even so, they'd had each other for a short while at least. They'd come together from opposite ends of a wasteland of emotional isolation: Han had never known love, so enamored of himself was he; Leia had never known love, so wrapped up in social upheaval was she, so intent on embracing all of humanity. And somewhere between his glassy infatuation for the one, and her glowing fervor for the all, they'd found a shady place where two could huddle, grow, even feel nourished.

But that, too, was cut short, now. The end seemed near. So much was there to say, they couldn't find a single word. Instead, they only joined hands, speaking through their fingers in these final minutes of companionship.

That's when Threepio and Artoo jauntily entered the clearing, beeping and jabbering excitedly to each other. They stopped cold in their tracks when they saw what the clearing had become ... and found all eyes suddenly focused on them.

'Oh, dear,' Threepio whimpered. In a second, he and Artoo had turned around and run right back into the woods from which they'd just come. Six stormtroopers charged in after them.

The Imperial soldiers were in time to see the two droids duck behind a large tree, some twenty yards into the forest. They rushed after the robots. As they rounded the tree, they found Artoo and Threepio standing there quietly, waiting to be taken. The guards moved to take them. They moved too slowly.

Fifteen Ewoks dropped out of the overhanging branches, quickly overpowering the Imperial troops with rocks and clubs. At that, Teebo – perched in another tree – raised a ram's horn to his lips and sounded three long blasts from its bell. That was the signal for the Ewoks to attack.

Hundreds of them descended upon the clearing from all sides, throwing themselves against the might of the Imperial army with unrestrained zeal. The scene was unabridged chaos.

Stormtroopers fired their laser pistols at the furry creatures, killing or wounding many – only to be overrun by dozens more in their place. Biker scouts chased squealing Ewoks into the woods – and were knocked from their bikes by volleys of rocks launched from the trees.

In the first confused moments of the attack, Chewie dove into the foliage, while Han and Leia hit the dirt in the cover of the arches that flanked the bunker door. Explosions all around kept them pinned from leaving; the bunker door itself was closed again, and locked.

Han punched out the stolen code on the control panel keys – but this time, the door didn't open. It had been reprogrammed as soon as they'd been caught. 'The terminal doesn't work now,' he muttered.

Leia stretched for a laser pistol lying in the dirt, just out of reach, beside a felled stormtrooper. Shots were crisscrossing from every direction, though.

'We need Artoo,' she shouted.

Han nodded, took out his comlink, pushed the sequence that signaled the little droid and reached for the weapon Leia couldn't get as the fighting stormed all around them.

Artoo and Threepio were huddled behind a log when Artoo got the message. He suddenly blurted out an excited whistle and shot off toward the battlefield.

'Artoo!' Threepio shouted. 'Where are you going? Wait for me!' Nearly beside himself, the golden droid tore off after his best friend.

Biker scouts raced over and around the scurrying droids, blasting away at the Ewoks who grew fiercer every time their fur was scorched. The little bears were hanging on the legs of the Imperial Walkers, hobbling the appendages with lengths of vine, or injuring the joint mechanisms by forcing pebbles and twigs into the hinges. They were knocking scouts off their bikes, by stringing vine between trees at throat level. They were throwing rocks, jumping out of trees, impaling with spears, entangling with nets. They were everywhere.

Scores of them rallied behind Chewbacca, who had grown rather fond of them during the course of the previous night. He'd become their mascot; and they, his little country cousins. So it was with a special ferocity, now, that they came to each other's aid. Chewie was flinging stormtroopers left and right, in a selfless Wookiee frenzy, any time he saw them physically harming his small friends. The Ewoks, for their part, formed equally self-sacrificing cadres to do nothing but follow Chewbacca and throw themselves upon any soldiers who started getting the upper hand with him.

It was a wild, strange battle.

Artoo and Threepio finally made it to the bunker door. Han and Leia provided cover fire with guns they'd finally managed to scrounge. Artoo moved quickly to the terminal, plugged in his computer arm, began scanning. Before he'd even computed the weather codes, though, a laser bolt explosion ripped the entrance-way, disengaging Artoo's cable arm, spilling him to the dirt.

His head began to smolder, his fittings to leak. All of a sudden every compartment sprang open, every nozzle gushed or smoked, every wheel spun – and then stopped. Threepio rushed to his wounded companion, as Han examined the bunker terminal.

'Maybe I can hotwire this thing,' Solo mumbled.

Meanwhile the Ewoks had erected a primitive catapult at the other side of the field. They fired a large boulder at one of the walkers – the machine vibrated seriously, but did not topple. It turned, and headed for the catapult, laser cannon firing. The Ewoks scattered. When the walker was ten feet away, the Ewoks chopped a mass of restraining vines, and two huge, balanced trunks crashed down on top of the Imperial war wagon, halting it for good.

The next phase of the assault began. Ewoks in kite-like animal-skin hang-gliders started dropping rocks on the stormtroopers, or dive-bombing with spears. Teebo, who led the attack, was hit in the wing with laser fire during the first volley and crashed into a gnarled root. A charging walker clumped forward to crush him, but Wicket swooped down just in time, yanking Teebo to safety. In swerving out of the walker's way, though, Wicket smashed into a racing speeder bike – they all went tumbling into the dense foliage.

And so it went.

The casualties mounted.

High above, it was no different. A thousand deadly dogfights and cannon bombardments were erupting all over the skies, while the Death Star laser beam methodically disintegrated the Rebel ships.

In the *Millennium Falcon*, Lando steered like a maniac through an obstacle course of the giant, floating Imperial Star Destroyers – trading laser bolts with them, dodging flak, outracing TIE fighters.

Desperately, he was shouting into his comlink, over the noise of continuous explosions, talking to Ackbar in the Alliance command ship. 'I said *closer*! Move in as close as you can and engage the Star Destroyers at point blank range – that way the Death Star won't be able to fire at us without knocking out its own ships!'

'But no one's ever gone nose to nose at that range, between supervessels like their destroyers and our cruisers!' Ackbar fumed at the unthinkable – but their options were running out.

'Great!' yelled Lando, skimming over the surface of the destroyer. 'Then we're inventing a new kind of combat!'

'We know nothing about the tactics of such a confrontation!' Ackbar protested.

'We know as much as *they* do!' Lando hollered. 'And they'll *think* we know more!' Bluffing was always dangerous in the last hand: but sometimes, when all your money was in the pot, it was the only way to win – and Lando never played to lose.

'At that close-range, we won't last long against Star Destroyers.' Ackbar was already feeling giddy with resignation.

'We'll last longer than we will against that Death Star and we might just take a few of them with us!' Lando whooped. With a jolt, one of his forward guns was blown away. He put the *Falcon* into a controlled spin, and careened around the belly of the Imperial leviathan.

With little else to lose, Ackbar decided to try Calrissian's strategy. In the next minutes, dozens of Rebel Cruisers moved in astronomically close to the Imperial Star Destroyers – and the colossal antagonists began blasting away at each other, like tanks at twenty paces, while hundreds of tiny fighters raced across their surfaces, zipping between laser bolts as they chased around the massive hulls.

Slowly, Luke and Vader circled. Lightsaber high above his head, Luke readied his attack from classic first-position; the Dark Lord held a lateral stance, in classic answer. Without announcement, Luke brought his blade straight down – then, when Vader moved to parry, Luke feinted and cut low. Vader counterparried, let the impact direct his sword toward Luke's throat ... but Luke met the riposte and stepped back. The first blows, traded without injury. Again, they circled.

Vader was impressed with Luke's speed. Pleased, even. It was a pity, almost, he couldn't let the boy kill the Emperor yet. Luke wasn't ready for that, emotionally. There was still a chance Luke would return to his friends if he destroyed the Emperor now. He needed more extensive tutelage, first – training by both Vader *and* Palpatine – before he'd be ready to assume his place at Vader's right hand, ruling the galaxy.

So Vader had to shepherd the boy through periods like this, stop him from doing damage in the wrong places – or in the right places prematurely.

Before Vader could gather his thoughts much further, though, Luke attacked again – much more aggressively. He advanced in a flurry of lunges, each met with a loud crack of Vader's phosphorescent saber. The Dark Lord retreated a step at every slash, swiveling once to bring his cutting beam up viciously – but Luke batted it away, pushing Vader back yet again. The Lord of the Sith momentarily lost his footing on the stairs and tumbled to his knees.

Luke stood above him, at the top of the staircase, heady with his own power. It was in his hands, now, he knew it was: he could take Vader. Take his blade, take his life. Take his place at the Emperor's side. Yes, even that. Luke didn't bury the thought, this time; he gloried in it. He engorged himself with its juices, felt its power tingle his cheeks. It made him feverish, this thought, with lust so overpowering as to totally obliterate all other considerations.

He had the power; the choice was his.

And then another thought emerged, slowly compulsive as an ardent lover: he could destroy the Emperor, too. Destroy them both, and rule the galaxy. Avenge and conquer.

It was a profound moment for Luke. Dizzying. Yet he did not swoon. Nor did he recoil.

He took one step forward.

For the first time, the thought entered Vader's consciousness that his son might best him. He was astounded by the strength Luke had acquired since their last duel, in the Cloud City – not to mention the boy's timing, which was honed to a thought's-breadth. This was an unexpected circumstance. Unexpected and unwelcome. Vader felt humiliation crawling in on the tail of his first reaction, which was surprise, and his second, which was fear. And then the edge of the humiliation curled up, to reveal bald anger. And now he wanted revenge.

These things were mirrored, each facet, by the young Jedi who now towered above him. The Emperor, watching joyously, saw this, and goaded Luke on to revel in his Darkness. 'Use your aggressive feelings, boy! Yes! Let the hate flow through you! Become one with it, let it nourish you!'

Luke faltered a moment – then realized what was happening. He was suddenly confused again. What did he want? What should he do? His brief exultation, his microsecond of dark clarity – gone, now, in a wash of indecision, veiled enigma. Cold awakening from a passionate flirtation.

He took a step back, lowered his sword, relaxed, and tried to drive the hatred from his being.

In that instant, Vader attacked. He lunged half up the stairs, forcing Luke to reverse defensively. He bound the boy's blade with his own, but Luke disengaged and leaped to the safety of an overhead gantry. Vader jumped over the railing to the floor beneath the platform on which Luke stood.

'I will not fight you, Father,' Luke stated.

'You are unwise to lower your defenses,' Vader warned. His anger was layered, now – he did not want to win if the boy was not battling to the fullest. But if winning meant he had to kill a boy who wouldn't fight . . . then he could do that, too. Only he wanted Luke to be aware of those consequences. He wanted Luke to know this was no longer just a game. This was Darkness.

Luke heard something else, though. 'Your thoughts betray you, Father. I feel the good in you . . . the conflict. You could not bring yourself to kill me before – and you won't destroy me now.' Twice before, in fact – to Luke's recollection – Vader could have killed him, but didn't. In the dogfight over the first Death Star, and later in the lightsaber duel on Bespin. He thought of Leia, briefly now, too – of how Vader had had her in his clutches once, had even tortured her . . . but didn't kill her. He winced to think of her agony, but quickly pushed that from his mind. The point was clear to him, now, though so often so murky: there was still good in his father.

This accusation *really* made Vader angry. He could tolerate much from the insolent child, but this was insufferable. He must teach this boy a lesson he would never forget, or die learning. 'Once again, you underestimate the power of the dark side . . .'

Vader threw his scintillating blade – it sliced through the supports holding up the gantry on which Luke was perched, then swept around and flew back into Vader's hand. Luke tumbled to the ground, then rolled down another level, under the tilting platform. In the shadow of the darkened overhang, he was out of sight. Vader paced the area like a cat, seeking the boy; but he wouldn't enter the shadows of the overhang.

'You cannot hide forever, Luke.'

'You'll have to come in and get me,' replied the disembodied voice.

'I will not give you the advantage that easily.' Vader felt his intentions increasingly ambiguous in this conflict; the purity of his evil was being compromised. The boy was clever indeed – Vader knew he must move with extreme caution now.

'I wish no advantage, Father. I will not fight you. Here . . . take my weapon.' Luke knew full well this might be his end, but so be it. He would not use Darkness to fight Darkness. Perhaps it would be left to Leia, after all, to carry on the struggle, without him. Perhaps she would know a way he didn't know; perhaps she could find a path. For now, though, he could see only two paths, and one was into Darkness; and one was not.

Luke put his lightsaber on the ground, and rolled it along the floor toward Vader. It stopped halfway between them, in the middle of the low overhead area. The Dark Lord reached out his hand – Luke's lightsaber jumped into it. He hooked it to his belt and, with grave uncertainty, entered the shadowy overhang.

He was picking up additional feelings from Luke, now, new crosscurrents of doubt. Remorse, regret, abandonment. Shades of pain. But somehow not directly related to Vader. To others, to . . . Endor. Ah, that was it – the Sanctuary Moon where his friends would soon die. Luke would learn soon enough: friendship was different on the dark side. A different thing altogether.

'Give yourself to the dark side, Luke,' he entreated. 'It is the only way you can save your friends. Yes, your thoughts betray you, son. Your feelings for them are strong, especially for—'

Vader stopped. He sensed something.

Luke withdrew further into shadow. He tried to hide, but there was no way to hide what was in his mind – Leia was in pain. Her agony cried to him now, and his spirit cried with her. He tried to shut it out, to shut it up, but the cry was loud, and he couldn't stifle it, couldn't leave it alone, had to cradle it openly, to give it solace.

Vader's consciousness invaded that private place.

'No!' screamed Luke.

Vader was incredulous. 'Sister? Sister!' he bellowed. 'Your feelings have now betrayed her, too . . . Twins!' he roared triumphantly. 'Obi-Wan was wise to hide her, but now his failure is complete.' His smile was clear to Luke, through the mask, through the shadows, through all the realms of Darkness. 'If you will not turn to the Dark Side, perhaps she will.'

This, then, was Luke's breaking point. For Leia was everyone's last unflagging hope. If Vader turned his twisted, misguided cravings on her . . .

'Never!' he screamed. His lightsaber flew off Vader's belt into his own hand, igniting as it came to him.

He rushed to his father with a frenzy he'd never known. Nor had Vader. The gladiators battled fiercely, sparks flying from the clash of their radiant weapons, but it was soon evident that the advantage was all Luke's. And he was pressing it. They locked swords, body to body. When Luke pushed Vader back to break the clinch, the Dark Lord hit his head on an over-hanging beam in the cramped space. He stumbled backward even farther, out of the low-hanging area. Luke pursued him relentlessly.

Blow upon blow, Luke forced Vader to retreat – back, onto the bridge that crossed the vast, seemingly bottomless shaft to the power core. Each stroke of Luke's saber pummeled Vader, like accusations, like screams, like shards of hate.

The Dark Lord was driven to his knees. He raised his blade to block yet another onslaught – and Luke slashed Vader's right hand off at the wrist.

The hand, along with bits of metal, wires, and electronic devices, clattered uselessly away while Vader's lightsaber tumbled over the edge of the span, into the endless shaft below, without a trace.

Luke stared at his father's twitching, severed, mechanical hand – and then at his own black-gloved artificial part – and realized suddenly just how much he'd become like his father. Like the man he hated.

Trembling, he stood above Vader, the point of his glowing blade at the Dark Lord's throat. He wanted to destroy this thing of Darkness, this thing that was once his father, this thing that was . . . him.

Suddenly the Emperor was there, looking on, chuckling with uncontrollable, pleased agitation. 'Good! Kill him! Your hate has made you powerful! Now, fulfill your destiny and take your father's place at my side!'

Luke stared at his father beneath him, then at the Emperor, then back at Vader. This was Darkness – and it was the *Darkness* he hated. Not his father, not even the Emperor. But the Darkness *in* them. In them, and in himself.

And the only way to destroy the Darkness was to renounce it. For good and all. He stood suddenly erect, and made the decision for which he'd spent his life in preparation.

He hurled his lightsaber away. 'Never! Never will I turn to the dark side! You have failed, Palpatine. I am a Jedi, as my father was before me.'

The Emperor's glee turned to a sullen rage. 'So be it, Jedi. If you will not be turned, you will be destroyed.'

Palpatine raised his spidery arms toward Luke: blinding white bolts of energy coruscated from his fingers, shot across the room like sorcerous lightning, and tore through the boy's insides, looking for ground. The young Jedi was at once confounded and in agony – he'd never heard of such a power, such a corruption of the Force, let alone experienced it.

But if it was Force-generated, it could be Force-repelled. Luke raised his arms to deflect the bolts. Initially, he was successful – the lightning rebounded from his touch, harmlessly into the walls. Soon, though, the shocks came with such speed and power, they coursed over and into him, and he could only shrink before them, convulsed with pain, his knees buckling, his powers at ebb.

Vader crawled, like a wounded animal, to his Emperor's side.

On Endor, the battle of the bunker continued. Stormtroopers kept irradiating Ewoks with sophisticated weaponry, while the fuzzy little warriors bashed away at the Imperial troops with clubs, tumbled walkers with logpiles and vine trip-wires, lassoed speeder bikes with vine-ropes and net-traps.

They felled trees on their foes. They dug pits which they covered with branches, and then lured the walkers to chase them until the clumsy armored vehicles toppled into the dug-outs. They started rockslides. They dammed a small, nearby stream, and then opened the floodgates, deluging a host of troops and two more walkers. They ganged up, and then ran away. They jumped on top of walkers from high branches, and poured pouches of burning lizard-oil in the gun-slits. They used knives, and spears, and slings, and made scary war-shrieks to confound and dismay the enemy. They were fearless opponents.

Their example made even Chewie bolder than was his wont. He started having so much fun swinging on vines and bashing heads, he nearly forgot about his laser pistol.

He swung onto the roof of a walker at one point, with Teebo and Wicket clinging to his back. They landed with a thud atop the lurching contraption, then made such a banging racket trying to hang on, one of the stormtroopers inside opened the top hatch to see what was happening. Before he could fire his gun, Chewie plucked him out and dashed him to the ground – Wicket and Teebo immediately dove into the hatch and subdued the other trooper.

Ewoks drive an Imperial Walker much the way they drive speeder bikes – terribly, but with exhilaration. Chewie was almost thrown off the top several times, but even barking angrily down into the cockpit didn't seem to have much effect – the Ewoks just giggled, squealed, and careened into another speeder bike.

Chewie climbed down inside. It took him half a minute to master the controls – Imperial technology was pretty standardized. And then, methodically, one by one, he began approaching the other, unsuspecting, Imperial Walkers, and blasting them to dust. Most had no idea what was happening.

As the giant war-machines began going up in flames, the Ewoks were reinspired. They rallied behind Chewie's walker. The Wookiee was turning the tide of battle.

Han, meanwhile, was still working furiously at the control panel. Wires sparked each time he refastened another connection, but the door kept not opening. Leia crouched at his back, firing her laser pistol, giving him cover.

He motioned her at last. 'Give me a hand, I think I've got it figured out. Hold this.'

He handed her one of the wires. She holstered her weapon, took the wire he gave her, and held it in position as he brought two others over from opposite ends of the panel.

'Here goes nothing,' he said.

The three wires sparked; the connection was made. There was a sudden loud WHUMP, as a second blast door crashed down in front of the first, doubling the impregnable barrier.

'Great. Now we have two doors to get through,' Leia muttered.

At that moment, she was hit in the arm by a laser bolt, and knocked to the ground.

Han rushed over to her. 'Leia, no!' he cried, trying to stop the bleeding.

'Princess Leia, are you all right?' Threepio fretted.

'It's not bad,' she shook her head. 'It's—'

'Hold it!' shouted a voice. 'One move and you're both dead!'

They froze, looked up. Two stormtroopers stood before them, weapons leveled, unwavering.

'Stand up,' one ordered. 'Hands raised.'

Han and Leia looked at each other, fixed their gazes deep in each other's eyes, swam there in the wells of their souls for a suspended, eternal moment, during which all was felt, understood, touched, shared.

Solo's gaze was drawn down to Leia's holster – she'd surreptitiously eased out her gun, and was holding it now at the ready. The action was hidden from the troopers, because Han was standing in front of Leia, half-blocking their view.

He looked again into her eyes, comprehending. With a last, heartfelt smile, he whispered, 'I love you.'

'I know,' she answered simply.

Then the moment was over; and at an unspoken, instantaneous signal, Han whirled out of the line of fire as Leia blasted at the stormtroopers.

The air was filled with laser fire – a glinting orange-pink haze, like an electron storm, buffeted the area, sheared by intense flares.

As the smoke cleared, a giant Imperial Walker approached, stood before him, and stopped. Han looked up to see its laser cannons aimed directly in his face. He raised his arms, and took a tentative step forward. He wasn't really sure what he was going to do. 'Stay back,' he said quietly to Leia, measuring the distance to the machine, in his mind.

That was when the hatch on top of the walker popped open and Chewbacca stuck his head out with an ingratiating smile.

'Ahr Rahr!' barked the Wookiee.

Solo could have kissed him. 'Chewie! Get down here! She's wounded!' He started forward to greet his partner, then stopped in mid-stride. 'No, wait. I've got an idea.'

IX

THE two space armadas, like their sea-bound counterparts of another time and galaxy, sat floating, ship to ship, trading broadsides with each other in point-blank confrontation.

Heroic, sometimes suicidal, maneuvers marked the day. A Rebel Cruiser, its back alive with fires and explosions, limped into direct contact with an Imperial Star Destroyer before exploding completely – taking the Star Destroyer with it. Cargo ships loaded with charge were set on collision courses with fortress-vessels, their crews abandoning ships to fates that were uncertain, at best.

Lando, Wedge, Blue Leader, and Green Wing went in to take out one of the larger destroyers – the Empire's main communications ship. It had already been disabled by direct cannonade from the Rebel Cruiser it had subsequently destroyed; but its damages were reparable – so the Rebels had to strike while it was still licking its wounds.

Lando's squadron went in low – rock-throwing low – this prevented the destroyer from using its bigger guns. It also made the fighters invisible until they were directly visualized.

'Increase power on the front deflector shields,' Lando radioed his group. 'We're going in.'

'I'm right with you,' answered Wedge. 'Close up formations, team.'

They went into a high-speed power-dive, perpendicular to the long axis of the Imperial vessel – vertical drops were hard to track. Fifty feet from the surface, they pulled out at ninety degrees, and raced along the gunmetal hull, taking laserfire from every port.

'Starting attack run on the main power tree,' Lando advised.

'I copy,' answered Green Wing. 'Moving into position.'

'Stay clear of their front batteries,' warned Blue Leader. 'It's a heavy fire zone down there.'

'I'm in range.'

'She's hurt bad on the left of the tower,' Wedge noted. 'Concentrate on that side.'

'Right with you.'

Green Wing was hit. 'I'm losing power!'

'Get clear, you're going to blow!'

Green Wing took it down like riding a rocket, into the destroyer's front batteries. Tremendous explosions rumbled the port bow.

'Thanks,' Blue Leader said quietly to the conflagration.

'That opens it up for us!' yelled Wedge. 'Cut over. The power reactors are just inside that cargo bay.'

'Follow me!' Lando called, pulling the *Falcon* into a sharp bank that caught the horrified reactor personnel by surprise. Wedge and Blue followed suit. They all did their worst.

'Direct hit!' Lando shouted.

'There she goes!'

'Pull up, pull up!'

They pulled up hard and fast, as the destroyer was enveloped in a series of ever-increasing explosions, until it looked finally just like one more small star. Blue Leader was caught by the shock wave, and thrown horribly against the side of a smaller Imperial ship, which also exploded. Lando and Wedge escaped.

On the Rebel command ship bridge, smoke and shouts filled the air.

Ackbar reached Calrissian on the comlink. 'The jamming has stopped. We have a reading on the shield.'

'Is it still up?' Lando responded with desperate anticipation in his voice.

'I'm afraid so. It looks like General Solo's unit didn't make it.'

'Until they've destroyed our last ship, there's still hope,' replied Lando. Han wouldn't fail. He couldn't – they still had to pick off that annoying Death Star.

*

On the Death Star, Luke was nearly unconscious beneath the continuing assault of the Emperor's lightning. Tormented beyond reason, betaken of a weakness that drained his very essence, he hoped for nothing more than to submit to the nothingness toward which he was drifting.

The Emperor smiled down at the enfeebled young Jedi, as Vader struggled to his feet beside his master.

'Young fool!' Palpatine rasped at Luke. 'Only now at the end, do you understand. Your puerile skills are no match for the power of the dark side. You have paid a price for your lack of vision. Now, young Skywalker, you will pay the price in full. You will die!'

He laughed maniacally; and although it would not have seemed possible to Luke, the outpouring of bolts from the Emperor's fingers actually increased in intensity. The sound screamed through the room, the murderous brightness of the flashes was overwhelming.

Luke's body slowed, wilted, finally crumpled under the hideous barrage. He stopped moving altogether. At last, he appeared totally lifeless. The Emperor hissed maliciously.

At that instant, Vader sprang up and grabbed the Emperor from behind, pinning Palpatine's upper arms to his torso. Weaker than he'd ever been, Vader had lain still these last few minutes, focusing his every fiber of being on this one, concentrated act – the only action possible; his last, if he failed. Ignoring pain, ignoring his shame and his weaknesses, ignoring the bone-crushing noise in his head, he focused solely and sightlessly on his will – his will to defeat the evil embodied in the Emperor.

Palpatine struggled in the grip of Vader's unfeeling embrace, his hands still shooting bolts of malign energy out in all directions. In his wild flailing, the lightning ripped across the room, tearing into Vader. The Dark Lord fell again, electric currents crackling down his helmet, over his cape, into his heart.

Vader stumbled with his load to the middle of the bridge over the black chasm leading to the power core. He held the wailing despot high over his head, and with a final spasm of strength, hurled him into the abyss.

Palpatine's body, still spewing bolts of light, spun out of control, into the void, bouncing back and forth off the sides of the shaft as it fell. It disappeared at last; but then, a few seconds later, a distant explosion could be heard, far down at the core. A rush of air billowed out the shaft, into the throne room.

The wind whipped at Lord Vader's cape, as he staggered and collapsed toward the hole, trying to follow his master to the end. Luke crawled to his father's side, though, and pulled the Dark Lord away from the edge of the chasm, to safety.

Both of them lay on the floor, entwined in each other, too weak to move, too moved to speak.

Inside the bunker on Endor, Imperial controllers watched the main view-screen of the Ewok battle just outside. Though the image was clogged with static, the fighting seemed to be winding down. About time, since they'd initially been told that the locals on this moon were harmless nonbelligerents.

The interference seemed to worsen – probably another antenna damaged in the fighting – when suddenly a walker pilot appeared on the screen, waving excitedly.

'It's over, Commander! The Rebels have been routed, and are fleeing with the bear-creatures into the woods. We need reinforcements to continue the pursuit.'

The bunker personnel all cheered. The shield was safe.

'Open the main door!' ordered the commander. 'Send three squads to help.'

The bunker door opened, the Imperial troops came rushing out only to find themselves surrounded by Rebels and Ewoks, looking bloody and mean. The Imperial troops surrendered without a fight.

Han, Chewie, and five others ran into the bunker with the explosive charges. They placed the timed devices at eleven strategic points in and around the power generator, then ran out again as fast as they could.

Leia, still in great pain from her wounds, lay in the sheltered comfort of some distant bushes. She was shouting orders to the Ewoks, to gather their prisoners on the far side of the clearing, away from the bunker, when Han and Chewie tore out, racing for cover. In the next moment, the bunker went.

It was a spectacular display, explosion after explosion sending a wall of fire hundreds of feet into the air, creating a shock wave that knocked every living creature off its feet, and charred all the greenery that faced the clearing.

The bunker was destroyed.

A captain ran up to Admiral Ackbar, his voice tremulous. 'Sir, the shield around the Death Star has lost its power.'

Ackbar looked at the view-screen; the electronically generated web was gone. The moon, and the Death Star, now floated in black, empty, unprotected space.

'They did it,' Ackbar whispered.

He rushed over to the comlink and shouted into the multi-frequency war channel. 'All fighters commence attack on the Death Star's main reactor. The deflector shield is down. Repeat. The deflector shield is down!'

Lando's voice was the next one heard. 'I see it. We're on our way. Red group! Gold group! Blue Squad! All fighters follow me!' That's my man, Han. Now it's my turn.

The *Falcon* plunged to the surface of the Death Star, followed by hordes of Rebel fighters, followed by a still-massing but disorganized array of Imperial TIE fighters – while three Rebel Star Cruisers headed for the huge Imperial Super Star Destroyer, Vader's flagship, which seemed to be having difficulties with its guidance system.

Lando and the first wave of X-wings headed for the unfinished portion of the Death Star, skimming low over the curving surface of the completed side.

'Stay low until we get to the unfinished side,' Wedge told his squad. Nobody needed to be told.

'Squadron of enemy fighters coming—'

'Blue Wing,' called Lando, 'take your group and draw the TIE fighters away—'

'I'll do what I can.'

'I'm picking up interference ... the Death Star's jamming us, I think—'

'More fighters coming at ten o'clock—'

'There's the superstructure,' Lando called. 'Watch for the main reactor shaft.'

He turned hard into the unfinished side, and began weaving dramatically among protruding girders, half-built towers, mazelike channels, temporary scaffolding, sporadic floodlights. The antiaircraft defenses weren't nearly as well developed here yet – they'd been depending completely on the deflector shield for protection.

Consequently the major sources of worry for the Rebels were the physical jeopardies of the structure itself, and the Imperial TIE fighters on their tails.

'I see it – the power-channel system,' Wedge radioed. 'I'm going in.'

'I see it, too,' agreed Lando. 'Here goes nothing.'

'This isn't going to be easy—'

Over a tower and under a bridge – and suddenly they were flying at top speed inside a deep shaft that was barely wide enough for three fighters, wing to wing. Moreover, it was pierced, along its entire twisting length, by myriad feeding shafts and tunnels, alternate forks, and dead-end caverns; and spiked, in addition, with an alarming number of obstacles *within* the shaft itself: heavy machinery, structural elements, power cables, floating stairways, barrier half-walls, piled debris.

A score of Rebel fighters made the first turn-off into the power shaft, followed by twice that number of TIEs. Two X-wings lost it right away, careening into a derrick to avoid the first volley of laser fire.

The chase was on.

'Where are we going, Gold Leader?' Wedge called out gaily. A laserbolt hit the shaft above him, showering his window with sparks.

'Lock onto the strongest power source,' Lando suggested. 'It should be the generator.'

'Red Wing, stay alert – we could run out of space real fast.'

They quickly strung out into single and double file, as it started becoming apparent that the shaft was not only pocked with side-vents and protruding obstacles, but also narrowing across its width at every turn.

TIE fighters hit another Rebel, who exploded in flames. Then another TIE fighter hit a piece of machinery, with a similar result.

'I've got a reading on a major shaft obstruction ahead,' Lando announced.

'Just picked it up. Will you make it?'

'Going to be a tight squeeze.'

It was a tight squeeze. It was a heat-wall occluding three fourths of the tunnel, with a dip in the shaft at the same level to make up a little room. Lando had to spin the *Falcon* through 360 degrees while rising, falling, and accelerating. Luckily, the X-wings and Y-wings weren't quite as bulky. Still, two more of them didn't make it on the downside. The smaller TIEs drew closer.

Suddenly coarse white static blanketed all the viewscreens.

'My scope's gone!' yelled Wedge.

'Cut speed,' cautioned Lando. 'Some kind of power discharge causing interference.'

'Switch to visual scanning.'

'That's useless at these velocities – we'll have to fly nearly blind.'

Two blind X-wings hit the wall as the shaft narrowed again. A third was blown apart by the gaining Imperial fighters.

'Green Leader!' called Lando.

'Copy, Gold Leader.'

'Split off and head back to the surface – Home-one just called for a fighter, and you might draw some fire off us.'

Green Leader and his cohort peeled off, out of the power shaft, back up to the cruiser battle. One TIE fighter followed, firing continuously.

Ackbar's voice came in over the comlink. 'The Death Star is turning away from the fleet – looks like it's repositioning to destroy the Endor Moon.'

'How long before it's in position?' Lando asked.

'Point oh three.'

'That's not enough time! We're running out of time.'

Wedge broke in the transmission. 'Well, we're running out of shaft, too.'

At that instant the *Falcon* scraped through an even smaller opening, this time injuring her auxiliary thrusters.

'That was too close,' muttered Calrissian.

'Gdzhng dzn,' nodded the copilot.

Ackbar stared wild-eyed out the observation window. He was looking down onto the deck of the Super Star Destroyer, only miles away. Fires burst over the entire stern, and the Imperial warship was listing badly to starboard.

'We've knocked out their forward shields,' Ackbar said into the comlink. 'Fire at the bridge.'

Green Leader's group swooped in low, from bottomside, up from the Death Star.

'Glad to help out, Home-one,' called Green Leader.

'Firing proton torpedoes,' Green Wing advised.

The bridge was hit, with kaleidoscopic results. A rapid chain reaction got set off, from power station to power station along the middle third of the huge destroyer, producing a dazzling rainbow of explosions that buckled the ship at right angles, and started it spinning like a pinwheel toward the Death Star.

The first bridge explosion took Green Leader with it; the subsequent uncontrolled joyride snagged ten more fighters, two cruisers, and an ordnance vessel. By the time the whole exothermic conglomerate finally crashed into the side of the Death Star, the impact was momentous enough to actually jolt the battle station, setting off internal explosions and thunderings all through its network of reactors, munitions, and halls.

For the first time, the Death Star rocked. The collision with the exploding destroyer was only the beginning, leading to various systems breakdowns, which led to reactor meltdowns, which led to personnel panic, abandonment of posts, further malfunctions, and general chaos.

Smoke was everywhere, substantial rumblings came from all directions at once, people were running and shouting. Electrical fires, steam explosions, cabin depressurizations, disruption of chain-of-command. Added to this, the continued bombardments by Rebel Cruisers – smelling fear in the enemy – merely heightened the sense of hysteria that was already pervasive.

For the Emperor was dead. The central, powerful evil that had been the cohesive force to the Empire was gone; and when the dark side was this diffused, this nondirected – this was simply where it led.

Confusion.

Desperation.

Damp fear.

In the midst of this uproar, Luke had made it, somehow, to the main docking bay – where he was trying to carry the hulking deadweight of his father's weakening body toward an Imperial shuttle. Halfway there, his strength finally gave out, though; and he collapsed under the strain.

Slowly he rose again. Like an automaton, he hoisted his father's body over his shoulder and stumbled toward one of the last remaining shuttles.

Luke rested his father on the ground, trying to collect strength one last time, as explosions grew louder all around them. Sparks hissed in the rafters; one of the walls buckled, and smoke poured through a gaping fissure. The floor shook.

Vader motioned Luke closer to him. 'Luke, help me take this mask off.'

Luke shook his head. 'You'll die.'

The Dark Lord's voice was weary. 'Nothing can stop that now. Just once let me face you without it. Let me look on you with my own eyes.'

Luke was afraid. Afraid to see his father as he really was. Afraid to see what person could have become so dark – the same person who'd fathered Luke, and Leia. Afraid to know the Anakin Skywalker who lived inside Darth Vader.

Vader, too, was afraid – to let his son see him, to remove this armored mask that had been between them so long. The black, armored mask that had been his only means of existing for over twenty years. It had been his voice, and his breath, and his invisibility – his shield against all human contact. But now he would remove it; for he would see his son before he died.

Together they lifted the heavy helmet from Vader's head – inside the mask portion, a complicated breathing apparatus had to be disentangled, a speaking modulator and view-screen detached from the power unit in back. But when the mask was finally off and set aside, Luke gazed on his father's face.

It was the sad, benign face of an old man. Bald, beardless, with a mighty scar running from the top of his head to the back of the scalp, he had unfocused, deepset, dark eyes, and his skin was pasty white, for it had not seen the sun in two decades. The old man smiled weakly; tears glazed his eyes, now. For a moment, he looked not too unlike Ben.

It was a face full of meanings, that Luke would forever recall. Regret, he saw most plainly. And shame. Memories could be seen flashing across it . . . memories of rich times. And horrors. And love, too.

It was a face that hadn't touched the world in a lifetime. In Luke's lifetime. He saw the wizened nostrils twitch, as they tested a first, tentative smell. He saw the head tilt imperceptibly to listen – for the first time without electronic auditory amplification. Luke felt a pang of remorse that the only sounds now to be heard were those of explosions, the only smells, the pungent sting of electrical fires. Still, it was a touch. Palpable, unfiltered.

He saw the old eyes focus on him. Tears burned Luke's cheeks, fell on his father's lips. His father smiled at the taste.

It was a face that had not seen itself in twenty years.

Vader saw his son crying, and knew it must have been at the horror of the face the boy beheld.

It intensified, momentarily, Vader's own sense of anguish – to his crimes, now, he added guilt at the imagined repugnance of his appearance. But then this brought him to mind of the way he used to look – striking, and grand, with a wry tilt to his brow that hinted of invincibility and took in all of life with a wink. Yes, that was how he'd looked once.

And this memory brought a wave of other memories with it. Memories of brotherhood, and home. His dear wife. The freedom of deep space. Obi-Wan.

Obi-Wan, his friend ... and how that friendship had turned. Turned, he knew not how – but got injected, nonetheless, with some uncaring virulence that festered, until ... hold. These were memories he wanted none of, not now. Memories of molten lava, crawling up his back ... no.

This boy had pulled him from that pit – here, now, with this act. This boy was good.

The boy was good, and the boy had come from *him* – so there must have been good in *him*, too. He smiled up again at his son, and for the first time, loved him. And for the first time in many long years, loved himself again, as well.

Suddenly he smelled something – flared his nostrils, sniffed once more. Wildflowers, that was what it was. Just blooming; it must be spring.

And there was thunder – he cocked his head, strained his ears. Yes, spring thunder, for a spring rain. To make the flowers bloom.

Yes, there ... he felt a raindrop on his lips. He licked the delicate droplet ... but wait, it wasn't sweetwater, it was salty, it was ... a teardrop.

He focused on Luke once again, and saw his son was crying. Yes, that was it, he was tasting his boy's grief – because he looked so horrible; because he *was* so horrible.

But he wanted to make it all right for Luke, he wanted Luke to know he wasn't really ugly like this, not deep inside, not all together. With a little self-deprecatory smile, he shook his head at Luke, explaining away the unsightly beast his son saw. 'Luminous beings are we, Luke – not this crude matter.'

Luke shook his head, too – to tell his father it was all right, to dismiss the old man's shame, to tell him nothing mattered now. And everything – but he couldn't talk.

Vader spoke again, even weaker – almost inaudible. 'Go, my son. Leave me.'

At that, Luke found his voice. 'No. You're coming with me. I'll not leave you here. I've got to save you.'

'You already have, Luke,' he whispered. He wished, briefly, he'd met Yoda, to thank the old Jedi for the training he'd given Luke ... but perhaps he'd be with Yoda soon, now, in the ethereal oneness of the Force. And with Obi-Wan.

'Father, I won't leave you,' Luke protested. Explosions jarred the docking bay in earnest, crumbling one entire wall, splitting the ceiling. A jet of blue flame shot from a gas nozzle nearby. Just beneath it the floor began to melt.

Vader pulled Luke very close, spoke into his ear. 'Luke, you were right ... and you were right about me ... Tell your sister ... you were right.'

With that, he closed his eyes, and Darth Vader – Anakin Skywalker – died.

A tremendous explosion filled the back of the bay with fire, knocking Luke flat to the ground. Slowly, he rose again; and like an automaton, stumbled toward one of the last remaining shuttles.

The *Millennium Falcon* continued its swerving race through the labyrinth of power channels, inching ever-closer to the hub of the giant sphere – the main reactor. The Rebel cruisers were unloading a continuous bombardment on the exposed, unfinished super-structure of the Death Star, now, each hit causing a resonating shudder in the immense battle station, and a new series of catastrophic events within.

Commander Jerjerrod sat, brooding, in the control room of the

Death Star, watching all about him crumble. Half of his crew were dead, wounded, or run off – where they hoped to find sanctuary was unclear, if not insane. The rest wandered ineffectually, or railed at the enemy ships, or fired all their guns at all sectors, or shouted orders, or focused desperately on a single task, as if that would save them. Or, like Jerjerrod, simply brooded.

He couldn't fathom what he'd done wrong. He'd been patient, he'd been loyal, he'd been clever, he'd been hard. He was the commander of the greatest battle station ever built. Or, at least, almost built. He hated this Rebel Alliance, now, with a child's hate, untempered. He'd loved it once – it had been the small boy he could bully, the enraged baby animal he could torture. But the boy had grown up now; it knew how to fight back effectively. It had broken its bonds.

Jerjerrod hated it now.

Yet there seemed to be little he could do at this point. Except, of course, destroy Endor – he could do that. It was a small act, a token really – to incinerate something green and living, gratuitously, meanly, toward no end but that of wanton destruction. A small act, but deliciously satisfying.

An aide ran up to him. 'The Rebel fleet is closing, sir.'

'Concentrate all fire in that sector,' he answered distractedly. A console on the far wall burst into flame.

'The fighters in the superstructure are eluding our defense system, Commander. Shouldn't we—'

'Flood sectors 304 and 138. That should slow them up.' He arched his eyebrows at the aide.

This made little sense to the aide, who had cause to wonder at the commander's grasp of the situation. 'But sir . . .'

'What is the rotation factor to firing range on the Endor Moon?'

The aide checked the compuscreen. 'Point oh two to moon target, sir. Commander, the fleet—'

'Accelerate rotation until moon is in range, and then fire on my mark.'

'Yes, sir.' The aide pulled a bank of switches. 'Rotation accelerating, sir. Point oh one to moon target, sir. Sixty seconds to firing range. Sir, good-bye, sir.' The aide saluted, put the firing switch in Jerjerrod's hand as another explosion shook the control room, and ran out the door.

Jerjerrod smiled calmly at the view-screen. Endor was starting to come out of the Death Star's eclipse. He fondled the detonation switch in his hand. Point oh oh five to moon target. Screams erupted in the next room.

Thirty seconds to firing.

Lando was homing in on the reactor core shaft. Else only Wedge was left, flying just ahead of him, and Gold Wing, just behind. Several TIE fighters still trailed.

These central twistings were barely two planes wide, and turned sharply every five or ten seconds at the speeds Lando was reaching. Another Imperial jet exploded against a wall; another shot down Gold Wing.

And then there were two.

Lando's tail-gunners kept the remaining TIE fighters jumping in the narrow space, until at last the main reactor shaft came into view. They'd never seen a reactor that awesome.

'It's too big, Gold Leader,' yelled Wedge. 'My proton torpedoes won't even dent that.'

'Go for the power regulator on the north tower,' Lando directed. 'I'll take the main reactor. We're carrying concussion missiles — they should penetrate. Once I let them go, we won't have much time to get out of here, though.'

'I'm already on my way out,' Wedge exclaimed.

He fired his torpedoes with a Corellian war-cry, hitting both sides of the north tower, and peeled off, accelerating.

The *Falcon* waited three dangerous seconds longer, then loosed its concussion missiles with a powerful roar. For another second the flash was too bright to see what had happened. And then the whole reactor began to go.

'Direct hit!' shouted Lando. 'Now comes the hard part.'

The shaft was already caving in on top of him, creating a tunnel effect. The *Falcon* maneuvered through the twisting outlet, through walls of flame, and through moving shafts, always just ahead of the continuing chain of explosions.

Wedge tore out of the superstructure at barely sublight speed, whipped around the near side of Endor, and coasted into deep space, slowing slowly in a gentle arc, to return to the safety of the moon.

A moment later, in a destabilized Imperial shuttle, Luke escaped the main docking bay, just as that section began to blow apart completely. His wobbling craft, too, headed for the green sanctuary in the near distance.

And finally, as if being spit out of the very flames of the conflagration, the *Millennium Falcon* shot toward Endor, only moments before the Death Star flared into brilliant oblivion, like a fulminant supernova.

Han was binding Leia's arm-wound in a fern-dell when the Death Star blew. It captured everyone's attention, wherever they happened to be – Ewoks, stormtrooper prisoners, Rebel troops – this final, turbulent, flash of self-destruction, incandescent in the evening sky. The Rebels cheered.

Leia touched Han's cheek. He leaned over, and kissed her; then sat back, seeing her eyes focused on the starry sky.

'Hey,' he jostled, 'I'll bet Luke got off that thing before it blew.'

She nodded. 'He did. I can feel it.' Her brother's living presence touched her, through the Force. She reached out to answer the touch, to reassure Luke she was all right. Everything was all right.

Han looked at her with deep love, special love. For she was a special woman. A princess not by title, but by heart. Her fortitude astounded him, yet she held herself so lightly. Once, he'd wanted whatever he wanted, for himself, because he wanted it. Now he wanted everything for her. *Her* everythings. And one thing he could see she wanted dearly, was Luke.

'You really care for him, don't you?'

She nodded, scanning the sky. He was alive, Luke was alive. And the other – the Dark One – was dead.

'Well, listen,' Han went on, 'I understand. When he gets back, I won't stand in your way . . .'

She squinted at him, suddenly aware they were crossing wires, having different conversations. 'What are you talking about?' she said. Then she realized what he was talking about. 'Oh, no. No,' she laughed, 'it's not like that at all – Luke is my *brother*.'

Han was successively stunned, embarrassed, and elated. This made *everything* fine, just fine.

He took her in his arms, embraced her, lowered her back down into the ferns . . . and being extra careful of her wounded arm, lay down there beside her, under the waning glow of the burning Star.

*

Luke stood in a forest clearing before a great pile of logs and branches. Lying, still and robed, atop the mound, was the lifeless body of Darth Vader. Luke set a torch to the kindling.

As the flames enveloped the corpse, smoke rose from the vents in the mask, almost like a black spirit, finally freed. Luke stared with a fierce sorrow at the conflagration. Silently, he said his last goodbye. He, alone, had believed in the small speck of humanity remaining in his father. That redemption rose, now, with these flames, into the night.

Luke followed the blazing embers as they sailed to the sky. They mixed, there, in his vision, with the fireworks the Rebel fighters were setting off in victory celebration. And these, in turn, mingled with the bonfires that speckled the woods and the Ewoks' village – fires of elation, of comfort and triumph. He could hear the drums beating, the music weaving in the firelight, the cheers of brave reunion. Luke's cheer was mute as he gazed into the fires of his own victory and loss.

A huge bonfire blazed in the center of the Ewok village square for the celebration that night. Rebels and Ewoks rejoiced in the warm firelight of the cool evening – singing, dancing, and laughing, in the communal language of liberation. Even Teebo and Artoo had reconciled, and were going a little jig together, as others clapped in time to the music. Threepio, his regal days in this village over, was content to sit near the spinning little droid who was his best friend in the universe. He thanked the Maker that Captain Solo had been able to fix Artoo, not to mention Mistress Leia – for a man without protocol, Solo did have his moments. And he thanked the Maker this bloody war was over.

The prisoners had been sent on shuttles to what was left of the Imperial fleet – the Rebel Star Cruisers were dealing with all that. Up there, somewhere. The Death Star had burned itself out.

Han, Leia, and Chewbacca stood off a short way from the revelers. They stayed close to each other, not talking; periodically glancing at the path that led into the village. Half waiting, half trying not to wait; unable to do anything else.

Until, at last, their patience was rewarded: Luke and Lando, exhausted but happy, stumbled down the path, out of the darkness, into the light. The friends rushed to greet them. They all embraced, cheered, jumped about, fell over, and finally just huddled, still wordless, content with the comfort of each other's touch.

In a while, the two droids sidled over as well, to stand beside their dearest comrades.

The fuzzy Ewoks continued in wild jubilation, far into the night, while this small company of gallant adventurers watched on from the sidelines.

For an evanescent moment, looking into the bonfire, Luke thought he saw faces dancing – Yoda, Ben; was it his father? He drew away from his companions, to try to see what the faces were saying; they were ephemeral, and spoke only to the shadows of the flames, and then disappeared altogether.

It gave Luke a momentary sadness but then Leia took his hand, and drew him back close to her and to the others, back into their circle of warmth, and camaraderie; and love.

The Empire was dead.

Long live the Alliance.

Warner Books now offers an exciting range of quality titles by both established and new authors. All of the books in this series are available from:

Little, Brown and Company (UK),
P.O. Box 11,
Falmouth,
Cornwall TR10 9EN.

Alternatively you may fax your order to the above address. Fax No. 01326 317444.

Payments can be made as follows: cheque, postal order (payable to Little, Brown and Company) or by credit cards, Visa/Access. Do not send cash or currency. UK customers and B.F.P.O.: please send a cheque or postal order (no currency) and allow £1.00 for postage and packing for the first book, plus 50p for the second book, plus 30p for each additional book up to a maximum charge of £3.00 (7 books plus).

Overseas customers including Ireland please allow £2.00 for postage and packing for the first book, plus £1.00 for the second book, plus 50p for each additional book.

NAME (Block Letters) ....

....

ADDRESS ....

....

....

☐ I enclose my remittance for ....

☐ I wish to pay by Access/Visa Card

Number ⬚⬚⬚⬚⬚⬚⬚⬚⬚⬚⬚⬚⬚⬚⬚⬚⬚⬚

Card Expiry Date ⬚⬚⬚⬚